CONGRESS AND THE POLITICS OF U.S. FOREIGN ECONOMIC POLICY 1929–1976

CONGRESS AND THE POLITICS OF U.S. FOREIGN ECONOMIC POLICY 1929–1976

Robert A. Pastor

WITHDRAWN

UNIVERSITY OF CALIFORNIA PRESS • Berkeley Los Angeles London

Written under the Auspices of the
Center for International Affairs,
Harvard University

University of California Press
Berkeley and Los Angeles, California

University of California Press, Ltd.
London, England

First Paperback Printing 1982

ISBN 0-520-04645-5

Library of Congress Cataloging in Publication Data

Pastor, Robert A
   Congress and the politics of U.S. foreign economic
policy, 1929–1976.

   Based on the author's thesis, Harvard.
   Bibliography: p. 355
   Includes index.
   1. United States—Foreign economic relations.
2. United States. Congress. I. Title.
HF1455.P28   337.73   79-63552

Printed in the United States of America

1   2   3   4   5   6   7   8   9

To My Parents

who provided the opportunities to pose questions and pursue answers.

CONTENTS

PREFACE

Only when answers are demonstrably inadequate do people return to the questions. The long and tragic involvement by the U.S. in Vietnam served that purpose: it prompted Americans to re-examine the fundamental questions of U.S. foreign policy. Questions of purpose—what goals should the United States pursue in the world? Which U.S. national interests should take precedence? Questions of content—what issues define our foreign policy agenda? What does "national security" mean? And questions of process—who makes U.S. foreign policy? What instruments should we use to further our interests?

As a student of foreign policy in the late 1960s, I was drawn to these questions. I found the answers provided by textbooks and conventional wisdom unsatisfactory; they were too rigid and unaware of the changes that had transformed the United States and the world. In J. William Fulbright's words, the "answers" had ossified, becoming "old myths" that were not helpful but misleading in trying to cope with "new realities." The goal of containing communism, which had guided the United States from World War II into Vietnam, had become an obsession, making the rational pursuit of that and other objectives more difficult and hazardous. The trusted and oft used instrument of military intervention seemed less useful. As to issues, U.S. foreign policy no longer was synonymous with national security policy; over the years, "national security interests" came to be used more as a symbol to mobilize public opinion than as a guide to making policy. New issues of interdependence began to preoccupy U.S. policy-makers. Finally, the idea that the President made U.S. foreign policy was impugned by the increasingly important role played by the Congress, by bureaucrats, and by interest groups. New roadmaps were necessary.

The first question of goals justifiably attracted the most urgent and careful attention. For the last decade, students of foreign policy seeking answers to this question have learned that an inordinate fear of communism had led the U.S. to ignore profound divisions within the Communist world, to misinterpret the vigorous pulse of nationalism in the Third World, and to ignore the real strengths of the United States—our humanitarian and idealistic origins—in dealing with other nations.

My own journey into foreign policy began with an extended search for an answer to this first question. This book, however, is directed toward the second and third questions—in particular to foreign economic policy as an increasingly important component of U.S. foreign policy, and to the Congress as an increasingly important actor in the formulation of U.S. foreign policy. The inquiry sparked by Vietnam has helped us to see the origins of the Cold War more clearly and has helped us to cope more effectively with new international realities. But there are still many who believe that economic policy is not an important component of U.S. foreign policy and that Congress has only a limited role to play in the formulation of that policy. The intention of this book is to correct those two misimpressions, and at the same time, to increase our understanding of U.S. foreign economic policy and how it is formulated and implemented.

I am pleased to note that, in the two years since the research for this book was completed, the two premises underlying the thesis of the book— that foreign economic policy would be an increasingly important element in U.S. foreign policy and that Congress would be an increasingly important actor—remain sturdy and valid. Moreover, they appear increasingly understood and accepted. In a poll taken in late 1978 by the Chicago Council on Foreign Relations, the general public and the foreign policy elite overwhelmingly selected international economic issues as the most important foreign policy issues facing the United States. In addition, from 1974 to 1978, those who felt Congress played a "very important role" in American foreign policy increased from 39 percent to 45 percent of the population. In the 1978 survey, 45 percent of the American foreign policy elite believed Congress was "very important" in foreign policy.[1]

In an acknowledgment of debts incurred in the course of researching and writing this book, I must begin with Joseph S. Nye, Jr., who as my teacher at Harvard pointed me in the right direction, and then as thesis advisor, friend and colleague, provided periodic and invaluable advice and encouragement. For giving of their time to comment on how I could transform the dissertation into a book, I would like to thank Samuel P. Huntington, Stephen D. Krasner, Robert Paarlberg, Charles Lipson, I. M. Destler, and Phillip Brenner. Under Abraham Lowenthal's direction and

[1]John E. Rielly (ed.), *American Public Opinion and U.S. Foreign Policy, 1979* (Chicago: Chicago Council on Foreign Relations, 1979), pp. 5–7.

with his valuable advice, I researched several studies for the Commission on the Organization of the Government for the Conduct of Foreign Policy, chaired by Ambassador Robert Murphy. These studies offered me the opportunity to develop the theoretical framework of interbranch politics which I use in this book. I should also like to thank Harvard University's Center for International Affairs for providing me an environment conducive to completing my research. Finally, without Karl Inderfurth's assistance, this book might not have cleared its final hurdle.

The book was completed on January 20, 1977, the same day that I began work on the National Security Council staff. It took over two years to find the time to edit the manuscript and make it readable. Let me emphasize that the research and ideas in this book were developed before entering the government. I am pleased that my experiences since completing the book have confirmed my arguments, but the views in this book are mine, and do not necessarily reflect those of any institution, least of all such coherent and unitary actors as the legislative and executive branches of the U.S. Government.

obtain votes for appropriations than it is for taxes, to facilitate consumption than to stimulate production, to protect a market than to open it. . . . The pressure of the electorate is normally for the soft side of the equations." For that reason, Lippmann concluded pessimistically that there is a tendency in the process to be drawn downward and inward.[2] Others who believe U.S. foreign economic policy is the "paradise of pressure groups" draw the same conclusions.[3] Still others believe that the erosion of U.S. hegemony in the world and Presidential leadership in the U.S. will bias U.S. policy in the same protectionist direction.[4]

In the field of foreign economic policy, the "equations" described by Walter Lippmann in 1955 have, if anything, become even more momentous. Testifying before Congress in 1972, Undersecretary of State U. Alexis Johnson said: "I expect that economic considerations may dominate foreign policy over the next decade, as security concerns have dominated the last two."[5] The trend toward the increasing importance of the economic agenda will span much more than a decade. In addition to asking whether we can maintain an adequate defense, U.S. foreign policy will need to address a fundamental question of economic policy: whether "collectively shared interests [can] prevail over narrowly defined interests."[6]

This book aims to answer that question: Can the United States formulate foreign economic policies which reflect a wider national interest in a more open and liberal international economic system, or will U.S. policies reflect the concerns of special interest groups? The importance of answering that question correctly will mount as economic issues and other issues of "interdependence" assume increasing importance on the U.S. and the international agenda.

In this book, I try to determine whether collective interests *will* prevail over particular interests by looking for clues in the past and in three sectors of U.S. foreign economic policy: trade policy from 1929, investment policy from 1961, and aid policy from 1945.

The clues led me down a path quite different from what I had expected. The conclusions of the book are that collective interests have largely prevailed over particular interests, and will probably do so in the future; that

[2]Walter Lippmann, *Essays in the Public Philosophy* (N.Y.: Mentor, 1955), p. 42.

[3]Lawrence D. Chamberlain, *The President, Congress, and Legislation* (N.Y.: Columbia University Press, 1946), p. 85.

[4]Stephen D. Krasner, *Defending the National Interest: Raw Materials Investments in U.S. Foreign Policy* (Princeton, N.J.: Princeton University Press, 1978), chap. 9.

[5]U.S. Congress, House, Committee on Foreign Affairs, *National Security Policy and the Changing World Power Alignment, Hearing—Symposium Developments*, 92nd Congress, 2d sess., May-August, 1972, p. 368. (Remarks by U. Alexis Johnson, Under Secretary of State for Political Affairs.)

[6]Joseph S. Nye, Jr., "Independence and Interdependence," *Foreign Policy* 22 (Spring 1976): 153.

U.S. foreign economic policy has been coherent and consistently liberal; that Congress's impact on policy has been positive and beneficial and that it is quite capable of resisting protectionist pressures and of taking a long-term and broader view of U.S. policy; and that policy is not made by pressure groups or bureaucrats, but rather by a subtle interactive process between two institutions, the Congress and the Executive, which behave for all practical purposes as unitary actors rather than as fragmented, self-interested bureaus and committees.

These conclusions run contrary to the conventional wisdom that holds that Congress and its members are so entangled with special interests and so preoccupied with re-election that the institution's vision is necessarily limited, short-term, and narrow. In domestic policy, Congress's limitations are viewed as bothersome and sometimes scandalous; in foreign policy, where the nation's very security is at stake, the failure of Congress to take a broad and long view puts the nation at risk. Indeed, the intersection where Congress meets foreign policy, according to the conventional wisdom, would seem like a natural place to look for accidents.

In the journey from the question to the unanticipated conclusion, I will explore thoroughly all the various dimensions of U.S. foreign economic policy: What it is? Who makes it? How can it be explained in a way that will not only increase our understanding of it but will also point us toward ways to improve both the policy and the process? And what of the future: what direction is U.S. foreign economic policy likely to take?

This chapter is devoted to two preliminary tasks. First, I will define U.S. foreign economic policy and explain why it justifies a systematic inquiry. Then, I will examine Congress's role in foreign policy and assess whether we are witnessing an assertive phase in a cyclical pattern or whether Congress's assertiveness in foreign policy-making is a more permanent characteristic.

In the next chapter, I step back from the data and examine alternative ways to interpret it. Rather than describe alternative "theories" or models to test the data, I describe five "lenses" that can be used to view U.S. foreign economic policy. The development of U.S. foreign economic policy can be viewed as a function of interest group pressure or bureaucratic politics. It can be viewed from a congressional perspective or from the perspective of the interaction between two institutions—Congress and the Executive. Finally, it can be seen as a reflection of the structure of the international system. Each lens not only helps us to view the issues from a different perspective, but each provides a road map of U.S. foreign economic policy. Some are obviously clearer, more useful and economical than others in getting to a selected destination and in helping us to see short cuts, roadblocks, or opportunities. Different criteria are identified for determining which of the lenses are the most useful and important.

Part II covers U.S. trade policy. Beginning with a brief survey of trade policy since the birth of the Republic, I focus on the major shifts in trade policy over the last fifty years, from the Smoot-Hawley trade bill of 1929–30 to the Trade Act of 1974 and its implementation. Every significant trade law is examined, described, and analyzed in order to determine what U.S. interests—collective or particular, international or local—were served and which lens was most useful in understanding and explaining both the process and the outcome.

Part III covers U.S. policies on foreign investment and foreign assistance. While trade policy remains the core of foreign economic policy and therefore receives a disproportionate share of attention in the book, it would be erroneous to mistake trade policy for all of foreign economic policy, as some have done.[7] A discussion of investment and aid policy not only provides a necessary supplement to the discussion on trade policy; it also provides an opportunity to test some of the propositions developed in the analysis of trade policy and to increase our understanding of the foreign economic policy-making process. In chapter 7, I define all of the different elements of U.S. foreign investment policy, recognizing that policy-makers have never approached it in as comprehensive a manner. Then, the balance of the chapter is used to analyze U.S. parent country investment policy in the period 1961–72. In chapter 8, I concentrate on the development of U.S. host country investment policy, trying to determine the extent to which policy-makers have understood and dealt with its international implications.

Chapter 9 describes and seeks to explain the different patterns and the most significant shifts in the direction of U.S. foreign aid policy since 1945. I identify four major initiatives which represent important periods in U.S. aid policy: the Marshall Plan for the economic recovery of Western Europe (1945–53); the Mutual Security Act to provide military assistance and materiel for friendly countries on the "rim" of the Communist powers (1951–61); aid for economic development in the developing world to deal, in part, with the causes of Communist insurgency (1961–73); and grant aid for the poorest people in the poorest countries (1973–76). In this chapter, I describe each of these initiatives, explain their origins, and analyze how they were formulated and implemented.

In chapter 10, I undertake a more intensive analysis of two case studies in order to obtain some additional insights into the foreign policy-making process. U.S. aid is often used to serve purposes other than economic development or military security. Two major concerns of the U.S. since

---

[7]Raymond Bauer, Ithiel de Sola Pool, and Lewis Anthony Dexter, *American Business and Public Policy* (Chicago: Aldine-Atherton, 1972) (hereafter BPD). This is one of the finest books on the politics of foreign economic policy, but even this study only covered U.S. trade policy, 1953–62.

World War II have been the protection of U.S. investment abroad and the promotion of human rights. How Congress, the Executive, and individual groups interact to formulate policy in these two areas is the subject of this chapter.

In Part IV, I try to draw all the material together. First, I describe in a summary statement foreign economic policy during the last half century; then, I identify the lens which has been most useful in explaining the policy; and finally, I draw some conclusions about how we should visualize the formulation of U.S. foreign economic policy and how both the policy and the process can be improved.

U.S. FOREIGN ECONOMIC POLICY: A DEFINITION AND A FRAMEWORK

Despite a history that begins with the birth of the Republic, U.S. foreign economic policy has seldom been subjected to a systematic definition. Indeed, there are few important terms which are used so often and so loosely.[8] In my journey through the literature on the subject, I found only one attempt at definition. Benjamin J. Cohen referred to foreign economic policy as a "hybrid"—as "the sum total of actions by the nation-state intended to affect the economic environment beyond the national jurisdiction," but also to be considered "part of a country's total foreign policy and to some extent [it] serves the same goals."[9]

Until recently, with a few notable exceptions, political scientists have generally left the field of foreign economic policy to economists. While acknowledging that politics is important and that foreign economic policy represents the interaction of politics and economics, these economists generally leave political analysis aside, approaching the subject in one of two ways. The "narrative school" *describes* foreign economic policies; definition or analysis plays little if any, role. Circular sentences often substitute for definition. For example: "Foreign economics is inseparable from domestic economics, and domestic economics is domestic politics, in the U.S. and everywhere." Or, "The political, in fact, in its true meaning embraces the economic."[10]

[8]For examples, see: Seymour E. Harris (ed.), *Foreign Economic Policy for the United States* (Cambridge, Mass.: Harvard University Press, 1948); and Benjamin Higgins, *United Nations and U.S. Foreign Economic Policy* (Homewood, Ill.: Richard D. Irwin, 1962). Neither defines U.S. foreign economic policy.

[9]Benjamin J. Cohen (ed.), *American Foreign Economic Policy: Essays and Comments* (N.Y.: Harper and Row 1968), pp. 1, 10.

[10]The first quote is from the Murphy Commission Report, p. 2; the second is from William Smith Culbertson, *International Economic Policies: A Survey of the Economics of Diplomacy* (N.Y.: D. Appleton and Co., 1931), p. vii. Other students of this school include:

as foreign economic policy when its predominant concern is affecting the problem of global inequality; it can be viewed as economic diplomacy when it is used to discourage human rights violations; or it can be considered intermestic policy if its intention is to stimulate U.S. exports (the "additionality" clause). Nonetheless, while recognizing the overlap, there is conceptual utility in making these distinctions and in recognizing that certain policies have different ends and emit different signals about U.S. purposes abroad.

3. *by destination:* North-North, East-West, North-South, or U.S.-Canada, U.S.-Latin America, etc.

An important distinction made in the course of describing U.S. foreign economic policy is geographical. The three most obvious and relevant distinctions are North-North (U.S. policies toward the democratic industrialized countries), East-West (U.S. policies toward the Communist world), and North-South (U.S. policies toward the developing world). The principles and institutions which inform our policies in the North-North area—Most-Favored Nation (MFN) trade treatment, General Agreement on Tariffs and Trade (GATT), national treatment on investment, harmonization of domestic policies—act as an important magnet on all our foreign economic relationships. North-South policy is directed more toward encouraging economic development, in part by modifying North-North rules to take into account the special needs of the developing world. East-West policy is different partly because the U.S. has to deal with government rather than private corporations and partly because the East-West strategic competition leads to greater use of economic diplomacy.

4. *by decision mode:* macro-policy, speech, congressional resolution, executive agreement, administration decision, etc.

Like the pigs on George Orwell's *Animal Farm*, all foreign policies are equal, but some are more equal than others. Obviously, a Presidential statement carries more weight than a statement by a congressman; a trade law is more definitive than "a sense of the Congress" resolution; the imposition of a countervailing duty is different than a petition to Treasury to consider a countervailing duty. Two distinctions need to be made: between policy statements and commitments (see fig. 1) and between micro-decisions and macro-policies.

The National Commitments Resolution of 1969 defines a commitment as an act that requires "the affirmative action taken by the executive and legislative branches."[14] A Presidential statement is obviously more significant than that of a congressman, but a good part of the reason is that the President has relatively more power

[14]U.S. Congress, Senate, *National Commitments*, Senate Report 91-129, 91st Cong., 1st sess., 16 April 1969, p. 5.

BINDING FOREIGN POLICY COMMITMENTS

Executive Control   Congressional Control

| Executive Orders | Administrative Actions | Executive Agreements | Treaties | Appointments | Legislation (new laws; annual authorizations) | Appropriations | Amendments | Joint Resolution |

NONBINDING FOREIGN POLICY COMMITMENTS

Executive Control   Congressional Control

| President or Secretary of State Speech or News Conference | Concurrent Resolution | Simple Resolution | Committee Report | Hearings | Floor Debate | Legislators' Speeches |

Figure 1 Binding and Nonbinding U.S. Foreign Policy Commitments

to obtain Congress's assent on a particular issue, or because the Congress may have already delegated responsibility to commit the United States. The power of other policy statements is not that they represent a decision like a commitment, but that they *signal* an intention to act.

It is useful to visualize a vertical dimension to figure 1 that distinguishes between micro-decisions, which are discrete statements or decisions (e.g., a tariff increase, an Export-Import Bank credit) and a macro-policy, which is a conclusion that one infers from a composite of discrete foreign policy statements and decisions on an issue. Thus, for example, a decision by the Treasury Department to impose countervailing duties on Brazilian footwear to the U.S. can be considered a discrete (micro) foreign policy of the U.S., while at the same time, the President states that the United States is committed to helping developing countries diversify their exports by expanding their access to the U.S. market. (One should not automatically conclude that such a micro-decision is inconsistent with the macro-policy. The countervailing duty would be imposed not to deny Brazil the opportunity to diversify its exports, although that may be its effect; it would be imposed because the Brazilians had subsidized footwear exports in a manner considered illegal by GATT and the United States).

5. *by principal decision-making arena:* Executive, congressional, private, state, local, etc.

A major premise of this book is that the *arena* in which a decision is made will help to explain *how* a policy is made, *who* makes it, and *what* it is—the three central questions of the book. This parameter is obviously closely related to the previous one. A policy enunciated by the President has a very different impact internationally than one promulgated by an interest group.

To summarize, U.S. foreign economic policy encompasses the totality of U.S. Government actions intended to affect the international economic environment either directly or by adjusting the way the U.S. economy relates to it. This policy can be defined in terms of issues, purposes, geographical destination, decision mode, or decision-making arena. In the second chapter, I will arrange these five parameters in a way that will yield hypotheses or propositions which will be used to find answers to the three questions of this book: What is U.S. foreign economic policy? How is it made? And who makes it?

FOREIGN ECONOMIC POLICY AS A SURROGATE

A systematic inquiry into U.S. foreign economic policy is justified not just because it hasn't been done before, nor just because foreign economic policy is assuming a new salience on the foreign policy agenda; it is justified because the insights derived from this study will be directly relevant and helpful in answering the broader question of whether the United States will be able to effectively cope with the emerging issues of interdependence.

Interdependence, defined as societal, economic and political sensitivity to events from other countries, has been increasing for two separate reasons: increased international transactions and increased domestic demands on national governments. These two factors reinforce each other and heighten the sensitivity between nations. The major consequence is that national governments are subjected to intense and conflicting pressures to turn outward to maintain their stake in the welfare of the international system and to turn inward to satisfy domestic economic and political demands.[15]

Foreign economic policy issues and the process by which they are made share with the new issues of interdependence a number of characteristics:

1. They are largely *routine* issues. If mismanaged or ignored, they can become crisis issues, but ordinarily one can expect a decision-making process which permits of sufficient time to analyze choices and interests and to coordinate and reconcile divergent views.

2. Since most of these issues involve the allocation of resources by the government, the end of the policy-making process generally requires *legislation*. Therefore, Congress has relatively greater influence in formulating policy on these issues than it does for most foreign policy matters, which do not require legislation.

3. The issues involve *trade-offs* between (a) particular *and* collective interests; (b) short-term, concrete *and* long-term, rule-sustaining interests; (c) economic *and* political, military/security, or environmental objectives; (d) domestic *and* diplomatic interests; and (3) autonomy *and* sovereignty.

   All decisions, of course, require trade-offs between competing objectives and interests, but these trade-offs differ from most foreign policy decisions in the extent to which domestic interests and values are involved, and they differ from domestic decisions in the extent to which those values associated with the maintenance of good foreign relations are involved.

4. The issues, therefore, sit on a *blurry line between domestic and foreign policy*, either considered a domestic policy with international

---

[15]About a decade ago, an important debate began on whether the post-World War II world had become more or less interdependent and what precisely we mean when we use that term. For a summary of the literature on that subject and the most systematic analysis of the term, see Robert Keohane and Joseph S. Nye, Jr., *Power and Interdependence: World Politics in Transition* (Boston: Little, Brown and Co., 1977).

Like their subject, the Congress, these scholars were responding to the two traumatic political events of the last decade: Presidential misjudgment in Vietnam and abuse of power in the Watergate affair. Like the New World, the Congress was called forth to redress the errors of the old one of the "imperial presidency." Nor was this the first time that Congress awakened from the slumber of the rubberstamp. The American political process has rebounded from a strong centralized government instituted during almost every emergency or war since the revolution to insist on the decentralization of power. In effect, this has meant a diminution of the Executive and a strengthening of the Congress.

As America tired with Vietnam in the late 1960s, the congressional resurgence resembled previous cycles. However, there is a significant difference. Since 1970, Congress has instituted three kinds of changes which could fundamentally alter its own capabilities as well as the way it relates to the Executive and its constituents. These changes could lead to either an extension of the assertive phase of the cycle, or it could mean that Congress will ride an upward sloping curve towards increased activity and independence.

Demands and Capabilities

Writing in the 1950s on the subject of Congress and foreign policy, both Robert Dahl and Roger Hilsman, in separate studies, concluded that the lack of independent sources of information precluded Congress from exercising independent judgment. Wrote Hilsman:

> This power over information and this plethora of expertise gives the Executive what might be called the intellectual initiative in foreign policy. The Congress as a whole can criticize; it can add, amend, or block an action by the Executive; but it can only occasionally succeed in forcing the Executive's attention to the need for a change in policy, and hardly ever in developing and securing the adoption of an alternative policy of its own.[21]

Up until the 1946 Legislative Reorganization Act, the House Foreign Affairs Committee and the Senate Foreign Relations Committee, as well as most other committees, didn't have a single professional staff member. When the Committees needed to write a report for a treaty or a bill, they asked the State Department to do it. In 1947, both Committees hired

---

contributed to the rise of the presidential mystique." (p. ix) For Neustadt's transformation, see the introduction of the 1978 edition of his book *Presidential Power*, rev. ed. (New York: John Wiley, 1976).

[21]Roger Hilsman, "Congressional-Executive Relations and the Foreign Policy Consensus," *American Political Science Review* 52 (September 1958), 729.

four professional staff, but the practice of having the State Department write reports for the Senate Foreign Relations Committee continued until 1955.[22]

While the executive branch had been the object of unprecedented reorganization and expansion, the Congress, in the early postwar period, was organized to cope with a legislative calendar more like that of the turn of the century than the postwar period. In the last decade, many more individual citizens have turned to their representatives for help, and the result has been an enormous expansion of the public agenda.[23]

The congressional response to this proliferation of problems and issues, locally, nationally, and internationally, was slow and reluctant at first, but since the 1970 Legislative Reorganization Act, it has been increasingly forceful and determined: more and better staff have been hired; new legislative support systems like the Congressional Budget Office and the Office of Technology Assessment have been established and older ones enlarged; new procedures have been developed to better utilize the resources of the Executive; and there has been an expansion of external research organizations which service the Congress.

Expansion of Staff In 1955, the House had 3,623 staff while the Senate had 1,962. Since then, staff levels have tripled in the House and more than doubled in the Senate, with an especially large increase since 1960.[24]

With regard to its implications on the congressional ability to make policy, the increase in the number of staff was not so important as its distribution to those Senators who had the fewest. Similarly, the House in 1971 adopted a series of reforms, one of which was to permit subcommittee leaders, chairman and ranking minority member, to each choose the subcommittee's own staff. By permitting subcommittee chairmen to hire individual staff, the House thereby permitted new areas of power to emerge.

[22]Interview with Carl Marcy, staff member and subsequently Chief of Staff of the Senate Foreign Relations Committee from 1953 to 1975; in Washington D.C., 1976.

[23]In 1953, 2,640 hearings were held in the Congress; in 1963, 3,869 were held; and in 1975, 6,325. (Congressional Quarterly, *Weekly Report,* 24 January 1976, pp. 152–155.) As one example of increased demands from constituents, former Senator William Brock noted that from 1971 to 1975, his constituent mail increased from nine hundred letters per week to three thousand. (Michael Malbin, "Senate Preparing for Study of Committee Staffing Problems," *National Journal,* 3 May 1975, pp. 647–651.)

[24]Congressional Quarterly, *Weekly Report,* 12 July 1975, pp. 1477. Also for a more up-to-date statistics and a more comprehensive break-down, see *The Senate Committee System:* Jurisdictions, Referrals, Numbers, and Sizes, and Limitations on Members, First Staff Report to the Temporary Select Committee to Study the Senate Committee System (Washington, D.C.: GPO, July 1976), p. 202. (Hereafter, *The Senate Committee System).*

For a breakdown by individual committees of growth in staff, see ibid., pp. 198–202. Also, see Harrison W. Fox, Jr. and Susan Webb Hammond, "Committee Professional Staffs: Attributes, Activities and Communication Patterns," paper prepared for delivery at the 1976 Annual Meeting of the American Political Science Association, Palmer House, Chicago, Illinois, 1–5 September 1976, table I, pp. 5–6.

research notification system, which is designed to facilitate the exchange of information and to avoid duplication.

External Resources: Public and Private, Special and General Interest Groups Similarly, there are many research institutions in Washington, D.C. which commission and publish monographs on public policy topics of current interest to the Congress; four have important influence on policy: the American Enterprise Institute for Public Policy Research, the Overseas Development Council, the National Planning Association, and Brookings Institution.

According to one congressman, the biggest change in the lobbying scene since 1968 is the emergence of public or general interest groups like Common Cause, Nader's Public Citizen, or the new foreign policy equivalent of Common Cause, New Directions; and the strengthening of others, like consumer groups, with longer histories.[31] Indeed, it was reported to have been in response to the increased power of public interest groups and consumer lobbies that many companies have recently set up lobbying offices in Washington.[32] The significance of these groups is probably greatest in the way they have altered the electoral equation but they have also had a great impact on providing expert information to Legislators on subjects like health care and tax reform. Representative Abner Mikva referred to Nader's Tax Reform Research Group as "almost the only source of expertise" available to Ways and Means Committee liberals.[33]

Tapping the Executive's Resources   Congress has also used a number of devices to better harness the informational resources of the executive branch for their own purposes. These include reporting requirements, broadened access to information because of the amended Freedom of Information Act, and the congressional and committee veto.

To summarize, since 1970, the Congress has established and expanded a number of legislative support systems and has utilized several kinds of legislative provisions to increase its informational capabilities to evaluate Executive policies and to offer alternatives. The increase in staff has

[31]Al Gordon, "Public Interest Lobbies: Nader and Common Cause Become Permanent Fixtures." Congressional Quarterly, Weekly Report, May 15, 1976, pp. 1197–1205; "Public Affairs Groups Expect Attention Under Carter," New York Times, 1 December 1976, p. B6. On "New Directions," see two articles in the New York Times by Gladwin Hill: "Citizen Action Unit Formed in Capital," 8 September 1976, p. 13; and "Group Hopes to Help Shape Foreign Policy," 21 November 1976, p. 40.

[32]Theodore Jacqueney, "Public Interest Groups Challenge Government, Industry," National Journal Report, 23 February 1974, 267–277. The point that most lobbying is "defensive" is substantiated by Lewis Anthony Dexter, "When the Job Is Chiefly Lobbying," in Raymond Wolfinger (ed.), Readings on Congress (Englewood Cliffs, N.J.: Prentice-Hall, 1971), p. 336.

[33]Al Gordon, "Public Interest Lobbies," p. 1205.

permitted individual Legislators to better utilize these support systems and to play a more active role as individuals and as an institution. Consequently, the two branches have begun to relate to each other differently.

Power Within the Congress

While Congress has been altering its bargaining power vis-à-vis the Executive since 1970, *the locus of power within the Congress* has shifted markedly as well. The passing of majority leadership with the death of Hale Boggs in 1973 to Representative Thomas P. O'Neill of Massachusetts signified the transfer of power in the House from Southern conservative chairmen to Northerners, many of whom were liberal. This coincided with a rather significant organizational shift in the locus of decision making in the Congress. In the House, Committee chairmen have seen their powers fragmented and dispersed in two directions: downward to other members of the Committees and to subcommittee chairmen, and upward to the party leadership. This was accomplished by new rules which democratized the internal workings of Committees and which introduced a measure of accountability of chairmen to their Committee members and to their party. Also, new patterns of staffing Committees have further decentralized the Committee-centered decision-making process of the House. Like the House though much more slowly, the Senate has imposed a degree of accountability on its chairmen and permitted a greater degree of independence for its members, particularly its less senior members. The effect of these changes is to enhance the capabilities of subcommittees and individual Legislators to propose and develop independent policies.

A Broadened Accountability: Transforming the Electoral Equation

The power of a special interest to prevail upon a Legislator is derived from several sources: its ability to mobilize or deny votes, and thus to credibly represent a constituency of importance to the Legislator; its ability to finance political campaigns; its ability to mobilize a disproportionately larger amount of money and votes than any potential countervailing group; its ability to generalize its grievance or interest in such a way that it is perceived as a national problem or opportunity; and, finally, the privacy, quietness, and complexity of the legislative process. When mark-up sessions are closed, there are few incentives for a Legislator in such a decision-making process to argue the public interest, since it would only alienate the special interest watching most intently. When the result is a fifty-page document, it is difficult if not impossible to identify whether or how a special interest has succeeded.

This electoral equation remained quite stable until 1970, when a number of new laws were passed which could significantly modify the incentive structure which guides the Legislators' performance.

Sunshine on the Legislative Process   While laws are public, the process by which they have been made was predominantly private. Thirty to forty percent of Committee meetings were regularly closed to the public.[34]

In 1970, the Legislative Reorganization Act began to open the door of the legislative process by permitting committees to allow the televising, broadcasting, and photographing of committee hearings.[35] One example of the importance of "sunshine" was a special interest amendment advanced by H. Ross Perot, a Texas millionaire and a generous contributor to political campaigns. Representative Abner Mikva noted: "The Perot amendment was not something new to tax-writing annals. What is new is that it was found out as quickly as it was because the process is open to the public."[36]

Countervailing and General Interest Lobbies   Mikva touched on the critical link between the openness of the process and the ability to discover and publicize a Perot-type amendment. In the case of tax loopholes, Ralph Nader's Tax Reform Research Group and Tax Analysts and Advocates provided the expertise and the *New York Times* disseminated the information. The impact on the Tax Reform Act of 1976 was considerable. For the first time, Senator Russell Long, Chairman of the Finance Committee, was impelled to reconsider a tax bill and delete many of the narrow-interest amendments which heretofore had escaped everyone's notice.[37] Without this relationship between general interest lobbies and the media, the public mark-ups would probably produce bills which were not terribly different from those resulting from private sessions.

Beginning in 1969, when Ralph Nader's one-man interest group became the Center for the Study of Responsive Law, public and general interest lobbies have proliferated in Washington, in numbers and influence, at an unprecedented rate.[38] Many older groups, like Consumers Union (265,000

[34]Norman J. Ornstein and David W. Rohde, "Seniority and Future Power in Congress," in Norman Ornstein (ed.), *Congress in Change* (N.Y.: Praeger, 1976), p. 73.

[35]Leroy Rieselbach, *Congressional Reform in the Seventies* (Morristown, N.J.: General Learning Press, 1977), p. 48.

[36]Congressional Quarterly, *Weekly Report*, January 10, 1976, p. 43; for a more extended discussion of the costs and benefits of open vs. closed sessions, see pp. 40–44.

[37]See an excellent series of articles by Eileen Shanahan in the *New York Times*, including "Tax Bills Pass in Senate With Contents Unknown," 20 July 1976, pp. 1, 15; "Long Offers Second Vote in Dispute Over Tax Aid," 21 July 1976, pp. 1, 38; "Advocates of Tax Reform Win Victories in House Committee and in Senate," 22 July 1976. Also see the *Washington Post* editorial, "Taxes and the Senate," 21 July 1976, p. A22.

[38]Theodore Jacqueney, "Common Cause," *National Journal*, 1 September 1973, 1294–1304.

members), the League of Women Voters (160,000 members), the Consumers Federation of America (225 organizations), and the Americans for Democratic Action (85,000 members) have expanded their membership and their legislative activities.[39]

Campaign Finance   The last link in the process by which special interests have traditionally leveraged their power is their eagerness to finance election campaigns and the confidentiality of financial transactions between contributor and candidate. In 1971, the Federal Election Campaign Act—the first electoral reform bill in forty-seven years—passed Congress. Watergate prompted Congress to re-examine that law and in October 1974, the Federal Elections Commission was established to enforce new rules on reporting and disclosure requirements and spending limits on contributions and expenditures.[40]

Conclusions: Cyclical or Secular?

What conclusions can be drawn about the permanence of these changes? One scholar summed up the reforms in the following way: "More legislators representing more interests have been allowed to participate meaningfully in legislative affairs, and they have been required to act more openly and publicly."[41] With the successful challenge to the seniority system and to the power of Committee chairmen, the locus of power within the Congress has shifted and dispersed, permitting power centers to grow up around issues and subcommittee chairmen. For example, Representative Donald Fraser became Chairman of the Subcommittee on International Organizations and Movements of the House Foreign Affairs Committee in 1971, and after recruiting staff, his subcommittee gradually became the center of expertise on the human rights issue in the House.

Power has been effected by the transformation of the concept of accountability. As a result of a more open legislative process, more general interest groups participating in that process, and the neutralization of campaign financing as an instrument for multiplying the impact of the wealthy, Legislators now have more discretion than ever before and are, in a sense, more directly accountable to their district or their state as a unit, rather than to an amalgam of distinct groups. Because of this democratization of the process, Legislators can take a longer and broader view of national policy.

[39]"League of Women Voters Has Come a Long Way," *Washington Post*, Sunday, October 24, 1976, pp. E1, 8. Frances Cerra, "A Lobbyist for Consumers," *New York Times*, Sunday, 31 October 1976, p. F7.

[40]See Bruce F. Freed, "Congress Clears New Campaign Finance Law," Congressional Quarterly, *Weekly Report*, 8 May 1976, pp. 1104–06. Also see "Congress Clears Campaign Financing Reform," Congressional Quarterly, *Almanac, 1974*, pp. 611–33.

[41]Rieselbach, *Congressional Reform in the Seventies*, p. 42.

In terms of affecting the way in which the Congress relates to the Executive, the most important set of reforms since 1970 have been those which have dramatically increased Congress's autonomous policy-making capability. The increase in professional staff and in legislative support systems has permitted the Congress to evaluate alternative policies more systematically and in greater depth than ever before. The new budgetary process permits Congress to sort out priorities in as rational a manner as the Executive. And finally, by increasing the use of the legislative veto and reporting requirements, the Congress has harnessed the Executive in a way that supplements the policy-making functions of the Congress.

In previous periods of congressional assertiveness, the Congress's focus in any struggle with the Executive was the particular issue that divided the two institutions. Congress never took the additional step of developing the resources necessary to transform its alternative vision into a workable set of policies. Beginning in 1970, however, Congress deliberately improved its autonomous policy-making and evaluating capability, and this represents a unique and significant change.

The growth in congressional capabilities has not been at the expense of the Executive; indeed, the congressional support systems are around one percent of those of the Executive's, and that percentage has increased only slightly, even in the current period of congressional assertiveness. It is therefore not a question of congressional vs. Executive assertiveness, but of two institutions with independent capabilities and biases competing or trying to merge their positions.

Thus the initial question—whether this phase of congressional assertiveness is cyclical or secular—does not seem as important a question as what assertiveness in fact means. Congress has been called "assertive" in the past when it refused to accept the Executive's policy. That explains why Congress's role has been viewed as negative when it is assertive, and constructive when it is passive.

What is fascinating is that in the current period, the American public has been more sympathetic to the Congress's policies than to the Executive's. In a series of polls taken by eight national polling organizations for the Senate Foreign Relations Committee in 1975, it was found that a majority of the country believed that the Congress was doing a good or fair job in handling foreign affairs and that the Congress should have "the strongest voice in foreign policy."[42] Perhaps, assertiveness has finally come to mean independence rather than obstruction. If so, that too represents a significant difference from prior periods of assertiveness.

There are several other ways the contemporary period differs from the past. Congress has adapted to the rhythms of change: its membership is

[42]Reprinted in *Congressional Record*, 8 October 1975, p. S17774.

changing; its rules are changing. Secondly, the procedures by which it distributes power internally, by which it makes policy, and by which it relates to the Executive and to outside groups, have undergone fundamental changes, and these presage a continued important role for Congress in foreign policy-making, and also suggest that Congress will be more capable of longer, broader vision than most observers of Congress have suggested.

In short, any analysis of U.S. foreign policy—particularly U.S. foreign economic policy, in the past as well as the future—will be incomplete without a full understanding of the role played by Congress. This book aims to provide that understanding.

VIEWING FOREIGN ECONOMIC POLICY: FIVE LENSES

To exist is one thing, and to be perceived is another.[1]

—*George Berkeley*

It ain't nothing till I call it!

—*Bill Klem, famous baseball umpire*

While there are any number of theories of congressional behavior and as formidable a number of theories of foreign policy, there are rather surprisingly no theories of congressional foreign policy, nor any theories of foreign economic policy,[2] and as logic would have it, no theories of congressional foreign economic policy. This is rather surprising in the light of the conclusions of the last chapter: that Congress is increasingly important in U.S. foreign policy; that foreign economic policy is increasingly salient; and that interdependence and national self-preoccupation will probably mean increasing importance in the future for Congress and foreign economic policy.

---

[1]George Berkeley, "The First Dialogue between Hylas and Philonius," in Paul Edwards and Arthur Pap (eds.), *A Modern Introduction to Philosophy* (Glencoe, Ill.: Free Press, 1957), p. 169. Klem's statement is in *New York Times*, Sunday April 25, 1976, p. V2.

[2]My point is not that there haven't been books or articles which suggest modes of understanding U.S. foreign economic policy because there have, and I hope to cover these in the course of describing the five theory-clusters in this chapter. But none of these theories is pointed directly at the dependent variable of U.S. foreign economic policy.

As I explained in chapt. 1, most of those who have written on foreign economic policy are narrators of events rather than conceptualizers. A good example is an article on "U.S. Foreign Economic Policy, 1776–1976" (in *Foreign Affairs* 55, January 1977: 395–417) by Charles P. Kindleberger. After briefly describing three models of U.S. foreign economic policy, he immediately discards them because "the country is not a unified actor with a single set of purposes, but an amalgam of shifting interests which engage customarily in ambiguous compromises." Therefore, he concludes (p. 395): "there is no escape from detailed description and analysis."

Nevertheless, from the mass of literature that sits on the corners of our subject, one can identify five separate clusters of theories which may be helpful in conceptualizing and explaining U.S. foreign economic policy and the process by which it is made. These five theory-clusters are (1) a structural theory of the international political economy; (2) bureaucratic politics and process; (3) congressional behavior; (4) interest groups and private organizations; and (5) interbranch politics.

Peter Katzenstein has argued that there has been an inordinate amount of attention paid to the international sources of foreign economic policy, and insufficient analyses of domestic sources and structures, which are of increasing importance given the loosening of the international economic system with the decline of American hegemony.[3] That four out of five theories described in this chapter are explicitly domestic in origin can be viewed as an attempt to right the imbalance described by Katzenstein. The fifth—structuralist theory—is introduced, despite the obvious shift in level of analysis, to maintain some semblance of balance, but more importantly, because it contains cogent and precise predictions with explicit and obvious implications for the domestic sources of foreign economic policy.

In this chapter, I will describe these theories and the questions and hypotheses each suggests, and review the relevant literature, so as to improve our understanding of the frontier of research on this subject. Prior to doing that, however, it would be useful to sketch the underlying purposes of theory and specifically those which underlie my selection.

Purposes of Theory

In an important essay on the uses of theory, J. David Singer wrote that there were essentially three jobs a theory should do: describe, explain, and predict. A theory should accurately depict events that have taken place; it should explain why they took place; and it should be prepared to predict under what conditions similar events in the future would occur.[4] In addition, a theory should be as parsimonious as possible, recognizing, as Morton Kaplan did, that "as we come closer to reality . . . we lose generality," but that "we cannot reason without generalization."[5]

[3]Peter J. Katzenstein, "International Relations and Domestic Structures: Foreign Economic Policies of Advanced Industrial States," *International Organization* 30 (Winter 1976): 1–46. Subsequently, Katzenstein has tried to correct this with a book he has edited on the domestic structures of the foreign policies of several advanced industrial states. Peter J. Katzenstein (ed.), *Between Power and Plenty: Foreign Economic Policies of Advanced Industrial States. (International Organization* 3 (Autumn, 1977) published by the University of Wisconsin Press).

[4]J. David Singer, "The Level-of-Analysis Problem in International Relations," in Klaus Knorr and Sidney Verba (eds.), *The International System: Theoretical Essays* (Princeton, N.J.: Princeton University Press, 1961), pp. 77–92.

[5]Morton A. Kaplan, "Problems of Theory Buildng and Theory Confirmation in International Politics," in Knorr and Verba, *International System*, pp. 6, 8.

But one must ask: describe, explain, and predict for what purpose? Theory is used for many purposes, and not infrequently the purpose a scholar intends for his theoretical work is closely related to his conception of his own role and that of the university in society. The Lurias, for example, identified three separate roles for a university—ivory tower, service station, or frontier post[6]—and one can easily visualize how theory can be used to serve each role.

Hans Morgenthau suggested that theory should provide "a map of the political scene not only in order to understand what the scene is like, but also in order to show the shortest and safest route to a given objective."[7] Depending on the view of one's role, that map could either resemble one taken by a satellite, one sketched by a person with a commanding position who could pinpoint landmarks and obstacles, or one taken by a trailblazer. The level of the analysis, of course, will be determined by the self-conception and in turn will determine the mode of analysis.

In *Essence of Decision*, Graham Allison subtly shifts his mode of analysis from theory to "conceptual lens" or "model" and from a "map" to the way one perceives the map.[8] In this book, I will try to synthesize that view of theory with Morgenthau's. The role of the scholar and of the university, in my view, is to cut lenses for society so that problems can be viewed more clearly and solutions seem more obvious. A good lens should help us to better understand the constraints and the possibilities in the decision-making process so that both policy and process can be improved in a way that helps clarify objectives and permits them to be more efficiently attained. A good theory should be economical (i.e., parsimonious) and accurate.

Technically, I am not using data to test alternative theories in a vigorous fashion as Allison did. Rather than concentrate on a single detailed case and systematically test hypotheses developed from each theory, I intend to describe the sweep of U.S. foreign economic policy over a long period, asking questions suggested by each lens, and exploring which set of questions and hypotheses seems most useful in understanding and explaining the body of material. I will therefore use the term "lens" more often than "theory."

If, as Louis Henkin once wrote, the Congress acts as the "rear wheels" with "substantial braking power" on U.S. foreign policy,[9] then perhaps the

[6]S. E. and Zella Luria, "The Role of the University: Ivory Tower, Service Station, or Frontier Post?" in *The Embattled University, Daedalus* (Winter 1970): 75.

[7]Hans Morgenthau, "The Nature and Limits of a Theory of International Relations," in W.T.R. Fox (ed.), *Theoretical Aspects of International Relations* (Notre Dame, Ind.: University of Notre Dame Press, 1959), p. 18.

[8]Graham T. Allison, *The Essence of Decision* (Boston: Little, Brown and Co., 1971).

[9]Louis Henkin, *Foreign Affairs and the Constitution* (N.Y.: W.W. Norton and Co., 1975), p. 123.

most efficient way to move this "strange contraption" forward is not to expend great quantities of energy—especially at current prices—by accelerating, but by understanding the mechanical processes and by devising a way to loosen the brakes. Henkin's metaphor should help to underscore the importance of selecting the correct lens with which to analyze U.S. policy.

STRUCTURE AND POLICY IN THE INTERNATIONAL SYSTEM

The structural lens differs fundamentally from the four others. It posits that there is a causal relationship between the structure of the international political system and that of the international economic system. According to this lens, the global world economy which was built upon the ruins of World War II did not so much reflect U.S. ideals and hopes for an open, free trading world as it reflected America's political hegemony and its desire to structure a system that would promote its interests. America's internationalism was, in the words of David Calleo and Benjamin Rowland, "specious" and just "a euphemism for imperialism."[10] Since the U.S. is no longer an hegemonic political power, and since the rigidly bipolar security-oriented world has given way to a polycentric, regionally decentralized, functionally diversified world, the international economy was, according to this lens, either going to break up into regional economic blocs;[11] or gradually succumb to protectionism and closure.[12] The movement to closure need not be precipitous, but the trend in that direction, according to this lens, is unequivocal.

If parsimony were the sole criterion for selecting a lens, the structural lens would undoubtedly finish first. Moreover, it has a cogency and a predictive quality which few of the other lenses possess. If the structural lens is accurate, then one would expect U.S. trade policy to be open and

[10]David Calleo and Benjamin Rowland, *America and the World Political Economy* (Bloomington, Ind.: Indiana University Press, 1973), p. 7.

[11]"Economic regionalism has already become seriously entrenched," in Douglas Evans, *The Politics of Trade: The Evolution of the Superbloc* (London: MacMillan, 1974), p. viii. Also, see David Calleo and Benjamin Rowland, *America and the World Political Economy* (Bloomington, Indiana: Indiana University Press, 1973); Ernest Preeg, *Economic Blocs and U.S. Foreign Policy* (Washington, D.C.: National Planning Association, 1974); Theodore Geiger, "Toward a World of Trade Blocs?" in *U.S. Foreign Economic Policy for the 1970s: A New Approach to New Realities*, A Policy Report by, an NPA Advisory Committee (Washington, D.C.: National Planning Association, 1971), pp. 67–78.

[12]Robert Gilpin qualifies his predictions but concludes that the world is moving away from "an interdependent world economy" and "in a mercantilistic direction." See Robert Gilpin, *U.S. Power and the Multinational Corporation: The Political Economy of Direct Foreign Investment* (N.Y.: Basic Books, 1975), pp. 261, 268. Also see an excellent article by Stephen D. Krasner which focuses more sharply on the question of "closure," "State Power and the Structure of International Trade," *World Politics*, 27, no. 3 (April 1976): 317–47.

global in the early postwar years and increasingly protectionistic as the "watershed" of 1971 approached.[13] After 1971, one would anticipate that U.S. foreign investment policy would become increasingly exclusive, restrictive, and nationalistic with regard to foreign investment in the United States, and less promotive and protective of U.S. multinational corporations abroad. Finally, one would expect that foreign assistance would be generous in the early postwar period and increasingly niggardly and regional in scope as the 1970s approached.

Of course, parsimony is not the only criterion; indeed, it is certainly less important than accuracy. Because this lens is inadequate for dealing with the complexities of U.S. foreign economic policy, I will shift my analysis from the international systemic level to the middle plane in international relations—the state and its foreign policy. At the level of domestic determinants and processes are the following four lenses: (1) bureaucratic politics and process; (2) congressional behavior; (3) interest groups; and (4) interbranch politics.

BUREAUCRATIC POLITICS AND PROCESS

With remarkably few exceptions, political scientists who have addressed the questions of what U.S. foreign policy is, and who makes it, have invariably adopted and applied decision-making theories as their mode of analysis, and have searched for answers in the executive branch. Indeed, in the two best theoretical works in the field of foreign policy decision making, foreign policy is defined as either the output of a bureaucratic process or the political resultant of bureaucratic bargaining.[14] The locus of decision-making is always the executive branch. Congress is hardly discussed, and when mentioned, it is treated theoretically as an appendage and empirically as a constraint on the action which takes place within the executive branch.

Why has the great weight of this literature on U.S. foreign policy-making come to rest on the executive side of the legislative-executive equation?

- Since 1900, but especially since 1933, the Executive has grown absolutely and in relation to the legislative branch in terms of staff, powers, and authority.

- The Executive has taken on many of the responsibilities of the Legisla-

[13]Richard Nixon, President of the United States, "1971—The Watershed Year . . ." in *U.S. Foreign Policy for the 1970s: The Emerging Structure of Peace*, A Report to the Congress, 9 February 1972, p. 2.

[14]Allison, *Essence of Decision;* and Morton Halperin, *Bureaucratic Politics and Foreign Policy* (Washington, D.C.: Brookings Institution, 1974).

ture. Legislation is increasingly drafted and initiated by the Executive; executive agreements to a great extent have come to displace treaties as important diplomatic instruments. "Policy" has come to mean administrative decision more than laws.

- In a security-threatened atmosphere, secrecy, unity, and dispatch became the critical ingredients of a foreign policy increasingly characterized by "crisis management."

Indeed, the cases which served as the basis for developing the bureaucratic models had two predominant characteristics: (1) They were *crises*. Decision-makers were initially surprised by the event and had a short time to respond.[15] (2) As perceived by the decision-makers and later by the general public, the very security of the nation was at stake.

These two characteristics are an ocean away from those identified previously with the issues of interdependence. And yet it is a tribute to the cogency of the bureaucratic argument that these models have been used on other noncrisis national security issues and have recently been extended to economic issues.[16] Like the pioneering works, the new generation of bureaucratic studies have largely ignored the Congress, though in the aftermath of Vietnam, a war ended by congressional determination over the objections of a united executive branch, one wonders how much longer foreign policy analysts can overlook the Congress. On issues ranging from war powers, to aid to Turkey or to Angolan rebels, to emigration of Russian Jews, and to human rights in general, the Congress has successfully made U.S. foreign policy over the objections of a united executive bureaucracy. In these cases, and in many others, "bureaucratic politics" as an explanatory theory of U.S. foreign policy is not only inadequate; it appears irrelevant.

But appearances, as we know, often deceive. Therefore, the bureaucratic lens will be used in this study as a question—does bureaucratic politics matter?—and as hypotheses rather than as an assumption.

H_1: *That an understanding of the divisions within the executive branch is essential to an understanding of U.S. foreign economic policy.*

[15]Seven days for Korea and thirteen for the Cuban Missile Crisis. See Glenn Paige, *The Korean Decision: June 24–30, 1950* (New York: Free Press, 1968).

[16]On noncrisis national security issues, see Halperin, *Bureaucratic Politics*. He examines the decision to seek appropriations and deploy the ABM Anti-Ballistic Missile System, while Alton Frye examines the congressional aspect of that case in chap. 2 of *A Responsible Congress: The Politics of National Security* (N.Y.: McGraw-Hill, 1975). For the model applied to economic policy, see, for examples: Jessica Pernitz Einhorn, *Expropriation Politics* (Lexington, Mass.: Lexington Books, 1974); I. M. Destler, et al., *Managing an Alliance: The Politics of U.S.–Japanese Relations* (Washington, D.C.: Brookings Institution, 1976); Griffenhagen-Kroeger, Inc., (Eleven) "Cases on a Decade of U.S. Foreign Economic Policy, 1965–74," in app. H, vol. 3 of the Appendices to the Report of the Commission on the Organization of the

H_2: *That the inconsistency in U.S. foreign economic policy is due to these bureaucratic divisions and the necessity of striking a bargain between competing bureaus.*

Before proceeding to the next lens, it would be useful to discuss briefly the distinctive contribution as well as the limitations of the bureaucratic lens, since the former will be helpful in understanding the other lenses and the latter will set distinct boundaries around an argument which its authors sometimes claim has universal applicability.

Contribution

Perhaps the most penetrating and enduring insight of the literature on bureaucratic politics is the simple point that foreign policy is often more the product of a dysfunctional decision-making process than of a rational assessment of instruments and objectives. The bureaucracy, which is delegated to conduct U.S. foreign relations, has interests of its own, and while diplomats acting as bureaucrats are unlikely to willfully sabotage U.S. foreign policy in pursuit of their organization's interests, they are also, according to the bureaucratic lens, unlikely to define U.S. policy objectives in a way that is incompatible with their own mission or "essence," however much this may depart from those policies mandated by law or executive order. This bureaucratic factor is critical, say these analysts, in understanding the apparent inconsistency in U.S. policy decisions.[17] In short, process and politics help explain much of policy.

Long before the invasion of the "model-builders," Robert Merton referred to this concept as "bureaucratic dysfunction" or the "trained incapacity" of bureaucrats to see the world as it is.[18] It is interesting that he, and those who have followed him, have focused almost exclusively on bureaucracy because the concept clearly has relevance to a broader range of experiences.

Rationality can be deflected, or refracted if you will, by rules, procedures, or biases of institutions as well as by the decision-making process of a large bureaucracy. Thus Congress, not a bureaucracy despite the popular fear it is becoming one,[19] is as capable of deflected rationality as the

---

Government for the Conduct of Foreign Policy (1975). (Hereafter, Hamilton Studies, Murphy Commission.)

[17]See I. M. Destler, "Country Expertise and U.S. Foreign Policymaking: The Case of Japan" (Washington, D.C.: Brookings Institution, General Series Reprint, 298, 1974).

[18]Robert Merton, "Bureaucratic Structure and Personality," in Merton (ed.), *Reader in Bureaucracy* (Glencoe, Ill.: Glencoe Free Press, 1952), pp. 18–26.

[19]See Max M. Kampelman, "Congress, the Media, and the President," in Harvey C. Mansfield, Jr. (ed.), *Congress Against the President* (N.Y.: Praeger, 1975), pp. 85–97. This fear, that the increase in congressional staff is "bureaucratizing" Congress is, in my

Executive. Scholars in the past have noted this. Indeed, the discovery and classification of congressional nonrationality most assuredly predates bureaucratic analysis.[20] Such nonrationality was explained in terms of special interests, and later in terms of constituent-roots or committee structure, but seldom in terms of an overall institutional "essence" in the sense that Halperin refers to the "bureaucratic essence" of the Defense Department.[21] We will find that this insight of refracted rationality will prove more useful, durable, and applicable to a wider range of phenomena than its father concepts of bureaucratic politics or organizational process.

Limitations

Passage of the National Commitments Resolution in 1969 over executive protests, of War Powers in 1973 over Executive veto, and finally, the enforced withdrawal of U.S. forces from Cambodia in August 1973 and denial of unlimited aid to Indo-China in the spring of 1975, demonstrated starkly the importance of Congress in foreign policy-making. Clearly, bureaucratic politics is at a loss to explain a foreign policy made by the Congress over the objections of a united bureaucracy. But to say that bureaucratic politics cannot explain all foreign policy is not to say that it can't explain anything. What is needed is a more precise taxonomy of policy which suggests when and how each institution (and lens) is likely to be important.

The National Commitments Resolution is a useful tool for developing such a taxonomy. It defines a commitment as one which requires "the affirmative action taken by the executive *and* legislative branches."[22] According to this definition, a speech by the Secretary of State or even the President cannot be considered a commitment until it has been ratified in some form by the Congress.

This definition challenges the conventional view that the President "makes foreign policy," as indeed it should, but at the same time a definition or policy-taxonomy which does not take into account the special place of the President and the Secretary of State is not terribly realistic. Therefore, it might be useful to use the National Commitments Resolution as an important criterion in distinguishing between *binding* foreign policy

---

opinion, entirely unjustified since the average number of congressional staff per elected official is about twenty, while in the Executive, it is several million.

[20]For just two examples: Woodrow Wilson, *Congressional Government: A Study in American Politics* (originally published 1885; reprint ed., Gloucester, Mass.: Peter Smith, 1973); E. E. Schattschneider, *Politics, Pressures and the Tariff: A Study of Free Private Enterprise in Pressure Politics, as Shown in the 1929–30 Revision of the Tariff* (Englewood Cliffs, N.J.: Prentice-Hall, Inc., 1935). (Hereafter Schattschneider.)

[21]Halperin, *Bureaucratic Politics and Foreign Policy.*

[22]U.S. Congress, Senate, *National Commitments*, Senate Report 91-129, 91st Cong., 1st sess., 16 April 1969, p. 5.

commitments and policy *statements.* (See fig. 1, p. 11)

By using figure 1, one can hypothesize that bureaucratic theories will have less relevance as one moves from left to right on the policy continuum. The converse hypothesis is also important: that congressional influence or involvement is likely to be greater as one moves from left to right. These continua are useful in understanding why policy-makers have varying amounts of influence on different kinds of decisions, regardless of the issue.

By adding a vertical dimension (foreign policy—domestic policy), we could refine our hypothesis on the relative importance of bureaucratic politics vis-a-vis congressional influence in the determination of U.S. foreign policy. If, as suggested above, domestic policy as contrasted with foreign policy is the object of more legislation and more congressional concern, then one could hypothesize that as foreign economic policy takes on more of the characteristics of domestic policy and less of foreign policy, the corresponding influence of Congress will increase.

THEORIES OF CONGRESSIONAL BEHAVIOR

Security issues have influenced the way scholars have thought about foreign policy. This is not only evident in the literature on bureaucratic politics; one can also see it in the studies of Congress and foreign policy.[23]

When asked about the extent to which the House Armed Services Committee influenced defense policy, one member answered: "We mostly reflect what the military people recommend; military policy is made by the Department of Defense. Our committee is a real estate committee."[24] According to that view, Congress makes procurement policy on military bases and weapons—rather than strategic policy.

In *A Responsible Congress,* Alton Frye documents how the experience in Vietnam discredited the "tyranny of the experts," a premise lurking behind the congressman's answer, and the result was increased congressional involvement in strategic policy issues. As regards the question of procurement, there are literally a "thicket of theories" which have grown up around that subject; one will be dealt with in this section, and another in the section on interest groups.[25] But both kinds of security issues are quite

[23]See A. Kanter, "Congress and Defense Policy, 1960–1970," *American Political Science Review* (March 1972); Craig Liske, "Changing Patterns of Partisanship in Senate Voting on Defense and Foreign Policy, 1947–69," in Patrick J. McGowan (ed.), *Sage International Yearbook of Foreign Policy Studies: Volume III* (Beverly Hills: Sage Publications, 1975); Vita Bite, et al., "Congress, the President, and the War Powers: A Bibliography" (Washington, D.C.: Foreign Affairs Division, Library of Congress, 22 September 1975).

[24]Lewis Dexter, "Congressmen and the Making of Military Policy," in Raymond Wolfinger (ed.), *Readings on Congress* (Englewood Cliffs, N.J.: Prentice-Hall, 1971), p. 376.

[25]For a description of this "thicket of theories," see James R. Kurth, "A Widening Gyre: The Logic of American Weapons Procurement," *Public Policy* 19 (Summer 1971).

different from the issues of economic interdependence. The nature of the trade-offs, the ways in which domestic and foreign actors relate to the decision-making processes, the relationship between domestic and international rule-making and rule-sustaining—all these variables add up very differently for foreign economic policy than they do for security policy.

Rather surprisingly, Congress's traditional strength in foreign economic policy has elicited comparatively little interest by scholars or analysts.[26] Even in the voluminous appendices to the report of the Murphy Commission on the Organization of the Government for the Conduct of Foreign Policy, written in 1974 and 1975, there was only one item which dealt explicitly with the subject of Congress and foreign economic policy, and that item was one and a half pages long.[27] When Congress was the subject of interest in the Murphy Commission studies, national security examples (including war powers and treaties) predominated, with an entire volume devoted to them.[28] When foreign economic policy was the subject, bureaucratic decision-making was used as the lens.[29]

All of these studies on Congress and defense or foreign policy have been outside the mainstream of congressional studies, which have been much less interested in studying specific policy areas than in studying congressional behavior in general.[30] To the extent that these authors use cases or empirical data, most of it is drawn from domestic issues. Unlike students of the Executive, who are virtually unanimous in their conclusion that the ostensibly united executive branch is actually rent by significant organizational fissures,[31] students of Congress, perhaps reflecting the insti-

[26]Those exceptions like BPD and Bruce Ian Oppenheimer, *Oil and the Congressional Process: The Limits of Symbolic Politics* (Lexington, Mass.: Lexington Books, 1974) will be discussed shortly.

[27]Senator James B. Pearson, "Foreign Economic Policymaking," in app. L, vol. 5, Murphy Commission, pp. 56–57.

[28]See the entire volume 5 of Murphy Commission, but particularly app. N.

[29]Hamilton Studies, Murphy Commission.

[30]Much of the literature on Congress has a sociological orientation, with a greater emphasis on the "roles" a congressman plays than on the policy he makes. Part of the reason for this orientation can be found in the kinds of data used by political scientists. In the postwar period, the main device researchers used in obtaining information on Congress was the interview, and rather than construct specific case studies, scholars used the technique to ask general questions about the ways Legislators approach or view their job. The result was that the interviewee often dictated the conclusions of the study rather than the interviewer inferring conclusions from the data. As Lewis Anthony Dexter, who has probably interviewed more Legislators over a longer period than any other political scientist, admitted: "It took me five years fully to see that I was not reporting on how Congressmen affect military policy but simply on how Congressmen define their role and responsibility in regard to military policy." In Wolfinger (ed.), *Readings on Congress*, p. 372.

[31]Stephen D. Krasner acknowledges these fissures, but is skeptical about their importance in explaining U.S. policy. See his "Are Bureaucracies Important? Allison Wonderland," *Foreign Policy* 7 (Summer 1972): 159–79.

tution, can be found scattered along the theoretical landscape. One can, however, identify and isolate three schools which explain congressional behavior on the basis of: (1) constituency; (2) committees; and (3) cue-taking. After describing each of these schools, I will explain how they can be combined into a single congressional lens.

Constituency: "The Electoral Connection"

David Mayhew, in one of the best recent studies on Congress, has a thesis unsurpassed in its precision: the best way to explain congressional behavior, he writes, is to understand that congressmen are "single-minded seekers of re-election."[32] All else follows from that single assumption. Congressmen are most active in trying to *secure particularized benefits* for their districts, in *claiming and advertising these benefits and themselves*, and in *taking positions* which will be popular in their districts. Since constituents do not monitor a congressman's behavior closely, there are few incentives for congressional follow-up unless interest groups are watching.

Consequently, the Congress is composed of people who are not so much interested in making national policy as in keeping their constituents happy. Since congressmen do not expect to be able to change national policy enough to improve the welfare of *their* constituents, the "logic of collective action" postulates that there is no incentive for them to even try, and thus they don't.[33]

Having said that, however, Mayhew then qualifies his argument by suggesting three reasons why the Congress as a whole is much more responsible than his analysis would imply: three vital committees in the House—Ways and Means, Appropriations, and Rules—keep a check on particularized legislation and over-spending; publicity and the growth of public interest groups keep constituents aware of the national implications of particularized legislation; and the delegation of responsibility to the Executive insulates Congress from certain particularized issues.[34] But having said this, Mayhew still comes down squarely on the side of the Congress as a localized institution, one not really capable of making national, let alone foreign, policy.[35]

[32]David Mayhew, *Congress: The Electoral Connection* (New Haven: Yale University Press, 1974), p. 5. Another book which stresses the importance of the constituency variable is Lewis A. Froman, Jr., *Congressmen and Their Constituencies* (Chicago: Rand, McNally, 1963).

[33]See Mancur Olson, *The Logic of Collective Action: Public Goods and the Theory of Groups* (Cambridge, Mass.: Harvard University Press, 1965).

[34]For a good example, see Mayhew, *Congress*, p. 177.

[35]George Galloway refers to this point as the "locality rule," and suggests that "the dominant operating forces in the system are centrifugal, pulling away from the center of national interest." See George B. Galloway, *The Legislative Process in Congress* (N.Y.: Thomas Y. Cromwell, 1953), p. 210.

This conclusion is shared by a number of other scholars as well as Legislators. Representative Les Aspin has written that Congress's "natural survival instincts dictate that a congressman will duck any tough issues that he can. Politically, it is often much safer to let the Executive do the leading."[36]

Another study attributes the failure of Congress to make national policy to its failure to adapt to the major changes of the twentieth century. Samuel Huntington suggested that Congress should concentrate on those activities which it does best: constituent service and administrative oversight, "which in practice, already constitute the principal work of most congressmen."[37] In a quantitative analysis of roll-call voting in the Senate in 1961–63, John Jackson found the constituency model the most successful in explaining voting behavior.[38]

To summarize, the constituency model suggests that the principal preoccupation of congressmen is to get elected, that his activities in Congress will reflect that fact, and that as a consequence the Congress is not likely to be an institution where national policy is debated and shaped, except when it is a pork barrel of particularized policies.

Francis Wilcox explained in an anecdote why the congressman is by necessity a political and parochial person:

> A member of Congress has to be concerned constantly over the next election (though a Senator may be forgiven a few lapses during the first year or two of his term). If a member is not so concerned, it will be said, depending on one's point of view, that he 'had great political courage' or that he is 'contemptuous of public opinion.' In either case, it will almost certainly be said of him after not very long that he is a former member of Congress.[39]

Committees

The essential problem is easily stated: How is a body of 535 equal representatives to make policy on hundreds of complicated technical issues for a nation of 220 million people? Even the first Congress, meeting in April 1789, with fifty-nine Representatives and twenty-two Senators, soon found

[36]Les Aspin, "Why Doesn't Congress Do Something?" *Foreign Policy* 15 (Summer 1974): 73.

[37]Samuel P. Huntington, "Congressional Responses to the Twentieth Century," in David B. Truman (ed.), *The Congress and America's Future* (Englewood Cliffs, N.J.: Prentice-Hall, 1965), p. 30.

[38]John E. Jackson, *Constituencies and Leaders in Congress: Their Effects on Senate Voting Behavior* (Cambridge, Mass.: Harvard University Press, 1972).

[39]Francis Orlando Wilcox, *Congress, the Executive, and Foreign Policy* (New York: Published for the Council on Foreign Relations by Harper and Row, 1971), p. 96.

itself unable to legislate on the floor of the Congress, and decided to organize ad hoc committees from time to time to draft bills from ideas and proposals suggested in the floor debate. By 1816, however, the Congress realized that ad hoc committees without filing systems and therefore lacking historical memory were inefficient, and Congress therefore established Standing Committees. Though the intention then was that the Congress of the Whole would still set the agenda and give general policy instructions to the committees, and that the committees would work out the details of the policy and report back to the full Congress, before too long the reverse of this process soon became the rule. It was the Committee which set the agenda, and as Woodrow Wilson wrote in 1884, "the House sits, not for serious discussion, but to sanction the conclusions of its Committees as rapidly as possible . . . so that it is not far from the truth to say that Congress in session is Congress on public exhibition, whilst Congress in its committeerooms is Congress at work."[40]

While congressional Committees have long been recognized as important, they did not attract serious, systematic analysis until Richard Fenno's path-breaking analysis of the House Appropriations Committee as a social system. This Committee faces conflicting pressures: the Executive bureaus want an increase in funding while the full House demands that the Committee adhere to a generalized norm of economizing. The Committee adapts to these pressures by generally cutting the annual budget estimates while increasing the funding level over previous years. The Committee acts as a restraining force on the Congress, and their decisions were therefore characterized by Fenno as "a balanced, conservative, incremental response to conflicting expectations."[41]

Fenno's study generated many others, each taking a different committee and analyzing it as an organization, which in the Barnardian sense seeks equilibrium by offering incentives to its members in proportion to their contributions.[42] In a synthesis of these studies plus several new ones of other committees, Fenno in *Congressmen in Committees* found that a committee's decisions were determined by the constraints of its environment (including relevant Executive bureaus and clientele groups), by deci-

[40]Wilson, *Congressional Government*, p. 69. For an early history of the development of the committee system, see Walter Kravitz, "Evolution of the Senate's Committee System," in Norman J. Ornstein (ed.), *Changing Congress: The Committee System* in The *Annals* of the American Academy of Political and Social Science 411 (January 1974): 27–38; and Joseph Cooper, *The Origins of the Standing Committees and the Development of the Modern House* (Rice University Studies, vol. 56, no. 3, 1970).

[41]Richard F. Fenno, Jr., *The Power of the Purse* (Boston: Little, Brown and Co., 1966), p. 44.

[42]Chester I. Barnard, *Functions of an Executive* (Cambridge, Mass.: Harvard University Press, 1950). For a list of studies on different committees, see John F. Manley, *The Politics of Finance: The House Committee on Ways and Means* (Boston: Little, Brown and Co., 1970), pp. 1–2, n. 2,3.

sion-making processes, and probably most of all by its members' goals. Using these variables, he discerned three different types of committees: those, like Ways and Means and Appropriations, whose members were principally "insiders," oriented toward influence in the House, and toward legislative success; those like Interior and Post Office, whose members were more constituent-oriented; and those, like Foreign Affairs and Labor and Education, whose members were primarily interested in public policy. He then compared the House Committees to their Senate counterparts, and found many similarities, but an overall difference. By and large, the Senate Committees were less important than their counterpart Committees in the House as a source of chamber influence; less preoccupied with success on the chamber floor; less autonomous within the chamber; less personally expert; less strongly led; and more individualistic in decision making.[43]

Fenno's study provides a framework for understanding why constituent-servicing is sometimes a decisive variable in explaining policy or an individual Legislator's behavior, and why it is sometimes inadequate. Clearly, there are some Legislators who are more oriented toward serving constituents than to making policies, and others whose preferences are the reverse. By cataloguing the differences in terms of committees, Fenno has provided useful criteria for distinguishing between different kinds of Legislators.

The model developed by Fenno also helps to explain the importance of process in understanding and explaining legislative outcomes. For example, the rule on cloture in the Senate *did have an important impact* on delaying the civil rights movement; committee chairmen *have made a difference on* such subjects as aid to education, medicare, and school prayer.[44] And thirdly, the "politics of recruitment," though obviously a much slower process, often has the largest impact. When Sam Rayburn was Speaker of the House, no one was appointed to the Ways and Means Committee who did not support free trade and the oil depletion allowance. When he died, a new criterion—support for medicare—was applied, and after a number of years, the complexion of Ways and Means as well as of Finance changed; medicare passed, and the oil depletion allowance was repealed.[45]

Cue-Taking

From a theory of committee behavior, which relies to a great extent on members' goals as an explanatory variable, it is but a short jump to the repackaged theory of "cue-taking," that Legislators' voting decisions are

[43]Richard F. Fenno, Jr., *Congressmen in Committees* (Boston: Little, Brown and Co., 1973).

[44]Also see Oppenheimer, *Oil and the Congressional Process*, p. 63; Lewis A. Froman, *The Congressional Process: Strategies, Rules, and Procedures* (Boston: Little, Brown and Co., 1967).

[45]Manley, *The Politics of Finance*, pp. 27, 35–53.

best explained by an analysis of the cues—e.g., colleagues, outside groups, Committee Reports—which guide him. I have referred to this theory as "repackaged" because in many ways it is just a more systematic, often computer-simulated model of an earlier sociological genre of scholarship on the Congress, which explored the Congress by interviewing Legislators and asking how they perceived their role, and how they made decisions.[46]

The "cue-taking" theory also has origins in a series of studies done by Lewis Dexter by himself and with Raymond Bauer and Ithiel de Sola Pool. They found that the information-processing and decision-making capabilities of Legislators were so overloaded that, by necessity, they had to be extremely selective of the information they received. Legislators adapted to this problem in two ways. First, they specialized. Ninety-seven out of one hundred congressmen interviewed by Stimson and Matthews said that they specialized in one area or another, and that they could identify the specialization of others. Secondly, for those other areas in which the congressmen had no particular expertise, they turned to other sources (cues), which they trusted to be in overall ideological agreement with their own philosophies.[47]

In a short paper for a symposium on the Congress and U.S. economic programs for the developing countries, Representative Barber Conable described in some detail his own decision-making process and in fact used the term "cue system" to refer to it. On foreign aid and other foreign policy bills, he often looked to his party for guidance primarily "because his own experience and the direct influences of his constituency are reduced with respect to such legislation."[48]

---

[46]See footnote #30; also see Charles Clapp, *The Congressman: His Work as He Sees It* (Garden City, N.Y.: Anchor Books, 1964), for a largely anecdotal study of congressmen; Roger H. Davidson, *The Role of the Congressman: How Our National Legislators View and Perform Their Tasks in the American Political System* (New York: Pegasus, 1969); William White, *Citadel* (N.Y.: Harper, 1957); Donald R. Matthews, *U.S. Senators and Their World* (N.Y.: Random House, 1960).

[47]BPD; Lewis Anthony Dexter, *The Sociology and Politics of Congress* (Chicago: Rand, McNally, 1969), part 2, "Through the Fog of Policy Demands: What Do Congressman Pay Attention To?" Contrast this with the following statement by Rep. Les Aspin: "Congressmen are rarely experts on anything except how their constituents are reacting." "Why Doesn't Congress Do Something?" *Foreign Policy* 15 (Summer 1974): 72. Aspin's statement reveals more frustration than fact, as he himself is one of Congress' most highly respected experts on military policy. Donald R. Matthews and James A. Stimson, *Yeas and Nays: Normal Decision-Making in the U.S. House of Representatives* (New York: John Wiley and Sons, 1975), p. 41.

[48]Rep. Barber Conable, "What Factors Influence a House Member in Dealing With Economic Programs for the Developing Countries," for the Symposium on the Congress and U.S. Economic Programs for the Developing Countries, October 1–2, 1972, sponsored by the Overseas Development Council at the Arlie House, unpublished papers (hereafter cited as Arlie House Papers), pp. 4–6. Another important study found that party identification in the late 1950s and early 1960s was the most important determinant of voting behavior for congressional elections, and that the foreign policy positions taken by Legislators were not an important influence in citizens' voting decisions. See Warren Miller and Donald Stokes, "Party Government and the Saliency of Congress," *Public Opinion Quarterly* 26 (Winter 1962): 531–546.

One serious failing with the cue-taking theory is its imprecision. Indeed, the definition of a "cue" is so broad as to be virtually all-inclusive. Matthews and Stimson, for example, say that it can be individuals, groups, a political party, a state delegation, "any communication—verbal or non-verbal—intended or unintended—that is employed by the cue-taker as a prescription for his vote."[49] Aage R. Clausen, in *How Congressmen Decide*, concludes that a congressman's decision depends on the issue, interest group relations, personal predilections, and the nature of his constituency. In short, the simulated model has returned to the broad-stroke analysis of earlier sociological works.[50]

The Congress as an Explanatory Variable: A Summary

Conventional wisdom has it that the Congress is so decentralized, uncoordinated, and personalistic that to speak of "the Congress" as a decision-making entity is to begin by assuming too much. After a brief survey of the literature on Congress, however, we've discovered that the problem is not that there isn't a theory to explain congressional behavior, but that there are too many.

This study, of course, is only concerned with congressional behavior to the extent that it affects U.S. foreign economic policy, whereas most of the others are concerned with Congress as the dependent variable. While recognizing the difficulty of the effort, let us therefore try to collapse the various theories into one with a set of hypotheses and questions which will become part of the intricate guidebook we are compiling to lead us through the history of U.S. foreign economic policy.

Fortunately, the congressional theories are not incompatible; indeed, they may even be complementary. In a 1965 study, John Saloma III found that 28 percent of a congressman's time and 41 percent of his staff's time were devoted to servicing constituents. One congressman said to him: "My experience is that people don't care how I vote on foreign aid, federal aid to education, and all those big issues, but they are very much interested in

---

[49]Matthews and Stimson, *Yeas and Nays* p. 51. Compare this, for example, with an earlier, less systematic study done by Donald R. Matthews by himself: " . . . the Senator's voting is affected by a number of different factors—his own personal background and beliefs, pressures from his constituents and lobbies, his party affiliation and leadership, committee recommendations, and the like . . . " *U.S Senators and Their World*, (N.Y.: Random House, 1960), p. 249.

John Kingdon concludes that a "consensual model" which is analogous to a "cue decision-making model" is determinant though he doesn't rule out the continued importance of a preconsensual (cognitive) process, which includes both personal and environmental factors. See John W. Kingdon, *Congressmen's Voting Decisions* (New York: Harper and Row, 1973), part 3.

[50]Aage R. Clausen, *How Congressmen Decide: A Policy Focus* (N.Y.: St. Martin's Press, 1973).

whether I answer their letters."[51] There are two possible inferences one could draw from that statement.

The first, which is more compatible with the theories described in this section, suggests that the Legislator will preoccupy himself with constituent-related problems and that he will only get involved in other problems or policies to the extent that they effect his re-election. Moreover, he will try to disaggregate policy problems so that he can present a "particularized benefit" to his district, and he will permit others to do the same so that they will also tolerate his indulgences. A corollary is that he will be more obeisant to outside pressure groups.

A second inference is that on national policy issues the Legislator is relatively free to follow his conscience and his "cues," and thus to make voting decisions based principally on his belief system. Furthermore, the restraining forces of the more prestigious committees plus the other factors mentioned as qualifiers by Mayhew will reinforce this course of action. The fact that the most desired committees are not the pork barrel committees but the "restraining committees" is one piece of evidence substantiating this inference.[52] A second is derived from the communications theory of Dexter (and of Bauer, Pool, and Dexter), which found that the Legislator selects cues more often than he is pressured into settling on one.

Both inferences point to diametrically different predictions, which will permit the conclusion of this study to be more precise than is usually the case. But few congressional scholars have followed the second line of reasoning to the conclusion suggested above, that Legislators have the discretion to be national policy-makers, and exercise it.[53] For the purpose of this study, then, the first inference—*that Legislators focus on re-election to such an extent that their outlook is necessarily narrow and short-term—will be considered the "congressional lens,"* whereas the second inference will be collapsed into the interbranch politics model described below. Studies on Congress and foreign policy by Robert Dahl and Holbert Carroll agreed that a "congressional theory" which identified an institution whose vision was short-term, immediate, concrete, and individualistic and whose involvement in foreign policy was, in Carroll's words, "episodic and fitfull," was essentially correct.[54]

[51]Cited by Mark J. Green, James M. Fallows, and David R. Zwick, *Who Runs Congress?* (New York: Grossman, 1972), p. 199.

[52]Charles S. Bullock III, "Committee Transfers in the U.S. House of Representatives," *Journal of Politics* 35 (February 1973): 85–120.

[53]There are, of course, exceptions. For example, see Gary Orfield, *Congressional Power: Congress and Social Change* (N.Y.: Harcourt Brace Jovanovich, 1975); and to an extent, David E. Price, *Who Makes the Laws? Creativity and Power in Senate Committees* (Cambridge, Mass.: Schenkman, 1972).

[54]Holbert N. Carroll, *The House of Representatives and Foreign Affairs* (Boston: Little, Brown and Co., 1966), p. 14; Robert A. Dahl, *Congress and Foreign Policy*, 2d ed. (N.Y.: W.W. Norton and Co., 1964), pp. 245–46.

INTEREST GROUPS

I tried to be more of a pluralist in 1972, but George Meany wouldn't return my phone call.[55]

—Senator George McGovern

What the gondoliers are to Venice, the beggars to Peking, the Negroes to Memphis, and the fleas to Amercamera, the lobbyist is to Washington . . . Home is the Lobbyist Home From the Hill.[56]

—David L. Cohen
Picking America's Pockets:
The Story of the Costs and
Consequences of Our Tariff
Policies, 1936

The history of the American tariff records the triumph of special interests over the general welfare.[57]

Henry J. Tasca

Stephen Bailey argues that interest group power is inherent in the legislative process: "When a national legislator thinks about the constituency that elected him, he rarely if ever sees in his mind's eye an undifferentiated mass of individual voters. He sees categories of interests. In some cases, he sees only a few dominant interests."[58] This idea is assumed by many to be more applicable to foreign economic policy than to any other foreign or domestic policy.

Beginning with E. E. Schattschneider's classic, *Politics, Pressures, and the Tariff*, a number of scholars have written about foreign economic policy as the hand-wrought product of special interests. What makes foreign economic policy particularly vulnerable and "permeable" is the relative absence of countervailing groups.[59] Two other conclusions which Schatt-

[55]Senator George McGovern, Remarks at the first plenary session of the Annual Meeting of the American Political Science Association, Convention at the Palmer House, Chicago, 2 September 1976.

[56]David L. Cohen, *Picking America's Pockets: The Story of the Costs and the Consequences of Our Tariff Policy* (N.Y.: Harper and Brothers Publishers, 1936), p. 47 and chap. 4.

[57]H. J. Tasca, *The Reciprocal Trade Policy of the United States* (Philadelphia: University of Pennsylvania Press, 1938), p. 1.

[58]Stephen K. Bailey, *Congress in the Seventies* (N.Y.: St. Martin's Press, 1970), p. 16

[59]Schattschneider, *Politics, Pressures and the Tariff*, BPD; David Truman, *The Governmental Process* (N.Y.: Alfred Knopf, 1951); Abraham F. Lowenthal," 'Liberal,' 'Radical,' and

schneider reached, but which were subsequently overlooked and then rediscovered by others, were that interest groups vary in effectiveness as a function of organization and motivation;[60] and that, in certain cases, government officials have considerable leeway to select the pressures to which they would prefer to respond.[61]

Nonetheless, political scientists remain captive to Schattschneider's first conclusion about the essential power of special interest groups to control the governmental process, in spite of the prize-winning study by Bauer, Pool, and Dexter (BPD) which began intuitively agreeing with Schattschneider, but ended as "a dissent."[62] After a rather intensive study of the politics of U.S. trade policy in the years 1953–62, BPD concluded that interest groups were remarkable only in their ineffectiveness and that the arrow of causality between the interest group and the Congress should in fact be "the reverse of what the public thinks."[63] The central group of protectionists in the U.S. was not pressuring the Congress; *it was in the Congress.* "Congressmen Richard Simpson and Cleveland Bailey and Senators Malone and Eugene Millikin," wrote BPD, "were far more important defenders of a waning ideology than were the more-or-less inert American Tariff League or the clamorous but relatively unsophisticated Strackbein committee."[64]

To explain why individual Legislators vote as they do, BPD suggested that a "complex sociopsychological mechanism" is at work,[65] a concept close to "cue-taking." To explain the aggregate policy decision of the Congress, they said that "congressional transformation processes" were responsible;[66] but while this concept offers great heuristic possibilities, the authors never really define what they mean by it.

Three other important points emerged from the study by BPD. First, one cannot realistically talk about business influencing U.S. policy without quickly realizing that within the business community, views are almost as diverse as within any other group or between groups.[67] Secondly, interest

---

'Bureaucratic' Perspectives on U.S. Latin Policy: The Alliance for Progress in Retrospect," in Julio Cotler and Richard R. Fagen (eds.), *Latin America and the United States: The Changing Political Realities* (Stanford: Stanford University Press, 1974); Lester W. Milbrath, "Interest Groups and Foreign Policy," in James N. Rosenau (ed.), *Domestic Sources of Foreign Policy* (N.Y.: Collier-MacMillan, 1967), p. 249.

[60]For example, Olson rediscovered this point in *The Logic of Collective Action.*

[61]This is the principal conclusion of BPD.

[62]BPD, p. 25.

[63]Ibid., p. 477.

[64]Ibid., p. 477.

[65]Ibid., p. 470.

[66]Ibid., ix.

[67]A number of different studies investigating the extent of business influence in U.S foreign policy have found that it is neither large nor united. See Joan Hoff Wilson, *American*

groups are not necessarily the venal lobbyists of Schattschneider's study; indeed, they play important and useful roles in the American political system,[68] fulfilling four "public services": organizing groups, articulating their grievances and interests, and mediating between groups; providing expert information to the Congress and the Executive; acting as "mutually suspicious watchdogs" who sniff out each other's subtle importunities and make these visible to preoccupied congressmen; and disseminating information on governmental decisions to the general public as well as to specific groups.[69] Thirdly, the influence of interest groups is neither decisive nor insignificant. According to Truman and Olson, their influence *depends* on the extent to which they can organize themselves and gain access to important decision-makers.[70] Nonetheless, Truman underlined BPD's main point: the Congress and the political system do not take instructions from interest groups; rather congressmen behave as active agents.

In an important review of BPD's book, Theodore Lowi argues that the intensive case study developed by BPD could only be understood in a theoretical framework which they don't provide. Lowi does.[71] BPD's conclusion that interest groups are inept is incorrect, according to Lowi, except for the case study used by BPD. In 1930, trade policy was a "distributive" issue, in which pork was sliced up for many different groups and put in a single barrel which was what no one intended but all found acceptable. By 1953–62, the trade bill had become a "regulatory" issue, which involved bargaining at the sector rather than the group level, and in which policy was general or aggregated, though also more difficult to predict and more amorphous. A third issue-area, redistributive issues, involves a redistribution of income or services from the privileged to the less advantaged; these

Business and Foreign Policy, 1920–1933 (Lexington, Ky.: University of Kentucky, 1971); Mira Wilkins, *The Maturing of the Multinational Enterprise, 1914–1970* (Cambridge, Mass.: Harvard University Press, 1974); N. Stephen Kane, "American Businessmen and Foreign Policy: The Recognition of Mexico, 1920–23," *Political Science Quarterly* 90 (Summer 1975): 293–313. Also see a recent survey of businessmen's attitudes which finds rather surprisingly that senior vice presidents of major American corporations have a remarkably uneconomically determined view of U.S. interests abroad. (Bruce M. Russett and Elizabeth C. Hanson, *Interest and Ideology: The Foreign Policy Beliefs of American Businessmen* (San Francisco: W. H. Freeman and Co., 1975). Compare this with David Horowitz, *Corporations and the Cold War* (New York: Monthly Review Press, 1969).

[68]David B. Truman, *The Governmental Process*, rev. ed. (N.Y.: Alfred Knopf, 1971). See part 1 for his analysis of the role of the interest group in the American political system. Truman defines an interest group as "any group that, on the basis of one or more shared attitudes, makes certain claims upon other groups in the society for the establishment, maintenance, or enhancement of forms of behavior that are implied by the shared attitudes." (p. 33)

[69]Bailey, *Congress in the Seventies*, p. 18, and all of chap. 2, "The Enveloping Interests."

[70]For a good, simple comparison of the relative effectiveness of two interest groups with ostensibly, equally legitimate grievances, see Clem Miller, "The Walnut Growers and the Chicken Farmers," in Wolfinger (ed.), *Readings on Congress*, pp. 349–51.

[71]Theodore Lowi, "American Business, Public Policy, Case Studies and Political Theory," *World Politics* 16 (1964): 676–715.

issues often become ideologically controversial.[72] Lowi constructs a policy framework which links up the actors and the politics with each issue. In other words, according to Lowi, policy determines politics rather than the other way around.

Lowi is simultaneously the most tireless critic of "interest group liberalism" as a normative theory and the most ardent admirer of its descriptive and explanatory power. In The End of Liberalism, he writes about how public policy has been appropriated by private interests.[73] In what he describes as "universalized ticket-fixing," private interests, having succeeded at fragmenting the American political system, then transform public power into tools serving their private ends. This theme is also developed by Grant McConnell and to a lesser degree by Douglas Cater, whose model of the political process is "subgovernments" or what Dorothy James calls "cozy little triangles," or Ernest Griffith, "policy whirlpools."[74] These are alliances that reach across both branches at the bureau and committee level, but alliances whose strings are ultimately pulled by private interests.

None go quite as far as Lowi, however, in recommending "juridical democracy" as an alternative form of governing in the interest of legalism and planning.[75] But whereas the analysis in all his works remains structural and revolutionary (or counter-revolutionary, depending on one's politics; a more neutral characterization would be nonincrementalist), his prescriptions, with the exception of the one mentioned above in The End of Liberalism, are surprisingly liberal, incrementalist and reformist. At one point, he admits that the reforms he suggests "would, if adopted, bring about a closer approximation to the best ideals of pluralism, in theory and in practice. This, of course, amounts to an admission that however hard we try, it is extremely difficult, perhaps impossible, to escape the pluralist political mold in a pluralistic and permissive society."[76]

Lowi's greatest contribution is in his attempt to move interest group theory beyond the mechanical conception of pressure politics to one where

---

[72]"Foreign Policy" is a fourth category mentioned by Lowi, but never really developed.

[73]Theodore Lowi, The End of Liberalism: Ideology, Policy, and the Crisis of Public Authority (New York: W. W. Norton and Co., 1969).

[74]Grant McConnell, Private Power and American Democracy (N.Y.: Vintage Books, 1970); Douglass Cater, Power in Washington: A Critical Look at Today's Struggle to Govern in the Nation's Capital (New York: Vintage Books, 1964); Dorothy James, The Contemporary Presidency (New York: Pegasus, 1969); and Ernest S. Griffith and Francis R. Valeo, Congress: Its Contemporary Role, 5th ed., (New York: New York University Press, 1975).

[75]Lowi, The End of Liberalism, chapter 10.

[76]Theodore Lowi, "Interest Groups and the Consent to Govern: Getting the People Out, for What?" in Robert Presthus (ed.), Interest Groups in International Perspective, The Annals of the American Academy of Political and Social Science 413 (May 1974): 100. In this article, Lowi concluded, perhaps semi-autobiographically, "that the only good pluralist is a pessimistic pluralist."

cases can be interpreted by issue, and outcomes analyzed in terms of the distribution of benefits. If the benefits are not allocated according to a rational formula, then Lowi argues that one may infer a relationship between those congressmen who made the policy, and those interest groups who benefitted.

Anyone who has examined interest group politics in any depth soon concludes, however, that all groups, regardless of their alleged clout, lose some of the time and win some of the time.[77] The important questions are why and how this occurs. The "distributive" issue-area or, as Paul Schulman calls it,[78] "divisibility paradigm," where a particular issue is disaggregated and pieces are traded for support, has a certain attractive cogency, and this aspect of Lowi's theory has been subject to a number of tests.

Gerard S. Strom analyzed the grants allocated by the Federal Waste Treatment Construction program (in which policy outputs are clearly divisible), and he found that Lowi's theory accurately predicted that members of the House Public Works Committee, which was principally responsible for the program, received a disproportionate share of the policy benefits.[79] In two other studies of military contracts, the theory was not confirmed.[80]

In another study, Bruce Russett reports no relationship between defense contract awards and Senate voting, although he does find a modest correlation between direct military payroll expenditures in a state, and voting patterns of Senators from that state.[81] And two different studies of the classic "pork barrel" legislation, public works and water projects, arrived at different answers to the same question: Was the project undertaken because it was a sound investment, or because it was a political boondoggle?[82]

Bruce Ian Oppenheimer takes two issues—the oil depletion allowance and water pollution legislation—and follows the development of policy over

[77]The Congressional Quarterly Weekly Report and the National Journal regularly carry in-depth analyses of interest groups in which these groups rather consistently exaggerate their unimportance while their opponents exaggerate their power. A close look at the group's priorities for previous years yields rather predictable results, that the group has won some issues and lost others. See, for example, Judy Gardner, "Israel Lobby: A Strong But Nebulous Force," Congressional Quarterly, Weekly Report, 30 August 1975, 1871–75; and Frank V. Fowlkes, "The Big Bank Lobby," National Journal, 6 December 1969, 295–9.

[78]For the term "divisibility paradigm" and its description, which basically derives from the Lowi typology, see Paul R. Schulman, "Nonincremental Policy-Making: Notes Toward an Alternative Paradigm," American Political Science Review 69 (December 1975): 1354–70.

[79]Gerard S. Strom, "Congressional Policy-Making: A Test of a Theory," Journal of Politics 37 (August 1975): 711–735.

[80]Barry S. Rundquist, "Congressional Influences on the Distribution of Prime Military Contracts" (Ph.D. dissertation, Stanford University, 1973), cited in Strom, ibid., p. 734.

[81]See Bruce Russett, What Price Vigilance? (New Haven: Yale University Press, 1970), pp. 56–90.

[82]James T. Murphy, "Congressional Pork and Project Discounting: A Comment on Ferejohn's Pork Barrel Politics," Harvard Journal on Legislation 12 (April 1975): 495–510.

a twenty-year period. Using an adaptation of Lowi's theory, he asks: why did the oil lobby win certain issues at certain junctures and lose others? His full description of the cases leads one to conclude that the reason the oil companies lost early in water pollution legislation was idiosyncratic: Sen. Edmund Muskie became chairman of the critical committee overseeing that legislation and was very interested in seeing it enacted. And the reason the oil companies lost in 1969 (when the oil depletion allowance was reduced slightly) was because of an overwhelming and cumulative congressional movement toward tax reform and because of the "politics of recruitment." Eight years after the death of Speaker Sam Rayburn, a sufficient number of nonoil state representatives were appointed to Ways and Means to be able to repeal the allowance.[83]

While pushing trade policy theory an additional important step, Lowi has, however, left us with more questions than answers. How and why does an issue move across the continuum from distributive to regulative, as he said trade policy did from 1930 to 1962? Can one manage this movement? How and why can a particular policy have both distributive and regulative qualities, or to put it differently, divisible and aggregated components? How can we explain the contours and the content of a particular aggregated policy, for example, trade policy?

Lowi's typology defined "distributive" and "regulative" as distinct issue-areas rather than characteristics or dimensions of a single policy. This limitation was corrected in a full book devoted to filling out his framework. In this book, Randall Ripley and Grace Franklin also add three new issue-areas: structural-distributive foreign policy, which involves decisions on the procurement, allocation, and organization of men, money, and materiel for the armed forces, and which is therefore quite similar to domestic distributive; strategic-regulative, a more generalized policy level in which strategic decisions relate directly to foreign policy and international politics; and crisis issues, in which the decision-making structure is quite simple: "It is the President and whomever he chooses to consult."[84] Ripley and Franklin borrow from an earlier study by Samuel Huntington on decision making in defense, and that explains the obvious bias in their foreign policy categories to defense-related rather than foreign economic policy-related issues. Despite a relatively weak chapter on foreign policy, their book is quite useful in three ways: it systematically lists the hypotheses and the predictions which are implicit in Lowi's framework;[85] and it provides a number of examples which help to further explain the framework. For example, it describes a number of cases of distributive issues in which the subgovernments were

[83]Oppenheimer, *Oil and the Congressional Process*, pp. 70–76.

[84]Randall B. Ripley and Grace A. Franklin, *Congress, the Bureaucracy, and Public Policy* (Homewood, Ill.: Dorsey Press, 1976), p. 143.

[85]Ibid., see table 4.1, p. 72.

challenged and defeated.[86] They unfortunately don't explain how policy-makers could manage the system in ways which would discourage the accumulation of distributive components.

Ripley and Franklin, however, return after their analysis to a position very close to that of Lowi: "In general," they conclude, "American public policy can be characterized as slow to change, as more responsive to special interests than to general interests, as more responsive to the privileged in society than to the underprivileged, and as tending to be defined as distributive and treated as such when possible."[87] What distinguishes that statement from similar ones by Lowi is the recognition of degree—more and less, rather than all or nothing—and the acknowledgment that counter-pressures, for example, from latent or general interests, occasionally produce very different results than one would expect from an interest group analysis.[88]

To summarize, then, the interest group lens posits that U.S. foreign economic policy is the result of the influence of interest groups. While subject to increased qualification and refinement, the lens still leads one to ask questions in which interest groups are central. For example: Which groups won, and which lost, and why and how? To what extent does the policy reflect the "arena" of decision making?[89] To what extent does the policy—whether it's a distributive or an aggregate issue—reflect the politics and the relative influence of the interest groups? To what extent can the distributive-aggregated policy dimension be manipulated? These are the questions which the interest group lens invites us to ask; and they will be asked in the case studies. In brief, if the resident aphorism for bureaucratic politics is "where you stand depends on where you sit," then for interest groups, it could be: "which way you lean depends on who's pushing you."

INTERBRANCH POLITICS

It is because in their hours of timidity the Congress becomes subservient to the importunities of organized minorities that the

[86]Ibid., chap. 4, pp. 82–88.

[87]Ibid., p. 165.

[88]The idea that latent or general interests emerge to countervail a special interest was first suggested by David Truman. Mancur Olson, however, in his intricate model refuted this idea: "Large or latent groups have no tendency voluntarily to act to further their common interests." *Logic of Collective Action: Public Goods and the Theory of Groups* (Cambridge, Mass.: Harvard University Press, 1968), p. 165. Olson therefore would not have been able to predict the success of Common Cause, Public Citizen, or any of the ecological or consumer groups, which have emerged in recent years.

[89]E. E. Schattschneider, *The Semi-Sovereign People: A Realist's View of Democracy in America* (N.Y.: Holt, Rinehart, and Winston, 1960).

President comes more and more to stand as the champion of the rights
of the whole country.[90]

—Calvin Coolidge

In order to lay a due foundation for that separate and distinct exercise
of the different powers of government, which to a certain extent is
admitted on all hands to be essential to the preservation of liberty, it
is evident that each department should have a will of its own. . . .
If a majority be united by a common interest, the rights of the minority
will be insecure.[91]

—James Madison
The Federalist Papers, #51

The last three lenses described above have several characteristics in
common. All identify the critical "loci of power"[92] in a single institution
or "black-box" whose behavior is then explained, and after analyzing its
"decision-rules," all found evidence for refracted rationality. Bureaucracies,
Congress, and interest groups do not make "rational" national policy, nor do
they even adequately reflect their own self-interest. But while the interface
between Congress and interest groups was exhaustively examined from both
directions, the interaction between Congress and Executive was overlooked
by these lenses.

There *are* such studies in both domestic as well as foreign policy, but
their emphasis appears to be on assessing the distribution of influence or of
"relative decisional dominance" between the Congress and the Executive in
each "policy stage" which invariably includes, though the jargon differs,
information-gathering, drafting, initiation, interest-aggregation, review,
decision, and veto.[93] The conclusions from such studies have varied. Most,
however, have concluded that congressional influence is greater than one
would expect, but still marginal compared to the Executive. Lawrence
Chamberlain, David Price, and Gary Orfield all examined domestic policy

[90]Quoted in Wilfred E. Binkley, *President and Congress,* rev. ed. (New York: Random
House, 1962), p. 381.

[91]Alexander Hamilton, James Madison, and John Jay, *Federalist Papers,* (N.Y.: New
American Library, 1961) #51, pp. 321, 323. My emphasis.

[92]The phrase "loci of power" is used by Theodore Lowi in "Four Systems of Policy,
Politics, and Choice," *Public Administration Review* 32 (July/August 1972): 305.

[93]Steven W. Hughes and Kenneth J. Mijeski, *Legislative-Executive Policy-Making: The*
Cases of Chile and Costa Rica (Beverly Hills: Sage Publications, 1973), pp. 7–11. See also
Raymond A. Bauer, "Study of Policy Formation: An Introduction," in Raymond A. Bauer and
Kenneth J. Gergen (eds.), *The Study of Policy Formation* (New York: Free Press, 1968); Price,
Who Makes the Laws?, pp. 4–6; James A. Robinson, *Congress and Foreign Policy making: A*
Study in Legislative Influence and Initiative, rev. ed. (Homewood, Ill.: Dorsey Press, 1967),
pp. 6–7.

areas, and their conclusions were repeated in a more recent study by Ripley and Franklin: "One general pattern we found that did not quite conform to our initial expectations was that Congress in general (not only at this subcommittee level) was a more important actor in all areas than the literature had led us to expect."[94]

In surveys of foreign policy, however, the most widely shared conclusion was that Congress's influence was, in the words of James Robinson, largely one of "legitimating, amending, or vetoing executive proposals."[95] The two cases of congressional initiative which Robinson found were later subjected to a detailed analysis by David A. Baldwin, who found reason to believe that the origin of these two ideas—the Development Loan Fund in 1957 and the Monroney Resolution in 1958 suggesting a soft-loan window for the World Bank—was in the executive branch or elsewhere.[96]

Baldwin's most telling point, however, was more subtle: *the whole question of initiative that has preoccupied all of these scholars is the wrong question.*[97] *The process by which the Executive and the Congress interact to shape policy is the more relevant question: who is pushing whom, for what purpose, and to what effect?* And in a recent article, Alton Frye suggests that even if congressional influence is only on the margins, as Robinson concludes, such influence shouldn't be dismissed as unimportant: " . . . in complex questions of foreign policy, the margins are frequently the

---

[94]Ripley and Franklin, *Congress*, p. 170. Similar conclusions were made by Gary Orfield in his study of social policy from 1960–74, *Congressional Power: Congress and Social Change* (N.Y.: Harcourt Brace Janovich, 1975); by Lawrence D. Chamberlain in *The President, Congress, and Legislation* (New York: Columbia University Press, 1946), pp. 45–54, a study of ninety different pieces of legislation between 1915–40. Of those ninety statutes, Chamberlain showed that 20 percent were due predominantly to the President, 40 percent were the product of Congress, 30 percent could be considered a joint product, and 10 percent could be attributed to the work of interest groups. David Price found that both Congress and the Executive shared responsibility for the development and passage of thirteen domestic bills in the 89th Congress, the high point of President Johnson's Great Society initiatives.

[95]Robinson, *Congress and Foreign Policy Making*, p. 14.

See, for example, Roger Hilsman, *The Politics of Policy Making in Defense and Foreign Affairs* (New York: Harper and Row, 1971), pp. 76–83. Also Robinson, *Congress and Foreign Policy-Making*. Barbara Hinckley in chapter 7, "Congress and Foreign Policy," of her book *Stability and Change in Congress* (New York: Harper and Row, 1971) concludes that Congress has grown increasingly involved in foreign affairs since World War II, but influence remains marginal.

[96]See David A. Baldwin, "Congressional Initiative in Foreign Policy," *Journal of Politics* 28 (November 1966). Also see Allan Furman, "Foreign Aid: New Directions or the End of an Era," unpublished paper for the Center for International Affairs, Harvard University, May, 1974, on the question of where to really assign the initiative for the Foreign Assistance Act of 1973.

[97]David Price, in *Who Makes the Laws? Creativity and Power in Senate Committees* (Cambridge, Mass.: Schenkman, 1972), chapt. 8, pp. 289 ff.; and Orfield, Fenno, Mayhew, and Ripley and Franklin have all moved away from the simplistic question of initiative to questions related to the legislative process, but scholars of Congress and foreign policy have been slower to follow.

vital edges, and Congress's ability to shape them is of real importance."[98]

There is solid theoretical ground for substituting a question related to the legislative process for the question on initiative that has preoccupied many scholars in the past. The question of initiative follows from the mechanistic, Newtonian model of the American Government as a system in which powers are separate and institutions check and balance each other, and in which power swings over time and particular issues from the Congress to the Executive and back again. However, as Richard Neustadt pointed out, our system more nearly reflects one of separate institutions sharing powers. Arthur Maass has refined and transformed this concept into a simple "organic" model in which there are two institutions, Congress and the Executive; two processes, the legislative and the administrative; and two roles, initiative and oversight. According to Maass, the general rule is that the Executive plays an initiating role in both the legislative and the administrative processes, while the Congress oversees both processes.[99] (See fig. 2.)

While useful in helping to conceptualize the governmental process, the model does not take us very far toward explaining or predicting policy content. In contrast, the bureaucratic politics model provides a framework for explaining policy on the basis of the interests of particular bureaus and their relative accessibility to the President. If Treasury, for example, has a Secretary who has greater access to the President than State, one is in a position to predict a particular policy which divides the two departments. There is no theory, however, for explaining the shape or the substance of the policy after it emerges from the Executive decision-making process and proceeds to the Congress, nor is there a theory available for explaining the extent to which the Congress affects the development of a policy as it winds its way through bureaucratic debates in the Executive.

Friederich's "rule of anticipated reactions," which was originally developed and subsequently applied to the manner in which the Executive's administration of policy is altered in anticipation of the way Congress is likely to respond, seems eminently transferrable to an analysis of the legislative process.[100] Since both branches actively participate in drafting legislation, the question Friederich's rule is helpful in answering is the extent and manner of cross-branch influence.

Using Friederich's rule and other ideas and insights from the literature

[98]Alton Frye, "Congress: The Virtue of Its Vices," *Foreign Policy*, no. 3 (Summer 1971): 108–21.

[99]Statement by Arthur Maass to the U.S. Senate, Subcommittee on Separation of Powers of the Committee on the Judiciary, *Hearings on the Separation of Powers*, 90th Congress, pp. 1–7, 113–45, 163–79.

[100]Carl J. Friederich, *Constitutional Government and Democracy* (Boston: Little, Brown and Co., 1941), pp. 589–91.

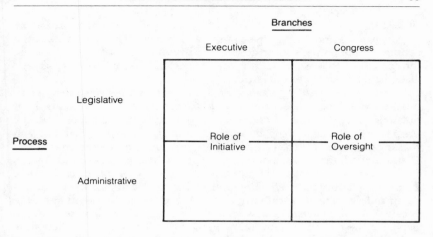

Figure 2   Legislative-Executive Process Model

on bureaucratic politics and on Congress, one could develop an eclectic lens which uses legislative-executive process as the explanatory device for understanding U.S. foreign policy. I will refer to it as the interbranch politics lens, and it will be based on *a definition of U.S. foreign policy as the resultant of a sometimes subtle or tacit, sometimes forceful or conflictual, always interactive process between two branches or institutions, the Executive and the Congress.* The best way to understand their interaction is not to view it from the level of a committee-bureau relationship,[101] or from the perspective of a tacit or real alliance between a congressman and an administration official, but rather from the perspective of *two institutions with distinct sets of institutional biases or predispositions* relating to one another. Like the standard operating procedures, repertoires, and programs of bureaus, these biases determine the Branch's behavior in foreign policy, the style of interaction, and the foreign policy priorities. *These biases lead each Branch to consistently rank its objectives differently.*

In foreign economic policy, for example, while both Branches consider the maintenance of an open global trading system and high levels of domestic employment important goals, the Executive is likely to put greater weight on the former or perhaps try to seek an equitable balance between the two objectives, whereas the Congress is likely to put more weight on the goal of domestic employment, sometimes to the exclusion of the first objective. *Whether the two branches will succeed in meshing these objec-*

[101]See Ripley and Franklin, *Congress,* chapts. 1–3.

tives into a relatively coherent policy will depend on the extent of responsiveness and trust between the two branches. The contours and the content of the policy will be determined by a number of factors including the degree of Executive leadership, congressional cohesion, institutional self-discipline, and economic conditions.

Any model that aggregates, as the interbranch politics model does, must inevitably sacrifice some richness for some elegance. Certainly, I am not suggesting that the Executive is a neat and coherent pyramid with the President perched at the top, requesting information and policy options, and making decisions that the various levels resting underneath implement. The literature on bureaucratic politics has exposed the gaps between the blocks in the pyramid almost to the extent that the blocks seem to tell us more than the pyramid. Peter Woll argues that the bureaucracy should be viewed as an independent political entity,[102] and those who have written on the Presidency, like Neustadt, have described its central problem as trying to persuade the bureaucracy to follow Presidential directives.[103] Others have argued that the Executive should be considered as a three-tiered political system—the President, the political appointee, and the career civil servant; each with his or her own political base and loyalties behaves differently.[104]

While acknowledging these differences, the argument here is that they are not as significant as the essential unity in the way those in the Executive Branch, from the President to the lowest level bureaucrat, interact with the Congress. And similarly, while acknowledging the important differences between House and Senate, between various Committees, subcommittees, individuals, subgovernments, etc., the Congress as a branch with its own "internal will" reacts to the Executive in a manner which has an overall consistency. The particular predispositions or biases of each branch will be detailed shortly, but *at their core is a fundamental Executive preference for as few laws as possible, because as soon as the policy moves to the congressional arena, the chances are that the Executive prerogative will be circumscribed.*

Having said that, one can still disaggregate and hypothesize that there are particular units in the executive branch (and within the Congress) which are likely to behave in such a way that they will accentuate the biases of their branch, and others in which the biases are likely to be more muted. For example, the State Department, for reasons which will be described, possesses all of the executive biases, only in excess. Two important executive biases are the preference for no legislation and for quiet admin-

---

[102]Peter Woll, *The American Bureaucracy* (New York: W. W. Norton and Co., 1963).

[103]Richard Neustadt, *President Power,* rev. ed. (N.Y.: John Wiley, 1976).

[104]Ripley and Franklin, *Congress.*

istration. Both Treasury and State possess both biases, but State carries them to such an extreme that its behavior—rather than just the issue—can sometimes lead to conflict with the Congress. Thus, when a shift in the unit of analysis from Executive to State occurs, it is for the purpose not of refuting but of refining and illustrating my argument, and giving a sense of where a particular agency or case fits on the continuum.

Briefly, let's examine two characteristics which both institutions have in common, then those biases which are special to each, and then hypothesize the potential consequences of interaction which would follow from those differences between the institutions.

Institutional Characteristics in Common

(1) *Active Agents.* Whereas interest group theory largely assumes Congress and the Executive as passive registers of external influence, and bureaucratic theory hardly has a role for Congress, *the interbranch politics model considers both institutions capable of independent and active influence in each other's decision-making arena, as well as in the private decision-making arena.*[105] Thus, the Congress and the Executive are both potentially active in the legislative and the administrative components of the governmental process.

(2) *Most Important Actors.* The Executive is the most important outside actor in the congressional decision domain, not only in terms of the number of interactions with the Congress but in terms of the magnitude of its influence, and the Congress is the most important actor of the many with which the Executive deals. A freshman congressman several years ago confirmed one side of the equation:

> *I had heard a lot about lobbyists before I came to Washington and expected to be besieged when I arrived. I was. To my amazement, the first ten lobbyists who came to see me were from the ten executive departments, offering assistance, literature, and advice on their legislative program.*[106]

---

[105]For a description of the three arenas as a conceptual device, see my "U.S. Sugar Politics and Latin America: Asymmetries in Input and Impact," pp. 221–32, in Murphy Commission Volume III, App. I, pp. 221–232. For a good example of active policy-making by the Executive, see Stepen D. Krasner, "Business-Government Relations: The Case of the International Coffee Agreement," *International Organization* 27 (Autumn 1973): 495–516.

[106]Quoted in Donald Smith, "Turning Screws: Winning Votes in Congress," *Congressional Quarterly, Weekly Report,* 24 April 1976, 954. Also see Frank V. Fowlkes and Harry Lenhard, Jr., "Two Money Committees Wield Power Differently," *National Journal,* 10 April 1971. "The Administration is the most active single lobbying force with which Ways and Means must contend." (p. 792)

And from the other side, one White House aide told a reporter that

> 99% of the pressure [he felt] came from Capitol Hill. . . . Some of these
> guys [Legislators] will just tell you flat out, they'll do everything they
> can to torpedo a bill if you don't give them what they want, whether
> it's hiring a constituent or building a bridge in their backyard.[107]

From the congressional direction, the contact will often be, as the above
quote suggests, the result of constituent pressure, but this is more often the
case in the administrative process than in the legislative process.

One indication of the increased importance of legislative-executive
interaction is the great expansion in the staff and responsibilities of the
Congressional Liaison offices in the White House and in the Executive
Departments.[108]

Institutional Biases

The most important difference between Congress and everyone in the
Executive, except the President, is also the most obvious: Legislators are
accountable, not only every two or six years, but in a sense, every day. They
are all elected, and all but a few take seriously the constitutional entreaty
that they are there to serve the people. Thus, constituent-servicing and the
"electoral connection" are indeed important factors in determining the way
Legislators approach the bureaucracy and the way the two institutions relate
to one another.[109]

People who work in bureaucracies don't always deserve the pejorative
appelation "bureaucrat"; but nonetheless, many do.[110] One proposition,
however, would be that compared to Legislators and congressional staff,
bureaucrats are more oriented to the status quo, less responsive to outside
pressures, and less responsive to nongovernmental (including business)

---

[107]Congressional Quarterly, *Weekly Report*, 24 April 1976, 947.

[108]See Abraham Holtzman, *Legislative Liaison: Executive Leadership in Congress* (Chicago: Rand McNally and Co., 1970); James P. McGrath, "White House and Executive Branch Public Relations and Lobbying Activities," (Washington, D.C.: Legislative Reference Service, Library of Congress, 10 October 1974); and for a good case study of the importance of Congress in the legislative process, see Stanley Surrey, "How Special Tax Provisions Get Enacted," in Wolfinger (ed.), *Readings on Congress*, pp. 352–62.

[109]David Mayhew, *Congress: The Electoral Connection* (New Haven: Yale University Press, 1974); Samuel P. Huntington, "Congressional Responses to the Twentieth Century," chap. 1 in David B. Truman (ed.), *The Congress and America's Future* (Englewood Cliffs, N.J.: Prentice-Hall, 1965).

[110]"If you want to be neutral about a government employee, call him a civil servant. If you want to heap abuse on him call him a bureaucrat. If you want to defend him, call him a "career official" or say with Alben Barkley, 'A bureaucrat is a Democrat who holds a job a Republican wants.' " William Safire, *Before the Fall*, (N.Y.: Belmont Tower Books, 1975), p. 247.

pressures than to governmental pressures. All those interviewed in the State Department and from business lobbying groups agreed that a bureaucrat is more likely to "get off the dime" if a congressman is pressing him, or if he knows the businessman can easily obtain the congressman's support should the bureaucrat prove unresponsive.[111]

The bureaucracy is less likely to think about ways that policy can be improved, partly because of its view that any changes in policy, particularly those made by the Congress, will more likely than not circumscribe Executive power. When I approached one State Department official for ideas on how the Congress might improve our trade policy, he said: "We never think about ways that the law can be changed. Our job is to implement the law, or to think up ways to get around it." The basic bureaucratic predisposition is that the fewer new laws and the less congressional involvement, the better.

Congress is also more volatile; its capacity for outrage is greater. Another State Department Foreign Service Officer (FSO) with experience working on Capitol Hill summed up this difference very aptly: "The difference between the Congress and the State Department is that if you make a mistake in the State Department, you're finished. In the Congress, you make a mistake every single day—only one if you're lucky—and you just come back the next day." What this means is that the caution of the FSO is reinforced by the institution, while the Congress's volatility and accident-proneness is also reinforced, and magnified when confronted with the unresponsiveness of the State Department.

Compared with the Executive, which is so jealous of its prerogative that in a crunch it would sacrifice policy for prerogative, there is much more ambivalence about prerogative in the Congress. Indeed, as Arthur M. Schlesinger has noted, the great shift in the balance of power away from the Congress was not so much because of Executive usurpation as because of congressional delegation and abdication.[112] Congress has particularly shown itself eager to delegate power to an administrative organization like the International Trade Commission, which Congress tries to insulate from the President, or to a negotiator like the Special Trade Representative, which Congress insulates from the State Department. From the Congress's perspective, an agency worth trusting with new power needs to demonstrate its ability to carefully and equitably weigh and balance various domestic interests with foreign interests.

[111]For example, Rep. Thomas P. O'Neil, Jr. acknowledged that he had interceded with a Cabinet officer on a problem brought to his attention by a constituent and a heavy contributor. O'Neil said: "I don't pressure people. I open the door for people." And Carla Hills, Secretary of Housing and Urban Development, said: "I simply called my people here and said, 'Let's get off the dime.' " (Martin Tolchin, "O'Neil Defends His Intercession in Campaign Contributor's Case," *New York Times*, 23 June 1976, p. 16.)

[112]Arthur M. Schlesinger, *The Imperial Presidency* (Boston: Houghton Mifflin, 1973), p. ix.

Consequences of Interaction: Hypotheses

1. *That U.S. foreign policy, though theoretically intended to be aimed abroad, will sometimes be pointed at the other end of Pennsylvania Avenue.*

Since it is the Executive who conducts foreign policy, it is often the Congress which has to enforce priorities and "tie hands," but the Executive participates in this game as well. In this game, the struggle over prerogative, more often than not, masks a more fundamental difference over policy or priorities.[113]

2. *That a kind of sparring match takes place as U.S. foreign policy develops.*

As the game goes on, there is an increased tendency for each branch, but particularly the President when the decision is being resolved in the congressional domain, to identify his own interest in a particular policy with the national interest, and to portray the actions of the other as undermining the national interest.

A good example is President Kennedy's statement at a Press Conference in August 22, 1962 while the Senate was considering the Trade Expansion Act:

> . . . *it seems to me it [the Trade Bill] is in a very important stage now, being considered by the [Senate Finance] committee. What concerns me most about the trade bill is if we will get a trade bill, we may get a bill so limited, which is so circumscribed. . . . If we fail to get the power that we need it will be a very bad blow to us all.*[114]

This sparring match may have an unintended impact on international negotiations. Sometimes it serves to strengthen U.S. bargaining leverage internationally, such as the case of negotiations with the Japanese and the Europeans on steel and textiles in 1970–73, with the Europeans on compensation for enlargement of the European Economic Community (EEC) in 1973–74, with the Japanese and European auto manufacturers on dumping in 1975, and with the EEC on countervailing duties on dairy imports.

Secretary of Treasury John Connally's description of his bargaining style in 1971 is also to the point: "The Europeans have a way of whipsawing you—they say they can't go ahead unless the Common Market agrees, but

[113]See my "Coping with Congress's Foreign Policy," *Foreign Service Journal*, 52, no. 12 (December 1975), pp. 15–18, 23.

[114]Congressional Quarterly, *Weekly Report*, 24 August 1962, 1424.

then any one of them can make sure the Common Market won't agree. So frankly, we used the Congress as our bargaining lever."[115]

Sometimes the impact is detrimental to U.S. national interests when the Congress's need for publicity and recognition conflict with the necessity of private diplomacy, or when the Executive's preference for secrecy conflicts with the Congress's desire for openness. More examples come to mind of this kind of case—for example, the Jackson–Vanik amendment on Jewish emigration from the Soviet Union, and the arms embargo to Turkey in 1974–75.[116]

3. *That frequently there is a congressional attempt to disaggregate a general policy, or to amend it or imprint upon it a constituent demand.*

This centrifugal tendency, however, can be prevented with strong congressional or executive leadership.

4. *That the restrictiveness of the law is directly related to the current or prior degree of Executive responsiveness to the congressional will on a particular issue and to the trust that this responsiveness elicits.*

Conversely, the greater the degree of cooperation between the branches, the greater the degree of discretion or delegation of powers to the Executive. The degree of trust and responsiveness between two branches as a determinant of policy cannot be stressed enough, and in the case studies to follow, we will often see the importance of this dynamic. There are few better statements of this point than that by Senator Russell Long in the course of Hearings on the nomination of several Treasury officials:

> *Chairman Long: One of our big objections, of course, and one of the reasons that Congress has not cooperated as much as the President would like for us to cooperate with him, has been that we sometimes have difficulty getting the administration to act. [Here he was talking about setting time limits on Treasury decisions for dumping and countervailing duty cases.]*
>
> *Of course, they [the Administration] have their own side of the argument but we would feel a lot better about passing a law to put*

[115]Quoted in William Safire, *Before the Fall*, p. 505.

[116]For a look at a similar debate on whether democracies can effectively cope with foreign policy, see Kenneth N. Waltz, *Foreign Policy and Democratic Politics: The American and British Experience* (Boston: Little, Brown and Company, 1967) on the affirmative side, and on the other side, Theodore Lowi, "Making Democracy Safe for the World," chap. 6, in his *End of Liberalism*.

more powers in the hands of the President if we could feel with some confidence that the President was going to use those powers as we had hoped he would use them when we gave them to him.[117]

5. *That cooperation in the legislative process by the Congress and responsiveness in the administrative process by the Executive will inevitably lead to a policy of the second best. Lack of cooperation may lead to self-defeating policies or to no policy whatsoever.*

This means that the President must try, in Lyndon Johnson's words, "to strike a balance between the bill he really wants and the bill he's got a good chance of getting . . ."[118]

HYPOTHESES AND PREDICTIONS: A SUMMARY

Each lens suggests a different set of questions to test a different set of hypotheses. Naturally, it would be impossible to answer these questions in as exhaustive a manner as they are answered in the books that fathered the theories. Graham Allison, it will be recalled, analyzed a single event, the Cuban Missile Crisis, to illustrate his thesis. Nonetheless, we can use a couple of basic questions from each lens and suggest a few outcomes predicted by using the lens.

Structuralism and the World Political Economy   *Hypothesis:* That the period of American political and military hegemony, 1945–71, is the only unequivocally open period in U.S. foreign economic policy. Since 1971, U.S. foreign economic policy would be increasingly characterized by movement toward protectionism.

Evidence/Question: Are there noticeable trends in U.S. foreign policy either toward openness or closure during the period from 1929 to 1976?

[117]U.S. Senate, Committee on Finance, *Hearings, Nominations of Jack F. Bennett, Edward C. Schmults, and Mrs. Catherine Bedell,* 93rd Congress, 2nd session, 4 June 1974, pp. 15–16.
      When Robert Dahl wrote *Congress and Foreign Policy* (N.Y.: W. W. Norton and Co., 1950, reprinted 1964), he examined the role of Congress in the isolationist legislation of the 1930s, but he arrived at a rather interesting conclusion: "It was, after all, primarily a deep-seated distrust of leadership that forced the rigid and inflexible provisions into the neutrality legislation of the pre-war period." (p. 248) I found a rather similar process at work with regard to Congress' role in foreign policy-making to Latin America. (Robert A. Pastor, "Congress's Impact on Latin America: Is There a Madness in the Method?" in Murphy Commission studies.)

[118]Doris Kearns, "Who Was Lyndon Baines Johnson, Part II," *Atlantic,* 237, no. 6: pp. 66–67. Comments by Marvin Feuerwerger on two hypotheses were very helpful.

Bureaucratic Politics and Process   *Hypothesis:* That an understanding of the divisions within the executive branch is necessary and sufficient for an understanding of U.S. foreign economic policy. That the inconsistency in U.S. foreign economic policy is due to these bureaucratic divisions and the necessity of striking a bargain between competing bureaus.

Evidence/Questions: How do the bureaus divide in the debate on particular foreign policy issues? Why did one executive department or bureau win, and another lose?

Congressional Behavior   *Hypothesis:* The more involved the Congress is in foreign policy making, the more distributive, narrow and short-term the policy.

Evidence/Questions: How was the Congress organized to deal with a particular issue, and to what extent did organization, i.e., committees, subcommittees, and the rules and procedures, affect congressional policy? To what extent did the Congress become involved in the executive debate? What were the sources of congressional interest and influence?

Interest Groups   *Hypotheses:* That foreign economic policy would reflect those interests which had greatest access, greatest economic resources, most adept organizational skills, or whose survival was at stake. That the private arena was the critical decisional locus for explaining U.S. foreign economic policy.

Evidence/Questions: Which interest groups were involved, and where did they stand on the particular issue? Did the decision reached in the private arena prevail in the public arena?

Interbranch Politics   *Hypotheses:* That foreign economic policy is best explained by the interaction between the two branches. That the degree to which respective priorities are integrated is a function of the degree of trust and responsiveness between the two branches. That Congress does consistently affect the debate within the Executive toward stressing domestic priorities, while the Executive weights the congressional debate toward the maintenance of the global economic system. The more responsive the Executive is to the congressional will, the more discretion the Congress is likely to delegate to the Executive. At the same time, the more influential general interest groups are, the more likely U.S. foreign economic policy will be reflective of long-term interests.

Evidence/Questions: How did Congress make a difference in the debate within the executive branch, and how did the Executive make a difference in the debate within the legislative branch? What were the policy priorities of each branch? To what extent was the relationship between

Congress and Executive based on trust and responsiveness? What accounted for accommodation and conflict between the branches?

THE DEPENDENT VARIABLE: SELECTING CASES

Which lens is most useful? To answer that question, it is necessary to be more precise in identifying what it is that I intend to explain—i.e., what is the dependent variable. The foreign economic policies that will serve as the raw data of this study are confined to three policy categories: U.S. trade policy, 1929–76; U.S. foreign investment policy, 1960–76; and U.S. foreign assistance policy, 1945–76.

While more manageable than analyzing all of U.S. foreign economic policy, each policy area is still unwieldy in its scope. To explain each policy, one needs some landmarks. In trade policy, the principal landmarks will be the trade bills, which define the parameters of U.S. trade policy. I will use different lenses to try to explain whether and why these trade laws, individually and collectively, were liberal or protectionist, short-term-oriented or more intent on long-term rule-making and sustaining, restrictive or discretionary, intent on helping particular groups or the collective interest.

In investment policy, many of the landmarks and issues are the same. On the issue of foreign investment abroad, the questions are whether U.S. policy will be protective or arms-length, promoting investment or restricting it, providing flexible or mandatory instructions to the President. On the issue of foreign investment in the U.S., the questions are whether the policy will be liberal or exclusionary, restrictive or discretionary, based on a double or a single standard.

Finally, on foreign assistance policy, the questions are whether the policy is restrictive or discretionary, at the service of a particular group or of the diplomatic or long-term interests of the United States. Like trade and investment policy, the case material will be primarily legislation, but the questions will relate to the administrative process as well as the legislative process. In foreign assistance policy, a more intensive analysis of two case studies—on investment disputes and on human rights—will be undertaken in order to search for some clues about the foreign policy-making process.

There are several reasons why these policy areas were chosen, and others were not. U.S. international monetary policy—one of the traditional quadrumvirate, with trade, aid, and investment, of foreign economic policy— was not chosen because it exhibits very few of the characteristics of the issues of interdependence, which are of central concern to this study. U.S. policy on the creation and maintenance of rules for the international monetary system is made by few actors, generally in the executive branch, with relatively little input by Congress or by private groups. This is both cause and consequence of the fact that it is more difficult to know what the impact of a change in the international monetary system will be on different groups in society.[119] In contrast, there are many societal groups that are aware of the impact of changes in trade policy, and therefore are actively involved in the political process, making officials acutely aware of their stake in a particular decision. Thus, the trade-offs are different, and monetary policy would therefore not provide a good test of either the theories or the question of whether the United States will manage economic interdependence.

There are many other policy areas—like agriculture, environment, oceans, etc.—which could have been selected, and one of these was the subject of a previous study which used a similar analytic framework,[120] but rather than risk being encyclopedic, this study has concentrated on the three most relevant policy areas of the traditional quadrumvirate of foreign economic policy.

So much of what is paraded as a foreign policy theory is actually a single case study, often occurring in a short time frame, writ large by generalization.[121] Even the Bauer, Pool, and Dexter book which remains probably the best study in the field does not cover U.S. foreign economic policy but only the politics of U.S. trade policy from 1953–62. Theodore Lowi, while trying to cast a wide net over many cases developed in other studies, does not examine the cases and, as a result, there are many which find the theory ill-fitting.[122]

Other studies have a tendency to bias their data, by selecting cases

[119]See John Odell, "The United States in the International Monetary System: Sources of Foreign Policy Change" (Ph.D. dissertation, Political Science Department, University of Wisconsin, 1976); John Conybeare, "U.S. Foreign Economic Policy and the International Capital Export Controls, 1963–1974" (Ph.D. dissertation, Harvard University, November 1976).

[120]See my "U.S. Sugar Politics and Latin America"; also Joseph S. Nye, Jr. and Robert O. Keohane examine the issues of oceans and money in Power and Interdependence (Boston: Little, Brown and Co., 1977), Part II.

[121]Lowi correctly criticizes David Truman for basing his model on interest groups in Governmental Process on a regulatory case developed by Early Latham in The Group Theory of Politics. See Lowi's "Four Systems of Policy, Politics, and Choice," Public Administration Review 32 (July/August 1972): 298–310.

[122]For example, Lowi argues that Kennedy's strategy on textile concessions was ineffective; it "probably got him only Georgia's votes." ("Public Policy and Political Theory," p. 683, n.8). He notes that on the crucial vote on the Mason motion for recommital, 37 of the 44 protectionist Democrats were Southern. What he neglects to mention is the fact that the textile bloc was composed of 128 congressmen, who had consistently voted as a bloc since the 1950s to oppose freer trade. The vast majority of this bloc supported Kennedy in 1962, including, or rather especially the bloc's leaders, Rep. Vinson and Rep. W. J. Bryan Dorn. (See Congressional Quarterly, Weekly Report, 27 April 1962, pp. 680–82; and Congressional Quarterly, Almanac, 1962, pp. 618–19.)

which will prove their theories rather than test them.[123] I have deliberately tried to avoid this pitfall by using cases which are diverse and which span the various instruments and potential relationships between the Congress, the Executive, and the private sector. For example, the private sector has traditionally played a large role in trade policy, which has often been characterized by legislative-executive compromise. Investment and assistance policy have often been subject to disagreement, sometimes conflict, between legislative and executive branches. Private sector involvement sometimes generates such conflicts; other times the private sector is not even involved in policy-making.

By spanning the period from 1929 to 1976, we will be able to explain why those variables associated with interest groups, which Schattschneider considered the most critical in his study of trade policy in 1929, were interpreted as unimportant by Bauer, Pool, and Dexter in the period 1953–62, and whether the variables viewed as important by the latter authors in the period 1953–62 were important in the period 1963–76.

With regards to foreign investment policy, there have been three studies of the decision-making process, and two concluded that bureaucratic politics was the most profitable framework of inquiry,[124] while the other concluded that multinational corporations were the determining factor.[125]

No comparable political theory other than legislative obstructionism has been offered for the inconsistencies in U.S. foreign assistance policy, and this policy area therefore offers fertile territory for analysis.

As I noted at the beginning of this chapter, I will not rigorously test each theory against the data; rather, I will move from one lens to another trying to determine the most useful one to explain the policies. In doing so, I will spend relatively more time and effort with the interbranch politics lens mainly because it is new. The concept emerged from an exhausting, if not exhaustive, study of the cases, and I will use this book to elucidate it.

Still, one can hardly argue that the cases in this study are self-serving. Indeed, they may be among the "least likely" to prove the utility of the interbranch politics lens.[126] The *most* likely would involve questions of institutional prerogative, particularly those raised by Congress (e.g., War Powers, Executive Agreements); those which engage the direct attention of

[123]Harry Eckstein, "Case Study and Theory in Political Science," in Fred I. Greenstein and Nelson Polsby (eds.), *Handbook of Political Science volume 7: "Strategies of Inquiry"* (Reading, Ma.: Addison-Wesley Publishing, 1975), pp. 79–138.

[124]Einhorn, *Expropriation Politics;* and Gregory F. Treverton, "United States Policy-Making Toward Peru: The IPC Affairs," in app. I, vol. 3 of the Hamilton Studies, Murphy Commission (1975), 205–11.

[125]Charles Lipson, "Corporate Preferences and Public Policies: Foreign Aid Sanctions and Investment Protection," *World Politics* 28 (April 1976): 396–421.

[126]Harry Eckstein, "Case Study and Theory," pp. 110, 119.

the American public (e.g., Vietnam); those involving a constituent in distress abroad; or those specific bills (more often private, sometimes public) which are pressed by a powerful interest (e.g., an amendment to the tax law).

Each chapter in this book, and particularly each of the cases, could easily have been the subject of a separate work. There is a clear trade-off that a researcher has to make between doing a single case intensively and doing a wide range of cases more superficially. Single, isolated case studies do indeed teach us something about a particular case, and the best of them, like Allison's and Neustadt's, lead us toward powerful general conclusions. But one just doesn't know the boundaries of their relevance, and the extent to which one can legitimately generalize. James Kurth has referred to the "thicket of theories" which have grown up trying to explain U.S. foreign policy. Many of these theories pretend a universality without clearly defining the limitations of their dependent variable, which may in fact be as specific as weapons procurement decisions, crisis decisions, or decisions on expropriation policy.

Obviously, I have chosen to examine a large body of case material in the hope that the conclusions that emerge will be solid enough to enable us to understand the politics of U.S. foreign economic policy—what it is and how it's made.

U.S. TRADE POLICY, 1929–76

I pass with relief from the tossing sea of Cause and Theory to the firm ground of Result and Fact.

—*Sir Winston Churchill, 1898*

3

U.S. TRADE POLICY, 1929–60

The methods by which tariff bills are constructed have become all too familiar and throw a significant light on the character of the legislation involved. Debate in the House has little to do with it. The process by which such a bill is made is private, not public; because the reasons which underlie many of the rates imposed are private.[1]

—*Woodrow Wilson, 1909*

Congressional [tariff] revisions are not only disturbing to business, but, with all their necessary collateral surroundings in lobbies, logrolling and the activities of group interests, are disturbing to public confidence.[2]

—*Herbert Hoover*
June 15, 1930

From 1789 until the completion of the Kennedy Round of Multilateral Trade Negotiations in 1967, the most important trade issue facing American Legislators, Administrators, and diplomatic negotiators was the tariff: whether and how to raise, lower, or eliminate tariffs on a particular product or group of products. In the nineteenth century, the tariff was not only considered synonomous with trade policy but also with U.S. foreign economic policy.[3] And, as both Woodrow Wilson and Herbert Hoover noted, the process by which tariff policy was made did not lend itself to much respect. Lawrence Chamberlain elaborated: "It is a commonplace that tariff legisla-

[1]Woodrow Wilson, "The Tariff Make-Believe," *North American Review*, October 1909.

[2]Congressional Quarterly, *Guide to the U.S. Congress* (1971), p. 178.

[3]See Tom E. Terrill, *The Tariff, Politics, and American Foreign Policy, 1874–1906* (Westport, Ct.: Greenwood Press, 1973).

tion in the United States has been the paradise of pressure groups."[4]

, Schattschneider's book was a systematic study of the influence of interest groups on the Smoot-Hawley Tariff bill of 1929, and it "set the tone for a whole generation of political writing on pressure groups."[5] It also cut the lens through which Americans have since visualized the making of U.S. foreign trade policy, and perhaps all of foreign economic policy. Yet a close study of the Smoot-Hawley Tariff in the context of a history of U.S. trade policy will leave one bewildered over the book's continued influence, since both the Smoot-Hawley Tariff and the book represented the end of an era, not a forecast of future policies. Indeed, Schattschneider completed his manuscript in September 1935, sixteen months after the passage of the Reciprocal Trade Agreements Act—a law viewed by another important author of the same period as a "profoundly significant political development of the first magnitude."[6] Not only did Schattschneider fail to recognize the significance of the new Act for future U.S. trade policy and the policy-making process, but he even predicted that the logrolling process he described for the 1930 Tariff Act was so entrenched that the U.S. was unlikely to ever see a rational, national trade policy: "The very tendencies that have made the [trade] legislation bad have, however, made it politically invincible."[7]

Not surprisingly, his analysis rested on several untested and faulty assumptions. His principal data source was the twenty thousand pages of public hearings which he called "the decisive step in the course of the bill through Congress." He viewed these documents as confidential rather than as public documents, which they were.[8] Of course, the public hearings on almost any subject other than televised impeachment are never decisive and hardly ever important; what counts is the (closed; now generally open) mark-up session, when the bill is redrafted by the committee. He focused on interest groups and Congress and totally excluded the role of the President, of partisanship, and of foreign reaction.

To understand the reasons for his oversights and to evaluate his judgment on the relative importance of interest groups on the trade policy-making process, we will begin this chapter with an analysis of Smoot-

[4]Lawrence Chamberlain, The President, Congress, and Legislation, (New York: Columbia University Press, 1946), p. 85.

[5]Raymond Bauer, Ithiel de Sola Pool, and L.A. Dexter, American Business and Public Policy (Chicago: Aldine-Atherton, 1972), hereafter cited as "BPD," p. 25.

[6]Henry Tasca, The Reciprocal Trade Policy of the United States (Philadelphia: University of Pennsylvania Press, 1938) pp. 7, 73.

[7]E. E. Schattschneider, Politics, Pressures, and the Tariff: A Study of Free Enterprise in Pressure Politics, as Shown in the 1929–30 Revision of the Tariff. (New York: Prentice-Hall, Inc., 1935), p. 283. The only mention of the 1934 Trade Act in Schattschneider's book is in a footnote on page 289 where he refers to it as "the intelligent approach to the problem."

[8]Schattschneider, Politics, Pressures, and the Tariff p. 13.

Hawley, and then examine all of the important modern legislative struggles in U.S. trade policy: 1934, 1945, 1953–55, 1962, and 1973–74. The period between the legislative renewals will be discussed only in so far as it sheds light on the policy and the process.

First, however, I will offer a definition of trade policy and provide a taxonomy so that one can more easily identify the extent to which one can generalize about trade policy from a study of the major trade laws.

FOREIGN TRADE POLICY: DEFINITION AND TAXONOMY

Benjamin J. Cohen concisely defines trade policy as "the sum total of actions by the state intended to affect the extent, composition, and direction of its imports and exports of goods and services."[9] And at that level of policy, the Council on International Economic Policy (CIEP) identified the objectives of U.S. trade policy as "multilateralism, nondiscrimination, and freer trade."[10] Yet at a different level, one can easily identify any number of governmental actions which have ignored, side-stepped, or undermined these objectives.

For example, in 1973, when the United States was trying to persuade the European Community to grant greater access to U.S. farm goods, the President announced export controls on soybeans. While the Executive was trying to persuade the Congress of the need for new liberal trade legislation in the early 1970s, it was at the same time trying to persuade the Japanese, the Europeans, and several other countries of the need for voluntary export restraint agreements. Both sets of examples indicate the degree and the seeming self-contradictory nature of U.S. Government involvement in trade policy. Although many have tried to explain the inconsistency by reference to bureaucratic politics,[11] another explanation would be that foreign economic policy is often marshalled to pursue a number of objectives. When these objectives conflict, trade-offs are necessary.

For the soybean case, the Administration used, or perhaps misused, export controls for the purpose of domestic price stabilization. The textile and steel voluntary export restraint programs were designed to protect two important industries from disruptive competition from imports. At the

[9]Benjamin J. Cohen, ed., *American Foreign Economic Policy: Essays and Comments* (New York: Harper and Row, 1968), p. 20.

[10]*International Economic Report of the President*, March 1976, 42.

[11]Hamilton Studies, Murphy Commission; I. M. Destler, et al., *Managing an Alliance*, Historically, the most conventional mode of explaining the inconsistencies in U.S foreign economic policy was "sectionalism," focusing on the different economic interests of different regions of the country. See, for example, Arthur D. Gayer and Carl T. Schmidt, *American Economic Foreign Policy: Postwar History, Analysis, and Interpretation* (1939).

TABLE 2   Trade Policy Taxonomy

A. IMPORT POLICY

    (1) *Promotion of Imports*: trade laws (harmonization, reduction, or elimination of tariffs and nontariff barriers), authorized on a one, three, or five year basis, and negotiated either bilaterally or multilaterally

    (2) *Restriction of Imports*: tariffs, nontariff barriers, quantitative restrictions, exchange controls, voluntary export restraint agreements, oil quotas, agricultural marketing orders (section 22 of Agricultural Adjustment Act), commodity agreements, sugar program, Buy-American Act

    (3) *Regulations which Affect Imports*: environmental, health, and safety standards and regulations, trade marks and patents

    (4) *Regime Creation, Maintenance, and Adjustment*: GATT, ITO, UNCTAD, commodity agreements and organizations

B. EXPORT POLICY

    (1) *Promotion of Exports*: trade negotiations (reduce or eliminate the tariffs or nontariff barriers of other countries); Export-Import Bank loans; Domestic International Sales Corporation, 1971; Treaties of Friendship, Commerce and Navigation; additionality ("tying" foreign assistance to purchase of U.S. goods); credits for arms sales; PL 480 (food assistance)

    (2) *Restriction and Regulation of Exports*: Strategic stockpiling (Defense Production Act, Export Control Act); antiinflationary (Export Administration Act); trade diversion for strategic purposes (Trading with the Enemy Act, amendments to the Economic Cooperation Administration Act); arms sales; nuclear technology

---

same time, these two agreements served a rather contradictory purpose of trying to maintain a nondiscriminatory trading system.

As table 2 shows, U.S. trade policy includes the promotion, restriction, and regulation of imports and exports. It also includes the creation, maintenance, and adjustment of the international trading system. While trade legislation entails only one set of U.S. trade policies (primarily promotion and restriction of imports; regime creation, maintenance, and adjustment; the promotion of exports), it is the principal rule-setting mechanism for domestic policy as well as for international negotiations abroad. As such, the central trade bills remain the core of U.S. trade policy and have, by far, a greater impact on the extent, composition, and direction of U.S. trade than any other U.S. trade policy.

It is necessary and useful to distinguish between the legislative and administrative functions which apply both domestically and internationally. Domestic legislative acts are trade laws; administrative acts include imposition of countervailing duties, antidumping, and export controls. International legislative acts are trade agreements; administrative acts are decided by GATT panels of investigation. The line of influence between domestic and international rule-making (legislative process) and rule-maintenance (administrative process) is multidirectional. (See fig. 3.) Domestically, we will find that the administration of trade policy is always influenced by and in turn influences the congressional consideration of a new trade bill. At the same time, investigations by GATT panels are always influenced by the multilateral trade negotiations which in turn are influenced by domestic rule-making (prescribing the negotiating authority of the U.S.) and administering (e.g., the imposition of countervailing duties on the exports of another country).[12]

TRADE POLICY, 1789–1929: A BRIEF SURVEY

In the eighteenth and nineteenth centuries, the United States, like most developing countries, used the tariff much as developed countries use taxes today: as the principal source of revenue and as an instrument for discouraging the consumption of luxury goods or products that would harm people or "infant industries." Even during the years 1837–61, a period of moderate tariffs in the United States and the world, tariffs contributed to 90 percent of all Federal revenue. The first Tariff Act in 1789 levied duties which averaged 8.5 percent, quite low by later standards, but this was gradually increased as the financial needs of the Federal Government expanded.[13]

Although the argument for protecting "infant industries" was heard as early as the first Tariff Act,[14] "protectionism" as a rationale, a principle, and an important tool of U.S. trade policy was not really employed until the Tariff of 1816. The War of 1812 and the decade of economic isolation and embargo which preceded it begat both a young industry in the northeast United States, which needed protection, and a "new nationalism" that

[12]For a study of GATT which also describes the interaction between GATT legal processes and negotiations on the one hand and U.S. legislative and administrative processes on trade policy on the other, see Robert E. Hudec, *The G.A.T.T.: Legal System and World Trade Diplomacy* (N.Y.: Praeger, 1975). For developments in the years 1973–74, see pp. 237–40.

[13]In contrast, tariffs in the late 1960s accounted for less than 1 percent of the Federal Government's revenue. See Congressional Quarterly, *Guide to the Congress*, p. 177. See also Louis Fisher, *President and Congress: Power and Policy* (New York: Free Press, 1972), p. 134.

For a good brief history of U.S. tariff policy from 1789 to 1970, see Sidney Ratner, *The Tariff in American History* (New York: D. Van Nostrand Company, 1972). For a much fuller description of U.S. tariff history from its beginning to 1922, see the classic *The Tariff History of the United States* by Frank W. Taussig, who was Professor of Economics at Harvard, and appointed by President Woodrow Wilson to be the first Chairman of the Tariff Commission (N.Y.: G.P. Putnam's Sons, 7th ed., 1922).

[14]Congress was only four days old when a Philadelphia Representative offered an amendment proposing additional duties on manufactured products "to encourage the productions of our country and to protect our infant manufacturers." The argument was given added strength in Alexander Hamilton's famous *Report on Manufactures* of 1791. See Fisher, *President and Congress*, pp. 134–35.

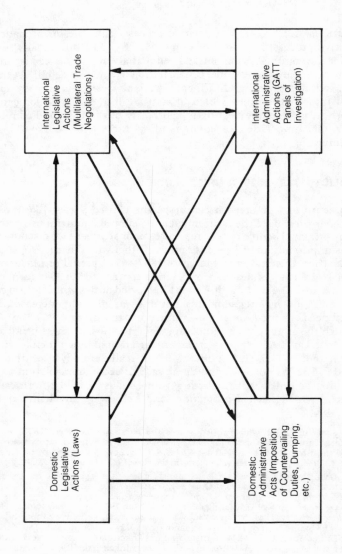

Figure 3 The Negotiating Process

provided the ideology.[15] The Tariff of 1816, which represented a marriage of economic and emotional needs, placed almost prohibitively high duties on woolen, cotton, and iron manufactures. An alliance between Northern industrialists and farmers and Western farmers kept tariffs high for a long period, over the objection of Southern planters and Northeastern merchants. Between 1816 and 1934, there were only two relatively brief periods— 1846–60 and 1913–22—when protectionism and high tariffs were not the rule.[16]

While interests shifted somewhat, sectionalism remained a powerful sculptor of U.S. tariff policy. Reflecting to a great extent the industrial, protectionist interests of the Northeast and Midwest, the Republican Party after the Civil War kept control of the Congress, the Presidency, and the tariff; Grover Cleveland and the Democratic Party tried a couple of times to change all three. The tariff issue was of such importance in this period that there were times when it was the only major campaign issue, as was the case in the Presidential election of 1888, which pitted Cleveland against the Republican Benjamin Harrison.[17]

The process by which Congress set tariff rates was largely unchanged until the Dingley Tariff of 1897, when Congress delegated authority to the President to negotiate trade treaties based on the principle of reciprocity. Eleven such treaties were negotiated, but not one was ever ratified.[18] In 1909, the Republicans repealed the treaty-making provision in favor of a "flexible tariff," which would be adjusted scientifically to equalize the costs of production between American and foreign products. The Congress delegated the power to adjust the tariff to the President and suggested the appointment of "experts" to write advisory reports on the costs of production of all potential imports. The 1909 law, the Payne-Aldrich tariff, set minimal tariffs to which rates of up to 25 percent could be added. While President

[15]Many liberal traders, like Thomas Jefferson, were persuaded of the importance of protectionism because of the demonstrated vulnerability of the U.S. economy to the fifteen years of embargo, European war, and piracy. Jefferson felt that the only way to minimize such dependence was to develop an indigenous manufacturing capability. (See Thomas Jefferson's letter to Benjamin Austin, 9 January 1816 in Merrill D. Peterson (ed.), *The Portable Thomas Jefferson* (N.Y.: Viking Press, 1975), pp. 547–50.)

[16]The 1846 Tariff, which not only heralded the beginning of moderate tariffs but also of relative prosperity and "manifest destiny," was passed partly as a reaction to extraordinarily high tariffs, partly because of a political compromise with Southern planters, and partly in anticipation of the repeal of the Corn Laws in Great Britain. See Ratner, *Tariff in American History*, pp. 23–24.

[17]Chamberlain, *President, Congress, and Legislation*, pp. 118–20. The debate on the tariff was always a heated one. See Frank Rosewater, "No More Free Rides on This Jackass or Protection Forever and Everywhere" (Cleveland, Ohio: Frank Rosewater, 1882). And from the other side, a more recent book by Oswald Garrison Villard, *Free Trade, Free World* (N.Y.: Robert Schalkenback Foundation, 1947). Villard concludes: "There can be no lasting peace without free trade."

[18]Fisher, *President and Congress*, p. 136.

Taft was an advocate of the "flexible tariff" as a way of "taking the politics out of tariff-making," he failed to gain congressional support for a Tariff Board in 1910, and decided instead to put the minimal tariff rates into effect.

Woodrow Wilson appeared in person before Congress, the first President to do so in over a century, to deliver a special message on tariff reform. He also followed the legislative process closely, often pressing individual Legislators to accept and translate into law the principle of tariff rate reduction. When the Underwood Tariff bill of 1913—as it was called—was threatened by protectionist amendments, Wilson publicly denounced the "industrious and insidious" lobbyists, and the bill passed intact.[19] Where the lobbyists failed, however, the disruption of the war succeeded in rendering the tariff reductions unnecessary, and by 1918, the Republicans again had a majority in Congress.

A bill which would have raised tariff rates passed the Congress in 1921 but was vetoed by Woodrow Wilson. The next year, the Fordney-McCumber bill, to which the Senate alone added twenty-four hundred amendments raising duties on as many products, became law. The act also resurrected the "flexible tariff" provision, giving the responsibility for determining the costs of production to the Tariff Commission, which had originally been established by the 1916 Revenue Act to give advice on tariff matters to the Congress. The President was empowered to revise rates upward or downward by as much as 50 percent whenever it was found that existing duties did not equalize the costs of production.[20] More prescient was a provision empowering the President to negotiate treaties based on the unconditional application of the most-favored nation (MFN) formula whereby any tariff concessions given to the products of one signator of the treaty would be given to another signator.

Although it was enthusiastically endorsed by all the Republican Presidents up to and including Herbert Hoover, the flexible tariff was a failure, technically and conceptually. With tariff lists of several thousand items, the Tariff Commission worked at a rapid pace and could only complete reports on thirty-eight items between 1922 and 1930. Of the thirty-eight revisions, the President increased tariffs in all but five cases.[21] Furthermore, since the purpose of trade is to take mutual advantage of the *differences* in costs of production, trying to equalize those costs by a duty defeats the very purpose of trade.

The 1930 Smoot-Hawley Tariff represents the high watermark of protectionism in the twentieth century for the United States (see table 3).

[19]Ibid., p. 137. For the text of Wilson's message, see Ratner, *Tariff in American History,* pp. 139–42.

[20]Congressional Quarterly, *Guide to the U.S. Congress,* p. 178.

[21]Fisher, *President and Congress,* pp. 142–43; Ratner, *Tariff in American History,* pp. 40–49.

Because of that and because just four years later, the Congress and the United States changed the policy and the policy-making process on tariffs fundamentally, we will examine Smoot-Hawley and the subsequent laws in greater detail.

THE SMOOT-HAWLEY TARIFF, 1929-30

"I might suggest that we have taxed everything in this bill except gall," said Senator Caraway from Arkansas.

"Yes," Senator Glass replied, "and a tax on that would bring in a considerable revenue."[22]

In 1928, when party platforms were still taken seriously, both the Democrats and the Republicans endorsed protectionism as a trade policy, although the Democrats did so in "pleasingly ambiguous language."[23] The new President Herbert C. Hoover called a special session of Congress on April 16, 1929 to redeem two of his campaign pledges: to help the farmer and to make "limited changes in the tariff."[24] The bill signed by Hoover fourteen months later, however, bore no resemblance whatsoever to the recommendations made in his special message of April 1929. Though there was a general increase in tariffs on agricultural products, the tariffs on industrial goods were raised so much higher that the farmers of the South, the Midwest, and the Northwest concerned over their rising costs of production, not to say living, ended up opposing the bill.[25]

The final bill included specific tariff schedules for over twenty thousand

---

[22]Quoted in "Senate Completes Revision of Tariff After Weary Fight of Six Months, Eighteen Days," *New York Times*, 23 March 1930, pp. 1, 30.

[23]The phrase is Chamberlain's *President, Congress, and Legislation*, p. 124. The Republican Party platform was perfectly clear: "We reaffirm our belief in the protective principle of the economic life of this nation. Adherence to that policy is essential for the continued prosperity of the country." The Democrats were equivocal, attacking the trusts and the monopolies for their "special tariff favors," and concluding: "We favor equitable distribution of the benefits and burdens of the tariff among all." (See the *Congressional Digest*, June–July, 1929, p. 172.)

In his memoirs, Hull claimed that the reason the Democrats accepted a statement that was equivocal on freer trade was because Alfred Smith, the party's Presidential candidate, and John J. Raskob, a millionaire and Chairman of the Democratic National Committee, had captured the party (Cordell Hull, *The Memoirs of Cordell Hull*, vol. 1 (New York: MacMillan Company, 1948), pp. 132, 140–41, 152–53). Actually, the Democratic platform could be considered "protectionist" only in that it endorsed the pseudo-scientific cost-equalization formula.

[24]William Starr Myers and Walter H. Newton, *The Hoover Administration: A Documented Narrative* (N.Y.: Charles Scribner's Sons, 1936), pp. 379–81.

[25]For an analysis of the final vote, see *New York Times*, 14 June 1930, pp. 1–2; and 15 June 1930, pp. 1, 25–27.

TABLE 3   Average U.S. Import Duty Collections, 1890-1970

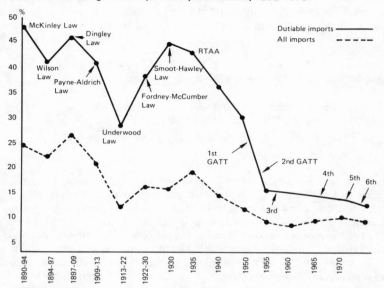

SOURCE: U.S. Tariff Commission, Report to the Subcommittee on International Trade of the Senate Committee on Finance: *Trade Barriers: An Overview, part 1.* TC Publication 665, Washington, D. C., April 1974, p. 80.

items, almost all of them increases. Under Smoot-Hawley, the average ad valorem rate on dutiable imports was 52.8 percent, the highest American tariffs in the twentieth century. The Senate had amended the House bill 1253 times, 1112 on the Senate floor. Senator LaFollette of Wisconsin called it "the worst tariff bill in the nation's history," and estimated that the cost to consumers would be about $1 billion.[26]

Proponents of the bill claimed that the nation, in the words of Senator Watson, was headed for "happy times." Watson pledged in June 1930 to a people still reeling from the stock market crash that "within thirty days" of passage of the bill, the United States "will be on the upgrade financially, economically, and commercially."[27] Representative Willis C. Hawley, Chairman of the House Ways and Means Committee and one of the bill's two sponsors, promised that the American people had nothing to fear since "the protection in this bill is nation-wide."[28]

[26]Quoted in *New York Times*, 25 March 1930, pp. 1, 2.
[27]*New York Times*, 14 June 1930, p. 1.
[28]*New York Times*, 15 June 1930, p. 25.

Yet the Democrats attacked the bill as "obnoxious and indefensible,"[29] and it wasn't long before their judgment was proven correct. Within months of passage of the bill, Canada, France, Mexico, Italy, Spain, Cuba, Australia, and New Zealand raised tariffs. By the end of 1931, twenty-six countries had enacted quantitative restrictions and exchange controls, and by 1932, the United Kingdom abandoned free trade and established the Ottawa system of Imperial tariff preferences.[30] In a book which described in great detail this wave of retaliation, Joseph M. Jones summarized its effect: "As a score of writers have pointed out, the world depression and the Hawley-Smoot tariff are inextricably bound up one with the other, the latter being not only the first manifestation of but a principal cause of the deepening and aggravating of the former."[31] From 1929 to 1933, U.S. exports fell from $5.2 billion to $1.7 billion; imports fell from $4.4 billion to $1.5 billion. World trade fell from $34 billion to $12 billion.[32]

Were these repercussions foreseeable? If so, how could Smoot-Hawley have happened? Schattschneider's assessment of the importance of lobbyists and special interests as responsible for the bill is supported by many of his contemporaries. Senator T. H. Carraway of Arkansas made the same point:

> The trouble is the system. The instances are many where protection is accorded to those industries that least need it, while others, really deserving, are passed or else not given the protection to which they are entitled. Just look at the schedules in the bill before the Senate. The rates in that bill bear no appreciable relation to imports.[33]

Critics of the bill began calling it the "Grundy Tariff" after the Senator who brazenly admitted that the people who gave money to congressional campaigns had a right to expect it back in tariffs.[34] At the same time, however, the daily press reports compelled the Congress in 1929 to investigate the activities of lobbyists. Few would have guessed that by the time the

[29]Statement by Senator Lawrence Harrison, Democratic Minority Leader, in *New York Times*, 23 March 1930, p. 1.

[30]Clair Wilcox, *A Charter for World Trade* (N.Y.: MacMillan, 1949), pp. 5–9.

[31]Joseph M. Jones, *Tariff Retaliation: Repercussions of the Hawley-Smoot Bill* (Philadelphia: University of Pennsylvania Press, 1934), p. 2.

[32]Figures cited in U.S. House of Representatives, Ways and Means Committee, *Hearings: Reciprocal Trade Agreements Act*, 1934, p. 3. The degree of protection offered to U.S. manufacturers by Smoot-Hawley was so high that almost all (70 percent) of the imports into the U.S. after the passage of the act were raw materials, which of course entered duty-free. John Day Larkin, *The President's Control of the Tariff* (Cambridge, Mass.: Harvard University Press, 1936), p. 7.

[33]L. C. Speers, "Tariff-Making: A Call for New Methods," *New York Times*, Sunday, Special Feature 11, 10 November 1929, p. 1.

[34]*New York Times*, 25 March 1930, p. 1. Chairman R. L. Doughton of the Ways and Means Committee began to call the bill the "Hawley-Smoot-Grundy Tariff Act." (*Congressional Record*, March 23, 1934, p. 5256). Also, see Hull, *Memoirs*, vol. 1, p. 132.

investigation had run its course, all the Senators would have been forced to disclose all of their financial holdings.[35] This investigation, however, only slowed the logrolling process; it didn't halt or reverse it. As Senator Walsh of Massachusetts, the only New England Senator to vote against the bill, explained: "The existing minuteness with respect to rates is partly an absurdity and partly a partisan fraud to cover what the tariff really is— namely a mass of private legislation."[36]

Schattschneider defined the process by which potentially conflicting interests were transformed into mutually supportive ones as "reciprocal noninterference"; and basically, it meant that conflicts were muted by giving a *little* pork—not as much as requested, but a little—to everyone.[37] "Policies must be so framed that they can be defended . . . ,"Schattschneider wrote. "Congress, therefore, seeks political support for the system, not by giving ample protection to a few industries whose stimulation is required by public welfare, but by giving a limited protection to all interests strong enough to furnish formidable resistance to it, and by making a virtue of the means by which the policy is executed."[38]

The Legislators were hardly unaware of the mechanics or the implications of the logrolling process, as is indicated by the following statement by Senator Waterman of Colorado:

> I have stated upon the floor of the Senate, and I have stated in the presence of Senators elsewhere, that by the Eternal, I will not vote for a tariff upon the products of another State if the Senators from that State vote against protecting the industries of any State.[39]

This pluralist theory of "reciprocal noninterference" is certainly parsimonious, but it doesn't explain the conflict which accompanied the bill, or the partisan nature of the vote, or Presidential behavior and its effect on the bill, or why a slightly more liberal bill with hardly any concessions to interest groups narrowly failed two years later, but a dramatically more liberal bill with *no* concessions to interest groups succeeded four years later.

Hoover's original proposal calling for modest revisions of the tariff schedule for farm products went to the House Ways and Means Committee and the Senate Finance Committee, both of which were controlled by Republicans from the Northeast industrial states. The Republicans caucused

---

[35]The first time Senators were forced into such a complete financial disclosure was in the wake of Woodrow Wilson's speech about "insidious" lobbyists. Fisher, *President and Congress*, pp. 137–38.

[36]Speers, "Tariff-Making", p. 1.

[37]Schattschneider, *Politics, Pressures, and the Tariff* p. 145.

[38]Ibid., p. 85.

[39]*New York Times*, Sunday, Sec. 3, 23 March 1930, pp. 1–2.

in both Committees, excluded the Democrats from mark-up, and set the tariff rates. The bills were bloated with amendments on the floor, but the final vote kept very close to party lines. In the House, after what seemed to many an interminable debate, the vote was 222-153 with only fourteen Democrats voting for it, and only twenty Republicans voting against it. The day before, Friday the thirteenth of June, 1930, the Senate voted 44-42 to pass it, with only five Democrats voting yes, and 11 Republicans no. Thus, partisanship was hardly insignificant, and the logrolling process was barely sufficient to gain its passage.

The bill was one of the most controversial issues in the nation for nearly two years, and the American and foreign press gave it front-page attention for a considerable portion of that time. The foreign reaction was slow to crystallize, but as the bill began to logroll, and it appeared likely to pass, formal diplomatic protests began to increase. By May 15, 1930, while the bill was deadlocked in Conference, thirty-three countries had sent protests, and this number grew to fifty-nine by June 3.[40] Reports of foreign discontent were often juxtaposed on the front page of the *New York Times* with reports of the bill's status in Congress. Discontent, however, was hardly confined to foreigners. Big business, particularly the automobile companies, became increasingly vocal in their opposition, and were joined by economists, 1,028 of whom sent an urgent letter to Hoover asking him to veto the bill.[41]

Most of these Senators who opposed the bill blamed Hoover, not the pressure groups. For sixteen months, according to Senator McKellar, Hoover "stood by in silence, without the vision, leadership, or courage to direct the Republicans in Congress to do what he had advised them to do. Necessarily this attitude of the President has brought about the chaos and confusion which have for months gripped the country."

"There has never been a time," McKellar continued, "in the slow stages of the present bill's progress when he [Hoover] could not have accelerated its movement, clarified its discussion in both Houses and directed its course to a completion compatible with the expectations of the country . . . "[42] And McKellar's judgment has been confirmed by several scholars who have studied this case.[43]

[40]*New York Times*, 15 May 1930, p. 5; 4 June 1930, p. 3.

[41]*New York Times*, 15 May 1930, p. 5; also 4 June 1930, p. 3. For the text of the letter, see Ratner, *President and Congress*, pp. 142–4. The economists' arguments for vetoing the bill included: (1) its cost to consumers; (2) international repercussions; (3) it would increase, not decrease unemployment; and (4) it would subsidize the most inefficient industries in the United States.

[42]*New York Times*, 9 May 1930, p. 4.

[43]In a characteristic understatement, Lawrence Chamberlain wrote: "Presidential leadership was not conspicuous in the formulation of the Hawley-Smoot Tariff Act of 1930." (*President, Congress and Legislation* p. 131) Gayer and Schmidt who examined Fordney-

A reading of Hoover's memoirs, however, suggests that while these conclusions are not inaccurate, they do require some refinement. In his memoirs, Hoover discounts the importance of the tariff increase, and he denies that Smoot-Hawley had anything to do with the deepening of the depression, which he attributes to international forces. Hoover's discussion of his role in the bill's passage was focused almost exclusively on a single aspect of the bill, the flexible tariff provision. "I believed," Hoover later wrote, "that the only way to get the tariff out of Congressional logrolling was through empowering this bipartisan commission [the Tariff Commission] to adjust the differential rates of dutiable goods upon the basis of the differences in costs of production at home and abroad."[44] Hoover wanted authority to reorganize the Commission, which would then have the authority to revise the tariff bill along the lines of the cost-equalization formula.[45]

To ensure that the final bill would reflect his views, he told a group of congressional leaders that he was prepared to veto it if his views were ignored. When the bill went to Conference, he followed it very closely, and as the Conference neared its end, he injected his views into the discussion with the full force of his office: "I wrote out the provision I wanted. I sent word that unless my formula was adopted, the bill would be vetoed. The result was a complete victory for the flexible tariff in the Conference Report."[46]

The victory was as elusive as it was ironic. The flexible tariff provision was proposed in 1922 by moderate or low-tariff people like Commissioner William C. Culbertson. It was, however, not only conceptually ill-founded, but it proved in the eight years since the passage of Fordney-McCumber to be a better instrument for protectionism than for free trade. By 1930, the alignment of forces had come full circle, with the protectionists promoting the flexible tariff, and the free traders opposing it.[47]

But there was another important issue involved in the flexible tariff, and it was the political divisions on this issue which contributed to Hoover's "victory." Many of those who opposed the high tariffs in the bill viewed the flexible tariff provision and the delegation of power to the President which it entailed as a potentially positive alternative to the kind of process which had lead to Smoot-Hawley. Senator Walsh, for example, said: "This would greatly mitigate, if not end, the log-rolling evil." Many

---

McCumber as well as Smoot-Hawley concluded with regard to the latter that "there was no effective leadership from the White House insisting on a national rather than a sectional point of view." (*American Economic Foreign Policy*, pp. 8–9)

[44]Herbert Hoover, *The Memoirs of Herbert Hoover: The Cabinet and the Presidency, 1920–33* (N.Y.: MacMillan, 1952), pp. 292–93. See chap. 41, "Reform of the Tariff."

[45]See Larkin, *President's Control*, pp. 3–5.

[46]Hoover, *Memoirs*, p. 295.

[47]John D. Larkin, *President's Control*, chap. 1.

Democrats were searching for new processes and procedures; some suggested open mark-up sessions; others, an expanded Tariff Commission.[48] Hoover's proposal was accepted by those who viewed the delegation of power to the President as a positive development, but most Democrats saw both the provision and Hoover's position as essentially protectionist, and they weren't wrong. Hoover's discomfort with the bill was clearly related to the legislative *process* rather than to the *policy*, the high tariffs. As Senator Reed Smoot was fond of pointing out, Hoover favored protection of U.S. industries. And Hoover never denied that.[49]

And that is the final reason for Smoot-Hawley. During the rather lengthy hearings in Ways and Means and Finance, the principle of protection was never seriously impugned. Said Senator Pine, who openly and frankly represented the oil interests: "The government cannot deny the equal protection of the law to any of its citizens."[50] Even the few lobbyists representing exporters or importers who argued for reductions of some tariffs did so as exceptions to a rule which they accepted: "The protective principle itself," they testified, "is not questioned, but . . . "[51]

As a young congressman in 1907, Cordell Hull of Tennessee devoted his first speech in the Capitol to the cause of free trade. His support for the cause never wavered; if anything, it evolved into a personal obsession. Hull took the Smoot-Hawley tariff as a personal defeat, referring to it as "perhaps the nadir of my Congressional career."[52] While isolated in the Democratic Party and in the House, Hull still wrote the Minority Report on the trade bill of the Ways and Means Committee, and it stands as an eloquent and intelligent defense of free trade and a clear-sighted recognition "of new and changed postwar conditions [which] clearly demand foreign markets rather than excessive tariff protection." "American economic policy," he wrote, "can no longer ignore the fact that since 1914 we have changed from a debtor and small surplus Nation to the greatest creditor and actual or potential, surplus-producing Nation in the world . . . "[53]

[48]Speers, "Tariff-Making: A Call for New Methods," p. 1.

[49]Wilfred E. Binkley, *President and Congress*, 283. Hoover's position on the tariff wasn't as unequivocal as the Republican Party's. (See n. 23.) Candidate Hoover supported the tariff for "farm relief," but beyond that, he asked for the people's trust: "I am sure the American people would rather entrust the perfection of the tariff to the consistent friend of the tariff than to our opponents, who voted against our present protection to the worker and the farmer, and whose whole economic theory over generations has been the destruction of the protective principle." (See *Congressional Digest*, June–July, 1929, p. 172.)

[50]Schattschneider, Politics, Pressures, and the Tariff p. 92.

[51]Ibid., p. 143. The voices of exporters and importers were heard, but to Schattschneider, the "significant fact" about these groups "is not their agitation but their lack of influence." (p. 159)

[52]Hull, *Memoirs*, p. 132.

[53]*Congressional Digest*, June–July, 1929, pp. 175–76. In contrast, Willis C. Hawley, who authored the Majority Report, wrote: "Foreign nations and producers have shown great interest in this readjustment, but since the tariff is a domestic matter, neither foreign officials nor the

In 1930, Hull was elected to the Senate in a Democratic sweep, which brought the Democrats to a majority in the Senate for the first time since 1916 and within two votes of the Republicans in the House. In 1932, the new, predominantly Democratic Congress passed the Collier Tariff Bill which reduced tariffs and introduced several other innovations in trade policy.

Hoover vetoed the Collier Bill on May 11, 1932 for the following five reasons:

1. It would lower tariffs, and in Hoover's words, "there has never been a time in the history of the United States when tariff protection was more essential to the welfare of the American people than at present." (Hoover was concerned that Europe's cheaper currency and wages would allow the Europeans to invade the American market.)

2. It would destroy the flexible tariff.

3. It called for an international conference on trade. Hoover explained why that idea was unacceptable: "The first legislative act of Washington's administration was a tariff bill. From that day to this, one of our firm national policies has been that tariffs are solely a domestic question in protection of our own people." Calling for an international conference or making international agreements would represent a "radical change in historic policies."

4. It included a provision for reciprocal trade agreements, which Hoover identified (incorrectly) with preferential agreements and therefore a departure from the "open door" commercial policy of the United States.

5. Since the Congress, in his opinion, showed no predisposition toward ratifying reciprocal trade treaties, Hoover believed it would be a "futile" exercise to negotiate them.[54]

THE RECIPROCAL TRADE AGREEMENTS ACT, 1934[55]

Our international relations, though vastly important, are in point of time and necessity secondary to the establishment of a sound national economy. I favor as a practical policy the putting of first things first. I

---

nationals of foreign nations were heard, except that representations of foreign governments were submitted through the State Department and made a part of our record."

[54]Myers and Newton, *Hoover Administration,* pp. 493–95.

[55]There is no political analysis of the 1934 Act in any way comparable to Schattschneider's on the 1930 law. Henry J. Tasca's study is more descriptive than analytical. He covers some of the chronology and describes the purposes of the bill, but he does not provide an explanation

> *shall spare no effort to restore world trade by international economic readjustments, but the emergency at home cannot wait on that accomplishment.*[56]
>
> —*Franklin D. Roosevelt*
> *Inaugural Address*
> *March 1934*

Six months after Hoover vetoed the Collier bill, the American people denied him a second term, though the deepening depression was doubtless more responsible. Governor Franklin D. Roosevelt of New York won handily with 62 percent of the popular vote and nearly 90 percent of the electoral vote, and the Democrats secured control of both Houses of Congress.

Roosevelt's position on trade was anything but clear—though this was also true of his positions on a wide range of issues. In an analysis of Roosevelt's book, *Looking Forward* (published in 1932) and his speeches, Harry Hawkins and Janet Norwood concluded: "Roosevelt was not well-versed in tariff matters, and he straddled the issue, at times calling for protectionism and the cost-equalization formula and at other times advocating the lowering of tariff barriers in order to increase trade."[57]

Cordell Hull had briefly worked with Roosevelt in the Democratic Party to try to reverse the quasi-protectionist position which it had taken in 1928 under the leadership of Alfred Smith and John J. Raskob. The subsequent appointment of Hull, who was so closely identified with free trade as Secretary of State, appeared to signal FDR's support for tariff reduction. At the same time, however, Roosevelt put national reconstruction at the top of his list of priorities in his inaugural speech, and kept Hull on an embarrassingly short leash at the London Economic Conference in the spring of 1933.

On November 11, 1933, as he was about to leave for a trip to Latin America, Hull was informed that Roosevelt had established an Executive

---

of why the law looked as it did or why Congress passed it. (See particularly chap. 3, pp. 29–44.) This is also the case with Hawkins and Norwood, though they do note that the "emergency aspects of the legislation were at least partly responsible for reducing Congressional resistance." (Harry C. Hawkins and Janet L. Norwood, "The Legislative Basis of United States Commercial Policy," in William B. Kelly, Jr. (ed.), *Studies in United States Commercial Policy* (Chapel Hill, N.C.: University of North Carolina Press, 1963), p. 84.)

For background information on the bill, and on the shaping of the new policy by FDR, Hull, and George Peek, see Arthur M. Schlesinger, Jr., *The Coming of the New Deal: The Age of Roosevelt* (Boston: Houghton Mifflin Co., 1959), pp. 184–94, 253–60. In addition, see Francis Bowes Sayre, *The Way Forward: The American Trade Agreements Program* (N.Y.: MacMillan, 1939), pp. 41–60. (Sayre was Assistant Secretary of State at the time, and is credited with drafting the bill.)

[56]Cited in Schlesinger, Jr., *The Coming of the New Deal*, p. 192.

[57]Hawkins and Norwood, "Legislative Basis of U.S. Commercial Policy" p. 69.

Committee on Commercial Policy, which included Hull, the Secretaries of
Treasury, Commerce, and Agriculture, the Chairman of the Tariff Commission, and the Administrators of the AAA and the NRA. The Committee's
mandate was to formulate a new trade policy for the U.S. As was his style,
Roosevelt also appointed George Peek, the Administrator of the AAA and an
economic nationalist, as chairman of another committee to coordinate trade
relations and to find markets for agricultural products either through
reciprocal agreements or barter arrangements. The latter was anathema to
Hull, who later wrote that Peek's appointment could not have bewildered
him more than if "Roosevelt had hit me between the eyes with a sledge
hammer."[58]

Hull's internationalist position on trade policy and his belief that
domestic recovery in the United States depended in part on an "open door"
policy abroad ultimately prevailed, although the debate with Peek continued
until the latter's resignation two years later.[59] In the winter of 1933–34,
FDR asked Hull to prepare a draft of legislation that could be sent to Capitol
Hill.

There was never any question in Hull's mind that the objective of U.S.
trade policy should be to reduce the barriers to the free flow of goods.
"Unhampered trade dovetailed with peace," Hull had said as a congressman.
"High tariffs, trade barriers, and unfair economic competition [dovetailed]
with war."[60] So the questions which the executive committee addressed in
drafting the trade bill related to identifying the best, the most feasible, and
the most practical method by which this objective could be accomplished.

While the unilateral reduction of U.S. tariffs would have been the
easiest way to accomplish the objective,[61] Hull and the others on the
committee saw it as impractical and almost definitely unacceptable to the
Congress. Hull preferred multilateral trade negotiations, and had suggested
the idea at the London Conference; but he learned there that "public opinion
in no country, especially my own, would at that time support a worth-while
multilateral undertaking." He was compelled to settle for what he called

---

[58]Hull, Memoirs, pp. 370, 352–54; for an overview, see Schlesinger, The Coming of the
New Deal, pp. 253–57; and Lloyd C. Gardner, Economic Aspects of New Deal Diplomacy,
p. 42.

[59]Schlesinger, The Coming of the New Deal, pp. 257–59.

[60]Richard N. Gardner, Sterling-Dollar Diplomacy; Anglo-American Collaboration in
The Reconstruction of Multilateral Trade (Oxford, England: Clarendon Press, 1956) p. 9. In his
Memoirs, Hull denied that he had ever said "that trade agreements would be an absolute
panacea against war." But he continued to believe that trade and peace were intimately related:
"Yes, war did come, despite the trade agreements. But it is a fact that war did not break out
between the United States and any country with which we have been able to negotiate a trade
agreement." (pp. 363–65)

[61]John W. Evans concluded that unilateral reductions would have made the most sense
for the United States in 1934. See his The Kennedy Round in American Trade Policy
(Cambridge, Mass.: Harvard University Press, 1971), pp. 5–6.

"the next best method": bilateral trade agreements based on the principles of reciprocity and most-favored-nation status (MFN).[62]

Another issue was whether tariff reductions should be made on a "horizontal" basis—i.e., all those products in a particular sector—or on a selective, item-by-item basis. The latter was chosen, largely because it was felt to be more acceptable to the Congress.[63] It was, of course, assumed that the Congress would be asked to delegate authority to the President to negotiate these agreements, but an important question was what role the Congress would play after the signing of the agreement. Should it be a treaty, requiring two-thirds of the Senate; a statute or a joint resolution, requiring the majority of the Congress; or an Executive Agreement, requiring no congressional involvement other than the initial authorizing legislation? The last alternative was chosen, and although it raised some constitutional questions, Assistant Secretary of State Francis Sayre, who drafted the bill, agreed that a treaty wasn't necessary since the Congress would make its will known by the passage of the law.[64]

According to one source, another alternative was considered: the legislative veto, which would have permitted the Congress to disapprove an agreement after it was negotiated. This idea was rejected by the Administration for the same reasons that treaties, joint resolutions, or legislation were rejected: it could have slowed, crippled, or prevented agreements, and the Executive wasn't willing to run the risk.[65] That also explains why the bill which was sent to Congress didn't have a time limit on the President's negotiating authority.

On February 28, 1934, FDR invited a group of congressional leaders to the White House to discuss the State Department's draft with the Executive Committee. In attendance were Vice President James N. Garner, Hull, Secretary of Agriculture Henry Wallace, George Peek, Frances B. Sayre, and the Democratic congressional leadership including Senators Joseph Robinson and Byron P. Harrison, Speaker Henry T. Rainey, House Majority Leader James Byrnes, and Chairman of the Ways and Means Committee, R. L. Doughton. The proposals and a legislative strategy were discussed and approved.[66]

On March 2, 1934, Roosevelt sent the Reciprocal Trade Agreements Bill to the House with a cover message indicating his complete and

[62]Hull, Memoirs, p. 356.

[63]Hawkins and Norwood, "Legislative Basis of U.S. Commercial Policy", p. 77.

[64]Ibid., p. 79.

[65]Ibid., pp. 88−89. Hawkins and Norwood do not footnote this point, and I have been unable to find confirmation by any other source. However, the idea that a legislative veto was considered by the Administration is plausible, as it had been used in the 1932 Legislative Authorization Act for the first time. It seems equally plausible that the Administration would only request it if they had no other choice, and in 1934, this was not the case.

[66]Hull, Memoirs, p. 357.

unequivocal support. The bill, which was actually just an amendment to the Tariff Act of 1930, would delegate to the President the power to negotiate foreign trade agreements which could reduce U.S. tariffs by as much as 50 percent of the Smoot-Hawley levels. (Hull had decided that the difficulty in trying to repeal the 1930 Act would have exceeded any possible benefit.)[67]

In contrast to the Hearings on the Smoot-Hawley bill, when Ways and Means accumulated over 11,000 pages of testimony and briefs in forty-three days and five nights and heard from hundreds of private witnesses but none from the executive branch,[68] in the Hearings on the Reciprocal Trade Agreements Act, Ways and Means heard from seventeen witnesses, of which seven represented the Administration, for just one week beginning on March 8, 1934.[69] Not only had the Congress and the President changed drastically, but the economic depression had riveted governmental attention on finding quick ways out of the emergency.

Hull was the lead-off witness, and after presenting a compelling statistical description of the sharp decline in American and world trade and production since the passage of Smoot-Hawley, he explained the rationale of the bill: its purpose was to expand "foreign markets for the products of the United States as a means of assisting in the present emergency in restoring the American standard of living, in overcoming domestic unemployment and the present economic depression . . . "[70]

There were many in the Congress who remained ardent protectionists and questioned Hull's free trade philosophy; others who saw this as just one more "program that is leading straight to Communism"[71]; but the most articulate argument questioned the constitutionality of the bill. Rep. Beck called it a "double violation of the constitution," because it delegated the congressional power to tax and the senatorial power of treaty ratification to the President.[72] Hull's counter-argument was premised principally on pragmatic grounds:

> . . . it is manifest that unless the Executive is given authority to deal with the existing great emergency somewhat on a parity with that exercised by the executive departments of so many other governments

[67]Ibid., p. 358. For text of Roosevelt's message, a copy of the bill and the final law (PL 316-73), see Tasca, Reciprocal Trade Policy of the U.S., pp. 299–308.

[68]Schattschneider, Politics, Pressures, and the Tariff, p. 36.

[69]U.S. House of Representatives, Ways and Means Committee, Reciprocal Trade Agreements Act: Hearings, 73d Congress, 2d sess., March 1934.

[70]Sec. 350a of Part III of Tariff Act of 1930; see Ratner, Tariff in American History p. 148.

[71]Remarks by Rep. Hancock from N.Y. who also said: "Millions of Americans are beginning to ask how far this bewildered Congress will go in surrendering its constitutional powers to the revolutionary group in the Executive Branch of the government." (Congressional Record, March 28, 1934, p. 5668.)

[72]New York Times, 25 March 1934, p. 3.

*for purposes of negotiating and carrying into effect trade agreements,
it will not be practicable or possible for the U.S. to pursue with any
degree of success the proposed policy of restoring our lost international
trade. It would seem to me that this is the one governing
consideration.*[73]

To underline his point, Hull alluded to a recent study by the Tariff
Commission, entitled *Regulation of Tariffs on Foreign Countries by Administrative Action* (1932), which described methods other governments used
and suggested that the United States would be at a comparative disadvantage
unless the Congress delegated such power.[74]

In the mark-up session, the minority party was not excluded as it had
been in 1930. A few amendments were adopted by the committee, one of
which was clearly intended to protect a special interest, the millers in
Buffalo, from Canadian competition.[75] The other amendments adopted were
policy-oriented, including one which "froze" the free list (products with no
tariffs), while at the same time prohibiting the President from negotiating
the elimination of any other tariff.[76]

The bill was voted out of committee on March 19th, but the report and
the vote were divided along partisan lines. The majority report adopted the
statistics, the arguments, and the entire bill of the Administration. The
Republicans, in a strongly-written minority report, stated their disagreement but stressed two points: (1) While the bill was advertised as an
"emergency measure," it was in fact permanent since the President was
given unlimited power for an indefinite period. (2) "It places in the hands of
the President and those to whom he may delegate authority the absolute
power of life and death over every industry dependent on tariff protection."[77]

The Democrats replied that the delegation of authority was constitutional, but on the floor of the House they accepted the brunt of the
Republican case, and adopted a series of compromise amendments. First,
Presidential authority to enter into trade agreements was limited to three
years. Secondly, the Congress expressly prohibited the Executive from
negotiating the issue of a country's indebtedness as part of a large commercial
package. Thirdly, agreements could be terminated after three years upon
giving six months notice. Otherwise, the agreements would remain in force
indefinitely.

[73]U.S. Congress, House Committee on Ways and Means, *Trade Agreements Act:
Hearings*, 73d Congress, 2d sess., pp. 5–6.

[74]Ibid., pp. 11–12.

[75]*New York Times*, 16 March 1934, p. 9.

[76]*New York Times*, 17 March 1934, p. 22.

[77]Report of the Ways and Means Committee on the Reciprocal Trade Agreements Act,
cited in *New York Times*, 20 March 1934, p. 4.

With the exception of these changes, the Democratic leadership kept the debate firmly under control, defeating the numerous other amendments offered by the Republicans.[78] The bill passed 274-111 on March 29th with a partisan vote, though eleven Democrats voted against the bill and two Republicans voted for it.[79] After the vote, Speaker Rainey and Majority Leader Byrnes met with the President who told them that he would be able to accept the House's amendments.[80]

Accommodationist tendencies were also evident in the Senate. The Finance Committee filed its report with the full Senate on May 2, and offered only one change from the House bill. Prior to concluding an agreement, the President would be required to issue a public notice of his intention to do so, and he would have to provide for a forum for outsiders to present their views on the proposed agreement.[81] The Senate debate was longer, more drawn out, more partisan, and many more amendments were defeated; but in the end, on June 4th, the bill passed 57-33. The *New York Times* called it "a Democratic victory from start to finish."[82] But unlike 1930, the Reciprocal Trade Agreements Act was seldom the subject of a front-page article let alone a headline. In fact, the amount of attention in 1934 to trade issues was a small fraction of what it was in 1930.[83]

Cordell Hull described the last stage of the bill's journey:

> At 9:15 on the night of June 12, I watched the President sign our bill in the White House. Each stroke of the pen seemed to write a message of gladness on my heart. My fight of so many long years for the reciprocal trade policy and the lowering of trade barriers was won. To say I was delighted is a bald understatement.[84]

In 1934, the interest groups which had filled the halls of Congress just four years before were conspicuous by their absence. It was known that the business groups split over the bill, with the National Association of

[78]*New York Times*, 30 March 1934, p. 1.

[79]Ibid.

[80]*New York Times*, 31 March 1934, p. 2.

[81]Sayre, *The Way Forward*, p. 58.

[82]*New York Times*, 5 June 1934, p. 1. Schattschneider's argument that the quieter the congressional decision-making process, the more likely interest groups will prevail, is not borne out in a comparison between the 1930 and 1934 tariff acts. (See E. E. Schattschneider, *The Semi-Sovereign People: A Realist's View of Democracy in America* (N.Y.: Holt, Rinehart and Winston, 1964).

[83]Not only was there less front-page attention, there was also less overall attention. The *New York Times* indexed more than nine full pages on the trade bill from October 1929 to June 1930, whereas less than three pages were devoted to the Reciprocal Trade Agreements Act of 1934.

[84]Hull, *Memoirs*, p. 357.

Manufacturers, the American Tariff League, the American Mining Congress, and National Wool Growers opposed; and the National Automobile Chamber of Commerce and the American Manufacturers Export Association in support.[85] But their influence was not discernable either in hearings or in the final bill.

It is therefore not surprising that there are few interest group political analyses of the 1934 Trade Act. The problem is in trying to explain how the same nation could formulate such a different foreign economic policy in a span of just four years. Lloyd Gardner, a radical historian who has studied the economic diplomacy of the New Deal, suggests that there was much more continuity than change from Hoover to Roosevelt. His thesis is that the long-time American tradition of the "open door" and the expansionist frontier thesis better explain U.S. policy than the supposed radical departure of the New Deal. Gardner glosses over Smoot-Hawley by saying that it wasn't the "real" Herbert Hoover. The real Hoover was Secretary of Commerce in the 1920s and was responsible for promoting exports and sending U.S. commercial attaches to virtually every country in the world.[86]

A more cogent explanation for the apparent inconsistency between Hoover's export-promotion period and his Smoot-Hawley period is suggested by Joan Hoff Wilson in her book, *American Business and Foreign Policy, 1920–33*. Wilson says that Hoover didn't draw a connection between domestic protectionism and its effects on America's exports and world trade. Furthermore, Hoover and the Republican Party of the 1920s and early 1930s chose to identify with the small and medium-sized manufacturers who were "business nationalists." By disaggregating the business community and assessing the relative effectiveness of different groups, Wilson is better positioned to explain not only the apparent inconsistency in Hoover's thinking but the important change between the tariff policy of the Hoover Republicans and the tariff policy of the Roosevelt/Hull Democrats.[87] She argues that the ideological preconceptions of the nation's leadership about America's role in the world—whether it be "unilateral internationalism," nationalism, or multilateralism—and about the roles of the Congress and the Executive in policy-making were of critical importance in explaining the different trade acts. Hoover was a "unilateral internationalist," in Joan Hoff Wilson's words, who was willing to let Congress raise the tariff rates to harmful levels without involving himself in the debate or trying to steer it to a more responsible outcome. Roosevelt, "an economic internationalist in principle, if not always in tactics and timing,"[88] worked closely with a more

[85]Chamberlain, *President, Congress, and Legislation*, pp. 131–132.

[86]Gardner, *Sterling-Dollar Diplomacy*, p. 8, and chap. 1.

[87]Joan Hoff Wilson, *American Business and Foreign Policy, 1920–1933*, pp. 75, 88–100.

[88]Schlesinger, *The Coming of the New Deal*, p. 253.

ideologically sympathetic Congress to develop a trade policy based on lower tariffs and reciprocity.

In 1934, Congress addressed the issue of trade policy at a general level, rather than a specific one. Though in substantial agreement with the bill sent by the President, the Congress did make several rather significant changes, including setting a three year time limit on the President's negotiating authority. The purpose of setting the time limit was to ensure that the President would have to return to the Congress for new authority, and at that time, the Congress could exercise its responsibilities of oversight. In addition, the "law of anticipated reactions" had impelled the Executive to make a nonpreferred choice on two of the three central questions which were faced in the drafting process: selective tariff-making rather than horizontal; bilateral agreements rather than multilateral or unilateral reductions. These were chosen largely because Hull sensed what could reasonably be asked of the Congress. And on the one question—Executive Agreements vs. treaties or statutes—where the Executive chose what it essentially wanted rather than what Congress might want, the Congress modified the Administration's bill. Despite the fact that this was a period of crisis in the U.S. and the power of the Executive was enormous and growing, the conclusion that emerges from a study of the 1934 trade act is one of a strong Congress shaping trade policy in accordance with its institutional imperative.

One writer called the Reciprocal Trade Agreements Act of 1934 "a revolution in tariff making";[89] another wrote that it "constitutes a significant turning point in the evolution of American commercial policy."[90] The law reversed an upward trend in American tariffs; since then, tariffs have steadily and consistently declined in importance as a barrier to trade. The law was the first time that the Congress as a whole recognized that it was not suited to set tariffs itself on an item-by-item basis; and for the first time, Congress delegated advance power to the President to raise or lower by as much as 50 percent all rates on agricultural as well as industrial goods, subject to no check other than a consultative one.

The House did not invoke a closed rule to pass the bill, nor did the Senate invoke cloture. It was Presidential and congressional leadership which kept the bill free of special interest amendments (which were introduced but defeated). The tenor of the debate had been inverted: the argument for protection, for the first time, became an argument of exception rather than principle.[91]

[89]Ratner, *Tariff in American History*, p. 148.

[90]James Constantine Pearson, *The Reciprocal Trade Agreements Program: The Policy of the United States and Its Effectiveness* (Gettysburgh, Pa.: Times and News Publishing Company, 1942).

[91]BPD, p. xiv.

And most important, the act irrevocably linked U.S. domestic rule-making to international negotiations. In 1932, President Hoover could say that tariff policy was wholly domestic policy; no President would ever say that again. The Reciprocal Trade Agreements Act ushered the United States into an era of "bilateralism" based on reciprocity.

On the day that the House agreed to the Conference Report, a number of foreign governments publicly expressed interest in trade negotiations.[92] By Executive Order, Roosevelt retained the Executive Committee on Commercial Policy and instructed it to begin planning long-term trade policy.[93] In addition, an inter-departmental Trade Agreements Committee chaired by the State Department was established as a coordinating council to give negotiating instructions to the State Department's Trade Agreements Division which would negotiate the agreements.[94] Lastly, a Committee on Reciprocity Information was set up to hear grievances from particular groups and thus to serve as a buffer from the negotiating process.[95] Chairman of the Tariff Commission, R. L. O'Brien, succinctly explained the importance of this Committee and how it would affect trade policy: "It substitutes the national welfare for special favors. It offers a fair hearing to every interest but permits no single one to be guiding."[96]

The Reciprocal Trade Agreements Act was extended by Congress routinely and by joint resolution rather than formal statute in 1937 and 1940 for three years and in 1943 for two years.[97] Between 1934 and 1940, the State Department negotiated twenty-two reciprocal trade agreements;[98] by 1945, the number rose to twenty-eight.[99]

THE 1945 TRADE ACT EXTENSION: POSTWAR ANXIETY

The point in history at which we stand is full of promise and of danger. The world will either move toward unity and widely shared prosperity or it will move apart into necessarily competing economic

[92]*New York Times,* 7 June 1934, p. 2.

[93]*New York Times,* 30 March 1934.

[94]Hawkins and Norwood, "Legislative Basis of U.S. Commercial Policy", pp. 101–102.

[95]Henry Tasca, *Reciprocal Trade Policy of the U.S.,* p. 61.

[96]Ibid., p. 73.

[97]Public Res. 10, 75th Congress, 1st sess., chap. 22; H.J. Res. 96, approved March 1, 1937; Public Law 61, 76th Congress, 2d sess., chap. 96, H.J. Res. 407; approved 12 April 1940. Public Law 66, 78th Congress, 1st sess., chap. 118; H.J. Res. 111; approved 7 June 1943. There were many amendments introduced each time, but all were defeated.

[98]Fisher, *President and Congress,* p. 146.

[99]Ratner, *Tariff in American History,* p. 152.

blocs. We have a chance, we citizens of the United States, to use our influence in favor of a more united and cooperating world. Whether we do so will determine, as far as it is in our power, the kind of lives our grandchildren can live.[100]

—*Franklin D. Roosevelt*
February 12, 1945

All too aware of the rise of isolationism after World War I and the rejection of the League of Nations by the Senate, Roosevelt was determined to keep history from repeating. Preparations and planning for the postwar period and for America's continued and active involvement in international affairs began almost as soon as the Congress declared war. Whereas Woodrow Wilson excluded the Congress from postwar planning, FDR consulted them and sought their participation in the planning and the negotiations for the United Nations, the International Monetary Fund, and the International Bank for Reconstruction and Development.

In some ways, the "first test" of Congress's commitment to internationalism in the postwar period was the extension of the Reciprocal Trade Agreements Act which was due to expire on June 12, 1945.[101] Almost all of the original negotiating authority mandated in the 1934 Act "has been used up," Roosevelt wrote.[102] Tariffs had fallen from an average of 59.1 percent in 1932 to 28.2 percent in 1945;[103] or to put in another way, the tariff rates on 64 percent of all dutiable imports were reduced by 44 percent.[104]

Congressional leaders conferred with State Department officials in February and expressed some anxiety that the extension might be more difficult than the three previous ones, particularly if the President asked for new authority. The departure of Hull as Secretary of State, a "tower of strength" in the words of Rep. Doughton, was one reason why they expected more problems. In addition, Congress was in a resurgent mood, more jealous of its prerogative, and more interested in putting its print on the emerging landscape of postwar commercial policy.[105]

In one of his last messages to Congress, on March 26, 1945, Roosevelt requested the renewal and strengthening of the trade act. Most of the arguments had been used before: we must buy in order to be able to sell;

[100]In a message accompanying the Bretton Woods proposals to the Congress, cited in Ratner, *Tariff in American History*, p. 155.

[101]R. L. Doughton's words, in *New York Times*, 23 May 1945, p. 13.

[102]Roosevelt's message to Congress, quoted in Congressional Quarterly, *Almanac*, 1945, pp. 224–26.

[103]Fisher, *President and Congress*, p. 149.

[104]Evans, *Kennedy Round*, p. 7.

[105]See John H. Crider, "Opposition Grows Over Trade Pacts," *New York Times*, 24 February 1945, p. 8.

prosperity must be built on specialization and trade; full employment requires our ability to export. The message requested new authority for three years to reduce tariffs by 50 percent of the 1945 tariff rate; and Roosevelt justified this new request by referring to our new responsibilities as a relatively prosperous ("we are now a creditor country") and powerful country. He asked for "a workable kit of tools for the new world of international cooperation to which we all look forward."[106]

Both the House Special Committee on Postwar Economic Policy and Planning and the Ways and Means Committee held hearings on the bill and recommended it to the full House. After Roosevelt's death, Harry Truman met with congressional leaders a number of times to stress the continuity of the government's trade policy, and to urge the Congress to extend the Trade Act.[107] Speaker of the House Sam Rayburn and Ways and Means Chairman R. L. Doughton led the debate, defeating twelve different amendments which would have given Congress veto power, reduced or eliminated the new authority, or helped several special interests. The House debate lasted three days, and after the vote to recommit failed, 212–181, the trade bill passed 239–153 on May 26, 1945.[108]

The Senate Finance Committee by a margin of one voted an extension without any new authority, but with equally strong leadership and an intensive lobbying campaign by the State Department, the Senate defeated the committee's bill by a vote of 47–33, and the next day passed the House bill 54—21, giving Truman what the *New York Times* called his "greatest victory in Congress" yet.[109] Senator Walter George of Georgia summed up the feeling of a Congress intent on constructing a new international economic order: "Events have lifted this issue entirely out of the field of mere tariff controversy. This is not a party issue, nor is it a question of the merits of high or low tariffs."[110]

While not precisely accurate, the Senator was more correct than at any time in the past. Fifteen Republicans crossed over to vote for the trade bill, reflecting a trend which had first become evident in 1943. Between 1934 and 1940, no more than five Republicans in either House had voted for a reciprocal trade bill. From 1943 through 1958, Republicans supported thirteen of sixteen rollcalls. It is true, as Louis Fisher points out, that many of the

---

[106]Ratner, *Tariff in American History*, pp. 153–55.

[107]Harry S. Truman, *Year of Decisions: Memoirs*, vol. I (N.Y.: New American Library, 1955), p. 175.

[108]*New York Times*, 27 May 1945, p. 1.

[109]*New York Times*, 20 and 21 January 1945, p. 1. The State Department's lobbying effort was directed by Assistant Secretary of State for Congressional Relations and International Conferences, Dean Acheson, who commented on his responsibilities: "This is a low life, but a merry one." (p. 156) See his *Present At The Creation* (N.Y.: New American Library, 1969), pp. 154–57.

[110]*New York Times*, Sunday, 13 June 1945, p. 33.

Republican votes were on behalf of "protectionist" provisions, like the "peril-point" in 1948 and 1949; but one should not underestimate the importance of the shift in the Republican position by mistaking the "peril-point" for a protectionist trend, since even this amendment recognizes the basic principle of reducing barriers to trade. While groups of Republicans were recognizing the nonpartisan nature of freer trade, however, there were significant defections by the Democrats from the newly industrialized border states. In 1945, the protectionist interests in these states were not yet articulated or organized, and congressional and Presidential leadership combined again to guide the trade bill through the maze of Congress rejecting temptations as well as diversions. (See table 4.)

POSTWAR TRADE POLICY, 1946–53

Bilateralism, the pursuit of freer trade through bilateral trade agreements, had in a sense approached the limits of its usefulness in 1945 at the same time that the 1934 negotiating authority had been "used up." Hull's first preference for a multilateral approach had become the most logical path; and indeed, Hull himself had laid the groundwork in spelling out America's objectives in multilateralism and universal and nondiscriminatory access in the first lend-lease agreement with Great Britain in 1941–42. Therefore, in November 1946, the U.S. invited twenty-two other countries to the first round of multilateral trade negotiations (MTN) in Geneva to begin in the spring of 1947. By the fall, a General Agreement was reached and signed. It consisted of a code of trade practices and schedules of tariff concessions (reductions) on more than forty-five thousand items accounting for more than one-half of world trade.[111] About 54 percent of U.S. dutiable imports were affected with a weighted average reduction of 35 percent.[112] These reductions were not as great as the combined reductions of twenty-eight bilateral agreements, but then the tariff rates in 1945–47 were, of course, about half of those of 1934.

The General Agreement on Tariff and Trade (GATT) was originally intended to have been part of a permanent International Trade Organization (ITO), which would make and enforce rules on international trade, much as the International Monetary Fund was doing for the international monetary system. After two years of negotiations, however, the final act of the United Nations Conference on Trade and Employment in Havana on March 24, 1948 was a document which was much more comprehensive than what the U.S. or most other nations had originally envisaged. Clair Wilcox, a writer and advocate of the Charter, said that the Conference had "produced and

---

[111]Congressional Quarterly, *Congress and the Nation, 1945–64*, pp. 194, 187–207.

[112]Evans, *Kennedy Round*, pp. 11–12.

TABLE 4   Congressional Votes on Trade Bills, 1934–58

	SENATE				HOUSE		
		Yeas	Nays			Yeas	Nays
1934	Democrats	51	5	1934	Democrats	269	11
	Republicans	5	28		Republicans	2	99
1937	Democrats	56	9	1937	Democrats	278	11
	Republicans	0	14		Republicans	3	81
1940	Democrats	41	15	1940	Democrats	212	20
	Republicans	0	20		Republicans	5	146
1943	Democrats	41	8	1943	Democrats	195	11
	Republicans	18	14		Republicans	145	52
1945	Democrats	38	5	1945	Democrats	205	12
	Republicans	15	16		Republicans	33	140
1948	Democrats	23	17	1948	Democrats	16	142
	Republicans	47	1		Republicans	218	5
1949	Democrats	47	1	1949	Democrats	234	6
	Republicans	15	18		Republicans	84	63
1951	Republicans	34	2	1951	Republicans	(voice count)	
1953	Republicans	(voice count)		1953	Republicans	179	25
1954	Republicans	37	2	1954	Republicans	126	39
1955	Republicans	38	7	1955	Republicans	109	75
1958	Republicans	36	10	1958	Republicans	133	59

SOURCE: Congressional Quarterly, *Almanac*, 1951, p. 215; Fisher, *President and Congress: Power and Policy* (N. Y.: Free Press, 1972) p. 148.

wrote into a single document, not one agreement, but six—one on trade policy, one on cartels, one on commodity agreements, one on employment, one on economic development and international investment, and the constitution of a new U.N. agency in the field of international trade."[113] Its comprehensiveness was a liability in the U.S. since there were many detailed features which many Americans found objectionable. But the main reason that the State Department didn't even bother to submit the charter for ratification to the Senate was because it contained too many exceptions for other countries and too many obligations for the United States. As Charles Kindleberger has written: "The United States would be held to the general rule; other countries would claim avoidance under saving clauses."[114]

[113]Clair Wilcox, *A Charter for World Trade* (N.Y.: MacMillan, 1949), p. vii.

[114]Charles P. Kindleberger, "U.S. Foreign Economic Policy, 1776–1976," *Foreign Affairs* 55 (January 1977): 409. Also see Gardner, *Sterling-Dollar Diplomacy*, chap. 17, "The End of ITO."

Thus, it would not be accurate to portray the American failure to ratify the Charter as a "protectionist" development, particularly since the GATT would, with U.S. support, serve the same purposes as the ITO was originally intended to serve.

The next four rounds of multilateral trade negotiations, until the Kennedy Round began in 1963, were not nearly as successful as the first GATT for a number of reasons. The first round was relatively painless, from the perspective of the United States, which held such a decisive economic advantage in world trade. From the perspective of the other twenty-one members of GATT, the sacrifices of reduced tariffs were deferred, and they were permitted to retain quantitative restrictions until they rebuilt their monetary reserves. The principle of diminishing returns set in immediately, making agreements on additional tariff concessions increasingly difficult for each successive round.[115]

The success of the first round and previous bilateral agreements coupled with the increasing difficulty in subsequent negotiations were both cause and consequence of a more strident domestic debate on trade policy in the United States. The 1945 renewal was called "the high point in the legislative basis of the trade-agreements program,"[116] and "the high-water mark of liberal trade sentiment in the U.S.,"[117] and in the sense that the bill passed virtually untouched, it is no doubt true. But to understand the legislative-executive struggle in the period following this renewal, one must first recognize that it took place within a context of gradually declining trade barriers and increasing trade. World exports, for example, increased from $21 billion in 1938 to $54 billion in 1948, to $96 billion in 1958 (see table 5).

Secondly, one needs to peel away the rhetorical debate between "protectionism" and "free trade," a debate which was never seriously joined in the United States after the 1930s, and examine more closely the difficult issue of adjustment to freer trade. After the 1940s, "protectionist" or "free trader" were labels people attached to others but never to oneself. In the 1945 hearings before the Ways and Means Committee, both Henry Wallace and Assistant Secretary of State Will Clayton both denied they were "free traders."[118] If pressed, they probably would have admitted they supported freer trade rather than free trade. Instead, they restated their belief in tariff protection when investigations showed this was necessary, i.e., when imports were seriously injuring a domestic industry.

Written in the 1934 Act by the Congress, one will recall, was a

[115]Evans, *Kennedy Round*, pp. 8–14.

[116]Hawkins and Norwood, "Legislative Basis of U.S. Commercial Policy" p. 104.

[117]Gardner, *Sterling-Dollar Diplomacy*, p. 373.

[118](Clayton) in *New York Times*, 19 April 1945, p. 9; (Wallace), *New York Times*, 24 April 1945, p. 19.

TABLE 5   World Exports (In Current Value Dollars*), 1938–78

Year	Value (in $U.S. million)
1938	21,100
1948	53,900
1958	96,000
1960	107,880
1965	156,490
1970	265,720
1972	355,310
1974	729,170
1976	991,000
1978	1,280,000

*only for market (i.e., non-Communist) economies

SOURCES: U.N. Department of Economic and Social Affairs, Statistical Office, *Statistical Yearbook, 1975* (N.Y.: U.N., 1976); *International Economic Report of the President,* March 1976, p. 10; GATT, *International Trade,* 1978.

provision (sec. 4) which guaranteed the opportunity for outside groups to present their views to the President before the completion of bilateral negotiations. If a particular industry could demonstrate that a concession would cause it "serious injury," then it was presumed that the President would not grant a concession on that item. (That, of course, was the reason that negotiations were to be on an item-by-item basis.)[119] This provision, which came to be called the "escape clause," was first generalized—rather than directed at a specific item—in the 1942 bilateral trade agreement with Mexico. The general clause permitted the modification or withdrawal of trade-agreements concessions in order to remedy serious injury to a domestic industry from increased imports resulting from that concession.[120] This clause was subsequently incorporated in a number of other bilateral agreements and in the multilateral agreement of GATT.

In 1945, in hearings before the Senate Finance Committee, the Administration agreed to incorporate the "escape clause" in all future bilateral and multilateral agreements. Because Congress believed that the law was being administered fairly and effectively, and because of the lack of any serious economic competition from abroad at that time, it was felt unneces-

[119]See John M. Leddy and Janet L. Norwood, "The Escape Clause and Peril Points Under the Trade Agreements Program," in William B. Kelly, Jr. (ed.), *Studies in U.S. Commercial Policy* (Chapel Hill, N.C.: University of North Carolina Press, 1963), pp. 124–5.

[120]Ibid., p. 125; Article XI of the GATT.

sary to mandate that provision into law. But administration spokesmen in the 1945 hearings were asked to go through the motions pledging that they would take no action which would be injurious to industry.

While an increasing number of Republicans had been converted to the belief in the necessity of America's involvement in world affairs, the Republican Party as a whole remained closely tied to the small and medium-sized manufacturer who continued to look abroad with suspicion. And, therefore, when the Republicans won control of the Congress in the 1946 fall elections, there was some trepidation about the future of the trade program. Rep. Jenkins (R-Ohio), a long-time opponent of freer trade, soon introduced a bill which would limit the Executive's negotiating authority and mandate a tightened escape clause. Truman was concerned about the bill's impact on America's prestige and leadership in Europe and in the Geneva negotiations, and he delegated responsibility to his Undersecretaries of State Dean Acheson and William Clayton, to negotiate a compromise with Senators Vandenberg, Chairman of the Foreign Relations Committee, and Millikin, Chairman of Finance. The compromise was in the form of an Executive Order, dated February 25, 1947, which established a formal governmental mechanism to act on applications of domestic industry for escape clause relief.[121]

In 1948, the Republicans extended the Trade Act for only one year and added a "peril point" provision, which required the Tariff Commission to determine in advance of a negotiation a precise tariff rate that could be safely agreed to without threat of injury.[122] The next year, when the Democrats regained control of Congress, they repealed this provision and passed a three-year Trade Act renewal, which because it was retroactive one year, would expire on June 12, 1951.

Between 1947 and 1951, twenty-one applications to increase tariffs under the escape clause were filed in accordance with the 1947 Executive Order. In only two of these cases (women's fur hats and hat bodies) did President Truman increase the tariff. As a result, in the 1951 law, Congress not only mandated the escape clause into law, it also brought back the "peril-point" provision.[123] Both amendments were adopted on the floor of the House. According to two accounts, the Congress adopted these provisions in part because of the failure of the Executive to recognize and adjust to the strength and legitimacy of the congressional concern. As the *New York Times* editorialized: "The distorted form in which this bill has passed the House indicates the degree to which the Administration has lost effective influence on Capitol Hill."[124]

[121]Ibid., pp. 126–27.
[122]Ibid., pp. 128–29.
[123]Ibid., pp. 128–29.
[124]*New York Times* editorial, 9 February 1951, cited in ibid., p. 133.

The Administration changed strategies in the Senate and met with greater success. Instead of trying to defeat the two provisions, the Secretary of State suggested language which was consistent with the intent of the Congress and the Executive Order. The language was accepted. The Tariff Commission was given broad discretion to determine whether injury occurred, or whether a tariff concession had caused or threatened to cause serious injury to the domestic industry. Then, the President had discretion to act upon the Commission's recommendation or reject it; if he chose the latter, he would have to inform the Congress of his reasons.[125]

TRADE POLICY BY FITS AND STARTS, 1953-60

In 1953, for the first time since the passage of Smoot-Hawley, the Republicans won control of both Houses of Congress and the Presidency. Eisenhower, like Hoover, was selected by the Republican Party in part because he was an internationalist, but also because he was in favor of limited government.

One week after his inauguration, Eisenhower invited the congressional leadership to the White House to discuss ways in which the two branches could cooperate with each other to assure good policy. He was very surprised to find that not only did many of the Republican Legislators enjoy their whiggish role as dissenters from executive leadership and policy-making, but that many disagreed with him on the need for a mutual security program and a low tariff program. " . . . And a few even hoped we could restore the Smoot-Hawley Tariff Act, a move which I knew would be ruinous," Eisenhower later wrote.[126]

The Trade Act was due to expire on June 12, 1953, but the Ways and Means Committee was preoccupied with oil import legislation.[127] Independent oil producers from Oklahoma, Texas, and Louisiana wanted an import quota as did those from coal mining states who wanted to prevent imports of residual oil, which was used frequently by industry as a substitute for coal. Eisenhower opposed the oil import quota, and instead urged the Congress in a special message on April 7 to pass a renewal of the Trade Act.[128] After a brief deadlock, Congress agreed to extend the act for one year if Eisenhower promised that no new substantive trade negotiations would be

[125]Ibid., pp. 133-38.

[126]Dwight D. Eisenhower, *Mandate for Change, 1953-56* (Garden City, N.Y.: Doubleday and Co. 1963), pp. 194-95.

[127]For a summary of the case, see BPD, pp. 30-34; Leddy and Norwood, "Escape Clause and Peril Points", pp. 133-38.

[128]BPD wrote that the Simpson bill lost because President Eisenhower took a strong stand against it, and the American oil companies, with subsidiaries in Venezuela (principally Standard Oil of New Jersey) organized a coalition of northeast Legislators. (pp. 32-33)

held. In addition, the President agreed to appoint a protectionist to the Tariff Commission, and accepted a Legislative-Executive Commission on Foreign Economic Policy of seventeen members, ten of whom were from Congress, to study and make recommendations on trade and foreign economic policy.

On August 7th, the President signed the bill into law, and appointed Clarence B. Randall, chairman of Inland Steel Corporation and a person known to be committed to freer trade, to be Chairman of the Commission on Foreign Economic Policy.

Randall drove the Commission, which was deeply divided between old-guard protectionists and proponents of an international trade policy, toward a deadline of January 1954. The final report, filed on time, was clearly internationalist in theme and direction, though there were a number of compromises in it, for example on length of authorization (three years instead of five or ten), and on the peril point and escape clause provisions, which many believed undermined the effectiveness of the broadened negotiating authority. The President asked Randall to coordinate the drafting of legislation, and on March 29, the day before the President's message was due to be sent to the Hill, Eisenhower invited several Republican congressional leaders to discuss the bill at the White House.[129]

When the bill reached the House, however, the Ways and Means Committee deliberately continued its hearings on taxes and social security, and ignored the trade bill. Finally, party leaders concerned about the effects of a difficult fight on trade in an election year, convinced Eisenhower to accept another one-year extension; and that passed on June 24th. This time, the President had obtained a commitment that the Congress would seriously consider a full bill in 1955.

In 1955, the Congress returned Democratic with low-tariff people like Rayburn and Lyndon Johnson as the leaders. But it was the first time that the textile industry had "entered the battle in full force,"[130] and this resulted in the relatively new and significant defection of a bloc of Southern Legislators. In hearings before the Ways and Means Committee, Secretary of State John Foster Dulles took a new tack and defended the peril-point and escape-clause provisions as important in permitting the U.S. to maintain a minimum level of self-sufficiency.[131] Eisenhower, in his *Memoirs*, elaborates on this theme:

> *We recognized, too, that the Soviet threat and the demands of free countries' national security impaired the free working of pure economic law by requiring individual countries to be at least partly*

[129]Eisenhower, *Mandate for Change*, pp. 292–94.
[130]BPD, 60.
[131]Leddy and Norwood, "Escape Clause and Peril Points", p. 139.

self-sufficient, able to produce goods for their armies and navies which other countries, if war should end forever, might better produce for them. To go full out in the direction of free trade, I insisted, the world would need permanent peace.[132]

The bill was voted out of the Committee 20–5, but on the floor of the House there was an attempt to get an open rule to add a multitude of restrictive amendments. This effort was blocked by the high-powered arm-twisting of Speaker Sam Rayburn, who said: "Only once in the history of the House in 42 years in my memory, has a bill of this kind and character been considered except under a closed rule."[133] Rayburn won by a single vote, and then won the final vote on the bill handily.

The Senate Finance Committee, however, made a great many changes. The escape clause provision was altered so that small segments of an industry rather than just an entire industry could seek tariff relief if they could show injury. Senator Matthew Neely (D-W.Va.) introduced the old Simpson bill on oil import quotas. Another amendment on several commodities (e.g., tariffs on lead and zinc) was accepted by the committee. The President began to accept a number of compromises, which surprised and disappointed many of his internationalist allies. The Neely amendment was transformed into one which gave the President authority to fix quotas on imports if in his opinion the domestic industries were vital to our national security.[134]

Eisenhower was expected to prefer the House version in Conference, but with a single deletion (agreed to by the Senate's representatives), the President accepted the Senate version, and it passed the Congress on May 15, 1955.[135] The law gave the President three years authority to reduce any tariff by 15 percent of the rate in existence on January 1, 1955—the reductions to be brought into effect in three annual installments.

In 1958, the Trade Act was extended for four years, and the President was empowered to reduce duties by 20 percent of their level on July 1, 1958. The escape clause was also amended in two important ways. The Congress finally gave itself a legislative veto, by two-thirds vote of a concurrent resolution, to force the President to implement a recommendation of the Tariff Commission. Secondly, the Congress extended the scope of the national security clause so that virtually any domestic industry could obtain

---

[132]Eisenhower, *Mandate for Change*, p. 209.

[133]BPD, p. 64. Rayburn's memory in this instance wasn't as good as his powers of persuasion.

[134]Using this provision, Eisenhower imposed oil import quotas in 1958. See Willard L. Thorp, "Trade Barriers and National Security," *The American Economic Review* 50 (May 1960): 433–42.

[135]Leddy and Norwood, "Escape Clause and Peril Points", p. 142.

protection from foreign competition if it were determined that such competition were weakening the internal economy and thereby impairing national security.[136]

Using the authority of the 1958 Trade Act, the U.S. and the European Economic Community negotiated for about nineteen months beginning in September 1960 in what has come to be called the "Dillon Round," after the chief U.S. negotiator, C. Douglas Dillon, who was Undersecretary of State in the last years of the Eisenhower Administration and John F. Kennedy's first Secretary of the Treasury. The contribution of the Dillon Round was not so much the reduction in tariffs, which was a lack-luster 10 percent, but the fact that it pointed up the inadequacies of existing legislation in the United States to cope with the great changes which had occurred in the international economic system since the core law, the 1930 Smoot-Hawley Tariff Act, had passed. The most important challenge facing the United States was the outstanding economic recovery of Western Europe and the establishment of the Common Market in 1958.

The EEC posed two problems for the United States: (1) the displacement of American exports and the need to negotiate appropriate compensation in terms of substitute concessions; and (2) the increased competition in the U.S. domestic market resulting from the increased productivity of European firms.

Tariff-negotiating authority was to expire in June 1962, and the question then was whether the United States could face up to the new challenge.

[136]Ibid., pp. 142-43.

4

TRADE EXPANSION OR CONTRACTION? 1961–71

"The tide is running in a protectionist direction," Jacob Viner warned in a *Foreign Affairs* article in July 1961, and the question he posed was whether the new President and the new Congress could halt or reverse this tide.[1]

BUREAUCRATIC BEGINNINGS

Trade policy was third on John F. Kennedy's list of economic priorities when he took office on January 20, 1961. In his State of the Union message, he said that he would begin by devoting most of his time to the other two: the recession in the U.S. and the balance of payments problem. Only in August 1961 did Kennedy ask Howard Peterson, a Philadelphia banker, to become his Special Assistant on Trade Policy and to begin drafting a bill.

Trade policy involved literally hundreds of different issues, but in the fall of 1961, two questions of scope and timing were fundamental and preliminary: (1) Should the legislation be merely a request for an extension with some modifications, or a dramatic new initiative, requesting more authority for a longer period to accomplish more goals? (2) When should such a request be made: in 1962, an election year in the United States and a decision year in Europe on whether England would be accepted as a new member to the Common Market, or in 1963, after the election and the decision?[2]

---

[1]"It is obvious, however, that there is keen awareness on the part of the President of the fact that in Congress, at least, and perhaps also in the country at large, the tide is running in a protectionist direction, supported no doubt by the current recession and our balance-of-payments difficulties." Jacob Viner, "Economic Foreign Policy," *Foreign Affairs* 39 (July 1961), 565.

[2]In developing the case study of the 1962 Trade Expansion Act, I found the following sources to be most useful. Ernest H. Preeg, *Traders and Diplomats* (Washington, D.C.:

Undersecretary of State George Ball had chaired a preinaugural Task Force on Trade Policy for Kennedy, and he along with Howard Peterson and his deputy Meyer Rashish (who had been Secretary of the Task Force) thought that a new initiative was necessary, though they were opposed by the bureaucracies who felt that an extension would be sufficient. Peterson pressed for an early initiative, recognizing that any trade bill would take time to get through Congress, but that the world was awaiting American leadership. Ball argued that an initiative in 1962 might undercut domestic support in England for joining the European Economic Community (EEC), and might also jeopardize England's chance for admission by giving the EEC a sense that it had other alternatives.[3]

On the question of asking for an extension or a new initiative, Kennedy decided, in Sorenson's words, that "the fierce fight, which even a simple extension would entail, might better be fought, and fought only once, for a wholly new trade instrument."[4] On the question of timing, the President was inclined toward the Peterson position, but decided to first see whether a couple of trial balloons would fly.

On November 1, 1961, Undersecretary of State George Ball addressed the forty-eighth meeting of the National Foreign Trade Council and spoke about the changes wrought in the international economy by the establishment of the European Economic Community. He said that the existing legislative authority was not adequate to the task of dealing with the common economic front of Western Europe, and he read a message from President Kennedy to the Convention which concluded by saying: "It is essential that we have new tools to deal with the problems of international trade in a new and challenging world."[5]

Ball said that he wasn't prepared to go "into any detail" at that time, but one week later, apparently the President had made up his mind.[6] In a press conference, Kennedy said: "My judgment is that the time to begin is

---

Brookings Institution, 1973), pp. 44–56; John W. Evans, *The Kennedy Round in American Trade Policy* (Cambridge, Mass.: Harvard University Press, 1971), pp. 139–59; Theodore Sorenson, *Kennedy* (N.Y.: Harper and Row, 1965), pp. 460–62; Arthur M. Schlesinger, *A Thousand Days* (N.Y.: Houghton Mifflin Co., 1965), pp. 771–75; BPD, pp. 73–79; Congressional Quarterly, *Almanac, 1962* and *Weekly Reports,* and the *New York Times.*

[3]There are, of course, a few discrepancies in the various narratives of the case. Schlesinger in *A Thousand Days* (p. 773) says that Peterson recommended that the trade bill be merely an extension of the existing act for 1962, whereas Preeg (p. 44) says that Peterson "after some initial wavering . . . also pressed for a new approach" along the lines Ball suggested. BPD's narrative is closer to Preeg's, concluding that "the President accepted Ball's bill with Petersen's timing." (p. 74)

[4]Sorenson, *Kennedy,* p. 461.

[5]Undersecretary of State George Ball, "Threshold of a New Trading World," Address Before the 48th National Foreign Trade Convention on November 1, New York, reprinted in *Department of State Bulletin,* 45 (20 November 1961): 833.

[6]Ibid., 836.

now . . . . One third of our trade generally is in [sic] Western Europe, and if the United States should be denied that market we will either find a flight of capital from this country to construct factories within that wall, or we will find ourselves in serious economic trouble."[7]

In early December, Representative Hale Boggs, an ardent supporter of the Administration's trade policy, began hearings in his influential Subcommittee on Foreign Economic Policy of the Joint Economic Committee. Many of the witnesses like former Secretary of State Christian Herter and former Undersecretary of State William Clayton expressed support for the trade initiative which the Administration was proposing.[8]

With balloons flying, President Kennedy himself commenced the campaign for a new trade bill with speeches on December 6 and 7 to the National Association of Manufacturers and to the AFL-CIO. "The Reciprocal Trade Agreements Act," he explained, "expires in June of next year. It must not be simply renewed—it must be replaced. If the West is to take the initiative in the economic arena, if the United States is to keep pace with the revolutionary changes which are taking place throughout the world, if our exports are to retain and expand their position in the world market, then we need a new and bold instrument of American trade policy."[9]

Substance

The Counsel's office in the State Department was given responsibility for drafting the bill, and the draft is said to have closely resembled the position paper of the Ball Task Force.[10] The bill, which was introduced in the House as H.R. 9900, delegated authority to the President to reduce tariffs (as of 1962) by 50 percent, staged over five years; but for those tariffs at 5 percent or less, the President could negotiate their elimination. As a special incentive to the EEC to admit the U.K., the United States would negotiate the elimination of tariffs on those products in which the U.S. and the EEC supplied 80 percent of world trade. (Few products would qualify unless the U.K. was a member of the EEC.) For the first time, negotiators were permitted to use whatever technique—either item-by-item or broad categories (linear reduction)—which would be more useful and successful in negotiations and in reducing tariffs. The United States was also pledged to

[7]Cited in Evans, *Kennedy Round*, p. 140. See also Peter Kenen, *Giant Among Nations* (Chicago: Rand, McNally, 1963).

[8]Evans, *Kennedy Round*, p. 141.

[9]"New Perspectives on Trade Policy: Address by President Kennedy to the National Association of Manufacturers, New York, December 6, 1961," reprinted in Richard P. Stebbins (ed.), *Documents on American Foreign Relations*, (N.Y.: Harper and Row, 1962), pp. 110–121. Quote is from p. 117. A similar speech was given to the AFL-CIO the next day.

[10]There is very little information on the bureaucratic debates on the bill. For Kennedy's message to Congress, the administration bill (H.R. 9900), and the final law, see Sidney Ratner, *The Tariff in American History* (New York: D. Van Nostrand Company, 1972), pp. 166–79.

eliminate tariffs on tropical products, provided that the EEC would do the same.

The Kennedy bill deliberately omitted the peril-point provision though it retained its four procedural stages which required that the Tariff Commission advise the President as to the probable economic effect of tariff reductions. And to soften the impact of increased imports, the bill included the then radical adjustment assistance provisions, first suggested in a paper by David McDonald for the Randall Commission, and later adopted as an amendment introduced in the Senate by Humphrey, Kennedy, and two others.

Strategy

As a Senator in the 1950s, Kennedy was aware of the growing distrust in the Congress of the State Department's handling of foreign economic policy and for that reason and others, he decided to operate the promotional campaign for the trade bill out of the White House. Peterson's staff was increased to ten, and rather than selecting George Ball, the President asked Secretary of Commerce Luther Hodges, former Governor of North Carolina, to be the chief administration spokesman on the Hill.

Most importantly, Theodore Sorenson noted, the trade bill was given top priority by the Administration:

> Like the antirecession program in 1961 and the tax cut in 1963 (and later in 1963, civil rights), the 1962 trade bill became the centerpiece of all that year's efforts—the subject of extra emphasis in the State of the Union Message, the subject of the year's first special legislative message, the subject of a pep talk with charts to Democratic legislators, the subject of several Presidential speeches, and the subject of an intense White House lobbying effort with priority over almost all other bills.[11]

Part of the Administration's strategy was to assist liberal trading groups; but an equally important part was to divide the opposition, and this often involved a number of nonlegislative concessions to groups which sought some protection from the trade winds. Since the 1950s, the political influence of the textile industry had increased to the point where it was a significant national force. (Indeed, as a Senator from Massachusetts, Kennedy had been very sensitive to their complaints about imports, even though imports in 1960 amounted to only about 7 percent of national production.)[12] On September 28, 1960, a resolution was adopted by the Southern Gover-

[11]Sorenson, Kennedy, p. 460.

[12]For discussion of textile strategy, see Congressional Quarterly, Almanac, 1962, p. 287.

nors Conference calling for import quotas and other restrictive measures to protect the textile industry. On December 3, 1960, President-elect Kennedy appointed one of those Southern Governors, Luther Hodges, to be his Secretary of Commerce. Two months later, Kennedy appointed Hodges as chairman of a Cabinet group to study problems of the textile industry and submit recommendations to him.

In the interim, the industry mobilized their congressional supporters to keep the pressure on the Administration. Representative Carl Vinson, the leader of the textile group in the House, a group with about 128 members, met with JFK on March 27 and later said: "Unless quotas are imposed that will provide the necessary protection to the textile industry in the United States, I think I can safely predict that at least some of the members who voted to extend the Trade Agreements Act of 1958 will have second thoughts if a bill to extend the Act is presented on the floor in 1962."[13]

On May 2, 1961, Kennedy announced a seven-point program to assist the textile industry, and although the plan didn't include quotas, it did promise negotiations leading to voluntary export restraint programs and greater access for foreign textiles to the European Economic Community. A seventeen-nation Textile Conference opened on July 17 in Geneva under the auspices of GATT. A short-term agreement was completed in nine days, but a longer-term agreement wasn't reached until February 9, 1962. This permitted the United States and other importing nations to freeze their textiles imports for two years, and after that, increase their imports by 5 percent annually.[14] On February 16th, Representative Vinson, W. J. Bryan Dorn, and seventy-three other congressmen who were from textile districts wrote a letter of thanks to the President.[15] And on March 31, 1962, the American Cotton Manufacturers Institute, which represented about 80 percent of the cotton textile industry, adopted the following resolution: "We believe that the authority to deal with foreign nations proposed by the President [in the Trade Expansion Act] will be wisely exercised and should be granted."[16]

This was not the first time that the textile industry—or parts of it—had threatened over-all trade policy; nor was it the first time that an Administration had successfully defused the challenge by nonlegislative concessions, but the long-term arrangement (LTA) under GATT was certainly the most extensive one of its kind.[17]

[13]Ibid.

[14]Ibid., pp. 287–88.

[15]*New York Times*, 16 and 17 February 1962, p. 1.

[16]BPD, p. 79.

[17]Voluntary agreements on the export of textiles from Japan to the U.S. were concluded in 1937 and 1957. See I. M. Destler, Hideo Sato, and Haruhiro Fukui, *The Textile Wrangle: Conflict in Japanese-American Relations: 1969–71* (Ithaca: Cornell University Press, 1979). See particularly chap. 1. For the effect of the wool tariff on trade negotiations in 1947–48, see Donald

With the most potent opponent of freer trade co-opted, Kennedy sent the Trade Expansion Act with a special message on foreign trade policy to the Congress on January 25, 1962. "A new American trade initiative" was justified, it began, in order to take account of "five fundamentally new and sweeping developments": (1) the growth of the European Common Market; (2) the growing pressures on the balance of payments; (3) the need to accelerate economic growth; (4) the Communist aid and trade offensive; and (5) the need to expand trade with Japan and the developing nations.[18] The message said that the new measure would "benefit substantially every state of the union, every segment of the American economy, and every basic objective of our domestic economy and foreign policy."[19] Those Americans who would benefit from the new bill would include the businessman, the farmer, the worker, and the consumer.[20] In concluding, he wrote:

> The purpose of this message has been to describe the challenge we face and the tools we need. The decision rests with the Congress. That decision will either mark the beginning of a new chapter in the alliance of free nations—or a threat to the growth of western unity. The two great Atlantic markets will either grow together or they will grow apart.[21]

Alignment of Interest Groups

The Administration had completed its decision-making process and had sent its product to the Congress. As the executive branch geared up to do battle in the Congress, so too did the various interest groups. The special interest groups often hired Washington lawyers to take their cases to committee Hearings and privately to individual Legislators. The general interest groups lined up, as they had many times in the past, on both sides of the issue.

The liberal trade lobby was lead by the Committee for a National Trade Policy, originally established in 1953 by the executives of large corporations with export interests. During each renewal of trade legislation, the CNTP enlarged its staff, and served as coordinator for the other freer trade groups

M. Blinken, *Wool Tariffs, and American Policy* (Washington, D.C.: Public Affairs Press, 1948), p. viii. For a description of the Long-Term Arrangement (LTA) under the auspices of GATT which entered into force on October 1, 1962 for a period of five years, and for a summary of national policies of the OECD countries prior to that to restrict cotton textile imports, see General Agreement on Tariffs and Trade, *A Study on Cotton Textiles* (Geneva, July 1966), pp. 79–84.

[18]Ratner, *Tariff in American History*, pp. 166–67.

[19]Ibid., p. 168.

[20]The order is not insignificant. Ibid., pp. 171–73.

[21]Ibid., p. 178.

and as liaison with the White House. In 1962, the AFL-CIO and the Chamber of Commerce worked with each other in general support of the bill, although each had pet provisions or modifications they intended to fight for in the bill.

The National Association of Manufacturers with about twenty-two thousand company members, representing both exporters and import-sensitive businesses, chose to remain neutral. The American Farm Bureau Federation also supported the President's proposal, though like the business-men and the labor unions, there were many farmers and farm organizations which defected and were vocal in their opposition.

On the other side of the issue were a number of organizations which either represented import-sensitive industries or were ideologically opposed to the concept of freer trade. The Trade Relations Council was the "grand-father" of the protectionist groups, having been founded as the American Protective Tariff League in 1885. In the 1920s, it changed its name to the American Tariff League, and in 1958 to the American Trade Council (ATC) to reflect a concern for a broader range of foreign economic policies. Its membership consists of several wealthy businesses, trade associations, and farm groups. The American Trade Council cooperated with the Nation-Wide Committee on Import-Export Policy, which was founded in 1953 and headed by O. R. Strackbein. Strackbein's staff generally consists of himself and a secretary, but his impact is said to be considerable. Finally, the Liberty Lobby founded in 1955 has consistently opposed trade legislation on the grounds that it views the delegation of tariff-making powers to the president as unconstitutional.[22]

"THE DECISION RESTS WITH THE CONGRESS"

Although intended to reduce government revenue by reducing tariffs, the Trade Expansion Act was still a revenue bill, and as such, it began its congressional journey in the House of Representatives' Committee on Ways and Means. Hearings began on March 12, 1962, and as with all major bills considered by the committee, a voluminous record of some 4,233 pages of testimony was compiled.

Europe was a principal topic of interest; other countries were often referred to as "third countries" and U.S. objectives were often defined in terms of assisting them to gain greater access to the Common Market. The rate of economic growth of the nations of the European Economic Com-munity (EEC) was twice the American rate. The framework for a common agricultural policy was accepted in 1962, and was a cause of some anxiety by

[22]Congressional Quarterly, *Weekly Report*, 9 March 1962, pp. 403–7.

committee members as was the reverse system of preferences between the
EEC and many developing and associated governments. The feeling was
widespread that the State Department in previous negotiations had been
more concerned in promoting Europe's growth than America's interests. A
popular comparison made by Committee members was that the EEC has a
22 percent tariff on automobiles while the U.S. rate was 6.5 percent.[23]

When George Ball testified, he insisted that "the United States has
come out very well in the [previous] four rounds of negotiations." He said
that Congress's feeling of loss was evident "in every industrial community
in the world." Still, the gains from increased exports clearly outweighed any
possible estimate of losses.[24]

Other issues of concern to the congressmen included the question of
the constitutionality of delegating tariff powers to the President, an argument which strict-constructionist Republicans continued to use even after
most of the protectionist lobbies had stopped. Adjustment assistance was a
controversial subject, with proponents arguing for it as a positive alternative
to the escape clause provision, and opponents suggesting that protection was
an American tradition while adjustment assistance was another form of
socialism.

Wilbur Mills, Chairman of the Committee on Ways and Means,
directed the legislative process with skill and effectiveness.[25] The Committee rejected a series of protectionist amendments, but it did make several
serious policy changes in the administration bill in two areas: delegation
of negotiating authority and most-favored-nation status for communist
countries.

Many congressmen and outside interests argued that the State Department, as the lead agency responsible for trade negotiations since 1934, was
unsympathetic and unresponsive to domestic interests and that the responsibility should be assigned elsewhere.[26] Of course, labor unions wouldn't
permit the Commerce Department to be the negotiator, nor would business
permit it to go to Labor. Treasury was thought to be primarily interested in
monetary questions and might therefore sacrifice our trading interests to
balance of payments considerations. After a conversation with President
Kennedy, Mills proposed the appointment of a Special Trade Representative
(STR) in the Executive Office of the President. The STR, appointed with the
advice and consent of the Senate, would be the chief representative of the

[23]Evans, *Kennedy Round*, p. 150.

[24]Congressional Quarterly, *Almanac*, 1962, p. 272.

[25]See John F. Manley, "Wilbur D. Mills: A Study in Congressional Influence," *American Political Science Review* 63 (June 1969).

[26]See, for example, Henry J. Taylor, "Pennsylvania, W. Virginia Miners Deprived of Jobs Because Our State Department Pampers British," *Pittsburgh Press*, 1 October 1962, reprinted in *Congressional Record* by Rep. John Dent, 4 October 1962, p. 22293.

U.S. at the multilateral trade negotiations, and (because of a Senate amendment) he would also chair the Cabinet-level interagency Trade Information Committee, which was also invented by the Ways and Means Committee to replace the Trade Agreements Committee as the central interagency coordinator on trade and the advisor to the President.[27]

The second major change provided that Congress could override a presidential decision against use of the escape clause by a majority vote, instead of the two-thirds vote as mandated in the 1958 law. This proposal was initially opposed by the President, but after realizing that the Congress had not attempted even once in nine opportunities to override in the period 1958 to 1962, the Administration's opposition softened, and the amendment passed.[28]

In previous trade negotiations, Legislators had attended as observers, not unlike journalists, lobbyists, or nongovernmental organizations, but that arrangement was no longer considered satisfactory. Thus, the third congressional initiative, which affected the negotiating process, provided official accreditation to the MTN for two congressmen of each party from the Ways and Means Committee and two Senators of each party from the Senate Finance Committee.

The President had requested discretionary authority to grant most-favored-nation status to Communist countries, but the House instead restored and tightened a provision which had first been in the trade legislation in 1951, denying MFN to all countries "dominated or controlled by international Communism," therefore excluding Yugoslavia and Poland. The President strongly opposed the House's position, and gained the agreement of the Senate Finance Committee, but the House prevailed in Conference.[29]

The Ways and Means Committee also added a provision which restrained the President for four years from negotiating a reduction in tariffs on any product which had received an affirmative injury finding by the Tariff Commission on an escape clause case. The Senate extended the limitation to five years.

The bill went to the House floor on June 27 with a closed rule, permitting only a motion to recommit, which was made by Representative Mason. Administration strategists, fearful of Republican Party opposition,

[27]See Chapter 5, "Administrative Provisions," Sec. 241, Trade Expansion Act (PL 88-794). Also, see Anne H. Rightor-Thornton, "An Analysis of the Office of the Special Representative for Trade Negotiations: The Evolving Role, 1962–1974," Edward K. Hamilton, (ed.), *Case Studies in U.S. Foreign Economic Policy*, app. H, vol. 3, in U.S. Commission on the Organization of the Government for the Conduct of Foreign Policy (Washington: G.P.O., 1975).

[28]Congressional Quarterly, *Almanac*, 1962, p. 276.

[29]In December 1963, the provisions of the Trade Act prohibiting MFN to Poland and Yugoslavia were removed. (See Evans, *Kennedy Round*, p. 157.)

were prepared to pare down the adjustment assistance provisions if that were necessary to gain their support. However, since the AFL-CIO said it might withdraw its support if the relatively strong adjustment assistance provisions were watered down, there was concern that the bill could unravel if this provision were altered. But the anxiety was for naught. Mason's amendment was defeated 171–253, and the bill then passed easily 298–125,[30] as many of those who opposed the bill but knew the dangers of appearing to oppose the "Atlantic Partnership" crossed over. Perhaps decisive was the "textile strategy," as a majority of the 128 members of the "textile lobby" voted against the Mason recommital, and the two leaders of the bloc, Representative Vinson and Representative W. J. Bryan Dorn, supported the Administration's bill.[31]

Two other particular interest groups, the Northwest timber industry and the oil industry, had considerable impact on the trade bill. Both had greater power in the Senate than in the House, but only the timber industry had a legitimate case that imports were causing serious injury. President Kennedy was not as responsive to the demands of the oil industry,[32] as he was to the lumber industry, announcing a six-point program for the lumber industry, including the preferential procurement of U.S. timber by the Defense Department and a pledge to negotiate a voluntary agreement on exports with the Canadians.[33]

For the first time in his administration, President Kennedy also accepted the recommendations of the Tariff Commission, and on March 19, 1962 announced that he would increase the tariffs on carpets and glass. When the EEC retaliated, as GATT rules permitted, with higher tariffs on a couple of American products, a reporter asked the President whether he would repeal the tariff increases. "No," the President answered, "it is going to stand. Carpets and glass . . . were very hard hit. We were quite aware of the fact that action would be taken by the Europeans. If we had had passage of the Trade Act, we could have then offered an alternate package which I think would have prevented retaliation."[34] Thus, Kennedy used the escape clause twice; once to show his responsiveness to injured industries, and a second time to underscore the urgency of passing the trade bill.

The Senate Finance Committee held four weeks of hearings on the

[30]Congressional Quarterly, *Almanac*, 1962, p. 279.

[31]Ibid., p. 288.

[32]Afterwards, Senators Kerr and Long made it sound as if they had "an understanding" with JFK that he would apply quotas for national security reasons. (Congressional Quarterly, *Almanac*, 1962, pp. 288–290.) While Kennedy didn't increase the quotas as the industry wanted, he didn't remove them either. Petrolum was also exempted from tariff cuts in the 1962 Act, although the central issue for oil was the quota not the tariff.

[33]Ibid., p. 290.

[34]Ibid.

trade bill from July 23 to August 16. The Finance Committee is generally regarded as more protectionist, but in 1962, the bill approved by the committee was considered satisfactory by the Administration. There had been a number of very close votes on amendments on the adjustment assistance provisions, but all were won by the liberal traders.

An exchange between Senator Paul Douglas and George Ball on the "dominant supplier" provision proved rather interesting because the traditional roles of the Executive fighting for more discretion and the Congress trying to limit it were reversed. The "dominant supplier" provision would have permitted the President to negotiate the elimination of tariffs on products in which the U.S. and the EEC together supplied 80 percent of the world's trade. Since few products would qualify unless the U.K. were a member of the EEC, Ball had written the provision as an incentive for the EEC to accept Britain.

Since the President had introduced the bill in January 1962, however, there had been a number of developments in Europe which appeared to presage the eventual rejection of British membership to the EEC. Douglas and Representative Henry Reuss therefore introduced an amendment which would permit the European Free Trade Association (EFTA), including Britain, to be counted along with the United States and the EEC as the "dominant suppliers." The President would then have authority to negotiate the elimination of tariffs on any product in which these three groups were responsible for 80 percent of the trade. Ball opposed it because he felt it would be more difficult to negotiate such arrangements with all of the countries of EFTA and also because it might be interpreted as trying to interfere in the U.K.–EEC negotiations. Douglas responded that the original proposal submitted by the Administration could be as easily interpreted as interfering with the EEC decision as his, but the Douglas–Reuss amendment provided wider flexibility and the opportunity for the elimination of a great many tariffs should the U.K. membership be rejected, as it in fact was. Douglas's views prevailed in the committee and in the Senate, but Ball persuaded the House delegates to Conference, and the Conference report deleted the Douglas amendment.[35]

The Finance Committee was pressured as much by exporters seeking access abroad as by importers seeking protection at home. Exporters wanted provisions granting the President special authority to retaliate with duties or import restrictions, for example, against those countries which maintained import restrictions on U.S. agricultural products. The Senate committee did, at least partially, respond by adding a provision which gave the President authority to increase duties on the fish products of a foreign country "which

---

[35]Ibid., 281; Evans, *Kennedy Round*, pp. 155–56; Henry Reuss, *The Critical Decade* (N.Y.: McGraw-Hill, 1964), pp. 43–46.

refuses to engage in good faith negotiations relating to conservation."[36] The Senate also gave additional authority to the President to enter into negotiations for orderly marketing agreements with foreign countries for those products in which the Tariff Commission found injury to a domestic industry. All of these unsought discretionary authorities were found acceptable by the President, and by the House.

The Finance Committee approved the bill 17–0 on September 14, 1962. On the floor of the Senate, an amendment by Prescott Bush (R-Conn.) to restore the peril point provision was rejected by a narrow 38–40. Other protectionist amendments were defeated by much larger votes. *Congressional Quarterly* explained why: "The union of various protectionist elements—such as textiles, coal and lumber—which, voting together, could have crippled the bill, failed to materialize."[37] On September 19, the Senate passed the bill, H.R. 11970, by a vote of 78–8, with fifty-six Democrats and twenty-two Republicans voting for the bill, and seven Republicans and one Democrat, Strom Thurmond, voting against. The final Conference Report was accepted by both Houses, and the act went to the President for his signature. There were no special product exemptions and no specific interest provisions in the final act, though it did reflect an amalgam of slightly different priorities. In some ways, especially the adjustment assistance provisions which to Kennedy's surprise survived the legislative maze,[38] it was better than what the President had asked for. And on September 19, 1962, Kennedy called it "the strongest trade bill" since the 1934 Reciprocal Trade Agreements Act since it "gives us the opportunity to develop closer and more harmonious trade relations with the nations of the Common Market and other nations throughout the world."[39]

One year after Jacob Viner warned of a new protectionist wave, a bill described by President Kennedy as "unprecedented" in scope and in its liberalness swept through the Congress in nine months.[40] How can we account for its success? We will save a definitive answer for chapter 7 when all the cases can be compared, but a tentative answer may be suggested here.

[36]For comparison of the House, the Senate, and the Conference bills, see the report by Wilbur Mills to the House, *Congressional Record*, 4 October 1962, p. 22280–82.

[37]Congressional Quarterly, *Almanac*, 1962, p. 283. In the Senate, the textile bloc did not unite against the bill. American Cotton Manufacturers Institute actively supported the bill, and administration spokesmen dropped hints that if they or other groups opposed the bill, the Long-Term Geneva Textile agreement might not be signed. (p. 288)

[38]Sorenson, *Kennedy* p. 461. Kennedy said that he "did not expect that revolutionary provision [on adjustment assistance] to pass."

[39]Congressional Quarterly, *Almanac*, 1962, p. 282.

[40]Cited in Harry C. Hawkins and Janet L. Norwood, "The Legislative Basis of United States Commercial Policy (Chapel Hill, N.C.: University of North Carolina Press, 1963), p. 114. In an analysis of the act, the two authors confirmed JFK's assessment: "The Trade Expansion Act extends to the President greater flexibility and tariff-reducing authority than any other legislation in the history of the trade-agreements program." (p. 122)

Certainly, Presidential leadership and strategy, congressional leadership particularly at the committee level, and an international environment which could lend credibility to the arguments made by the bill's supporters were all very important. President Kennedy gave the issue his highest attention, organized a White House-centered promotional campaign, and divided and co-opted the opposition by nonlegislative concessions. Chairman Mills steered the bill through his Committee, but he did allow changes which altered, albeit slightly, the priorities of the policy-package. In the Senate, congressional priorities were asserted more forcefully, while Presidential discretion was permitted. In the final act, Congress had a larger role than ever before, with accredited delegates to the negotiations and a Special Trade Representative free of the State Department's influence and within reach and influence of Congress and domestic considerations. The movement toward relaxation of tensions with the Soviet Union or Eastern Europe was slowed and in some ways halted for the moment. Congress, in short, left its print and some of its priorities.

THE KENNEDY ROUND: TOO MUCH OF A GOOD THING

The period between the signing of the Trade Expansion Act in October 1962 and April 10, 1973, when President Nixon sent the Trade Reform bill of 1973 to the Congress, is one of the most complicated, ambiguous, and chaotic decades in the history of U.S. foreign economic policy. It began in euphoria, continued through one of the most successful international trade negotiations in world history, and then centrifugal forces in the U.S. and elsewhere threatened to pull the international trading system, so recently improved, irrevocably apart.

President Kennedy called the Trade Expansion Act "the most important international piece of legislation . . . affecting economics since the passage of the Marshall plan,"[41] and his emphasis on the international dimension was both correct and ominous. While it provided sufficient negotiating authority to conclude after four very trying years, "the most successful trade negotiations in history,"[42] it did not provide for sufficient congressional or public involvement to ensure the development of a supportive consensus;[43] nor did it provide sufficient flexibility in its "escape valve" mechanisms to

[41]Congressional Quarterly, *Almanac*, 1962, p. 262.

[42]Harald B. Malmgren, *International Economic Peacekeeping in Phase II* (N.Y.: Quadrangle Books, 1972), p. 16; see also Preeg, *Traders and Diplomats*, chap. 16, "An Evaluation."

[43]Rep. Thomas B. Curtis of Missouri was a member of the Ways and Means Committee since 1953 and was instrumental in shaping the 1962 act. He had served as congressional observer to the 1956 negotiations, and was instrumental in shaping the 1962 act. He has written a book, *The Kennedy Round and the Future of American Trade*, with John Robert Vastine, Jr. (N.Y.: Praeger, 1971), which unfortunately for our purposes only describes the international

alleviate the strain of increased imports in certain sectors or to give the Congress the impression that the act was being administered fairly. Between 1962 and 1969, there were fifteen petitions for adjustment assistance, and all were rejected by the Tariff Commission. Not a single affirmative vote was cast in the twelve escape clause cases that were brought before the Tariff Commission in the six years following the passage of the Trade Expansion Act, and although not quite as restrictive, the other potential "escape valves"—antidumping, the national security waiver, unfair trade practices, countervailing duties—permitted little to escape until around 1969.[44]

The administration of the act domestically only reinforced the growing feeling in the Congress that U.S. negotiators in Geneva were losing. As Senator Russell Long, Chairman of the Finance Committee, colorfully depicted the negotiations: "This nation in its trade and aid programs has played the part of an Andy Gump until it is on the verge of becoming an international Barney Google . . . "[45] Paradoxically, a new and potent protectionist mood and bloc appeared to emerge from an extremely productive and successful round of multilateral trade negotiations.

On June 30, 1967, the expiration date for U.S. negotiating authority, the United States joined with forty-five other nations in signing the General Agreement of 1967 concluding the Kennedy Round.[46] Prior to 1967, the most successful trade negotiations for the U.S. in terms of the scope of tariff reductions occurred twenty years earlier in the first MTN when tariffs were reduced on products constituting about 54 percent of the U.S. total dutiable imports. In the Kennedy Round, with many more governments participating and tariffs much lower than in 1947, the tariffs on 64 percent of all dutiable imports were reduced. John Evans thinks that "the decisive reason" for the

---

negotiations. He doesn't try to describe or explain the politics which shaped the Trade Act and affected the international negotiations.

Moreover, although perfectly positioned to comment on the impact of the congressional delegation, he has little to say other than that the relationship between the delegation and the negotiators "was highly experimental but successful." (p. 11) Nor does he make much of an attempt to explain the complete failure on the issue of the American Selling Price System (ASP) to gain Congress's support, when presumably that was one of his responsibilities. Sen. Herman Talmadge, however, strongly disagreed with Curtis's assessment of the congressional advisory system. (See U.S. Senate, Committee on Finance, *Hearings on the Trade Reform Act of 1974*, p. 224.)

[44]For an excellent article detailing and summarizing the various cases, see Frank V. Fowlkes, "Administrative Escape Valves Relieve Pressures of Imports on Domestic Industries," *National Journal*, 24 July 1971, pp. 1544–50. Also see *National Journals*, 7 March 1970, pp. 501–504; 4 December 1971, p. 2402; and 23 September 1972, pp. 1496–1503.

[45]Quoted in Preeg, *Traders and Diplomats*, p. 160.

[46]The importance of the deadline of 30 June 1967 as an action-forcer was one of the themes of Preeg's book, and he aptly began his book with the following quote by Samuel Johnson: "When a man knows he is to be hanged in a fortnight, he concentrates his mind wonderfully." (p. 1)

extensive commodity coverage was the linear method of tariff reduction adopted in 1963.[47]

Not only were the reductions wide, but they were also quite deep. The average tariff cut for all industrial products was about 35 percent, and although this represented only about one-quarter of world trade, it represented 80 percent of the trade of those products which still had tariffs.[48] On agricultural products (excluding grains), the average reduction by the major industrial countries amounted to about 20 percent and affected almost half of the dutiable imports of the four majors—the United States, the U.K., EEC, and Japan.[49]

After 1972, when the final stage of the tariff reductions would come into effect, the overall average of tariffs for the following countries would be as follows:

TABLE 6   Average Tariffs — Due to Kennedy Round

Country	Average Duty as of 1972	Percentage Reduction
U.S.	9.9%	36%
EEC	8.6%	37%
U.K.	10.8%	39%
Japan	10.7%	39%

SOURCE: Preeg, *Traders and Diplomats,* pp. 208-211.

The very success of the Kennedy Round in reducing tariffs created two problems. Several industries, feeling the chill of freer trade, scrambled for protection; and secondly, non-tariff barriers (NTB's) increased in importance. As one writer graphically put it: "The lowering of tariffs has, in effect, been like draining a swamp. The lower water level has revealed all the snags and stumps of nontariff barriers that still have to be cleared away."[50]

Robert E. Baldwin chooses to call nontariff barriers nontariff distortions, and defines the concept broadly and economistically as "any measure (public or private) that causes internationally traded goods and services, or resources devoted to the production of these goods and services, to be

[47]Evans, *Kennedy Round,* p. 281.

[48]Ibid.

[49]See Preeg, *Traders and Diplomats* chaps. 13–15 for a detailed assessment of the results, and chap. 15 of Evans, *Kennedy Round.*

[50]B. A. Jones, *New York Times,* 10 July 1968, as quoted by Robert E. Baldwin, *Nontariff Distortions of International Trade* (Washington, D.C.: Brookings Institution, 1970), p. 2.

allocated in such a way as to reduce potential real world income."[51] NTB's (or NTD's), therefore, include not only those measures such as quotas, export subsidies, or border tax adjustments, whose purpose is to directly affect the volume and composition of trade, but also those regulatory policies—safety, health, or pollution standards, regional development subsidies, or discriminatory procurement—whose purpose and orientation is predominantly domestic (to set standards or assist an industry or region) but which nonetheless have an impact abroad. And Baldwin encourages us to think broadly about nontariff distortions as virtually all national policies which affect in a negative way the efficient allocation of resources.[52] Like tariffs, nontariff distortions can be utilized for short-term advantage by a particular government, but only at the risk of retaliation, and thus an ultimate diminution of world income.

To summarize, nontariff distortions have increased in importance, not only because of the lowering of tariffs, but because of the increased economic integration of societies in different countries and because of the increasing responsiveness of governments towards their citizens' needs and wants.[53] The international negotiations of these policies will also be quite different from negotiating tariff concessions. Increasingly, the goals will be harmonization and coordination of national policies rather than their reduction or elimination. For example, in the case of export subsidies, governments will want to retain the means to promote certain kinds of exports, but will want to eliminate the competitive aspect of bidding for higher interest rates. This can be accomplished by agreeing on certain rules for the amount and volume of subsidies and level of interest rate, while acknowledging the legitimacy of the device.[54]

Two nontariff barrier policies—an antidumping code and the American Selling Price (ASP) system of customs valuation—were the subject of important negotiations during the Kennedy Round, even though they were not addressed in the Trade Expansion Act. When the Congress learned that the Executive was negotiating NTB's, the Senate adopted by voice vote on June 29, 1966 S.Con. Res. 100 urging the President to instruct U.S. negotiators in Geneva to bargain only on provisions authorized in the Trade Expansion Act of 1962.[55]

---

[51]At the same time, Baldwin recognizes that his definition is "unmanageable" and only deals in his study with those "measures that significantly distort international trade." Baldwin, *Nontariff Distortions,* p. 5. The word "significantly" unfortunately goes undefined.

[52]Baldwin does, however, acknowledge the importance of other social and distributive goals for society, though it is more as a qualification or a departure from his economic analysis.

[53]For another view, which sees the alleged decline of tariffs and rise of NTB's as exaggerated, see Evans, *Kennedy Round,* pp. 303–9.

[54]See chap. 4 of Harald Malmgren, *International Economic Peacekeeping in Phase II.*

[55]S. Con. Res. 100, 29 June 1966, S. Rept. 1341. Congressional Quarterly, *Almanac,* 1967, pp. 810–814. Also, Evans *Kennedy Round,* pp. 299–301.

The warning was ignored, and two elaborate packages were negotiated in Geneva, an antidumping code and the repeal of the ASP. It was only with the greatest difficulty that the Executive worked out a compromise with the Congress on the antidumping code, and the compromise, in effect, rendered their exercise in Geneva meaningless. The Congress agreed to accept the code only on condition that it did not conflict with the 1921 U.S. antidumping statute. In the event that the two did conflict, the administering agency (either the Treasury Department or the Tariff Commission) would have to apply the statute rather than the code.[56]

The legislative-executive negotiations on the ASP package were less successful. Established by law in 1922 to protect the "infant" benzenoid chemical industry which had been started during the war, the American Selling Price system permitted relatively low tariffs, but extraordinarily high protection by computing tariff rates on the basis of the price of the American product rather than the price of the import.[57] (Thus, an ASP of 20 percent on an item which costs $1 to import but sells for $2 in the U.S. would actually be taxed 40 percent.) The repeal of the ASP was bargained against two separate European packages; one would go into effect regardless of whether the Congress acted favorably on the repeal of the ASP; the second package was conditional on congressional approval. "During the course of negotiations," said the senior staff member of the Senate Finance Committee in charge of trade issues, "the Executive didn't consult with us at all."

Thus, not surprisingly, the Congress didn't move independently to repeal the ASP, and President Johnson, his attention fixed elsewhere, delayed until May 28, 1968 before he submitted a bill, the Trade Expansion Act of 1968 (H.R. 17551), which requested the repeal of the ASP, an extension of negotiating authority until June 30, 1970, and the relaxation of the criteria by which industries and workers could obtain adjustment assistance. The Ways and Means Committee heard testimony on the bill from more than three hundred witnesses for a nineteen day period from June 4 to July 2.

Not only did the Congress not repeal the ASP, it enacted a bill (H.R. 10915) which would have transferred the cotton quota of Egypt and the Sudan to American producers, and it almost passed several bills setting quotas on dairy products, textiles, and iron and steel products. Johnson vetoed the cotton bill and warned that no protectionist bill would "become law as long as I am President."[58]

[56] See Curtis and Vastine for details, *Kennedy Round*, pp. 205–15.

[57] See Curtis and Vastine, *Kennedy Round and the Future of American Trade*, pp. 93–126. Since 1922, the ASP valuation system has been extended to cover rubber-soled footwear, canned clams, and knitted gloves.

[58] Quoted in Congressional Quarterly, *Almanac*, 1968, p. 729. In same volume, for a summary of the various quota bills, see "Trade Expansion, Protectionist Moves Blocked," pp. 729–34.

Mills deliberately tabled the administration bill, fearing that with the protectionist sentiment increasing in the Congress, the chances of at least one industry attaching an import quota to the bill were very good. "The Congress always has trouble approving import quota legislation affecting a single industry," he explained, prophetically. "However sympathetic individual Representatives or Senators are to the textile import problem, there are other industries which are seeking the same form of relief and which also have supporters in the Congress. Thus, it appears difficult, if not impossible, to work out an import quota law for one industry and prevent its extension to the products of other industries."[59]

Viewed from the perspective of the Congress, the international trade winds were not blowing favorably in the period between the signing of the Kennedy Round and the introduction of the Trade Act of 1973. In 1967, the EEC enacted a value-added tax, which had the effect of promoting their exports and discouraging imports. In addition, by then, American farmers began to feel the restrictive and discriminatory effects of the Common Agriculture Policy, which had been initiated in 1962.[60] At the same time, the Japanese economy had been accelerating; throughout the 1960's, her rate of growth was more than twice that of the U.S.,[61] and the balance of trade since 1965 had been continually and increasingly in Japan's favor.[62] While admiring Japan's achievements, U.S. businessmen and Congressmen were frustrated by the continued restrictiveness and exclusionary policies of the Japanese government.[63]

Continued balance of payments problems and an over-valued currency were two additional factors that fueled protectionist sentiment in the U.S., contributing to the introduction of more than forty different bills recommending quotas for specific products. None of these bills passed, but as the November election of 1968 arrived, both Presidential candidates found themselves forced to promise special efforts, if elected, to secure voluntary export restraint agreements on a wide variety of products, but particularly for man-made fibers, woolen textiles, and steel.[64] And quantitative restric-

[59]Evans, *Kennedy Round*, pp. 303–4.

[60]One indication of the impact of CAP on American exports is the decline by 40 percent of U.S. exports of CAP-related products in the years 1967–70. Protection in 1971 of the agricultural goods covered by the Common Agricultural Policy was reported to be roughly three times what it was in the early 1960s. Harald B. Malmgren, "Coming Trade Wars? Neo-Mercantilism and Foreign Policy," in Richard N. Cooper, *A Reordered World: Emerging International Economic Problems* (Washington, D.C.: Potomac Associates, 1973), p. 27. For another description of the CAP, see Gerald Meier, *Problems of Trade Policy* (Oxford: Oxford University Press, 1973), pp. 208–13.

[61]*International Economic Report of the President, 1975*, p. 123.

[62]Ibid., p. 135.

[63]Evans, *Kennedy Round*, p. 323.

[64]Nixon's "southern strategy" campaign pledge of 1968 was to extend and broaden the

tions were increasing at such a rapid rate that a number of scholars expressed a concern that the first principle of GATT, nondiscrimination, might be seriously and irrevocably undermined.[65] From 1963 to 1970, the number of quantitative restrictions on imports into the U.S. on specific industrial categories increased from seven to sixty-seven.[66]

A RESURGENCE OF NEO-MERCANTILISM, 1969—71

While there were a number of valiant initiatives on behalf of freer trade, "chaos" is probably the best way to describe the foreign economic policy of the first several years of the Nixon administration. There were others, of course, who saw more consistency, although they were unhappy and pessimistic about their own conclusions. C. Fred Bergsten, for example, who was the Senior Economist on the National Security Council from 1969–71, wrote that "since 1962, U.S. trade policy has been moving steadily away from the liberal trade approach which had characterized it since 1934 . . . "[67] And Harald Malmgren, a Senior Fellow at the Overseas Development Council, noted in the winter of 1970–71 that "today, we are seeing a resurgence of mercantilism, whereby governments meet domestic economic demands with conscious policies of manipulation, passing the costs of these policies as much as possible on to other countries."[68]

Despite Congress's reputation as the playing field for protectionists and interest groups, the Presidency was as frequently contacted by special groups; and often, as in the case of steel, it was the President who took the initiative to stem imports. Steel imports had increased from 3.2 million tons or 4.7 percent of U.S. steel consumption in 1961 to 17.9 million tons or 16.7 percent of consumption in 1968. On January 14, 1969, after months of negotiations, the State Department announced a three-year voluntary agreement with Japanese and European steel producers to limit exports of steel to approximately the 1967 level with an allowable increase of 5 percent each

long-term agreement on cotton textiles to man-made fibers and woolen textiles. See Meier, *Problems of Trade Policy*, pp. 97–103.

[65]See Meier, *Problems of Trade Policy* pt. 2; C. Fred Bergsten, "Crisis in U.S. Trade Policy," *Foreign Affairs* 49 (July 1971): 619–35. Robert Baldwin comments on the danger of proliferating Quantitative Restrictions (QR's) and why they should be transformed, as intended originally by GATT, into tariffs and bargained down. (pp. 42–46)

[66]See John C. Renner, "National Restrictions on International Trade," in *United States International Economic Policy in an Interdependent World*, Report submitted to the Commission on International Trade and Investment Policy, vol. 1 (Washington, D.C.: July 1971), p. 666. (Hereafter Williams Commission Report.)

[67]C. Fred Bergsten, "Crisis in U.S. Trade Policy," p. 619.

[68]Harald Malmgren, "Coming Trade Wars?" p. 26.

year.[69] Several weeks later, President Nixon asked his new Secretary of Commerce Maurice Stans to make good his campaign pledge on textiles; but the negotiations proved easier promised than done, and in the next several years, the pressure from trying to induce agreement with the Japanese would be a major sore in U.S.–Japanese relations.[70]

On November 18, 1969, President Nixon sent a "modest" trade message to the Congress which he hoped would reverse the drift towards protectionism. The trade message was relatively unique not only in its modest scope, but in the curious way it tried to mix free trade with protectionist rhetoric and instrumentalities. Nixon requested that negotiating authority, which had expired on June 30, 1967, be extended to June 30, 1973, and expanded to permit both downward revisions in the tariff schedule as compensation for tariff hikes resulting from the use of the escape clause, and increases in duties on products of countries which unfairly discriminate against U.S. goods. It was tacitly understood that the latter provision, which was retaliatory in effect if not in intent, would be used as additional leverage in the various trade and monetary negotiations underway with Japan.

The bill, H.R. 14870, also asked for a relaxation of the escape valves— both adjustment assistance and the escape clause itself—so that injured industries could more easily obtain administrative relief, and therefore not have to request legislative quotas. An important provision was the repeal of ASP, a measure which greatly concerned the Europeans not only because of the size and importance of the package itself but because of its implications for the ability of the U.S. Executive to negotiate future nontariff barriers. And with the repeal was a request for authority and a resolution of intent for the President to mount "a serious and sustained effort to reduce nontariff barriers to trade."

Since peaking at $7.1 billion in 1964, the U.S. trade surplus had steadily declined until it stood at $1.3 billion in 1969. To stimulate exports, Secretary of the Treasury David Kennedy proposed a concept called DISC, the Domestic International Sales Corporation, which would provide a deferral on taxes for goods which were exported. This too was incorporated in the President's message, which was advertised as "an interim" law while the Executive began to prepare for new legislation for a new round of trade negotiations.[71]

The Administration's bill found itself lost in a crowd of trade legislation in the Ways and Means Committee. Almost three hundred members of the

[69]Richard S. Frank, "Consumers Union Attack on Steel Quotas Could Release Protectionist Pressures," *National Journal*, 29 July 1972.

[70]I. M. Destler, et al., *Managing an Alliance: The Politics of U.S.-Japanese Relations* (Washington, D.C.: Brookings Institution, 1976).

[71]For a summary of the Nixon Trade bill, see Congressional Quarterly, *Almanac*, 1969, pp. 1050–67; also *National Journal*, 29 November 1969, pp. 219–20.

House, among them twenty members of the committee, had introduced quota legislation of one sort or another in the 91st Congress. Altogether, the Committee had fifty-nine bills related to steel imports, forty-seven to textile imports, forty to milk and dairy imports, twenty-four to footwear, and fifty-five empowering the president to set ceilings on imports competing with troubled industries on the basis of percent-of-domestic-market. And on April 13, 1970, Wilbur Mills, a long-time advocate of freer trade, introduced H.R. 16920 with 184 co-sponsors, a bill which would have imposed quotas on imports of leather shoes and textile goods *unless* voluntary limitations were agreed to with Japan and other countries.

Throughout the spring and early summer, the Committee held hearings and took testimony. For the first time since 1930, the Administration's arguments on trade policy began to disclose some wavering and ambivalence, and certain cleavages between agencies became visible. The State Department and the Office of the Special Trade Representatives (STR), which was unfortunately very weak in this period,[72] remained solidly opposed to any form of quota legislation, but the Commerce Department, in testimony by Assistant Secretary Kenneth N. Davis, Jr., hinted that quotas might be one way to improve the U.S. trade balance.

Behind that ambivalence stood a difficult question and a precarious strategy. The GATT prohibited legislated quotas because of their tendency to be permanent and to proliferate; but GATT did permit "voluntary" export restraint agreements. When confronted with an almost intransigent bargaining position by the Japanese, the U.S. adopted a strategy of feinting toward legislated quotas as a way to induce Japanese agreement. Mills went along with the strategy in introducing his bill, though he was uncertain whether the Administration could retain control of the process and prevent legislated quotas once it started.[73]

After hearing 377 witnesses for a month, the Ways and Means Committee closed its doors and drafted a bill. On August 11, 1970, the Committee reported a bill, which Representative Al Ullman described in a dissent as "restrictive, ill-timed, and provincial." The bill repealed ASP, but it also set import quotas on shoes and textiles, limiting future imports to the 1967–68 levels. It also included a provision which came to be called the "Byrnes Basket," empowering the Tariff Commission to recommend tariff quotas on certain products under certain conditions, and compelling the President to accept the commission's recommendations in all but a few cases.

---

[72]One of the reasons for the organization's weakness was that the STR's director, Carl Gilbert, was ill during this period. For other reasons, see Anne H. Rightor-Thornton, "An Analysis of the Office of the Special Representative for Trade Negotiations: The Evolving Role, 1962–74," in Hamilton Studies, Murphy Commission.

[73]Meier, *Problems of Trade Policy*, p. 152. Also see n.88 in this chapter.

The repeal of the ASP illustrates the power of the State Department and the executive branch to override special pressures when sufficiently motivated. To a great extent, their success in persuading the Congress depends on the legitimacy of their case—whether certain interests are really at stake—and on the amount of leverage they can bring to bear on outside groups. In the words of one State Department official, their case was simple: "If repeal of ASP is rejected, it is hard to see how anyone would want to negotiate with us again."[74]

On the same day that the Committee, in executive session, voted down the repeal of ASP, Bryce Harlow, Counsellor to the President, and Stanley Nehmer, Deputy Assistant Secretary of Commerce, launched a campaign to reverse that decision. At that point, the bill contained a quota provision for man-made fibers, which were manufactured and used by the textile companies, and it contained an oil quota as well. Harlow, Nehmer, and Secretary of Commerce Stans called all the major textile and oil companies which would be beneficiaries of the Mills bill, and told them that the President would veto the bill unless ASP was repealed, and that the President was counting on them to put pressure on the chemical companies. Stans was very frank in explaining the strategy to the *National Journal:* "We called the chemical companies, and we told the textile industry very flatly that they would not get their quotas unless the President got a bill he could sign. We talked to both the [textile] mill people and the apparel people and let them know that they should go to work on it. We did the same to a lesser extent with the oil companies."[75] Stans then testified on May 12 and asked that the quota on man-made fibers be dropped from the bill. The Committee complied. After getting assurances from the chemical and textile industries that they would accept the repeal of ASP, Stans asked for the quota to be reinstated, and on the last day of the mark-up, August 11, the Committee wrote a bill with a quota for man-made fibers and gave the President authority to repeal ASP.

The battle over ASP was a pyrrhic one since the bill as a whole was judged very unsatisfactory by the Administration, and Assistant Secretary of State Phillip H. Trezise predicted that foreign reaction would be "quite hostile" if it passed.[76] Another indication that President Nixon may have given up on the Mills bill was his appointment on May 21, 1970 of a Presidential Commission on International Trade and Investment Policy to be chaired by Albert L. Williams, Chairman of IBM.

But the obituary on the Mills bill was premature. In the debate on the

[74]This case study was compiled by Frank V. Fowlkes, "House Turns to Protectionism Despite Arm-Twisting by Nixon Trade Experts," *National Journal,* 22 August 1970, pp. 1815–21.

[75]Ibid., p. 1816.

[76]Ibid., p. 1821.

House floor on November 18, 1970, Mills made a long, and apparently sincere, defense of his bill. Attempting to respond to the Administration's objections, he said that the quotas in the bill were all temporary for five years; that with unemployment rising, future trade bills were likely to be even more protectionist; and that the advantages accruing to foreign countries with cheap labor required some offsetting arrangements for the U.S. Others expressed their irritation with Japan which still maintained illegal quotas on ninety-eight different products. When the vote came on November 19, 1970, the Mills bill passed 205-165.

It wasn't quite a classic logroll since the bill arrived on the floor with a closed rule. But many of the special interest amendments—e.g., a quota on glycine by Representative Brock (Tenn.) or on mink by Representative Byrnes (Wisc.) were added in the Committee. Nor was the bill classically protectionist or inwardly-oriented; indeed, it was as much a reaction to international economic developments and to what was perceived as unfair trade practices by our allies as it was an attempt to respond to domestic pressures. It was also a clear signal to the President and to the STR that tougher negotiating was expected of them.

Aware that time was running out, the Senate Finance Committee began working on the bill before the House finished. Senator Long said that he felt that the United States was being mistreated by our trading partners, and he took the quota-laden trade bill, detached the provisions on Domestic International Sales Corporation (DISC) and the one repealing ASP, and cemented it as a rider to the Social Security bill. As Bob Best, the Staff Director of the Finance Committee, said at the time: "The social security bill was the last train out of the station." (If the social security bill passed the Senate, the House would not have been permitted to add the ASP and DISC provisions since the original social security bill passed by the House didn't contain those provisions.) In the meantime, William Timmons, Chief of Congressional Liaison in the White House, tried but failed to delay the vote on the Mills bill in the House. Negotiations with the Japanese on textiles were visibly stepped-up, and the Administration said it was seriously considering a new Japanese proposal made on November 15. The Senate Finance Committee reported its "Christmas Tree bill" on December 9, but the session ended before it could be considered by the full Senate.[77]

The bill that failed was called "the most protectionist act since the depression of the 1930's."[78] In retrospect, congressional participants claim that they did not seriously believe that the bill would pass.[79] Its principal

[77]For details on the bargaining on the Senate side, see "White House May Lose Gamble: Protectionist Bill Is Emerging," *National Journal*, 21 November 1970, pp. 2555–57.

[78]Ibid., p. 2555.

[79]Interviews.

purpose was to send a message to the State Department, to the White House, and to our allies, especially the Japanese, but also the Europeans. The message was absorbed fastest by the Tariff Commission which began to process petitions quicker and with more even-handedness.[80]

But the problems confronting U.S. trade policy were more fundamental and would require a series of "shocks" before the protectionist-freer trade equation could be rebalanced.

THE WATERSHED YEAR AND THE DEATH OF SANTA CLAUS

In his annual Foreign Policy Report to the Congress, issued on February 9, 1972, President Nixon called 1971 "the watershed year,"[81] and in the area of foreign economic policy few could quarrel with that characterization. The "chaos" which had so accurately described the various policies in 1969 and 1970, also seemed appropriate for the first half of 1971. The New Economic Policy proclaimed on August 15, 1971, however, represented a sharp break from the past, a collapse of both the Bretton Woods system and a strategy of incremental adaptations; and an aggressive attempt to start anew. If the NEP didn't make the various foreign economic policies which followed any more consistent than those in the past, at least it provided a framework with which one could better understand the reasons for its inconsistency.

On January 10, 1971, the President tried to impose some order on his policies by establishing a new structure, the Council on International Economic Policy.[82] Directed by Peter Peterson, the council's purpose was to oversee and coordinate all foreign economic policy and to ensure that foreign and economic considerations be carefully weighed and balanced in the making of policy.[83] In April 1971, Peterson presented to the President a

[80]See Frank V. Fowlkes, "Administrative Escape Valves Relieve Pressures of Imports on Domestic Industries," *National Journal*, 24 July 1971, pp. 1544–50.

[81]Richard M. Nixon, *President's Foreign Policy Report to Congress: The Emerging Structure of Peace*, 9 February 1972, p. 2.

[82]To a limited extent, the National Security Council had helped coordinate some foreign economic policy, but due to Kissinger's lack of interest in the field, and due to the resignations of his two senior economic specialists, Fred Bergsten and Robert Hormats in April 1971, there was, for a time, a leadership and coordinating vacuum which was made worse by the weakness in these years of STR, but which was filled for a time by CIEP.

CIEP remained the central formal coordinating group for foreign economic policy until December 1972 when Treasury Secretary Schultz became Chairman of the Council on Economic Policy. In this period, 1971–72, however, Secretary of the Treasury John Connally dominated foreign economic policy, and no coordinating body was really used.

[83]International Economic Policy Act of 1972 (PL 94-412). Also see Dom Bonafede, "Peterson Unit Helps Shape Tough International Economic Policy," *National Journal*, 13 November 1971; pp. 2238–48.

132-page report entitled "The United States in a Changing World Economy." The message of the report was basically a sophisticated structural explanation of the Congress' behavior the previous year. The U.S. share of the world's wealth and income was declining sharply, and the United States needed to adjust to this changed position by making it clear that economic issues and interests should take precedence over traditional diplomatic niceties. The report asked: "Are we advocating our own economic interests as forcefully as we should? . . . Even posing the question suggests that other industrialized nations have been more vigorous in the pursuit of their economic interests."[84]

George Shultz, then Director of the Office of Management and Budget, put it more bluntly: "Santa Claus is dead."[85]

Textiles and steel remained high on the diplomatic agenda. Wilbur Mills reintroduced his bill on textile quotas in 1971 at the request of the administration and also began to negotiate directly with the Japanese. On March 8, 1971, Japan announced a three year export restraint program on textiles which would begin on July 1. The Japanese relayed the announcement directly to Mills in the hope that it would defeat any protectionist legislation.[86] The Japan Textile Federation insisted that their decision was not economically justified, but that it was done primarily to respond and to halt American protectionism. (There were also rumors that Prime Minister Sato had promised such an agreement to President Nixon in exchange for the American decision to return Okinawa.)[87] American textile producers and unions immediately rejected it, and three days later, President Nixon formally rejected the proposal and repeated his support for the reintroduction of the Mills bill on textile quotas. Mills, however, believed that the Japanese decision was both courageous and satisfactory, and that President Nixon was jealously rejecting what he himself could not deliver: "Having responded on many occasions to requests from Administration officials during the past two years to assist in furthering a negotiated settlement of this problem, I am both surprised and disappointed at this [Nixon's] decision." Mills also said that he did not intend to press for any new legislation but with tongue firmly implanted in cheek, he said: "I await with considerable interest the presentation of such a program by the Administration."[88]

Voluntary steel agreements usually had a three-year life, the duration of the U.S. steelworkers' labor contract. The long strike of 1959 had so

[84]Ibid., p. 2241.

[85]Ibid., p. 2238.

[86]Meier, *Problems of Trade Policy*, pp. 148–52.

[87]Ibid., p. 149.

[88]Ibid., p. 152.

shaped the perception of steel buyers that in the year preceding the renegotiation of each labor contract, buyers would strain the market in order to hedge against a strike, and imports would increase dramatically. This occurred again in 1971, and the voluntary agreement broke down. "Early in 1971," Nathaniel Samuels, Undersecretary of State for Economic Affairs and subsequently U.S. negotiator for a new steel agreement, recalled, "the steel industry people and the labor leaders came to see us [State Department officials] because of the problems that they foresaw arising in the course of 1971."[89] Samuels began negotiations with the Japanese Iron and Steel Exporters Association and the Association of the Steel Producers of the European Coal and Steel Community to limit their exports of steel to the United States. A new three-year agreement was finally consummated on May 6, 1972, intended to extend until December 31, 1974.

In July 1971, the Williams Commission presented its report on international trade and investment policy to the President. The Williams Commission was composed of twenty-seven people, mostly businessmen, although there were several academics and two labor union leaders, I. W. Abel of the United Steel Workers and Floyd E. Smith of the International Association of Machinists and Aerospace Workers. The labor representatives appended a sweeping minority dissent from what was fundamentally an internationalist document. The commission recommended that the U.S. in conjunction with its major trading partners undertake a new round of multilateral trade negotiations with the purpose of preparing "the way for the elimination of all barriers to international trade and capital movements within twenty-five years."[90] The report, "U.S. International Economic Policy in an Interdependent World," also stressed that the United States had carried a disproportionate share of the burden of maintaining the international economic system and henceforth, "this responsibility must be shared by the major trading nations . . . "[91]

The Commission assigned "high priority to measures the United States must take to increase the strength and the resilience of its economy."[92] Many of their recommendations illuminated the path towards the New Economic Policy (NEP) announced by President Nixon on August 15, 1971. The NEP identified three fundamental economic problems facing the U.S. economy, and set forth three solutions: (1) to counter inflation, the President imposed a wage-price freeze; (2) to begin the movement towards international monetary reform, the President suspended the convertibility of the dollar into gold; and (3) to encourage a readjustment of exchange rates and

---

[89]For more details, see Richard S. Frank, "Consumers Union Attack on Steel Quotas Could Release Protectionist Pressures," *National Journal*, 29 July 1972, pp. 1229–36.

[90]Williams Commission Report, p. 10.

[91]Ibid., p. 17.

[92]Ibid., p. 8.

the U.S. balance of payments, the President imposed a temporary 10 percent surcharge on imports into the U.S.[93]

The President also announced on August 15 that the U.S. would impose mandatory textile quotas by October 15, 1971 unless the Asian governments reached agreement on voluntarily reducing their exports. On that deadline, agreement was reached with Japan, and the resulting agreement was signed on January 3, 1972, at which time the surcharge was also lifted.[94] But the tactic "left the Japanese angry, resentful and determined to retaliate sooner or later."[95] Similar agreements were subsequently reached with Taiwan, South Korea, and Hong Kong.

The August 1971 decisions were viewed abroad as unilateral and nationalistic,[96] and certainly did nothing to discourage the protectionist drift in the U.S. Prior to 1970, the labor union leadership had successfully kept any protectionist inclinations its membership in check, partly because of the necessities of the Cold War and partly because freer trade was an unquestioned tenet of the Democratic Party coalition of which they were a part. Indeed, the Federation's lobbyists worked hard to help pass the Trade Expansion Act of 1962.[97]

By the late 1960s, the leadership joined its membership and came out in support of quotas and limitations and restrictions on the free flow of goods and capital. And the change in their policy stance, according to one Congressional Staff member, was hardly done quietly: "The Union leadership had held the line so long against the locals that when they got religion, they really got it; and they decided that the bogeyman was the Multinational Corporation."

Labor argued that the most important changes in the international economy were the internationalization of technology, the emergence of the multinational corporation and the international bank, and the management of national economies and society's welfare by governments; and these changes "have made obsolete old theories of free trade and protection."[98] Labor argued in a brief to the Senate Finance Committee:

> In reality, labor is not mobile internationally, markets are not free from government interference, and exchange rates are relatively fixed. Without the underlying assumptions being correct, the theory cannot

[93]Edward Knight and Margaret Brady, "The New Economic Policy," (Congressional Research Service, Library of Congress, 30 August 1971).

[94]Meier, *Problems of Trade Policy*, p. 153.

[95]Ibid., pp. 161–62. No noticeable retaliation followed.

[96]Knight and Brady, "Foreign Reaction," pp. 257–69.

[97]"AFL-CIO's Turnabout on Free Trade," *National Journal*, 15 January 1972, pp. 112–14.

[98]Williams Commission Report: dissent by Commissioners I. W. Abel and Floyd E. Smith, p. 341.

*and does not serve as a useful guide to the policy-makers in any
country. Its real acceptance appears limited to academic circles.*[99]

In their dissent to the Williams Commission Report, I. W. Abel and
Floyd E. Smith argued: "Sharply rising foreign investments of U.S. companies—as well as advances in transportation and communications and the
increase in patent and license arrangements with firms in other countries—
have caused the rapid transfer of American technology, production, and
employment to foreign operations."[100]

Others have explained the desertion of the AFL-CIO from freer trade in
terms of its membership composition, which is primarily from declining
manufacturing industries—and its increasing unrepresentativeness of a
national economy propelled by a dynamic and expanding service sector.[101]

The problem, as Nat Goldfinger, Director of Research for the AFL-CIO
saw it, was simply the relative immobility of labor as a factor of production
compared to capital, technology, and even management.[102] The mechanism
by which capital and technology were transferred, and, according to the
AFL-CIO, jobs were lost, was the Multinational Corporation (MNC). In May
1971, the AFL-CIO Executive Council met and issued a nine-point statement
clearly designating the Multinational Corporation as the target of future
policy and regulation. In his testimony before Senator Ribicoff's Subcommittee on International Trade of the Senate Finance Committee, George
Meany on May 18th stated his position: "We want the U.S. government to
protect the interests of American workers against the export of American
jobs."[103]

Labor's offensive against the MNC stimulated a great number of
studies and almost created a new industry to research the newly-discovered
phenomenon. The Tariff Commission began a massive study in response to
a request by Senator Ribicoff.[104] Since 1965, the Harvard Multinational
Enterprise Project directed by Raymond Vernon had been compiling data,

[99]U.S. Senate, Committee on Finance, *Foreign Trade: A Survey of Current Issues to Be
Studied by the Subcommittee on International Trade*, 14 May 1971, p. 2.

[100]Williams Commission Report: dissent by Commissioners I. W. Abel and Floyd E.
Smith, p. 340.

[101]C. Fred Bergsten, "Crisis in U.S. Trade Policy,"; Lawrence B. Krause, "Why Exports
Are Becoming Irrelevant," in Richard N. Cooper (ed.), *A Reordered World* (Washington, D.C.:
Potomac Associates, 1973), pp. 92–99.

[102]Nat Goldfinger, "A Labor View of Foreign Investment and Trade Issues," Williams
Commission Report, pp. 913–28.

[103]Quoted by Harry Lenhart, Jr., "Labor Fears Loss of Jobs in U.S. as Firms Expand Their
Overseas Facilities," *National Journal*, 17 July 1971, pp. 1486, 1485–93.

[104]U.S. Senate, Committee on Finance, *Report on Multinational Corporations Submitted
by the Tariff Commission: Implications of Multinational Firms for World Trade and Investment and for U.S. Trade and Labor*, February, 1973.

and beginning in 1971 with the publication of Vernon's book *Sovereignty At Bay*, the Project began to publish its results.

In the Congress, Representative Hale Boggs's Subcommittee on Foreign Economic Policy of the Joint Economic Committee held rather extensive hearings in July 1970, as did a comparable subcommittee in the House Foreign Affairs Committee in the spring of 1969. Senators Church, Humphrey, and Javits expressed interest in studying the subject in a subcommittee of the Senate Foreign Relations Committee, but because of Chairman J. William Fulbright's rather traditional approach to foreign policy, such a subcommittee had to await Jack Anderson's revelations of ITT's escapades in Chile before it would be voted into being.

The United Nations appointed in July 1972 a twenty member Group of Eminent Persons to study the impact of MNC's on the development process and on international relations. As a result of its report, issued in 1974, the U.N. has established a Commission on Transnational Corporations and an Information and Research Center. Virtually every international organization, including UNCTAD, the OAS, International Labor Organization, UNIDO, the U.N. Commission on International Law, and the OECD, have since established committees or working groups to study the MNC.[105]

The MNC itself has hardly remained passive in the face of what many businessmen consider is an unjustified onslaught. The International Economic Policy Association, a research group financed by Multinational Corporations, established a Center for Multinational Studies in July 1971 and stated their raison d'etre in their first first pamphlet: "The attack [against MNC's], if unanswered, will at the least unnecessarily shackle international business through regulations, reporting schemes, registration and taxation, to the great detriment of the best interests of the United States."[106] The Chamber of Commerce, the Emergency Committee on American Trade, the National Policy Association—all began commissioning studies to counter the attack by the labor unions.

The spread of multinational corporations and the debate which followed in its wake represented a joining of the two issues of trade and investment for the first time in U.S. domestic policy-making. The Trade and Investment Act of 1972, which was drafted by the AFL-CIO and introduced by Representative James A. Burke, with sixty-five co-sponsors in the House and Sen. Vance Hartke and two co-sponsors in the Senate on September 28, 1971, was the clearest evidence that the two policy issues would demand simultaneous consideration.[107] One of the purposes of the bill was to repeal the incentives

---

[105]Council of the Americas, "Status on International Governmental Activities Regarding Multinational Corporations," mimeo, December 1, 1975.

[106]Lenhart, "Labor Fears Loss of Jobs", p. 1489.

[107]It will be recalled that the issues were joined in the ITO Charter, and that was one of the reasons for its failure. (See Clair Wilcox, *A Charter for World Trade* (N.Y.: MacMillan,

for U.S. corporations to invest abroad and thus to "export jobs," and the three instruments to accomplish this would be the elimination of the tax deferral on income earned by subsidiaries of U.S. MNC's abroad, the replacement of the tax credit for these subsidiaries with a deduction, and the elimination of tax exemptions for U.S. citizens living or working abroad. The bill would have relaxed the escape clause and other "valves" along the lines suggested in the 1970 trade bill, and would have empowered the President to regulate all transfers of capital and prohibit the licensing of patents if that would have a negative impact on domestic employment. Most important, the Burke-Hartke bill would have established a new three-member Foreign Trade and Investment Commission, composed of one representative each from labor, industry, and the public, which would have strong powers to regulate imports.

The Administration publicly and vociferously opposed the Burke-Hartke bill, but privately an interagency Task Force on Adjustment Assistance was set up in September 1971. In August, President Nixon appointed William D. Eberle, who was Chairman of American Standard, Inc. and had recently chaired a Task Force on Foreign Trade Policy for the Committee for Economic Development, as his Special Trade Representative. Eberle's task was to begin preparations for the next round of Multilateral Trade Negotiations.

SUMMARY: THE CLAMOR FOR CLOSURE

The "fierce fight" which Kennedy had waged to gain passage of the Trade Expansion Act contained the seeds of its own undoing in its extraordinary success. When the tariff barriers came tumbling down, and the war in Vietnam placed an almost unbearable strain on an over-valued dollar, injured industries found the "escape valves" closed, and sought new forms of protection and new scapegoats. One such target was the MNC; another, the trilateral trading partners of the United States, which had become competitive while retaining the protective barriers of an earlier recovery period. In 1963, for example, while the United States had quantitative restrictions on 7 product categories, the European Community had them on 76 categories and Japan on 132.[108]

The result was that Legislators introduced hundreds of bills which would have mandated quotas on a wide variety of products. None of these

---

1949). For a summary of the Burke-Hartke bill and its politics, see Charles Culhane, "Labor and Industry Gear for Major Battle Over Bill to Curb Imports, Multinationals," *National Journal,* 15 January 1972, pp. 108–19.

[108]Williams Commission Report, p. 666.

bills passed, but there was no mistaking the signals which were emitted from the Congress: the international economic system needed readjusting, and if other nations were unwilling to do it, then the U.S. would have to force the issue.

During this chaotic decade, however, the *end* of the process of adjustment was never clear, while the clamor of protectionism always was. This clamor for closure, however, was only one swing in the cycle. To understand the complete development of U.S. trade policy, one must follow the process beyond Burke-Hartke to the passage of the Trade Act of 1974.

THE TRADE ACT OF 1974: WHAT WENT RIGHT?

I have said repeatedly that I didn't get to be Chairman of the Ways and Means Committee to preside over the destruction of any segment of our American industry.[1]

—*Wilbur Mills, 1970*

I am going to stand for the general interest. . . .[2]

—*President Richard M. Nixon*
Press Conference, January 1973

On April 10, 1973, President Richard M. Nixon, already under fire because of Watergate, sent the most complex trade bill in U.S. history to the Congress.[3] He requested "unprecedented negotiating authority" for five years to conduct multilateral trade negotiations to harmonize, reduce, or eliminate all tariffs and nontariff barriers, to redefine and readjust domestic

---

[1]Quoted in Frank V. Fowlkes, "Pressure Mounting on Congress to Enact Import Quota Legislation," *National Journal*, 16 May 1970, pp. 1034–36.

[2]Quoted in Richard P. Nathan, *The Plot That Failed* (New York: Wiley, 1975), p. 85.

[3]The Trade Act of 1974 was first introduced as the Trade Reform Act (TRA) of 1973, but circumstances intervened. Similarly, the "Nixon Round" of multilateral trade negotiations, which was expected to follow the passage of the Trade Act, was subsequently renamed the "Tokyo Round," the site of the conference in September 1973 in which the GATT nations issued a declaration of intent to pursue another round of trade negotiations. [See App. C, 1974, Annual Report of the Council on International Economic Policy for a text of the declaration.])

The President sent a "special message" on trade to the Congress on April 10, 1973. This became the Trade Reform Act (TRA) of 1973, H.R. 6767, but it was reported out of the Ways and Means Committee with significant changes as H.R. 10710 in October 1973. It passed the House in December 1973, and the Senate and Conference in December 1974. The "Trade Act of 1974," PL 93-618, was signed by President Ford on January 3, 1975. This book will often refer to the bill and the act as TRA.

and international rules of trade, and to give additional preference to the U.S. market to the exports of the developing world.

The times were hardly propitious for such a far-reaching bill. Vietnam and then Watergate had transformed a largely passive and agreeable Congress into an often irascible, assertive institution, highly skeptical of demands to extend the Presidential prerogative. The worst depression since the 1930s coupled with double-digit inflation, scarcities of vital raw materials, and within nine months, a quadrupling of the price of petroleum—all this did not auger well for a bill that asked America to open its doors wider to foreign goods. "We are witnessing an outbreak of short-sighted nationalism that seems oblivious to the economic, political and moral implications of interdependence," wrote Richard Gardner in the spring of 1974 as the bill was being considered in the Senate.[4]

And yet the Trade Act, which passed the Congress in December 1974, *was* an internationalist document which did in fact delegate unprecedented powers to the President (though it also granted significant new responsibilities for Congress). Not only was the President given a five-year mandate to enter into trade agreements to reduce all tariffs above 5 percent ad valorem by as much as 60 percent, the largest percentage ever granted in a trade bill, and to *eliminate all tariffs below 5 percent,* but for the first time in U.S. history, he was granted authority to negotiate agreements to harmonize, reduce, or eliminate *all barriers* to free trade.

Moreover, since the final decisions on the trade bill were made in the closing moments of the 93d Congress, making the bill virtually "veto-proof" (since the Executive had to settle for whatever it got), the London *Economist* expressed a general European anxiety that the Senate would hang all kinds of "baubles" on this Christmas tree. Surprisingly, the *Economist* wrote after the Senate vote, "the trade bill got through astonishingly free of such baubles."[5] Looking back at the long and arduous struggle between the forces of internationalism and the forces of protectionism, Edwin L. Dale, Jr. of the *New York Times* admitted that in 1974, to his own astonishment, "the protectionist forces essentially lost the battle."[6]

How did this happen? Why, despite prophecies of doom and neo-mercantilism,[7] did the U.S. Congress, which has been characterized as constituent-rooted, short-term and special-interest-oriented, and provincial, pass a law giving a post-Watergate, post-Vietnam President unprecedented

---

[4]Richard N. Gardner, "The Hard Road to World Order," *Foreign Affairs,* 52 (April 1974): 556.

[5]*The Economist,* 28 December 1974, p. 30.

[6]*New York Times,* Sunday, 23 May 1976, p. F17.

[7]Harald B. Malmgren, "Coming Trade Wars: Neo-Mercantilism and Foreign Policy," *Foreign Policy,* no. 1 (Winter 1970); C. Fred Bergsten, "Crisis in U.S. Trade Policy," *Foreign Affairs* 48 (July 1971).

authority to "promote the development of an open, non-discriminatory, and fair world economic system?"[8] What went right?

As the last and most recent case of trade policy that will be examined, this case will be explained and analyzed in much greater detail than the others.

BUREAUCRATIC PREPARATIONS, 1971–73

William D. Eberle was appointed Special Trade Representative (STR) in August 1971 and was given a two-part mandate: (1) to meet with the leaders of our principal trading partners to see whether there was sufficient interest in a new round of multilateral trade negotiations (MTN), and if not, to try to generate interest; and (2) to consult with the Congress and begin preparing trade legislation which would provide the requisite negotiating authority. Congressional leaders told Eberle that they couldn't seriously consider a trade bill unless there were clear signs of international interest.[9]

It wasn't hard to find international interest. In February 1972, the United States, the EEC, and Japan issued a Joint Declaration in support of a new round of multilateral trade negotiations, which would involve tariff as well as nontariff barriers, agricultural as well as industrial products. The leaders agreed to meet with the other contracting parties of GATT in November to organize a preparatory committee which would set the guidelines for the next round.[10]

By this time, however, it was clear that the United States had sustained its first trade deficit—in 1971 of $2 billion—since 1888. In December 1971, the U.S. dollar had been effectively devalued by 10-12 percent, and although most analysts predicted that this would help right the trade balance in a couple of years, in the interim it just underlined America's vulnerability. These events plus the sluggishness of the economy convinced Eberle and a number of his advisors that the time was not yet ripe to send a new trade bill to the Congress. As Secretary of Commerce Peter Peterson commented in January 1972: "Any kind of trade legislation submitted now might well be amended to include permanent quotas on all kinds of things."[11]

Eberle recognized that regardless of when the bill would be submitted,

---

[8]This is part of the title of the Trade Act of 1974, PL 93-618.

[9]Interview with William D. Eberle, Washington, D.C., June 1976. This is one of the only interviewees I will specifically identify since almost all of the interviews I had with over thirty people from Congress, the STR, Treasury Department, and State Department were given with promises of confidentiality.

[10]*International Economic Report of the President,* 1973, p. 44.

[11]Quoted in *National Journal,* 22 January 1972, p. 156.

extensive work would be required beforehand, and he therefore hired two deputies: William Pearce, a member of the Williams Commission and a vice-president of Cargill, to handle the domestic track; and Harald Malmgren to prepare for international negotiations. A bureaucratic problem became immediately apparent, and it would plague the drafting process until the bill was finally introduced in April 1973. Technically, STR (the office of the Special Trade Representative) was responsible for negotiating, while the Council on International Economic Policy (CIEP) was responsible for coordinating the formulation of foreign economic policy. In January 1972, Peter Flanigan, who had worked as Nixon's Special Assistant for three years, became the Executive Director of CIEP, which was also designated the body for coordinating the trade bill. This not only introduced an additional bureaucratic layer between STR and the President, but because of Flanigan's past experience, it also made the drafting process unnecessarily and injuriously sensitive to the short-term and sporadic whims of a highly political election year. The result was repeated delay and disruption. Flanigan, unlike Eberle, had access to the President, and as a former political operative, was very sensitive to political winds.

Moreover, throughout this period, Flanigan was constantly trying to bring STR under CIEP's wing, and one official of STR said that at least 25 percent of his time was spent just fighting off the merger. While Malmgren chaired the interagency committee responsible for formulating options for the international negotiations, Deane Hinton, Deputy Director of CIEP, chaired the interagency group responsible for drafting a trade bill. Papers were requested from those departments with particular responsibility or expertise on particular issues—e.g., Treasury for countervailing duties or balance of payments issues; State for generalized preferences. After a long and relatively unproductive period, Pearce persuaded Flanigan in the summer of 1972 to use the Williams Commission's report as the basis for the interagency debate, rather than repeat its work.

Three quite distinct bureaucratic cleavages developed during the debate on the trade bill. The Commerce Department's position was perhaps as close to a protectionist one as the executive branch had seen since 1932. In the past, Commerce had often argued on behalf of protection of a few firms or industries, but by 1972, the Department adopted a more generalized approach. Concerned that the U.S., as a nation, had lost its competitive edge and that our standard of living couldn't be maintained unless new measures were taken to prevent "market disruption" by imports, Commerce argued for the liberalization of procedures for granting relief by quotas and tariff-quotas for industries suffering from import competition. The Department of Labor supported this position, although in a Republican administration with a relatively weak departmental Secretary (Brennan), Labor was not a major actor in the debate.

When one considers Nixon's strong internationalist predilections,[12] one is led to ask why a protectionist argument had an important impact on the Administration's debate. Was it in anticipation of the congressional debate? The reason, according to administration officials, had nothing to do with the Congress; it was simply that the President was "not accessible." And on the one or two occasions when a top official took an issue to the President, he found the President incredibly uninformed.

The bureaucratic fighting between STR and CIEP opened up additional access points for Commerce to argue its views. But in the end Commerce's impact was greater* on the tone of the bill than on the substance. The internationalist view prevailed, but the bill did reflect Commerce's heightened sensitivity to the grievances of declining industries, by loosening the four escape valves—escape clause eligibility, adjustment assistance, antidumping, and countervailing duties.

The position of the Treasury Department in this bureaucratic debate largely reflected the militantly aggressive style of its secretary, John Connally. According to Connally, our trading partners were taking advantage of us, and this must end. A tough bill with threatening language and many varieties of retaliatory capabilities would be necessary not only to gain Congress's support, but to promote our interests in the forthcoming multilateral trade negotiations (MTN). In the bill which was sent to Congress, the Treasury's position was evident in the elaborate import and export restrictions which the United States would impose if another government either maintains "unreasonable tariffs" or engages in discriminatory economic policies, and it was reflected in the request for new authority to use trade policy as a tool for dealing with international payments imbalances. But the stridency of Treasury's position was toned down with the replacement of Connally by George Shultz in 1972. Also gone, however, was much of Treasury's power. Treasury officials said that they no longer found other departments deferring to them as much as when their boss was Connally, whom everyone knew had the President's full support. The personality of a departmental secretary has a more pervasive impact on bureaucratic debates *at all levels* than one would expect.[13]

The third position was fundamentally an internationalist one and was

---

[12]While Nixon's internationalist credentials were sound and unquestioned, his knowledge of foreign economic policy was not nearly so solid. At a Press Conference on 20 July 1970, he said: "We're an exporting nation rather than an importing nation. . . . Consequently, I have always opposed quota legislation as a general proposition." *(Public Papers of the Presidents, Richard M. Nixon,* 20 July 1970, p. 606.)

[13]Jessica Einhorn discovered this in an analysis of a different issue, expropriation policy. See Jessica Pernitz Einhorn, *Expropriation Politics* (Lexington, Mass.: Lexington Books, 1974), p. 95.

represented by STR, State, Agriculture, and the Council of Economic Advisers. The lesson they drew from the experience of the Mills bill in 1970 was essentially what Kennedy instinctively had known in 1961–62.[14] To get an important trade bill through the Congress requires a gargantuan executive effort and significant congressional discipline. One dabbles with *legislative* protectionism—i.e., a product quota—only at the great risk of seeing the entire legislative process unravel. If one has to co-opt a particular industry, like steel or textiles, it is best to offer non-legislative concessions and keep the bill "pure." STR also felt that a broadened adjustment assistance program would be necessary as a way to compensate those interests which would look to the Congress for some relief.

Four Issues

The trade bill that was sent to Congress on April 10, 1973 was more than forty pages long and addressed literally hundreds of issues, requiring as many decisions. The three positions represented different slants and emphases, which the final bill integrated. There were also several distinct issues in which bureaucratic cleavages were evident, though not that important. Four issues turned out to be pivotal in the debate on the trade bill: the delegation of negotiating authority for tariffs and nontariff barriers (NTB's) to the executive, and procedures for approval and disapproval by the Congress; adjustment assistance and the variety of "escape valves," including import relief and unfair trade practices; Title IV, the granting of most-favored nation treatment to Communist countries; and Title V, the granting of a generalized system of tariff preferences (GSP) for developing countries.[15] We shall follow the debate on those four critical issues as the bill winds its way through the bureaucracy and the Congress and then seek to determine which of the actors and arenas were most influential in shaping the law.

Negotiating Authority   The crux of this trade bill, as was true of every trade bill since 1934, was the delegation of negotiating authority to the President. However, because tariffs in 1973 were at their lowest levels in U.S. history, the questions which the drafters and Legislators faced were somewhat different than in prior cases: (1) whether to request the elimination of low *tariffs* and the sharp reduction of high tariffs, and more

---

[14]For 1961–62 strategy, see BPD, p. 78; and Theodore Sorenson, *Kennedy* (N.Y.: Harper and Row, 1965), pp. 460–62.

[15]In the Administration's bill, H.R. 6767, "Trade Relations with Countries Not Enjoying MFN" (which were all Communist countries) was Title V and GSP was Title VI. With a congressional rewrite, both titles were moved up a notch.

importantly, (2) what negotiating procedures should be devised to harmonize, reduce, or eliminate *nontariff* barriers.

Nontariff barriers (NTB's) include both those measures, like quotas, export subsidies, or border tax adjustments, whose purpose is to directly affect the volume and composition of trade, and those policies, like safety, health, or pollution standards or regional development policies or discriminatory procurement, whose purpose and orientation is predominantly domestic but which nevertheless have an impact abroad.[16] Nontariff barriers, in short, are U.S. domestic law, and in 1966, when U.S. negotiators began negotiating the elimination of one such NTB, the American selling price (ASP) system of customs valuation, the Congress warned that they had no such authority.[17] Nonetheless, negotiations proceeded, and while they succeeded at Geneva, U.S. negotiators failed to sell it to the Congress. The question was how to prevent that from happening again.

STR advised the President to provide an option that would allow Congress to veto an agreement on NTB's, while the State Department and CIEP insisted that the limits of congressional involvement should be to provide a mandate and beyond that, to be consulted on an informal basis. The act of negotiating or deciding upon the final agreement, viewed by the State Department as an Executive Agreement rather than a treaty or a new law, was in the words of one official "none of Congress's business." The President apparently split the difference. He asked Congress for a prior mandate to negotiate the repeal of ASP and other NTB's, but he said that *in some cases*, he would permit the Congress the option of a negative veto within ninety days.[18] On the question of the consultation procedures, the president gave STR a blank check to develop appropriate procedures, and STR then passed the check on to the Congress. On the question of negotiating tariff reductions, the President requested unlimited authority.

Adjustment Assistance and Import Relief   The issue of adjustment assistance stimulated disagreement among agencies. STR and the Depart-

---

[16]Robert E. Baldwin, *Nontariff Distortions of International Trade* (Washington, D.C.: Brookings Institution, 1970).

The GATT Secretariat, which studied NTB's since the end of the Kennedy Round in 1967, classified more than eight hundred specific NTB's into thirty-three categories. For a list, see U.S. Senate Committee on Finance, *Hearings: Nomination of Frederick B. Dent*, 94th Congress, 1st Sess. 18 March 1975, pp. 10–13.

[17]When the Congress learned that the Executive was negotiating the elimination of an NTB in 1966, the Senate adopted by voice vote on 29 June 1966, S. Con. Res. 100 urging the President to instruct the U.S. negotiators in Geneva to bargain only on provisions authorized in the Trade Expansion Act of 1962. See Congressional Quarterly, *Almanac*, 1967, pp. 810–814; and John W. Evans, *The Kennedy Round in American Trade Policy* (Cambridge, Mass.: Harvard University Press, 1971), pp. 299–301.

[18]TRA of 1973, Message from the President of the U.S. to the Congress, House Document 93-80, pp. 16–17, sec. 103.

ments of Labor and State all insisted that the inclusion of a generous trade assistance section was the only way a trade bill could pass the Congress. Secretary of Treasury George Shultz was the primary opponent of an expanded adjustment assistance program; he felt it was expensive and unnecessary. Why, he asked, should workers and firms get special assistance because of increased imports rather than because of technological changes or because of a government decision such as the closing of a military base or the reduction of loans to small business? He argued that all unemployed workers should get the same benefits regardless of cause of unemployment. Shultz was supported by OMB, which was concerned about budgetary constraints, and by Peter Flanigan and Deane Hinton, who argued on political grounds that a liberal adjustment assistance program wouldn't win Labor's support anyway. STR conceded that the AFL-CIO could not be persuaded, but they argued that it might win over as many as one hundred congressmen who could use the adjustment assistance package to show their constituents that the trade bill was not insensitive to job displacement.

As one industry spokesman who closely followed the bureaucratic debate told the *National Journal*: "There was fighting all the way up to the end. It [adjustment assistance] was in and out of the bill."[19] At the meeting where the final decision was made, most of the Cabinet officers attended. Secretary of Labor Brennan was expected to make the case for an expanded program, and he was briefed beforehand by his assistants, but even though STR nudged him in the meeting, Brennan hardly uttered a word, and the case was lost by default. A minimal program was accepted. The federal government would augment, if necessary, state unemployment compensation payments to workers to ensure that they receive at least half of what their weekly wage was before, or two-thirds of the state's average weekly wage, whichever is lower for the number of weeks set by each state for jobless benefits (generally twenty-six weeks). Some retraining and relocation allowances were included.

Title IV—Most-Favored Nation (MFN) Status for Communist Countries

The single issue which so dominated the congressional debate on the trade bill that the rest of the bill often seemed unimportant in comparison, was the Jackson-Vanik amendment, which prohibited the granting of MFN to any government which denies its citizens the right of emigration or imposes more than a nominal emigration tax. Though part of a trade agreement between the U.S. and USSR signed in Moscow on October 18, 1972, the

---

[19]Charles Culhane, "Labor Shifts Tactics on Administration Bill, Seeks Concessions on Imports, MNC's," *National Journal*, July 28, 1973, p. 1094. The particular case was also developed from interviews and from another article by Richard S. Frank, "Administration Torn Between Domestic, Overseas Interests in Drafting Trade Bill," *National Journal*, 13 January 1973, pp. 44–52.

granting of MFN to the Soviet Union did not have to be a part of the TRA. And many argued that it should be kept separate. Rep. Sam Gibbons of the Ways and Means Committee called the inclusion of this provision, which became Title IV, "a blunder, a serious blunder, that the White House should have avoided if they had read any signals up here."[20]

And the signals were manifest. On October 4, 1972, Senator Jackson introduced an amendment with seventy-five cosponsors denying the Soviet Union MFN while it barred emigration or imposed an emigration tax. On the same day, Rep. Charles A. Vanik introduced the same bill in the House with 130 cosponsors. With the start of the 93rd Congress, Vanik reintroduced the bill and obtained 259 co-sponsors. (The number increased to 289 during the session.)

But there were other signals. Henry Kissinger, then Special Assistant to the President, who had taken no interest in the trade bill until it came to this question, argued that detente was very popular in the country and on Capitol Hill, and that the inclusion of this provision would improve the chances of passage of the TRA. Eberle and Pearce had contacted several members of the Ways and Means and the Finance Committees and concluded that Title IV might jeopardize the entire bill, but they were overruled by the President, who evidently agreed with Kissinger.

Title V: Generalized System of Tariff Preferences   The idea that industrialized countries should eliminate tariffs on manufactured goods just for developing countries was first advanced in 1961, but it was Raul Prebisch, the first Secretary General of the United Nations Conference on Trade and Development, who mobilized international political support behind the concept.[21] In 1967, President Johnson pledged American support for the idea, and this pledge was repeated in an address by President Nixon in October 1969 before the Inter-American Press Association, and it was included in the "modest" bill sent to the Congress in November. A tariff preferences bill was supposed to be submitted in early 1972, but at that time, Assistant Secretary of State Charles Meyer said that the balance of payments problem "coupled with a sluggish economy created not only an unreceptive mood but a strong isolationist sentiment in Congress. . . . In this unfavorable climate, the Administration considered that not only was passage of a preference bill unlikely but that submission of a bill . . . might be unwise."[22] By April 1972,

[20]Congressional Quarterly, *Almanac*, 1973, p. 834.

[21]See Joseph S. Nye, Jr., "UNCTAD: Populist Pressure Group," in Robert Cox and Harold Jacobson (eds.), *The Anatomy of Influence* (New Haven: Yale University Press, 1973). See also United Nations Conference on Trade and Development, *Toward a New Trade Policy for Development:* Report by the Secretary General of the United Nations Conference on Trade and Development (N.Y.: United Nations, 1964). Also see Sidney Weintraub, *Trade Preferences for Less-Developed Countries: An Analysis of U.S. Policy* (N.Y.: Praeger, 1967).

[22]Quoted in *National Journal*, 22 January 1972, p. 156.

ten industrialized governments plus those of the European Community had enacted a system of tariff preferences.[23]

In the discussions on tariff preferences in the Administration, the principal issue was the amount of flexibility. STR wanted a "competitive need test" whereby tariff preferences would be suspended when imports of any article from a particular country reached either 50 percent of total U.S. imports or $25 million, whichever was less. The State Department opposed this as too restrictive, denying developing countries the opportunity to exploit economies of scale. STR won.

There were two other items of special concern to particular people or departments, which were incorporated since there was no resistance. Peter Flanigan considered the trend towards preferential trading arrangements "abhorrent," particularly so in the case of reverse preferences whereby certain developing countries were granted special market preferences to industrialized countries in return for special concessions.[24] The bill therefore had a section which denied GSP to any country that maintained reverse preferences by January 1, 1976. The Treasury Department was especially concerned about the increased trend of nationalizations in the developing world and wrote language (sec. 604(5)) in the bill which required the President to take into account a government's treatment of American foreign investment before granting the GSP.[25]

WEIGHTING THE BUREAUCRATIC DEBATE: CONGRESSIONAL INFLUENCE

In a Press Conference on April 10, 1973, the day President Nixon transmitted the Trade Reform Act of 1973 (TRA) to the Congress, the President said: "And just as we have consulted closely with the Congress in shaping this legislation, so the executive branch will consult closely with the Congress in exercising any negotiating authorities it receives."[26] And Secretary

[23]Fascell's subcommittee on Inter-American Affairs of the House Foreign Affairs Committee held hearings on *Trade Preferences: Latin America and the Caribbean*, 93rd Congress, 1st sess., June 25 and 26, 1973, and then Fascell testified before the Ways and Means Committee on the results of his subcommittee's deliberations. Rep. Charles Whalen introduced and explained Title V (GSP) before the House floor, p. 72.

[24]Quoted in Richard Frank, *National Journal*, 13 January 1973, p. 52. See also International Economic Report of the President, 1973, pp. 46–47.

[25]Treasury's preoccupation with this issue in the first Nixon administration is well documented by Jessica Einhorn in *Expropriation Politics*. The State Department, which fought Treasury every step of the way through the decision on the President's statement in expropriation policy, didn't even notice that Treasury had inserted its point in the GSP section of the Trade Act. (Interviews)

[26]The President's Trade Message to Congress (transmitted on 10 April 1973, printed as H. Doc 93-80, 93rd Congress, 1st sess.) is reprinted along with briefings by Secretary of State

Shultz echoed the same sentiments in his testimony before the Ways and Means Committee: " . . . in the process of putting this bill together, we did a lot of consultation with Members of the Congress, and we benefitted from that . . ."[27] Just *how* did the Executive benefit? What was Congress's impact on the executive branch's legislative process?

In answering these questions, one must distinguish between the *timing* and the *kinds* of communication. For our purposes, there were two periods: the drafting process and the period prior to introduction of the bill. In the latter period, several high administration officials, including William Eberle, the President's Special Trade Representative, William Pearce, Deputy STR, and Peter Flanigan, Executive Director of the Council on International Economic Policy, fanned out and briefed several dozen key congressmen and Senators (primarily the leadership and ranking members of Ways and Means and Senate Finance) in very general terms about the bill. The purpose was basically to "give them a chance to know what was going on and let them make some comments" and "to de-fuse any potential resistance." Some changes were made as a result of these contacts, but they were minor.[28]

Other than that, the extent of communication between the two Branches was remarkably low, and the direction of contact was almost always *from* the executive branch. With few exceptions, Legislators didn't participate unless consulted. One explanation, or perhaps rationalization, for this passivity, suggested by several congressional staff, is the Congress's conception of the separation of powers; Legislators may feel that it is unnecessary to insert themselves in the legislative process in the executive arena, since in the final legislative arena, they govern.

The idea that he who defines—that is, he who drafts the first draft—determines the parameters of the debate, and in effect has a disproportionate share of the policy-making power, is not persuasive to the Congress because Legislators believe they have sufficient time and opportunity to alter policy as they wish. Besides, Congress is so filled with the business of its own arena that it has little time to involve itself in the Executive's arena, particularly since the Executive's arena is predominantly a closed one, and the costs of gathering information there are inordinately high.

William P. Rogers, Under Secretary of State William J. Casey, Deputy Assistant Secretary of State Julius Katz, Assistant Secretary of State Willis C. Armstong, and Special Trade Representative William D. Eberle to foreign ambassadors at the State Department on April 10th, in the *Department of State Bulletin*, 30 April 1973, pp. 513–32. (Hereafter DSB, Trade Message) The President's quote is on p. 516.

[27]U.S. House of Representatives, Committee on Ways and Means, *Hearings: Trade Reform Act of 1973*, part 1, p. 184.

[28]It also gave Mills an opportunity to unveil portions of the bill on the House floor, thereby enhancing his own credibility as the congressional leader who was most up-to-date and aware of the Executive's deliberations on the bill. It also gave him an opportunity to begin lobbying for it. See *New York Times*, 22 March 1973, p. 65.

Though not actively involved in the executive arena, the Congress has many mechanisms—from speeches to simple, concurrent, or joint resolutions, to legislation—by which it can send a signal to the executive that an issue is of particular concern. For example, in February 1973, while the Executive was putting the trade package together, Representatives John Culver, Charles Whalen and forty-three other congressmen introduced legislation calling for a strengthening of the adjustment assistance programs.[29] The Executive can overlook or ignore the message, as it did on adjustment assistance, but it does so at the risk of introducing another potentially controversial element into the trade bill.

And while congressmen and Senators may only be infrequently consulted, "Congress" as a word, a concept, a distantly powerful institution is frequently employed by bureaucratic bargainers to win points and influence policy. The word and the symbol "Congress" are powerful bargaining chips. One bureau, trying to squash the proposal of another, will argue that Congress will never buy it. The other bureau, trying to keep its proposal alive, will reply that it should be retained since the Executive has to give the Congress something to change. The first will say it will antagonize the Congress; it will be counterproductive. And so on. One might presume from this exchange that the various bureaucratic bargainers would leave the meeting, telephone a few Legislators, and return to another meeting with a strengthened argument. But such is not the case.

In the trade bill drafting process, Peter Flanigan kept most of the chips, using "Congress" the most frequently, but after trying to identify the most likely Legislators who would be consulted, I found that "they" were, by and large, Wilbur Mills.[30] On those cases described above, there was hardly any consultation, and those signals emitted by Congress were either not received or grossly misinterpreted. On the issue of unlimited negotiating authority for the President, one official asked Harry Lamar, the senior staff from the Ways and Means Committee, whether they could get it, and received the reply: "You have rocks in your head if you think you'll get this through Congress." Lamar was ignored, though he was right.

If one were to choose a single congressman to consult on the trade policy, Chairman Mills was certainly the most logical candidate, but even given his extraordinary hold on the Ways and Means Committee in 1972, there were still good reasons to turn to other congressmen as well as Senators.

On one issue, Mills did have a decisive impact: the taxation of foreign-source income. In order to appear responsive to the message of Burke-Hartke

[29]*New York Times*, 28 February 1973, p. 53.

[30]No doubt there were officials in the Executive who contacted other Legislators at different times, but those officials whom I interviewed told me that Peter Flanigan seemed to use this strategy the most frequently and the most effectively.

and to try to demonstrate a sufficient concern for Labor's interests, Mills asked that such a provision be included in the trade bill, and the Administration complied.[31] Mills, however, only wanted it for "presentational purposes," and therefore didn't monitor the Administration's final decision on this issue, which was unfortunate for the Administration because they were made to appear unnecessarily foolish and ineffective. The packages they offered on taxation of foreign income were weak and were offered sloppily and insincerely.[32] The best George Meany said about them was that "the President's proposals do not meet the grave problems of trade which we have detailed time and again."[33] And even though the taxation provision was applicable to only a handful of businesses who used "tax havens," all the business community united in vigorous opposition. So the result was that both friends and enemies were antagonized.[34]

The taxation example, in which the Executive displayed surprising ineptness in handling the Congress and interest groups, was hardly unique. Nixon spoke to the thirty-five member Executive Council of the AFL-CIO on February 19, 1973 in an attempt to win support for the trade bill. Apparently, he spoke only about the militant aspects of the bill—the retaliatory capabilities, the powers to raise tariffs, impose quotas, etc.— because Meany and the other members left the meeting encouraged and enthusiastic. "From the point of view of a trade unionist, who likes to go to the bargaining table with options open and with authority to give and take, I think that the idea itself is attractive," Meany said after listening to Nixon.[35] Of course, when the bill was introduced, and it was clearly an internationalist document, Meany took his leave.[36]

In early January, as the Administration was making its final decisions on the bill, Peter Flanigan publicly announced that the administration was considering three alternatives: a comprehensive trade package; a "barebones bill"; and no legislation at all. On the last alternative, Flanigan said: " . . . it [legislation] would help, but I don't think it's essential."[37] It is not clear

[31]Interviews. Also see Charles Culhane, "Labor Readies Stronger Jobless Pay Plan, Rejects Version Offered With Nixon Trade Bill," *National Journal*, 19 June 1973, pp. 821–30.

[32]Nixon mentioned the provision at a News Conference on 12 April 1973, promising that he would send a bill to Congress soon. Finally, on May 7, a few notes arrived unsigned to the committee, and no one in the Administration made any attempt to find a sponsor for the provisions.

[33]Charles Culhane, "Labor Readies Stronger Jobless Pay Plan", p. 821.

[34]See Richard Frank, "Multinationals Mobilize To Preserve Favorable Tax Status on Overseas Income," *National Journal*, 14 July 1973, pp. 1019–28.

[35]Quoted in Charles Culhane, "Labor Shifts Tactics on Administration Bill, Seeks Concessions on Imports, MNC's," *National Journal*, 28 July 1973, pp. 1091–92.

[36]*New York Times*, 12 April 1973, p. 75.

[37]Quoted in Richard Frank, "Administration Torn Between Domestic, Overseas Interests," *National Journal*, 13 January 1973, p. 44. Also for irony's sake, the same issue carries

whether Flanigan's statement was a gaffe or a threat. His comments were certainly not well received on Capitol Hill.

There had been some question in December 1972 whether President Nixon would give the trade package the kind of priority in 1973 that it required, but on April 10, 1973, Nixon answered those doubts by beginning three days of comprehensive briefings involving virtually every Cabinet member and many sub-Cabinet officials.[38] Of course, Watergate would overtake the best of intentions, but at least the bill began its journey with the united and complete support of the President and the executive branch.

Each Cabinet member spoke to a different audience, and it is rather interesting to juxtapose the different emphases. Secretary of State William Rogers, briefing foreign ambassadors at the State Department, accented the "exceptionally broad authority" that the bill delegated to the President, particularly in negotiating nontariff barriers. "Now, in certain cases, and you will see from the bill, he [the President] can do this [negotiate the "reduction, harmonization, or elimination of nontariff barriers"] without any legislative approval after this bill is enacted. In other cases, he would be able to do so if the agreement is not vetoed by one House of Congress within 90 days."[39] And in the same briefing, Undersecretary of State William Casey said that customs valuations procedures such as ASP would be subject only to Presidential determination.[40]

In contrast, President Nixon stressed the rationale for the bill: it "can mean more and better jobs . . . can help American consumers . . . can mean expanding trade and expanding prosperity . . . [and] can help us reduce international tensions and strengthen the structure of peace."[41] To accomplish these objectives, "significant new negotiating authorities" would be necessary, but he quickly added: " . . . such delegation [has been recognized for "several decades now"] as . . . indispensable." The only question is one of degree, and Nixon pledged that he only asked for what "is necessary and proper to advance the national interest."[42]

Rep. Al Ullman, who would soon be chairing the Ways and Means Committee, was the first to react to the bill, and he expressed skepticism of increasing the President's authority: "My problem with the proposals is the degree to which we are delegating broad new powers to the executive."[43]

another article on an attempt by the White House to improve its liaison with the Hill. (Dom Banafede, "Administration Realigns Hill Liaison To Gain Tighter Grip on Federal Policy," pp. 35–43.)

[38]Department of State Bulletin - see fn #26 DSB, Trade Message.
[39]Ibid., pp. 523–24.
[40]Ibid., p. 526.
[41]Ibid., p. 513.
[42]Ibid., pp. 515–16.
[43]Congressional Quarterly, *Almanac*, 1973, p. 838.

Ullman's statement prompted a sensitivity in the Administration to congressional prerogative which had been conspicuously absent during the drafting stage. When one reporter asked Peter Flanigan whether President Nixon was seeking "unprecedented power" in the trade bill, Flanigan called the charge "blatant nonsense."[44]

IN THE CONGRESSIONAL ARENA: THE HOUSE

When the Speaker assigned the Trade Reform Act of 1973 (H.R. 6767) to the House Ways and Means Committee, the committee was in the midst of hearings on Tax Reform. Those hearings continued for thirty-five working days from March 5 to May 1, and just the index of the witnesses and the material submitted for the record amounted to forty-six pages; the full record was 7,247 pages.

The volume of the record is only one sign of the busiest and most important committee in the House, if not the entire Congress. Ways and Means, which is the most prestigious and attractive of congressional committees,[45] derives its power from three sources: its jurisdictional control of all revenue laws including issues of taxes, trade, medicare, social security, national health insurance, and the oil depletion allowance; the fact that the House often accepts its product without amendment;[46] and its role as Committee on Committees to choose all committee assignments for the Democrats in the House.[47] According to Richard Fenno, congressmen recruited to Ways and Means tend to be more interested in personally influencing the business of the House of Representatives than in making policy or servicing constituents.[48] Partly because of the prestige of the Committee and partly to carry out its role as Committee on Committees, the Democrats tended to be leaders from different regions of the country. In the 93d Congress, for example, Al Ullman represented the Northwest; William Green, Pennsylvania and the mid-Atlantic states; and Joe Waggoner, the deep South. The Republicans tended to recruit members from safe districts.

[44]*New York Times*, 8 May 1973, p. 65.

[45]See John F. Manley, *The Politics of Finance* (Boston: Little, Brown and Co.), p. 54; Eileen Shanahan, "Mills's Power: Why the Others Wanted Him to Have It," *New York Times*, 25 December 1974, p. 32. Frank V. Fowlkes and Harry Lenhart, Jr., "Two Money Committees Wield Power Differently," *National Journal*, 10 April 1971, pp. 779–807.

[46]John F. Manley, "The House Committee on Ways and Means: Conflict Management in a Congressional Committee," *American Political Science Review* 59 (December 1965): 930–1.

[47]This responsibility was transferred to the Democratic Caucus in 1975. One Congressional Staff denied that the power to assign members to the committee was a source of great influence, since the assignments are only a one-shot decision.

[48]Richard Fenno, Jr., *Congressmen in Committees* (Boston: Little, Brown and Co., 1973).

The committee, therefore, is reasonably representative of the full House, though a tinge older and more conservative;[49] and its members are well respected. This partly explains the Committee's extraordinary effectiveness. Between 1961 and 1968, there were only two cases in which the legislation reported out by the Committee was rejected by the House.[50]

Another important factor in explaining the Committee's effectiveness was its chairman from 1958–1975, Wilbur Mills. Because of the Committee's influence in the House, it has often been the battle ground between the political parties. In 1930, the Republicans excluded all the Democrats from the Committee when it began marking-up the trade bill. The Democrats weren't quite so blatant in 1934 and thereafter, but partisan divisions remained the operating style of the Committee until Mills assumed the chairmanship. John Manley, who has written a book and several articles on the Committee and on Mills, believes that his influence stemmed primarily from his flexibility and his willingness to subordinate his own particular interest in a policy in order to achieve bipartisan consensus.[51]

Mills's leadership skills are most evident when one considers the respect, indeed reverence, which he received from members of the Committee who could agree on little else. In retrospect, one member said that Mills was "able to overwhelm [other Committee members] by his own personal intellect and his experience," and because he had abolished all subcommittees, and centralized all the staff under his leadership, no one else on the Committee could draw upon alternative sources of information.[52] In trade policy, for example, many of those who actively participated in the Committee's deliberations readily admitted that practically no one on the Committee except Mills knew anything about trade policy.[53]

Because of these factors—a Committee without subcommittees, the politics of consensus, and a Committee on Committees composed of regional leaders—power flowed from the House to the Committee to the chairman. That is why the Administration only felt it needed to consult Wilbur Mills.

Beginning with 1973, however, this particular configuration of power began to come apart. Mills's abortive 1972 Presidential election campaign led many of his colleagues for the first time to question his judgment. In

[49]Roger H. Davidson, "Representation and Congressional Committees," in Norman J. Ornstein (ed.), *Changing Congress: The Committee System,* The *Annals* of the American Academy of Political and Social Science 411 (January 1974), p. 52.

[50]Manley, *The Politics of Finance,* pp. 206–11; Edward F. Morrison, "Energy Tax Legislation: The Failure of the 93d Congress," *Harvard Journal on Legislation,* 12 (April 1975): 376.

[51]Manley, *Politics of Finance,* p. 380.

[52]Quote by Rep. Sam Gibbons in Morrison, "Energy Tax Legislation," p. 373.

[53]Exceptions were Gibbons and Barber Conable.

January 1973, the House agreed to establish the House Select Committee on Committees to study the organization of the House and committee jurisdiction, and Richard Bolling, a long-time rival of Mills, was named chairman. Although acknowledged to be competent and effective, Ways and Means was also viewed by most congressmen as having more issues and policy than it could realistically handle. Therefore, during the 93rd Congress, the Ways and Means Committee was very sensitive to this criticism, and pushed itself much harder to prove its ability to handle its portfolio.[54]

The Democratic caucus, which was increasingly influenced by the liberal Democratic Study Group, decided in February 1973 to amend the House rules to make it easier to challenge the right of a committee chairman to receive a closed rule,[55] and since Mills more than any other chairman had relied on the closed rule as the principal instrument to keep his committee's product clean, this rule change was viewed by many as a personal setback. Finally, in July, *after* twenty-four days of hearings on the trade bill and 5,317 pages of testimony, *but before* committee mark-up, Mills entered the hospital for a back operation. Although he returned periodically, he didn't really reassume the chairman's responsibilities again until April 1974, long after the committee and the House had dealt with the trade bill.

With considerable understatement, Representative Barber Conable said: "The Committee is in a state of transition."[56]

There was time enough to learn. The bill went through three stages in the House: hearings, mark-up, and floor debate. Mark-up is unquestionably the decisive stage for all bills, but particularly for a bill like the Trade Act, which went to the House floor with a "modified close rule," permitting only a couple of amendments.

In debates on trade policy in recent years, countervailing interests almost always emerge to contest an interest demanding special attention. The original interest then is impelled to refine its case, and the debate moves to a more technical level. To read the public hearings is to understand with compelling clarity what distinguishes the Congress from the Executive. *What a congressman says and the policy he proposes depends on who's listening, but more so, on to whom the congressman has listened.* Hearings are for hearing, and if congressmen don't always absorb the details, they can't help but be reoriented and sensitized. Let's examine one interest as an example: shoes.

The American Footwear Industries Association was represented, appropriately, by Richard W. Shomaker, who was also President of Brown Shoes Company, St. Louis, Missouri. The Association claims to represent the

[54]Interview Daniel J. Balz, "Ways and Means Seeks to Maintain Power and Prestige," *National Journal*, 22 June 1974, pp. 913–20.

[55]Morrison, "Energy Tax Legislation,", p. 380–81.

[56]Quote of Barber Conable, in Balz, "Ways and Means," p. 913.

manufacturers of 95 percent of the leather and vinyl footwear produced in the United States[57]—which amounts to 520 companies with about 900 plants and 200,000 workers in 40 states and 239 Congressional districts.[58] Their case was hardly unique. Imports were increasing at an alarming rate: in 1968, imports amounted to 22 percent of the domestic market; in 1970, 30 percent; in 1972, 36 percent. Jobs were disappearing, from 233,000 in 1968 to 200,000 in 1972—a 14 percent loss. Their grievances were well documented. Not only were they trying to compete with countries with low wage levels, but also with many developing countries, which were subsidizing their exports or giving tax rebates or cash remissions.

"The remedy we seek," Mr. Shomaker said, "lies in action by this Congress because, despite the serious injury caused the nonrubber footwear industry by growing imports, the executive branch has failed to be responsive to existing procedures for dealing with such problems and has not taken action to provide our industry with relief from the injury caused by these disruptive imports."[59] Escape clause proceedings had begun in July 1970 when the House was considering the previous trade bill, but by the time the Tariff Commission made a decision, on January 15, 1971, and the decision was a split vote, the trade bill had died in the Senate, and the President let the escape clause decision end in a like manner. What the Association requested in 1973 was not a quota, but a requirement in the new bill which forced the President to make a decision on such cases within a 120-day time limit.[60] They also asked the Congress to follow the President's decision to exclude footwear from GSP.[61]

The President of the United Shoe Workers of America testified next in support of Burke-Harke and annual quotas.[62] But he was followed by the Volume Footwear *Retailers* Association and the Footwear Group of the American *Importers* Association, both of whom testified on behalf of the consumer and requested the termination of the ASP which lifted tariffs on footwear by 58-100 percent ad valorem.[63]

With countervailing interests engaged in debate, the discussion moved quickly to detailed issues like the kinds and amounts of subsidies by exporting countries and the kinds of shoes being produced and imported. But

---

[57]Both Schattschneider and BPD have effectively questioned the credibility of associations to in fact represent all the organizations they allege to represent.

[58]U.S. Congress, House of Representatives, Committee on Ways and Means, *Hearings: Trade Reform,* H. R. 6767, part 14 of 15, 12–15 June 1973, 93d Congress, 1st sess., pp. 4699–4811.

[59]Ibid., p. 4700.

[60]Ibid., p. 4706.

[61]Ibid., p. 4700.

[62]Ibid., p. 4738.

[63]Ibid., p. 4811.

the hearings were remarkably well attended, and the congressmen were prepared with good questions. It was clear that the purpose of going into detail was to develop a generalizable point about policy, or about the way administrative procedures of the Tariff Commission should be altered, or about the way negotiations led by STR should go forward. Congressmen would petition the Tariff Commission or send letters to STR on behalf of a constituent interest, but only in exceptional cases did they intervene or even interfere; their purpose was to go through the motions of serving an interest and to make certain that the process was responsive, fair and equitable.[64]

The Ways and Means Committee spent twenty-four days taking public testimony, and thirty-seven days privately writing a bill, completing it on October 5, 1973. The Committee's changes reflected their legislative orientation as well as the legislative-executive negotiating process.

For the first time on a trade bill, the Committee was required by new House rules to make a choice between an open mark-up or an executive session. On June 18, by a vote of 15-9, the Committee followed the lead of its Acting Chairman Al Ullman, who said that a closed session would get more work done with less demagoguery. Ten spokesmen for the Administration were permitted to attend and to participate. The Committee, in comparison, had only one permanent staff member, Harry Lamar, plus two people detailed from the Tariff Commission. Also, Anthony Solomon, former Assistant Secretary of State for Economic Affairs, was hired as a consultant by Mills, but he departed after Mills became ill.

William Eberle and Peter Flanigan decided to send William Pearce, Eberle's deputy, as the chief Administration spokesman—probably more for personality reasons than for bureaucratic ones. Pearce was the perfect negotiator; he was flexible, but even when he took a hard position, he could do so without antagonizing anyone. Pearce chose as his deputy John Jackson, who had taken leave from the University of Michigan, where he taught a course on trade law and had written a textbook on the GATT, to serve as Counsel for STR. Pearce decided to play the role of the advocate, and Jackson that of the scholar, to whom the Committee turned for information and legal interpretations. Mary Jane Wignot of the Tariff Commission and later of the Ways and Means Committee was the Issues Coordinator for the executive branch recruiting specialists from different departments as the issues before the Committee changed. The interaction between the Committee and the Administration was described by one participant as

[64]It is also interesting to note that despite the importance of constituent-servicing as a determinant of congressional behavior, Legislators don't unduly interfere with the administrative process. As Catherine May Bedell testified: "In the three years I have been Chairman of the Tariff Commission, I can think of no single instance in my case where either the executive branch or the legislative branch ever attempted to exert improper pressure, or pressure of any kind." (U.S. Senate, Committee on Finance, *Hearings: Nominations of Jack F. Bennett, Edward C. Schmults, and Mrs. Catherine Bedell,* 93d Congress, 2d sess., June 4, 1974, 21.

"intimate." Another said that "the level of debate was extremely high and good-humored."[65]

Ullman was under a lot of pressure to produce a good, responsible bill, and at the same time, he was eager to gain the respect of the Committee, since, in a sense, he would be up for re-election as Chairman at the beginning of the 94th. His style was much more democratic and open than Mills's, and the Committee members, according to one, "rather liked operating as a committee. They liked being consulted about things rather than being the tail on Wilbur Mills's comet."[66] The administration spokesmen were treated as equal participants, being permitted by Acting Chairman Ullman to make points or ask questions at their discretion. They saw their role as trying to maintain the integrity of the bill, responding to questions by identifying the cost of various alternatives. Because the exchange was so open and so free-wheeling, their more expert views generally prevailed.

William Pearce said that the bill which emerged from the Ways and Means Committee was in many ways an improvement over the Administration's bill.[67] His point was that the give-and-take between the two branches, with different orientations, made the policy more sensitive to domestic interests while still granting the Executive the range of negotiating authority necessary to conduct successful international negotiations.

As the Administration's principal negotiator with the committee, Pearce was given a good deal of discretion, although he kept George Shultz, who chaired the executive committee responsible for overseeing the Hill strategy, informed on almost a daily basis of the committee's discussions.

How did the House change the bill? First and most important, they strengthened the adjustment assistance provisions. Rep. John Culver's Subcommittee on Foreign Economic Policy of the House Foreign Affairs Committee held thorough hearings on the subject, and Culver's recommendations were seriously considered by the Committee. The United Auto Workers lobbied hard for adjustment assistance as the only way to withstand the pressures of protectionism. Leonard Woodcock, UAW President, said: "No matter how deeply I and the other leaders of the U.A.W. may believe in liberal trade policies, the U.A.W. will not be able to resist the protectionist

---

[65]This close relationship between the Committee and the Executive has precedents. (See Manley, *The Politics of Finance*, p. 350.)

[66]Quoted in Morrison, "Energy Tax Legislation," p. 380.

[67]Interview. The *New York Times* in an editorial agreed that the Ways and Means bill was an improvement over the Administration's draft (*New York Times*, 23 September 1973, sec. IV., p. 16) and Secretary of the Treasury George Shultz also used the opportunity in testifying before the Senate Finance Committee on 4 March 1974 to compliment the House for its work. He called the House bill "an excellent vehicle for accomplishing what is needed and needed soon." The House changed the administration bill "but with only a few exceptions, its changes were positive contributions to the legislation itself . . . " (U.S. Congress, Senate, Committee on Finance, *Hearings on the Trade Reform Act*, part 1, p. 166.

tide to which, regrettably, a large part of the American labor movement has already succumbed, unless the nation's trade policy is humanized as well as liberalized."[68] Whereas the Administration had insisted that imports must contribute "substantially" to job loss before workers could be eligible, the House mandated that imports must contribute "importantly" for workers as well as businesses to be eligible. In addition, the benefits were increased dramatically over what the Administration originally requested. With this provision strengthened, Ullman felt justified in taking the bill to the floor and saying that it was "needed to assure job opportunities for American workers."[69]

Both Mills and Ullman knew that the Administration's request for unlimited negotiating authority would be altered, and it was. On tariffs, the Administration's request for unlimited authority for five years was circumscribed to permit the President to eliminate tariffs of 5 percent or less, to cut by 60 percent if the current rate is 25 percent or less, and to cut by 75 percent if the current rate is more than 25 percent. No tariff above 25 percent can be cut below 10 percent. On the much more difficult subject of nontariff barriers, the Executive was given the power to convert NTB's to tariffs, but there would be no advance authority to eliminate NTB's or ASP. Rather, the President would have to consult with the two committees before entering into agreements, and then either House of Congress could reject the agreement by majority vote. Ullman explained the dilemma of the Ways and Means Committee:

> To withhold the needed Presidential authority would weaken the capacity of the U.S. to defend its economic interests in trade negotiations; to grant such authorities without developing effective congressional controls over their use would be irresponsible. The Committee has attempted to respond to both challenges in reporting the Trade Reform Act of 1973.[70]

The tax provisions on multinational corporations were also dropped by the Committee because they had "no friends and many enemies," and because the bill was felt complicated enough without them.[71] There was almost unanimous agreement among all those interviewed that the AFL-CIO was totally ineffective in lobbying against the bill. Apparently, labor's initial strategy was to ignore the Administration's bill, and instead to try to obtain support for Burke-Hartke. At the start of the 93rd Congress, however,

[68]*National Journal*, 28 July 1973, pp. 1095–96.

[69]*Congressional Record*, 10 December 1973, p. 40501.

[70]*National Journal*, 24 November 1973, p. 838.

[71]Ibid., pp. 1751–52; interview.

three months before the Administration's bill was even sent to the Hill, Burke-Hartke was reintroduced, but it had lost twenty sponsors (from eighty to sixty in the House).

The next strategy employed by James A. Burke was to try to graft his bill in the form of two amendments onto the Administration's bill in Committee. One amendment would have triggered quotas when imports exceeded current levels. The other would have related product quotas to a specific foreign-import share of the U.S. market. Both amendments would not have permitted any Presidential discretion, i.e., they would have been automatically implemented. Both amendments were rejected 7-16.[72] From then on, organized labor made no attempt to improve the bill, and Ullman was moved to say: "I don't think they seriously ever tried to improve the bill. I think their effort from the beginning was to kill it." This was confirmed in a statement by Rep. Joseph Karth, who along with five other congressmen from the Committee sympathetic to labor, met with two representatives of the AFL-CIO on June 12. Karth related the meeting: "I think there was unanimity of opinion that the Burke-Hartke bill was not going to pass. It was agreed that if they had any amendments that would make the Administration's bill more favorable, we would be happy to take a look at them, and if they met with our approval, offer them during the course of the committee meetings." After that, Karth didn't hear from labor again until the final vote on the House floor when labor requested that he vote against the bill. Karth voted for the trade bill.[73]

Not only was the protectionist argument undermined by the failure to mount an effective lobbying effort, but economic developments and recent foreign and domestic policies also conspired to disperse the protectionist winds which had been blowing through the Congress for the previous six years. The twin devaluations of December 1971 and February 1973 significantly improved the competitiveness of U.S. exports, and by the second quarter of 1973, when the trade bill was in the Ways and Means Committee, there were reports of a trade surplus, which amounted to $1 billion by the end of the year, a considerable improvement from the $6.4 billion deficit in 1972. Furthermore, for three years following April 1969, Japan gradually cut its illegal (under GATT) trade restrictions, from 120 in number to 33, while at the same time making unilateral tariff reductions on 124 items in April 1971, 238 in 1972, and 102 in 1973.[74] And with the encouragement of liberal trade groups, the Tariff Commission and the Treasury Department began to process cases under the escape clause and the adjustment assistance provi-

[72]National Journal, 24 November 1973, p. 1752. The New York Times reported the vote at 16-6. (17 July 1973, p. 55)

[73]Ibid.

[74]National Journal, 7 July 1973, p. 978.

sions much more frequently and with more positive results for injured industries.[75]

The problem of steel imports had been resolved in 1972, and on January 1, 1974, a long-term GATT textile agreement on man-made fibers, wool, and cotton textiles for fifty nations went into effect. Senator Herman Talmadge of Georgia remarked to Secretary of Commerce Dent that he "feels that this agreement holds great promise, and I want to compliment you [Dent] for your part in getting that arranged."[76] "Steel and textiles," Harry Lamar said, "once you keep them out of a trade bill, you can resist the efforts of the other interests." And according to another participant, "once it became apparent that we were getting agreement on these, everything else became easier."

One consequence of the improved trade balance, and the increased responsiveness of the Administration and foreign governments to the complaints of injured U.S. industries or unassisted exporters, was that the Congress approached the issue of the escape clause more realistically, and indeed, significantly improved the Administration's language and clarified the intent. The Administration had requested authority to raise tariffs without limit, to impose quotas, and to negotiate orderly marketing arrangements when an industry was injured because of imports. The Ways and Means Committee defined limits to each power, then organized them in order of preference, and included an opportunity for a congressional veto.

As expected, the various interests complained about the inadequacy of consultations during the Kennedy Round and requested that a more reliable mechanism be established for the "Nixon Round," which it was then being called. The Committee mandated elaborate oversight and consultation procedures between the Congress, which would have ten accredited advisers to the negotiations, and the STR. It also drafted without the opposition of the Executive an elaborate three-tiered consultation mechanism for private groups.[77]

The most controversial congressional initiative was, alas, the most predictable. The Jackson-Vanik amendment to Title IV prohibited the granting of most-favored-nation status to any nation which denies its citizens the right of emigration. Except for that provision, Henry Kissinger, who was then Secretary of State in everything but name, would not have become involved with the Trade Act at all. *Because* of that provision, he almost succeeded in killing the bill. But as Rep. Barber Conable said: "The

---

[75]See "Commission's Recent Votes Relax Tariff Pressures in Congress," *National Journal*, 7 March 1970, pp. 501–02; "Tariff Commission Work Load Growing," *National Journal*, 4 December 1971, p. 2402; and Richard S. Frank, "Treasury Steps Up Dumping Law Enforcement to East Pressures at Home and Abroad," *National Journal*, 23 September 1972, pp. 1496–1503.

[76]U.S. Senate, Finance Committee, *Hearings on the Trade Reform Act*, part 2, p. 413.

[77]See Richard S. Frank, "Industry Seeks Greater Voice in Trade Talks to Influence Decisions on its Products," *National Journal*, 20 October 1973, pp. 1561–69.

President and Henry Kissinger have not kept track of what was going on here. They did not realize that MFN was being opposed not just by the Jewish community, but by a very impressive coalition."[78]

On October 3, 1973, the House Ways and Means Committee voted 20-5 to report the Trade Reform Act. On October 10, the Report (H.Rept. 93-571) was filed and immediate consideration of the bill was requested and granted for October 17th. The President then requested a delay because Title IV (MFN to the U.S.S.R.) contained language which he found objectionable. Ullman responded that Title IV was in the bill only because the Administration had requested it. But as Ullman explained: "Because the President specifically tied his request for delay to matters of grave national security in the Middle East and the possibility of the outbreak of general war, there was no way that either the Speaker or the Committee on Ways and Means could refuse the request."[79] This first request for a delay came in the midst of the Yom Kippur war, and Kissinger thought that the passage of the bill might anger the Russians and complicate the peace settlement. In the meantime, the AFL-CIO urged the Rules Committee to reconsider sending the bill to the floor under an open rule, permitting amendments. Their strategy was to delay or kill the bill, and they were getting unintended assistance from the administration.[80]

Then, on October 25, Nixon asked Albert to drop the entire Title IV. Albert denied Nixon's request, saying that he would face a revolt if he tried to do that since there was strong support for the amendment.[81] The Administration tried to mobilize support to defeat the Vanik amendment by October 30, but failed, and requested a third delay to the great frustration of Ullman and Mills, who warned the President: "We have the votes now, but the longer we delay, the more difficult our problem becomes."[82]

The debate in the Administration paralleled the one in Congress, and grew more heated and polarized. Kissinger and Flanigan believed that detente was too important and too fragile to be exposed to a bitter debate in the House and they urged the President to delay the bill until Ullman and the House leadership mobilized support to defeat the amendment. The other departments—including STR, Commerce, Agriculture, Labor, and Treasury—believed that the trade bill was too essential to be jeopardized by an issue which could easily be detached and treated separately.[83]

Finally, Flanigan joined Eberle, Shultz, Mills, and Ullman and almost convinced Nixon to over-rule Kissinger. Nixon sent Speaker Albert a letter

---

[78]*National Journal,* 24 November 1973, p. 1751.

[79]*Congressional Record,* 10 and 11 December 1973, pp. 40500–40505.

[80]Congressional Quarterly, *Almanac,* 1973, pp. 844–45.

[81]*National Journal,* 24 November 1973, p. 1751.

[82]Ibid., p. 1752.

[83]Ibid., p. 1741. Interviews confirmed this point.

on December 2 requesting that he take up the bill and suggesting a compromise.[84] Two days later, Kissinger turned Nixon around again, and Nixon wrote Albert that he would veto the bill if it reached him with the provisions aimed at curbing free trade with the U.S.S.R.[85] Nixon's threat had no impact on the House debate or the vote.

On December 10, the House began debate on the trade bill under a "modified closed rule," which permitted the consideration of three amendments proposed by the Ways and Means Committee to give the House the opportunity "to work its will" on three controversial provisions: the Vanik amendment, the entire Title IV, and Title V. The debate was limited to seven hours, of which three were given to Ullman, as Acting Chairman of the Ways and Means Committee, three to the Ranking Minority Member of the Committee, and one to Rep. John Dent, a protectionist congressman from Pennsylvania.

The first subject of debate was the rule itself: should it be accepted, or should the bill be open to other amendments? The debate was laced with references to the Smoot-Hawley Act, "one of the worst pieces of legislation ever passed," which was granted an open rule. "We do not want to repeat that mistake here today," said Rep. Delbert Latta.[86]

Rep. John Anderson warned the House that if it fails to accept a closed rule, "I have no doubt about the effect. A glut of amendments will rain down upon this body that would have the purpose of exempting and protecting every product and labor sector from both the real and imagined dangers of freer trade."[87] Rep. Sam Gibbons explained why the process would be unavoidable: "Under an open rule, it becomes incumbent upon every member sitting here to try to defend the interest of his own district. What happens, though, is that sometimes, we get a horrible monstrosity, such as Smoot-Hawley . . . " Rep. Ullman, Gibbons continued, has "resisted with skill and determination any attempts to put into this bill the kind of things . . . that members of Congress are inclined to do when they are protecting their own district's interest . . . "[88]

The closed rule was accepted by a vote of 230-147, and Ullman proceeded to explain and defend the bill. He decried the preoccupation with detente, and criticized the argument that the bill represented a significant delegation of authority to the President. He pointed out that each Title had a congressional veto provision in addition to guidelines, limitations, requirements of investigations and public hearings, consultations, and disapproval

[84]*New York Times*, 4 December 1973, p. 1; and for a description of the bureaucratic debate, *New York Times*, 15 December 1973, p. 2.

[85]*New York Times*, 5 December 1973, p. 71.

[86]*Congressional Record*, December 10 and 11, 1973, p. 40494.

[87]Ibid., p.. 40495.

[88]Ibid., p. 40499.

procedures. "In reality," Ullman argued, "the bill will constitute a return to this Congress of its rightful role in carrying out its constitutional responsibilities over tariffs and trade."[89]

On the House floor, both sides were well prepared though there was not a good deal of communication or debate between the two sides, and it's unlikely whether any minds were changed. Ullman explained portions of the bill for those congressmen who were confused or uncertain, and he delegated responsibility for explaining different parts to several members of the Ways and Means Committee.

Those who argued against the bill, as James A. Burke did, said that it "simply reheats and re-serves the trade philosophy pursued by this government with such unfortunate results for the past decade." The adjustment assistance provisions were, in the light of one million jobs lost since 1965, "a cruel hoax"; the delegation of authority to the President was "a domestic Gulf of Tonkin resolution."[90]

Among those who supported the bill, there were still several recurrent themes of uncertainty. One fear was that the negotiators and the administrators of the bill would be insensitive to particular needs. The second was that the Administration might sacrifice U.S. domestic and foreign economic interests for foreign policy reasons. "It is my hope," said Rep. Chamberlain, "that renewed emphasis on trade after this bill passes will prompt our officials to pay more attention to commercial policy beneficial to our own economy and less attention to foreign policy in our dealings with other countries."[91] This is not an isolationist statement; it is a recognition of passing hegemony and it is a message to the President urging him to adapt his foreign policy machinery, not to say goals, to a new era of more genuine reciprocity. The congressional impulse was by nature of its institutional bias, perhaps, always more attuned and more comfortable in a nonhegemonic world, as Rep. Brotzman's statement suggests:

> Often as we discuss the problems of world trade, it becomes an interesting colloquy and discussion about international events. The real fact is that this particular bill touches flesh and blood people that we here represent. It touches them as to what they are going to pay for the products they buy. It touches them as to their own jobs.[92]

In this trade bill, however, the Congress was also quite interested in the direction, scope, and pace of the evolving relationship between the U.S. and the Soviet Union. By accepting the Vanik amendment overwhelmingly

[89]Ibid., p. 40502.
[90]Ibid., pp. 40532–33.
[91]Ibid., p. 40540.
[92]Ibid., p. 40496.

319-80-33, the Congress was not tying the Executive's hands, as many said. It was simply legislating different priorities. No doubt there were many groups and congressmen who used this amendment for purposes other than those professed, and this was more often the case in the Senate, as we shall see; nonetheless, the Congress was not persuaded by the Administration's principal argument: "One argument we hear repeated quite often is that trade leads to peace. Mr. Chairman, there has been no substantive evidence that trade necessarily leads to peace."[93] And more important, the Congress, as Rep. Clarence Long pointed out, had a constructive and justifiable reason for redefining the means and the ends of U.S. foreign policy to the Soviet Union: "A vote prohibiting trade credits without free emigration is a clear statement from Congress that the U.S. should drive much more realistic bargains with the Soviets in return for economic concessions."[94]

At the end of the seven hours alloted for debate on December 11, 1973, the House voted and passed the Trade Reform Act, H.R. 10710, "to promote the development of an open, nondiscriminatory, and fair world economic system, and to stimulate the economic growth of the United States"—272 ayes to 140 noes.

IN THE CONGRESSIONAL ARENA: THE SENATE

The Finance Committee

The Ways and Means Committee has been described as "a quiet pond compared with the cauldron of the Senate Finance Committee."[95] The Finance Committee has a reputation of being more protectionist, more receptive to special interests, and less cooperative with the Executive.[96] These characteristics are a function of the distribution of power within the Senate and within the committees, to the rules which govern the Senate's and the committees' operations, and to the orientation and attitudes of Senators to the Senate and to the President.

Whereas the locus of power in the House has been, at least until recently, the Ways and Means Committee and its chairman, in the Senate, "individualism" has reigned.[97] Senate Committee Chairmen, like Russell Long, possess great reserves of potential power, but the Senate norm of

[93]Remarks by Ben Blackburn, 41557. See Joseph S. Nye, Jr., *Peace in Parts* (Boston: Little, Brown, and Co., 1971) for a more systematic analysis of this proposition, but one which confirms Blackburn's point.

[94]*Congressional Record*, 10 December 1973, p. 40547.

[95]Frank Fowlkes and Harry Lenhart, Jr., "Two Money Committees Wield Power Differently," *National Journal*, 10 April 1971, p. 795.

[96]Manley, *The Politics of Finance*, pp. 267−288.

[97]Randall Ripley, *Power in the Senate* (N.Y.: St. Martin's Press, 1969).

individualism keeps this power in check. "Senate norms neither force them [Chairmen of Committees] to become complete democrats nor allow them to become complete autocrats."[98]

The dispersion of power makes the Senate less resistant to a logrolling process, and this tendency is reinforced by the flexibility of the rules which govern its operations. The Finance Committee and the Senate as a whole have nothing comparable to the closed rule, which insulates, to a considerable extent, the House and the Ways and Means Committee from short-term or special pressures or interests. Unlimited debate is the rule in the Senate unless cloture (two-thirds of the Senate before 1975; three-fifths since) is invoked. And unless cloture is invoked, an unlimited number and kinds of amendments are permitted. Thus, the policy process in the Senate encourages rather than impedes special amendments. This is often openly acknowledged, sometimes in ways which approach the humorous, as when Senator Ribicoff began a question to Eberle during the Finance Committee hearings in March 1974 with the following remark: "Mr. Secretary, we have already heard about tobacco from Georgia [Talmadge], and chickens from Arkansas [Fulbright]. Let's get down to ballbearings from the state of Connecticut."[99]

Stanley Surrey, former Assistant Secretary of Treasury for Tax Policy, referred to the policy of the Finance Committee which emerges from this process as "a composite of personal results," whereas Ways and Means produces "a committee result."[100]

Another important difference is that the Senate tends to be more jealous of its constitutional prerogative, particularly in commerce and foreign affairs. It is therefore not surprising that the negative veto on nontariff barrier agreements which was legislated by the House was viewed as inadequate to the Senate. The Finance Committee insisted that new legislation would have to pass the Congress in order for a nontariff barrier agreement to take effect. This was initially unacceptable to the Administration for a number of reasons, one of which was the fear that the Congress would delay for years the passage of an agreement, thereby impeding international negotiations. After intense negotiations, STR agreed to accept a congressional approval (as opposed to just a veto) procedure as long as there was a time limit that would require a congressional decision within ninety days. The Committee accepted this compromise, and mandated a procedure of sixty days for implementing legislation and ninety days for revenue bills. The Senate Report explained why a disapproval mechanism like the one in the House bill was unsatisfactory, and why an affirmative determination by the entire Congress was constitutionally and politically necessary: "Virtually

[98]Ibid., p. 129.

[99]U.S. Senate, Committee on Finance, *Hearings: Trade Reform Act of 1973*, part I, p. 233.

[100]Quoted in Fowlkes and Lenhart, "Two Money Committees Wield Power Differently," p. 795.

all nontariff barriers in the U.S. are matters of law. If the Congress were to delegate to the President the power to change domestic law, subject only to a Congressional [negative] veto, it would not only be a reversal of the constitutional roles of the legislative and executive branches, but also an abrogation of legislative responsibilities."[101] And this was satisfactory to Eberle: "As long as they can't hold us up on procedures, that's the key."[102]

The Senate Report also stated that consultations should not be deferred until the completion of the agreement or be confined to only a few select members. The negotiators "must work to gain the confidence and respect of all members, as well as keeping members fully informed."[103] In addition, the negotiators should establish procedures which would "insure maximum participation by the private sector in these negotiations."[104]

The Relationship with the Executive

The Ways and Means Committee accepted the affirmative veto in conference and a staffer acknowledged that failure to legislate an affirmative veto in the first place was an "oversight." That may have been true, but it was also symptomatic of a very different relationship between the two committees and the executive branch. William Pearce had resigned from STR after the bill cleared the House, and the spirit of comity departed with him, though this was due more to his reasons for leaving (disgust over Watergate) than to the qualities of his successor. By March 4, 1974, when the first of nineteen days of hearings on the Trade Reform Act began in the Finance Committee, the evidence pointing toward an abuse of Presidential authority unprecedented in American history was clear and persuasive to all but a few. It would be a mistake, however, to argue that Watergate was responsible for congressional assertiveness in the Trade Act, or even that it played a large role in the development of the legislation. As noted before, its principal effect on the executive debate was in keeping the President so preoccupied listening to tapes that the trade policy-making process was completed before reaching him. In the House, the Ways and Means Committee may have been slightly more sensitive to the issue of delegating new powers to the president; and in the Senate, the Finance Committee was less willing to work closely and cooperatively with the Executive, but Watergate was only one of many reasons (and a relatively minor one at that) for the adversary nature of the relationship.

The relationship between the Executive and Finance was different for other reasons. Finance didn't need to rely as much on the Administration for

---

[101]U.S. Senate, Committee on Finance, *Report* on the Trade Reform Act of 1974, H.R. 10710, No. 93-1298, November 26, 1974, 107–8. (Hereafter Senate *Report*)

[102]*National Journal*, 4 October 1974, p. 1486.

[103]Senate *Report*, p. 111.

[104]Ibid., p. 103

information and analyses because Finance accepted the House's bill, and instead concentrated their concern on amendments and on particular issues. Secondly, the Finance Committee had more staff with more time to study and evaluate the bill. Thirdly, as the 93d Congress drew to a close and the passage of the legislation became more urgent, Finance found itself dealing from a position of increasing strength. At the initiative of the United States, the nations of GATT were prepared to begin negotiations in early 1974 to the considerable embarrassment of STR, which had generated international enthusiasm for a new round. The negotiations were in limbo awaiting the arrival of the U.S. team with negotiating authority.[105] Thus, STR needed a bill.

In summary, the bargaining process between the Executive and the Senate Finance Committee when the bill went into executive session was, in the words of one participant, "much more difficult than was the case in the House." "It wasn't the full, careful deliberation," said another participant. All the staff of the Finance Committee were in attendance, although none of the legislative assistants of the committee members were permitted to attend. There were three staff from the Tariff Commission, who helped in explaining the implications of alternatives. A full representation from STR was there, often including Eberle, Malmgren, John Jackson, and Jackson's Deputy, Allan Wolfe. Officials from the State Department, Treasury, Commerce, and Labor attended when appropriate, but the State Department, not fully resigned to playing a back-up role, remained extremely suspicious of the discussions.

The Impact of External Events

Watergate was hardly the only external event affecting the legislative process or the outcome. The successful utilization of the oil producers' cartel for economic gain and for political purposes impelled the administration and the Congress to take another look at the trade bill, this time from the perspective of securing adequate access to supplies. The anxiety over "one, two, many OPEC's" grew more intense during 1974 as the number of producers' associations increased and as the developing world appeared to become more united.[106] Furthermore, scarcities and unusually high prices for raw materials coupled with synchronized inflation in the industrialized countries did not auger well for an internationalist position. Nor was President Nixon's Project Independence, which was taking shape in the

[105]For an article on the GATT and trade officials "marking time," see Richard Frank, "July May be Crucial Month in Setting Fate of GATT Talks," *National Journal*, 13 July 1974, pp. 1038–46.

[106]For a debate on whether the world would see many more OPEC's, see Stephen Krasner, "Oil is the Exception," *Foreign Policy* no. 14 (Spring 1974): 68–84; and C. Fred Bergsten arguing that "The Threat Is Real," *Foreign Policy* no. 14 (Spring 1974): 84–90.

spring, likely to encourage a multilateral, internationalist view of world trade problems.[107]

Perhaps the greatest problem for the Administration, however, was in trying to develop with the Congress a long-term domestic policy on foreign trade while being involved, at the same time, in some of the most difficult international economic negotiations for a generation. By the spring of 1974, the various trade disagreements between the United States and the European Community had so multiplied as to make almost credible Kissinger's warning the year before to the Senate Finance Committee that the Atlantic Partnership was in danger of coming apart.[108]

There were three issues: the amount of compensation—in terms of tariff concessions—due to the United States as a result of the trade-diversion effects of the enlargement of the European Community (EC) in January 1973; the reverse preferences scheme as well as the more general policy of the EC to negotiate special and discriminatory trading relationships with individual countries; and the increasing tendency of the European governments to pursue bilateral energy policies at the expense of cooperation or even consultation with the United States.[109] The compensation question proved the most vexing, though the United States tried many different strategies to obtain a satisfactory settlement. Kissinger's "New Atlantic Charter" speech of April 23, 1973 attempted to link this issue as well as monetary and energy problems with the continued American security presence in Europe. Kissinger anticipated that the "linkage" concept might be misinterpreted and rejected, and he was right.[110]

After a year of ignoring America's complaints, the EC made an offer to the United States on December 13, 1973. The United States responded that the offer was a step forward, but inadequate.[111] The issue was clearly at the front of the collective mind of the Senate Finance Committee as they commenced hearings. In the hearings on the TRA, Chairman Russell Long devoted much of his opening statement to Europe and the implications of the current impasse on future trade negotiations:

> The bloom is off the rose of 'Atlantic partnership,' as our friends in
> Europe concentrate on bilateral deals with oil producing nations and

[107]*New York Times,* 13 May 1974, p. 49.

[108]See Richard Frank, "Foreign Trade: Truce or War?" *National Journal,* 30 March 1974, pp. 457–67. Kissinger's testimony on p. 458.

[109]See Robert J. Lieber, *Oil and the Middle East War: Europe in the Energy Crisis* (Cambridge, Mass.: Harvard University Center for International Affairs, 1976).

[110]See Frank Fowlkes, "Administration Trade Strategy Taking Shape to Strengthen U.S. Bargaining Position," *National Journal,* 7 July 1973, pp. 973–80.

[111]Richard Frank, "Foreign Trade: Truce or War?" *National Journal,* 30 March 1974, p. 458.

> *their former colonies. I'm not at all sure they want to negotiate on a basis of fairness and reciprocity. If they were sincere, they would offer us fair compensation for the $1 billion trade loss that we will suffer from the enlargement of the European Common Market.*
>
> *I recognize that the United States must play a major role in leading the world and shaping its economy. Our country is the world's largest single market . . .*
>
> *I still desire an 'open, nondiscriminatory, and fair world economic system,' but I am tired of the United States being the 'least favored nation' in a world which is full of discrimination. We can no longer expose our markets, while the rest of the world hides behind variable levies, export subsidies, import equalization fees, border taxes, cartels . . .*
>
> *I realize we have barriers of our own. Yet I invite you to take a look at the number of foreign cars on our streets and ask why there are practically no Datsuns in Europe and practically no Volvos in Japan.*
>
> *What I am saying is that trade legislation comes before the committee bearing a heavy burden. It must be demonstrated that the next decade of our trading relations will be different from the last . . .* [112]

The Europeans apparently listened to Long and to the other Senators. On May 31, 1974, the United States and the EC reached agreement for compensation for the United States in the form of tariff reductions for U.S. tobacco, citrus, paper, and other products.[113]

The Finance Committee and its membership and rules of procedure; the relationship between the Committee and the executive branch; and domestic and international economic and political events—all of these factors affected the Committee and the Senate as the bill was rewritten. What changes were made by the Senate, and which of these factors best explain these changes? Let's examine again the four central issues: the delegation of negotiating authority; adjustment assistance, import relief, and unfair trade practices; Title IV and the Jackson-Vanik amendment; and Title V: the generalized system of tariff preferences.

Negotiating Authority and the Congressional Veto   The discussion between the Senate and the Executive on the proper procedure for ratifying trade agreements on nontariff barriers was actually a part of a more wide-ranging debate on the 'distribution of power between the two branches.

[112]U.S. Senate, Committee on Finance, *Hearings on the Trade Reform Act,* part I, p. 2.

[113]*National Journal,* 8 June 1974, p. 864. Europeans expressed concern that an influential member of Congress had balked at writing a trade bill for the Multilateral Trade Negotiations unless the EC showed itself more agreeable on the issues of compensation.

Virtually every delegation of authority in the Senate bill (subsequently agreed to by the House) also circumscribes the power of the President with a congressional veto—either a congressional affirmative determination or a congressional option to override. Watergate, the most obvious explanation for this congressional desire to keep the Executive on a leash, is also the least satisfactory. There is much more evidence in the legislative history of the trade bill for an explanation grounded in the widespread Congressional feeling that the Executive had continually, and often unnecessarily, sacrificed U.S. domestic interests in order to reach international agreement. Thus, the prevalence of the congressional veto in the trade bill is explained by its two purposes: to ensure that future executive policy reflects the priorities mandated in the trade bill; and to ensure that U.S. domestic interests get a fair hearing.

The Congress had been increasingly bothered by the State Department's bureaucratic desire to maintain tensionless relations with foreign governments rather than pursue a particular U.S. interest more vigorously. Senator Ribicoff characterized the Executive's negotiating strategy in the past as "bargaining with our trading partners to see how much advantage they could give away without Congress making too much of a fuss."[114]

Congressional distrust often focuses on the State Department, and if one examines the hearings that the Finance Committee held on the "Czechoslovak Claims Settlement," one can more readily understand the sources and the character of this distrust. After the Communist coup in February 1948, $80 million of American property was nationalized by the Czech government without compensation. The U.S. Government responded by seizing $100 million of Czech gold, which in fact was being held in the U.S. since the war as part of a three-country trust (with Great Britain and France).

When the Czechs approached the U.S. Government requesting MFN, the State Department realized that Congress would insist on the settlement of the nationalized property, and they therefore negotiated an agreement in which the Czechs would pay approximately $34 million, or about 42 percent of the $80 million of U.S. property nationalized in 1948. Such a settlement was incomprehensible to the Senate Finance Committee.

The Chairman (Russell Long): You are holding enough assets of that government to insist on paying off 100 cents on the dollar of those claims. You are in a position to withhold it from them. Yet you want to settle for 42 percent. Why does anybody think he has made a satisfactory settlement when he gets 42 percent and he is in a position

---

[114]*Congressional Record,* 13 December 1974, p. S31380.

to withhold more than 100 percent! You are in a position to withhold $100 million from them to protect $80 million worth of claims.

Mr. Armitage (Deputy Assistant Secretary of State for European Affairs): Between 80 and 90 million, yes.

I think the simplest answer to that is that in our judgment, the settlement that we got with the Czechoslovaks is the best settlement that we can get. And if we are to reopen these negotiations, in effect, the financial agreement which we have would collapse, and it would be a long time before we would be able to get a settlement at all.[115]

For two days the State Department strained itself, trying to defend that agreement. Congressional skepticism never waned.

An additional issue which gripped Congress was whether the United States should insist that tariff negotiations proceed by "product sectors" (e.g., agriculture, chemicals, etc.) or by the linear method used in the Kennedy Round. The source of this concern was the agricultural exporters who felt that because the agricultural and industrial sectors were separated in negotiations during the Kennedy Round, "agriculture was sold down the river."[116] The American Farm Bureau wanted to link the two sectors in the next round and to bargain U.S. tariff concessions on industrial goods for tariff concessions on agricultural goods by the EC and Japan.

The Executive, of course, wanted to retain as much negotiating flexibility as possible. Said Eberle: "Limiting the negotiations too closely to a sector basis could cause damage to the over-all goals of the trade reform act . . . and of the negotiations. An approach tilted too strongly toward sector negotiations could result in least common denominator results in the negotiations."[117] The House finally approved a broad grant of authority but included the caveat that in the negotiations "to the extent feasible, balance should be sought for major product sectors." The Senate allowed slightly more flexibility, and in the report made clear that the language "is intended to mean that agriculture shall be included in the negotiations. It is not a directive for cross-sectoral trade-offs between agriculture and industry."[118]

At the same time, various Senators extracted commitments from STR on "the manner in which specific provisions of the Trade Act should be implemented" on particular products. These commitments were deliberately not written into the law for fear it might result in logrolling. However, after

[115]U.S. Senate, Committee on Finance, *Executive Hearings: Czechoslovakia Claims Settlement*, 93d Congress, 2d sess. 11 and 26 September 1974, 2.

[116]Richard Frank, "Distrust Leads Congress to Tie Strings to New Authority," *National Journal*, 5 October 1974, p. 1488.

[117]Ibid., but for a fuller discussion of this issue, see pp. 1484–88.

[118]Senate *Report*, p. 79.

the sudden and unexpected resignations of Eberle and Malmgren in January 1975, the Senators asked the new Special Trade Representative, Frederick B. Dent, to accept a letter identifying these commitments at his nomination hearings. This letter included the following promises: STR did not intend to cut tariffs to zero for import-sensitive goods; cuts on footwear "would be weighed very, very carefully, and would be subject to full consultations with advisers from the footwear industry"; negotiations on dairy products would only proceed after full consultations with Senators Mondale and Nelson and only if the dairy policies of major competitors were "also on the table"; the multilateral textile agreement would not be adversely affected by the MTN.[119]

The letter also gave additional credence to a statement made by Senator Lawton Chiles of Florida when the bill was considered on the Senate floor:

> *The citrus people do not want their fate determined by some complicated trade negotiation in some far off place with other governments. They are having trouble enough coping with the forces at work in our own economy. I want the people in the citrus industry in my state to know that I have heard their call. I pledge myself to stand watch on trade negotiations as they go forward . . . our top trade negotiators have assured me that they will make every effort to see that the citrus industry fully participates in the negotiations as prescribed by law . . .* [120]

There was only one case where the tacit agreement between Congress and the Executive to avoid mentioning a specific product in the law itself was violated, but it was not done by the Committee. Unlike the House, the Senate has a tradition of permitting the consideration of any amendments on the Senate floor. Because time was running out on the 93rd Congress, the Senate voted cloture (Rule XXII) which set time limits on the debate and only permitted germane amendments. Still, thirty amendments were considered and twenty-eight were accepted. Among them was an amendment by Sen. John Pastore which excluded specific products from the generalized system of tariff preferences. When it became known that Pastore intended to introduce an amendment which would exclude watches and import-sensitive steel and textile products from GSP, Senator Humphrey persuaded him to add import-sensitive electronic articles and Senator Robert Byrd argued for glass products. Pastore agreed, and fortunately the log stopped rolling there.

[119]U.S. Senate, Committee on Finance, *Hearings: Nomination of Frederick B. Dent*, 94th Congress, 1st sess., 18 March 1975, 5–7, 50–52, 55–56.

[120]*Congressional Record*, 20 December 1974, p. S22510. Indeed, they had assured him. See ibid., p. 6.

But GSP, as we will see shortly, was viewed differently than the more "domestic" side of the trade bill, and a departure from the tacit rule was therefore more justifiable.

Adjustment Assistance, Import Relief, and Unfair Trade Practices   Despite the fact that the AFL-CIO put all of its lobbying strength into trying to defeat the Trade Act, and therefore didn't lobby for an improved adjustment assistance provision, the Congress devoted a good share of its time to doing just that.[121] Whereas the Administration had insisted that imports must contribute "substantially" to job loss for workers to be eligible for adjustment assistance, the House mandated that imports must contribute "importantly" for workers as well as businesses to be eligible; and the Senate accepted the House's version but also included a provision for adjustment assistance to communities. In addition, the Senate incorporated a "trade statistics monitoring system," which would monitor the flows of imports to identify potentially abrupt and disruptive increases, and a provision which defined responsibilities of firms that decide to close domestic plants and relocate outside the United States. These were all included in the final act as were a dramatic increase in benefits for adjustment assistance over that which the Administration had originally requested.

Similarly, while the Administration had relaxed the provisions for escape clause eligibility and relief from the standards established by the Trade Expansion Act of 1962, the Congress insisted that the provisions did not go far enough. The Administration asked for authority to raise tariffs without limit, to impose quotas, negotiate orderly marketing arrangements and other instrumentalities including adjustment assistance if it were demonstrated that U.S. producers were injured and that imports were a "primary" cause of injury. (The 1962 law required that imports, *due to previous tariff concessions*, must be a *"major"* cause of injury.) The Congress relaxed it so that producers could be eligible if imports were found by the International Trade Commission to be a "substantial" cause of injury; and they tightened and set priorities on the use of the various instrumentalities. (Title II, Ch. 1) The President still retained the authority to reject the recommendations of the Commission if he found a rejection to be in the national economic interest, but the Congress gave itself the power to override a Presidential determination.

A similar pattern held for the issue of the proper governmental response to unfair trade practices of other governments, particularly in

---

[121]The United Auto Workers did lobby for adjustment assistance, but they were not joined by their colleagues in the AFL-CIO. See Charles Culhane's two articles in the *National Journal*, "Labor Readies Stronger Jobless-Pay Plan, Rejects Version Offered with Nixon Trade Bill," 9 June 1973, 821–30, and "Labor Shifts Tactics on Administration Bill, Seeks Concessions on Imports, MNC's," 28 July 1973, 1091–8.

subsidizing exports and in dumping (foreign goods sold at lower price in the U.S. than in country of origin). The United States had two laws of long-standing which were designed to deal with these problems: the countervail-ing duty law of 1896 to impose a duty proportionate to the export subsidy, and the antidumping law of 1921 to assess duties of "dumped imports." The Treasury Department was charged with investigations, and if unfair practices were identified, then duties would have to be assessed. The problem was that there was no administrative discretion, but there was also no time limit, so that most petitions were postponed indefinitely. The President sought to "modernize" these provisions by setting strict time limits, although allowing for considerable Presidential discretion in implementa-tion. The House accepted this provision, but added a right of court review for those domestic industries which received a negative decision from the Treasury Secretary. At the Administration's urging, the House also added a provision which would give the Treasury Secretary the discretion to suspend the law during the multilateral trade negotiations.

The milk producers took their case to the Senate. Despite clear evidence of subsidization by the Europeans, the Executive showed great reluctance to use the weapon. "All the rhetoric about the possible use of such measures, will not replace the visible, positive fact that it is not being used."[122] In a meeting with Senators Mondale and Nelson, the dairy industry representatives and the Senators agreed that the five-year mora-torium (during MTN) should be deleted from the bill, and the imposition of countervailing duties be made mandatory upon a finding of export subsidization.

The Committee was prepared to accept their recommendation, but the Administration fought it intensely. A compromise was reached and written in the bill, and subsequently it became law. STR gave up its demand for a moratorium in exchange for discretionary authority to suspend the imposi-tion of duties if three conditions are met: the foreign government is taking steps to reduce or eliminate the subsidy; there is "a reasonable prospect" of reaching such an agreement; and the imposition of duties might jeopardize multilateral negotiations on this issue. Each House of Congress also retained the right to override the Secretary of Treasury's decision. Senator Nelson supported the compromise, announcing that "They [the Administration] have to have some flexibility."[123]

When the Administration testified before the Senate Finance Commit-tee and asked for even greater Presidential discretion to table such decisions,

[122]Statement by Patrick B. Healy, Secretary of the National Milk Producers Federation, quoted in an excellent article on TRA by Richard S. Frank, "Distrust Leads Congress to Tie Strings to New Authority," *National Journal*, 5 October 1974, pp. 1488-89.

[123]Ibid., p. 1490.

Senator Abraham Ribicoff responded angrily: "What is the use of seeking liberalization of this clause if you have been so reluctant to apply even a stricter clause?"[124] The Congress did not pass a special import quota for footwear or for any other special product. What it did do was insist that the law be administered as intended. This often meant that the language was tightened; the administrative discretion was limited; and the opportunity for congressional override was mandated. The Congress did not intend that every petition by every industry be accepted by the International Trade Commission; nor did they want to see a repetition of the 1960s when virtually every petition was denied.[125]

Evaluating the work of the International Trade Commission a year after the passage of the Trade Act, Senator Russell Long stated:

> I am pleased to observe that you Commissioners have in your determinations since the passage of the Trade Act of 1974 observed both the letter and spirit of the Trade Act as it emerged from the Congress. Sometimes the Commission has found that domestic industries were not being hurt and in other cases it was found that the injury was taking place. Each case has been judged on its own merits . . . [126]

Within the year, a total of fourteen industry investigations under the escape clause were completed, as compared with only one such investigation in the preceding twenty months.[127] Injury was found in only two cases, and in only one of these—specialty steel imports—did the President recommend restrictive quotas as the relief mechanism. As table 7 indicates, there has been an increase in the number of petitions received for action under the antidumping and countervailing duty provisions as well as for other unfair import practices, but neither affirmative determinations of injury nor restrictive trade actions have increased very much.

By providing for the impartial and relatively nonpolitical relief of protectionist pressures and by the generous use of adjustment assistance (see table 8), congressional changes in the Trade Act of 1974 helped impede any ostensible slide to protectionism. At the same time, by legislating for

[124]U.S., House of Representatives, *Hearings on Trade Reform Act* of 1973, H.R. 6767, June 1973, part 14 of 15 vols., p. 4700.

[125]U.S. Senate, Committee on Finance, *Hearings on Trade Reform Act* of 1973, H.R. 10710, March 1974, part I, p. 233.

[126]The Senate Finance Committee reported: "It is not intended that the escape clause criteria go from one extreme of excessive rigidity to complete laxity." (Twentieth Annual Report of the President of the United States on the Trade Agreements Program—1975, p. 38.)

[127]U.S. Senate, Committee on Finance, *Hearing: Authorization of Appropriations for the U.S. International Trade Commission,* 94th Congress, 2nd session, March 5, 1976, p. 2.

TABLE 7   Summary of Antidumping, Countervailing Duty, Escape Clause and
Unfair Import Practices 1973–1975

	CALENDAR YEAR		
	1973	*1974*	*1975*
Antidumping:			
Petitions received	20	10	25
Negative decisions	9	2	3
Affirmative decisions	25	5	8
Injury or likelihood of injury	13	3	2
Discontinuances	5	3	0
Countervailing duty:[a]			
Proceedings initiated	1	5	38
Negative decisions	0	1	10
Affirmative decisions[b]	0	4	9
Terminations	0	4	15[c]
Escape Clause:[d]			
Investigations initiated	2	0	13
Negative decisions	1[e]	0	4[e]
Affirmative decisions	1[e]	0	2[e]
Unfair import practices:[f]			
Investigations initiated	15	9	11
Negative decisions	0	0	0
Affirmative decisions	0	0	0

[a]Data for 1975 includes first week of 1976.

[b]Includes waivers under the Trade Act of 1974.

[c]Does not include nine rejected petitions.

[d]Data for 1975 through January 26, 1976.

[e]Tie vote.

[f]Includes actions taken under Section 337 of the Tariff Act of 1930, as amended, and Section 301 of Trade Act of 1974.

SOURCE: *International Economic Report of the President*, March 1976, p. 45.

themselves a new and active role in the negotiating process, the Congress
improved the prospect of negotiating a trade package which would be
acceptable domestically.

Title IV and the Jackson-Vanik Amendment   Secretary of State Henry
Kissinger said that he would probably recommend a Presidential veto if the
Trade Bill contained the Jackson-Vanik amendment. "I believe that the bill
as it has emerged from the House would do serious and perhaps irreparable

TABLE 8   Tariff Commission Determination on Worker Adjustment Assistance Petitions, Fiscal 1963–75

Fiscal Year	DENIED		AFFIRMED		EVENLY DIVIDED	
	Petitions	Workers	Petitions	Workers	Petitions	Workers
1963-69	6	1,410	0	0	0	0
1970	2	700	6	2,012	5	1,100
1971	40	17,735	7	3,041	24	13,502
1972	41	16,125	9	6,815	0	0
1973	35	15,899	11	6,393	9	5,301
1974	24	7,034	8	2,630	3	1,260
First half 1975[a]	10	3,423	9	6,260	0	0
1963-75[b]	158	62,326	50	27,151	41	21,163[c]

[a]July 1974–December 1974.

[b]Through December 1974.

[c]Slight variations in estimated workers in this classification appear in Department of Labor documents.

SOURCE: Data supplied by U.S. Department of Labor. Reprinted in Daniel J. B. Mitchell, *Labor Issues of American International Trade and Investment* (Baltimore, Maryland: Johns Hopkins University Press, 1976), p. 52.

damage to our relations with the Soviet Union," he said.[128] And it was only by intellectual agility that he avoided being cornered by Senator Harry Byrd, who then completed the argument he was pursuing without Kissinger's help: "Well the fact that you would recommend a veto, as you stated you would do, certainly suggests to me that you regard that part of the bill as more important than all of the rest of the bill, combined."[129]

The battle over the Jackson-Vanik amendment which jeopardized the passage of the trade bill twice and probably delayed the Trade Bill for as much as a year is a case study in itself.[130] The case shows two institutions with two different sets of goals and priorities struggling unsuccessfully to mesh those goals. Interestingly enough, this was the only issue in the Trade Bill which was handled exclusively by the State Department. (The STR was the primary administration spokesman for the rest of the bill.)

[128]U.S. Senate, Committee on Finance, *Hearings on the Trade Reform Act*, part 2, p. 457.

[129]Ibid., p. 474

[130]Joseph Albright, "The Pact of Two Henrys," *New York Times Magazine*, 5 January 1975, pp. 16–34. See also Paula Stern's *Water's Edge: Domestic Politics and the Making of American Foreign Policy* (Westport, Ct.: Greenwood Press, 1979).

Jackson's objective was to slow detente, to embarrass the Russians and, if possible, Kissinger; to get the Russians to accept freer emigration; and undoubtedly, personal political considerations were not irrelevant. Kissinger and the Administration wanted to use MFN to hasten detente with the Russians, and did not believe that MFN should, in his words, "be made dependent on the transformation of the Soviet domestic structure."[131]

All the maneuvering through the fall of 1973 and the summer of 1974 was like some kind of shadow-boxing, but in the end, both sides won and lost. Jackson "won" in slowing detente and embarrassing the Russians as well as Kissinger, but in the process, he embarrassed himself since the Russians cut emigration and renounced MFN and the entire agreement on January 14, 1975. Kissinger "won" in that he embarrassed Jackson and obtained an example he could use to prove his point that the Congress has no business making foreign policy. He lost in not being able to fulfill his promise to the Russians, in slowing detente, and in significantly harming his relations with many Legislators, who felt that he had deceived them.[132] Because this issue totally dominated the debate on the Trade Bill in the Congress, obscuring other much more important issues, and monopolizing the very limited time of Henry Kissinger and the Legislators, the biggest loser may have been U.S. trade policy.

Generalized System of Preferences (GSP/Title V)   Kissinger and the State Department didn't devote time or bargaining chips to Title V, the generalized system of tariff preferences (GSP). Rather surprisingly, the House passed GSP with hardly a change. One explanation was lack of time; another that GSP had the strong support of several influential congressmen, including Rep. Dante Fascell and Charles Whalen, Jr.[133]

By the time the bill reached the Senate, however, the impact of the OPEC cartel had been felt, and the strength of that feeling is evident in

[131]U.S. Senate, Committee on Finance, *Hearings on TRA*, part II, p. 474.

[132]The Finance Committee had been trying to get Kissinger to testify for several months; he had agreed in principle but kept postponing the hearing. Finally, on 3 December 1974, as time was running out on the 93d Congress, Kissinger testified, mostly on the implications of the Jackson amendment. Later, the Senators learned that Kissinger had been notified by Russian Ambassador Dobrynin before his testimony that the Soviet Union planned to renounce the agreement for MFN linked to free emigration. Kissinger didn't even hint that this could be a possibility, and as a result a number of Senators felt that he had deceived them. (U.S. Senate, Committee on Finance, *Hearing: Emigration Amendment to the Trade Reform Act of 1974*, 3 December 1974; interviews).

[133]Fascell's subcommittee on Inter-American Affairs of the House Foreign Affairs Committee held hearings on *Trade Preferences: Latin America and the Caribbean*, 93d Congress, 1st sess. 25 and 26 June 1973, and then Fascell testified before the Ways and Means Committee on the results of his subcommittee's deliberations. Rep. Charles Whalen introduced and explained Title V (GSP) before the House floor.

the following statement by then Senator Mondale in hearings in the Finance Committee:

> What OPEC stands for, it seems to me, is an outrageous, uncivilized, extorting, monopolistic strategy to take a critical world commodity, increase the price out of any economic proportion, not only to generate revenues but to extort political concessions as well, to the point that the oil prices are doing more to break up NATO and the Common Market than the Russians ever could do.[134]

Senators reached for any lever they could to vent their rage. Many also attempted to respond constructively to the kind of threat Mondale believed it represented. One result was that the TRA is laced with references to the need to negotiate for access to supplies as well as to markets. (See Title III, Sec. 301–302; Title V.) Another was the exclusion of all OPEC countries from the GSP. Had the exclusionary provision distinguished between those OPEC countries which embargoed the United States and those which hadn't, the response internationally would not have been as unfavorable, and it might possibly have had some impact on OPEC. But the entire developing world had identified with this first successful effort by a producer's association to alter the terms of trade, and thus this exclusionary provision was viewed by developing nations as an attempt by the U.S. to reassert an obsolete and unjust international economic system. All the member governments of the Organization of American States with the exception of the U.S. met in January 1975, after the enactment of the Trade Act, and unanimously condemned the OPEC-exclusionary amendment as "discriminatory." The Latin American governments then cancelled the upcoming conference of the "New Dialogue" in Buenos Aires.[135]

In addition, the Senate excluded from GSP all Communist countries, all members of international cartels like OPEC "which disrupt prices and supplies," and all countries which do not try to prevent the international trade of narcotics.

On December 13, 1974, after staving off two protectionist amendments, one by Sen. Hartke and another by Sen. McIntyre, which would have prevented the President from reducing tariffs on those imports which already account for one-third or more of domestic consumption—after rejecting these amendments, the Senate accepted the Trade Reform Act, renamed the Trade Act, by a vote of 77-4.

The bill went to Conference for two days to resolve the differences. The conference accepted the Senate's OPEC-exclusionary amendment to

---

[134]U.S. Senate, Committee on Finance, *Hearings on TRA*, part I, p. 180.

[135]David Binder, "Twenty Latin Countries Condemn U.S. Trade Act," *New York Times*, 24 January 1975, p. 3.

"prevent the U.S. from exposing our markets to countries who act to hurt us and the rest of the world in international trade by forming cartels, by drastically reducing prices, or by denying us access to supplies."[136] The conference also accepted the Senate's amendments renaming the Tariff Commission the International Trade Commission ("because tariffs are no longer the major impediments to trade")[137], and strengthening the Commission by lengthening the terms of office of commission members to nine years and giving it an independent budget (i.e., free of alteration by OMB or the President). Rep. Barber Conable explained in the House that these changes "were approved in large part because we were trying to remove the Tariff Commission from possible influence by the State Department, which it was felt had failed to fully represent American consumer interests."[138]

The Conference Report and the final bill were returned to both Houses on December 20, the last day of the 93d Congress, for a vote. In the Senate, Long introduced the report: "The House and the Senate conferees met for two long days on this bill, and I am proud to say that they held substantially to the Senate version."[139] At approximately the same time of day, Representative Ullman addressed the House: "The conference report, Mr. Speaker, . . . is essentially a victory for the House and the Congress."[140]

On that final day of debate, Congressmen and Senators who made statements did so for one of three reasons: (1) To explain their continued opposition to the bill, even while recognizing the hopelessness of the task. Senator Vance Hartke, for example, offered a new title to the Bill, "the Unemployment Act of 1974 . . . because unemployment is exactly what the effect of this bill will be."[141] (2) To establish a history—a legislative record— for a particular interpretation of the bill, or to put in writing a tacit agreement or assurance. (3) To try to influence the future implementation of the act. Senator Mike Gravel used the opportunity to reiterate concern for a future settlement on claims from Czechoslovakia:

> I would also like to ask the Chairman and at the same time voice my views for the benefit of the State Department, which I know is in attendance, and that is, when they go back and negotiate for a fair settlement, that they observe the definition of what a fair settlement

---

[136]Senator Long's summary of the Conference report in *Congressional Record*, 20 December 1974, p. S22508.

[137]*Trade Act of 1974, Summary of the Provisions of H.R. 10710,* prepared by the Staffs of the Committee on Finance, 30 December 1974, p. 6.

[138]*Congressional Record*, 20 December 1974, p. H12577.

[139]Ibid., p. S22507

[140]Ibid., p. H12573

[141]Ibid., p. S22509

is, and that is going to be $64 million, which is the principal amount which is due the Americans that have had their property taken, and as long as I am on the Committee and a member of this body, any agreement that comes back . . . I, for one, and I am sure others will join me, intend to make a major point of this issue . . .

Senator Long: I stand with the Senator on that.[142]

The Conference Report passed the House 323-36 and the Senate 72-4. President Ford signed the Trade Act of 1974 (PL 93-618) on January 3, 1975. When the Trade Act began its journey through the Congress twenty months before, it was called the Trade Reform Act, and it was expected to signal the beginning of the "Nixon Round" of trade negotiations. By the time the Congress completed its work, the "reform" was gone; it was renamed the Trade Act, and the upcoming round of trade negotiations was rechristened the "Tokyo Round," symbolizing in one bold stroke a country that had arrived and a President who had departed.

SYMBOLS AND CYMBALS: THE CLASH OF INSTITUTIONS

The Trade Act of 1974 represents the fourteenth time since 1934, but the first time since the reported passing of American political hegemony, that the Executive has requested authority from the Congress to negotiate international agreements to reduce tariffs. One of the reasons that the clamor for protection was so loud prior to its passage is that U.S. tariffs were already at their lowest levels in U.S. history, offering little insulation from the cold winds of sharply increasing imports. And yet in the Trade Act of 1974, the President was given greater authority than ever before to reduce those tariffs above 5 percent by as much as 60 percent (the previous highest was 50 percent of a much higher tariff level), to eliminate tariffs below 5 percent and to work within the GATT framework to harmonize, reduce, or eliminate all those national policies, from government procurement to antitrust to environmental pollution standards, which distort the free flow of international trade.

In addition, the Trade Act contained safeguard and assistance provisions to help industries and workers *adjust* to changes in trade, not *protect* them from those changes. The negotiating and ratification process were also significantly changed for the first time since 1934 to permit greater participation and oversight by Congress and by private groups, including labor, business, consumers, and agriculture. Thus, in many ways, the Trade Act of

[142]*Congressional Record,* 20 December 1974, p. S22508–9.

1974 can be considered as liberal, internationalist, and far-sighted a foreign economic policy as any in which the Congress has participated since the passage of the Bretton-Woods Agreement Act in July 1945.

Whither the interest groups, the protectionists, the short-term, parochial congressional perspective? How do we explain the Trade Act of 1974? What went right?

The interest groups seeking protection were certainly as active as in any period in the past; and including, for the first time, the labor movement, they were certainly more numerous and ostensibly more powerful. The administration bill, however, was so comprehensive and so detailed that its introduction altered the terms of the debate, and the protectionists never adapted. Instead of working on the margins of the Administration's bill, pressing for taxation of foreign income, improved adjustment assistance, and other items of concern, the AFL-CIO concentrated its attention and power on passing the Burke-Hartke bill. After Burke's two amendments were defeated, 6-16, in Committee, organized labor tried, but failed, to defeat the Administration's bill.[143]

The Legislators improved the adjustment assistance provisions of the bill not because they were pushed by labor, although the UAW was in favor of it, but because they realized that those provisions were important for a balanced bill.

One might argue that the protectionist winds were not only dispersed by the failure of these groups to mount an effective lobbying campaign but by economic trends and international events. The twin devaluations of December 1971 and February 1973 significantly improved the competitiveness of U.S. exports and turned America's $6.4 billion deficit in 1972 into a $1 billion surplus in 1973. And Japan significantly reduced its illegal (under GATT) trade restrictions in the years 1969–72.[144] But by the last quarter of 1973, while the bill was in mid-passage, the winds of economic misfortune returned as a hurricane. Depression, double-digit inflation, and a quadrupling in the price of petroleum followed the trade bill through the Senate, undermining the argument that a good trade bill is the result of an improving economic picture.

One could argue correctly that two major interests—steel and textiles— were accomodated outside the legislative framework in 1973–74, just as President Kennedy had handled them in 1961–62. But one should recognize that these two industries are not exactly your run-of-the-mill special interests. The textile industry, for example, employs 2.4 million workers (as

---

[143]Rep. Al Ullman, in frustration, talked of the role of organized labor: "I don't think they seriously ever tried to improve the bill. I think their effort from the beginning was to kill it." (*National Journal*, 24 November 1973, p. 1752).

[144]*National Journal*, 7 July 1973, p. 978.

of 1971), which was one in eight of all U.S. manufacturing jobs. And 60 percent of these jobs were located in small-town and rural areas.[145] Steel, on the other hand, had annual sales of $20 billion and a workforce of almost half a million in 1971.[146] If the steel and textile industries were special interests, they were also national interests.

Furthermore, one should recognize that the voluntary export restraint agreements for steel and textiles were not static cartels, but rather "orderly marketing arrangements," which permitted *a gradually increasing percentage of imports each year* at an orderly and controlled rate.

The Nixon Administration correctly realized that to obtain a good trade bill, a few—as few as possible—industrial interests, which were capable of disrupting the bill, would have to be dealt with outside of it. Indeed, by making the voluntary restraint agreements contingent on the passage of the Trade Act, the Administration gave these interests a stake in its passage. Such a strategy worked in 1962,[147] and it contributed to the success of the trade bill in 1974. Also, as in 1954 with the Randall Commission on Foreign Economic Policy, and in 1961 with the Ball Task Force on Foreign Economic Policy, the 1973 Trade Reform Act was preceded by a Presidentially-appointed commission, the Williams Commission on International Trade and Investment Policy. All of these commissions wrote the outline and much of the details for the subsequent trade bill, and more importantly, provided some semblance of public support for the policy.

Bureaucratic politics provides a valuable theoretical framework for mapping and interpreting the struggle within the executive branch, but in the case of the trade bill, it is obviously inadequate for the simple reason that the bill which emerged from the bureaucratic debate was significantly different from the law that was enacted.

Theories of Congressional behavior were helpful in explaining the differing operations and products of the Ways and Means and Finance Committees. Constituents, generally more influential as groups, were more important in stimulating Legislators to consider certain policy concerns

[145]*United States International Economic Policy in an Interdependent World,* Papers Submitted to the Commission on International Trade and Investment Policy, vol. 1, (Washington: G.P.O., July 1971), pp. 304, 314.

[146]*National Journal,* 29 July 1972, p. 1236.

[147]Lowi argues that Kennedy's strategy on textile concessions was ineffective; it "probably got him only Georgia's votes." ("Public Policy and Political Theory,", p. 683, note 8) He notes that on the crucial vote on the Mason motion for recommital, 37 of the 44 protectionist Democrats were Southern. What he neglects to mention is the fact that the textile bloc was composed of 128 congressmen, who had consistently voted as a bloc since the 1950s to oppose freer trade. The vast majority of this bloc supported Kennedy in 1962, including, or rather especially the bloc's leaders, Rep. Vinson and Rep. W. J. Bryan Dorn. (See Congressional Quarterly, *Weekly Report,* 27 April 1962, pp. 680–82; and Congressional Quarterly, *Almanac,* 1962, pp. 618–19.)

than individual interests. With strikingly few exceptions, specific interests were addressed at the policy level (e.g., escape clause standards), where the Administration's position and arguments carried the greatest weight, rather than at the case level (e.g., raising a tariff on a product).

While an analysis which disaggregates the Congress by committees, rules, or chambers, or the Executive by bureaus, adds richness and detail to the case study, the critical cleavage, if one could choose only one, was undoubtedly that between the Congress and the Executive. In the end, the Trade Act of 1974 represented the give-and-take of these two institutions, acting as such, with different biases and different priorities. In certain issues, like adjustment assistance, import relief, and negotiating authority, the priorities of the two institutions *qua* institutions were clear-cut. The Congress stood for a more automatic and more generous allocation of adjustment assistance; more flexible and equitable import relief criteria, mechanisms and benefits; and more participation and power to the general public and to Congress in the negotiating process.

The Executive, on the other hand, gave highest priority to obtaining maximum flexibility to negotiate or administer the law. On import relief, the Executive wanted to retain discretionary authority. On adjustment assistance, the Executive found political, budgetary, and ideological reasons to oppose it. On these issues, there were compromises, and integration of priorities, and a better bill as a result.

The major changes in the trade bill occurred as a result of interbranch politics. Even in the debates *within* the executive branch, the major determinant was the "law of anticipated reactions." Because the Executive knew it had to write a bill that would not be rejected out-of-hand by the Congress, it included a section on adjustment assistance, some loosening of the escape valves, and some congressional participation in the negotiating process. Without a Congress, the Executive would probably have omitted these provisions.

The Congress made many more changes. As table 9 points out, the critical changes in the two fundamental issues of negotiating authority and adjustment assistance were made by Congress. Congress limited the executive authority to negotiate tariff reductions; it denied advance authority to negotiate NTBs; and it increased congressional and public involvement in negotiation and ratification of agreements. The Senate, with a firmer grip on prerogative than on detail, tightened and formalized the responsibilities of Congress. But again, the changes between House and Senate are marginal compared to those made by the Congress. On adjustment assistance, the Congress turned a minimal program into one which significantly expanded benefits for workers and businesses and relaxed the eligibility requirements. The same pattern held for Congress's change of the escape clause eligibility provision, and on the administration of unfair trade practices; U.S. industries

TABLE 9   Changes in the Trade Act, 1974

Issues	Executive	CONGRESS	
		House	Senate
1. Negotiating Authority Tariffs	Unlimited Authority for 5 years.	Strict limitations on depth of cut.	Slight change.
Non-Tariff Barriers	Advance authority to negotiate ASP.	No advance authority; negative veto.	Affirmative determination required.
Product Sector	Opposed any limits on product sector.	"Balance should be sought for major product sectors."	Agriculture should be included; specific product commitments.
Congressional Participation	Practically none.	Negative veto; formalized procedures.	Affirmative determination plus formalized procedures.
2. Adjustment Assistance and Escape Valves	1. Minimal program on *adjustment assistance*; for eligibility, imports must contribute "substantially" to job loss.	1. Expanded benefits of program for workers and businesses; plus easier to get.	1. Same
	2. *Escape Clause Eligibility* relaxed from 1962: if imports were a "primary" cause of injury, then Executive would negotiate to raise tariffs, etc.	2. Expanded — if imports "substantial" cause of injury. Set priorities on use of instruments.	2. Same
	3. *Unfair trade practices.* On export subsidies, dumping, countervailing duties: strict time limits, but administrative discretion.	3. Limited discretion; although suspended law during MTN.	3. Tightened discretion during MTN — required 3 conditions to be met — Congress could override.

would find it easier to get a fair hearing and to get benefits. Finally, on the issue of MFN to Communist countries, the Congress was united against a united Executive. Unfortunately, different goals were not integrated. On Title V, the Senate closely examined the generalized tariff preferences and attached a number of amendments specifying the terms under which GSP should be granted as well as denied.

An important point to keep in mind in understanding why there was room for compromise on these issues and why there is reason for hope in the management of interdependence is that Congress is guided by an "internationalist standard." This standard is for nontariff barriers what reciprocity was for tariffs. It means, quite simply, that Congress will more readily accept less government protection or promotion of a domestic interest if it can be satisfactorily demonstrated that other governments are pursuing the same course. And conversely, Congress will insist on helping U.S. domestic interests if other governments are doing it. The discussion below between then Secretary of Commerce Frederick Dent and Sen. Russell Long illustrates this point:

> *Secretary Dent: Now with respect to the Government purchasing policy offshore, we agree with you that this has been discriminatory toward American industry. We are participating in a multilateral study in the OECD designed to develop a code at the international level where all of this will be equalized. Last summer, in taking bids for a new generator at Grand Coulee, for the first time, we made the foreign bidders specify what their government's policy would be with respect to purchasing similar items in their country. So we let them know that there is no monkey business any more; this Government is interested in the jobs here . . . [that is why] we have a major projects division in our Bureau of International Commerce. They identify sales and we go after them tooth and nail.*

> *The Chairman: I am pleased to hear that, Mr. Secretary. That is good news.*[148]

At other times, the two institutions were unable or unwilling to compromise, like the Jackson-Vanik amendment and the GSP/OPEC. It is not surprising that this was more often the case with foreign policy issues, particularly those in which the State Department had special responsibility.

[148]Senator Long continued, tiptoeing on the edge of hypocrisy:
"Now I would like to ask your help in selling some sugarcane harvesting and processing equipment, because I am satisfied that we manufacture the best in the world in Louisiana, and all things being equal, would make a sale, but we have not been getting as much help from our Government as the other fellow has been getting from his and they have been making inroads on us.
As a matter of fact, I think Secretary Butz might even be a little more effective in that area, because if we are going to follow the pattern of the existing Sugar Act where we assign

For Congress, the *process* of negotiating domestically and internationally is often as important, sometimes more so, than the *outcome* of these negotiations. The democratic process requires the participation and reconciling of different interests and objectives, and often means that the outcome will be second-best. However, virtually all negotiations in which the State Department has a lead role, regardless of whether the issues are economic or security-related, are conducted in a secretive, insular fashion, keeping the Congress as well as the general public at arms length. (Even the hearings on the Czechoslovak Claims Settlement were held in executive session, though it is difficult after having read the released transcript to explain why.) This secretive style is no longer realistic nor viable, particularly for issues of economic interdependence.

A second reason why it was difficult to integrate the foreign policy positions of the two institutions is because both GSP and the granting of MFN were seen as aid or resource-transfer issues rather than trade issues. In the latter, the internationalist standard and reciprocity are guiding principles; in an aid-issue, however, there is a feeling that if it's our resources, then we should have a hand in setting the conditions for receipt of these resources. In a speech in December 1975, Senator James Abourezk put it succinctly: "The Congress has the responsibility and the right to determine the conditions under which U.S. assistance is to be given."[149]

While the Executive agrees with the principle and acts upon it, it believes that use of aid-as-an-instrument should be done privately and subtly (and by itself). Since it doesn't consult with Congress on the tactics and strategies of using aid, Congress is therefore forced to legislate its priorities publicly and loudly. That is why compromise has been less likely in this field than in the other.

What went right? The Trade Act of 1974 provided the guidance and authority to drastically reduce the artificial barriers to trade. Why, despite the prophets of doom, did Congress pass such a law? The reasons, in brief, were: executive leadership, though in this case it was largely and ironically without the Chief Executive; congressional cohesion and the ability through rules and procedures to resist centrifugal pressures; and the effectiveness and the responsiveness of the legislative-executive process.

---

quotas to people, if I could send him over there as salesman before he recommends what their quotas are going to be, my guess is he can sell all we can manufacture.

Secretary Butz: . . . I might sell so much that it would displace production in Louisiana.

The Chairman (Senator Russell Long): All I am asking for is the same type of thing that these other countries are doing to help their people get the business . . . . Will you assure us that you will use that leverage [the sugar quota] as best you can to help our people get some business and make it a two-way street?"

(U.S. Senate, Committee on Finance, *Hearings on TRA*, part 2, pp. 441–44.)

[149]*Congressional Record*, 5 December 1975, p. S21276.

6

U.S. TRADE POLICY, 1929–76: SUMMARY AND TENTATIVE CONCLUSIONS

THREE QUESTIONS

What is U.S. foreign trade policy? Who makes it? And how can it be explained?

The journey from Smoot-Hawley to the Trade Act of 1974 was a long and sometimes hazardous one, in which landmarks often appeared as obstacles or roadblocks. Along that road, tariffs gradually descended from a peak of 49.5 percent to less than 10 percent, and world trade spiralled upward at a much more rapid rate. As the paramount economic power in the world, the United States made decisions on trade policy which contributed to both developments.

Viewed from the perspective of aggregate trade and tariff statistics over a fifty-year period of time, U.S. trade policy appears more consistent, liberal, and successful than has been suggested by others who have analyzed U.S. trade policy by particular periods or policies. For example, Hawkins and Norwood analyzed the period from 1946 to 1960 and concluded that it represented the revival of protectionist sentiment. Jacob Viner warned of a neoprotectionist wave in 1961, as did C. Fred Bergsten and Harald Malmgren a decade later. One study that focused on both the textile agreements and the efforts of the footwear industry to obtain protection from imports concluded, as E. E. Schattschneider had done forty years earlier, that interest groups made U.S. trade policy little more than a patchwork quilt of special interest policies.[1]

---

[1]Douglas Wilson Kessler, "American Business and U.S. Foreign Trade Policy: Cotton Textiles and Nonrubber Footwear, 1960–70," (A Senior Honors Thesis for the Harvard University Government Department, March 1970).

Yet, the analysis in the last three chapters spanned the entire period, and it is clear that the United States had a very different kind of trade policy than a patchwork quilt, and that the best explanation of this liberal trade policy is hardly interest group theory. By surveying a full fifty years of U.S. trade policy, one is better positioned to understand the patterns which dictate the shape of trade policy and the variables which are most important in the policy-making process.

A SURVEY

In eighteenth and nineteenth century America, U.S. trade policy was used to provide the federal government with sufficient revenue to do its business. Secondly, it was used to protect certain industries or firms from foreign competition. The instrument was the tariff, and it was manipulated periodically, generally in an upward direction. Though Congress was the arena of decision-making, the Legislators represented sections of the country rather than constituents, individual groups, or the Congress as an institution. By the end of the nineteenth century, however, a sectionalist U.S. had been transformed into a country of economic groups and these groups coalesced within particular parties so that the Republicans became the party of high tariffs and big business, and later of small and medium-sized firms. The Democrats became the party of low tariffs and activist Presidents.

Smoot-Hawley is significant because it represents the culmination of these developments; at the same time, it represents their last, worst gasp. Interest groups were rampant; Presidential leadership was nonexistent. Congress raised the tariff to its highest point in the twentieth century, while Hoover fought to retain a meaningless provision permitting the Tariff Commission to adjust the tariff so as to equalize the costs of production between foreign and domestic goods. The logrolling process, described by Schattschneider, undermined public confidence in the Congress and the government. Foreign governments protested and threatened; professional economists in the United States warned the President of dire consequences. Hoover ignored or ridiculed all such threats or warnings.

Two years after the passage of Smoot-Hawley, a Democratic Congress sent Hoover a bill ("the Collier bill") reducing many of the tariffs which the Republicans had raised, but Hoover, true to his party and principles, vetoed it.

Thus, the Reciprocal Trade Agreements Act which passed in 1934 became the real watershed in U.S. trade policy history for a number of reasons. It was the first time Congress didn't debate tariffs in a tariff bill; instead it formally delegated tariff-making authority to the President. In comparison, Congress's delegation of authority in adjusting tariffs to the

Tariff Commission in the 1922 and 1930 Tariff Acts was a meager, indeed, trivial grant. In 1934, the President was empowered to negotiate trade agreements with other countries, and these agreements unlike treaties or statutes were neither subject to ratification or congressional veto. Secondly, it represented the beginning of a long process by which tariffs and ultimately all barriers to trade would be reduced on a gradual and reciprocal basis. The President could begin by negotiating the reduction of tariffs by as much as 50 percent of their 1934 level.

Whereas Hoover had hoped that his "flexible tariff" would lift the tariff-making process out of the politics of logrolling and into the scientific hands of the Tariff Commission, Roosevelt had moved forcefully to ensure that tariff reduction would be the goal of U.S. trade policy, and that the President would be the executor. In 1930, while the President had initiated the process, the Congress had clearly taken charge, and the final policy, with the single exception of a modified, flexible tariff, represented the will of the Congress. In 1934, the President proposed, and to a considerable extent also disposed. In comparison to the extraordinary grants of authority delegated the President in domestic affairs in 1933 and 1934, the power over the tariff perhaps seemed insignificant, and that plus the fact that the trade bill was sold as an "emergency" measure are important reasons why the bill passed easily through Congress.

Still, there were a number of important changes or modifications in trade policy which were the result of congressional proposals, reflecting a very different set of priorities than those of the Executive. These changes were of two kinds: those made by the Executive in anticipation of congressional action, and those done by the Congress. Of the first group, the fact that bilateral agreements would be the mode, rather than multilateral agreements or unilateral reductions, was attributed to the expectation of congressional attitudes. Secondly, the Executive requested authority to negotiate reductions on an item-by-item basis, when it clearly preferred linear reductions. This second change was satisfactory to the Congress, but not sufficient. The Congress also mandated a procedure whereby individual interests and groups could be permitted to give testimony on proposed tariff reductions to an Executive Committee on Reciprocity. Also, the Congress sought successfully an informal pledge from the Executive that tariff reductions would not be made on products in which certain industries were being significantly injured by imports.

The most important change Congress made in the trade bill was in circumscribing the grant of authority to the President. Roosevelt had in effect asked for permanent negotiating authority, but Congress preserved what was left of their power over trade policy by giving him only three years and requiring the President to return, if he wished, for renewal.

Interest groups were curiously absent in the congressional deliberations on the Reciprocal Trade Agreements Act, and this was as portentous as any of the other changes described above. In future renewals of trade bills, interest groups would be organized at the sector level, and lined up on both sides of the issue, cancelling out their specific influence in all but two kinds of cases. When specific interest groups, like the dairy industry or footwear, had a genuine complaint, they forced the Congress to address the source of their grievance at a general level, for example, by changing the law on countervailing duties or on adjustment assistance. In other words, they focused the Congress's attention and forced it to address the issue in a way that would ensure the responsiveness of the administrative process. Secondly, for those industries like steel or textiles which were clearly national in scope, specific pressure forced the President to define an industrial policy for these sectors and to negotiate this policy internationally.

The Trade Act was renewed routinely in 1937, 1940, and 1943. In 1945, the President asked for new authority to reduce tariffs by 50 percent of the 1945 rate, and after considerable anxiety, Congress passed it with the strong and vigorous leadership of House Speaker Sam Rayburn. As in 1934, the combination of strong congressional and vigorous Presidential leadership defeated a spate of amendments, and in 1945, the bill passed unchanged. Except for the intensity of the debate and the very real prospect that restrictive amendments would be added to the bill, the fact that the bill passed unmarred would have been one sign of the arrival of American political hegemony on a global basis. To be sure, the leap by U.S. negotiators from bilateral to multilateral agreements was one such indication of global power status.

Of greater consequence, however, was the character of the domestic debate in the U.S. following the first round of multilateral trade negotiations in Geneva in 1947. The debates resulted in short-term renewals, meager grants of new negotiating authority, rejection of an international organization for trade, the inclusion of peril-point provisions, and the tightening of the escape clause. The Congress behaved in the period from 1948 through 1961 as if the U.S. were anything but a global superpower.

Yet one must view these "restrictions" in the appropriate context. For one, multilateral negotiations continued on almost a regular basis in this period; five trading rounds were concluded prior to the passage of the Trade Expansion Act in 1962. Secondly, the Congress *did* expand the President's power to reduce tariffs by an additional 15 percent in 1955 and an additional 20 percent in 1958. Thirdly, the escape clause provision was not new to this period. It had been accepted informally by both branches since the 1934 Act, and the process by which informal agreement became Executive Order and finally statute was more a function of Executive unresponsiveness than congressional protectionism. Fourthly, the congressional veto can hardly be considered an inherently restrictive step. What is surprising is not the congressional demand for such an option, but the fact that it was such a feeble request (two-thirds to override), and why the Congress waited until 1958 to mandate it. In brief, the argument that the period 1947–1961 represented a "revival of protectionism" seems unfounded; it is true that the system didn't leap forward as it had done in 1934, 1945, and 1962, but nonetheless, the process of expanding the conduits of trade was a steady and deliberate one in this period.

The Trade Expansion Act of 1962 was, in a sense, the first "modern" trade bill in terms of its complexity and comprehensiveness. Kennedy asked for sufficient authority—the reduction of tariffs by 50% of 1962 rates—to eliminate tariffs as a significant barrier to trade. For the first time, the Administration requested authority to negotiate on the basis of linear reduction rather than an item-by-item basis; and for the first time, the President requested an adjustment assistance package which would presumably help industries and workers who were substantially injured as a result of increased imports. The Congress accepted these requests, but made several other major changes. A new office of the Special Trade Representative was created in the Executive Office of the President, and the power to coordinate and to negotiate U.S. trade policy was moved out of the State Department to the STR. Secondly, the Congress mandated that the President couldn't negotiate the reduction of tariffs of those products in which an affirmative determination of injury had been found by the Tariff Commission.

In 1962, the Congress enlarged its own role in trade negotiations not only by moving the Executive's negotiator out of the State Department, where the Congress perceived its influence as marginal, but also in mandating official accreditation to the MTN for two congressmen and two Senators. Moreover, the congressional option to override a President's decision on the escape clause was changed from requiring a two-thirds vote to merely a majority vote. Finally, Congress imposed its sense of priorities with regard to the direction and tempo of policy initiatives toward the Communist bloc. In this, as in the redistribution of negotiating authority, the 1962 Trade Act was a portent of more dramatic policy changes to come.

Why did the Trade Expansion Act succeed in 1962 when Jacob Viner had warned barely a year before that its chances were not good? Clearly, a high-powered Presidential commitment was an important factor, but in order to defeat the multitude of protectionist amendments offered on the floor of the Senate, two other factors were needed: Congressional leadership and cohesion, and nonlegislative concessions on textiles and timber.

The very success of the Trade Expansion Act and the "Kennedy Round" which followed its passage made a follow-on period of consolidation and adjustment inevitable. It is not surprising that observers of U.S. trade policy mistakenly described this period of consolidation as a trend toward world closure brought on by the waning economic and political hegemony of the U.S. The Burke-Hartke bill, introduced in September 1971, one month after the announcement of the New Economic Policy, appeared, from this perspective, as the first genuine assault on liberal trade since 1934. But it was more signal than sign.

The Trade Act of 1974, which delegated unprecedented authority to the President to reduce, harmonize, or eliminate tariff and nontariff barriers is inexplicable in a structuralist framework which argues that the global economy is headed toward regional blocs or closure. Clearly, the act fell on the wrong side of the "watershed." The new law increased Congress's involvement in the making of trade policy without unduly restricting or inhibiting the Executive. Indeed, the Congress drafted procedures which would make the kind of failure in repealing ASP from 1968–71 less likely. "Escape valves" which had been closed by the "success" of the Trade Expansion Act were not opened full throttle by the 1974 law, but they were made to work as intended. The Congress also improved the Executive's draft on the adjustment assistance provisions.

In summary, one can follow a distinct, consistent, and clear line from the 1934 Trade Act to its 1974 successor in the desire by the Congress for reducing barriers to trade, for empowering the President to negotiate first bilateral and then multilateral agreements, for permitting exemptions for those industries, firms, or workers which are severely injured by the impact of imports, and for gradually but determinedly increasing the powers of the Congress to oversee the administrative process to ensure that the law is executed equitably. At the same time, Congress increased its participation in the negotiating process in order to ensure that domestic law or interests would be promoted vigorously in international arenas. The nontariff, nonlegislative concessions to specific groups like the textile industry, to specialty steel, to timber, or oil are minor developments compared to the scope of multilateral trade negotiations; they are certainly not sufficiently important to justify impugning the consistency or the goal of openness of overall U.S. foreign trade policy.

The real inconsistency or paradox in U.S. trade policy is not to be found in these exceptions, but is rather in the cry-to-sigh cycle which is evident virtually every time the Congress and the President consider a major trade bill. First there is the *cry* of protectionism which economists and other internationalists raise when Legislators introduce restrictive or protectionist bills or amendments. But then, the *sigh* of relief follows the passage of a liberal trade law. An explanation of that paradox will yield clues to the policy-making process.

SIGNALLING AND THE CRY-AND-SIGH PARADOX OF U.S. TRADE POLICY

To understand the process by which U.S. trade policy has been made, one must begin with a crucial distinction, one often overlooked or obscured by those who periodically warn us of a new protectionist resurgence. The distinction is between the initiation of a bill and the passage of a law, between the emission of a signal and the commitment of a policy. A Legislator introduces a bill to send signals forcefully to different groups, governments, the executive branch or particular bureaus or departments. The purpose is to inform injured or adversely-affected groups that the Congress or a particular Legislator is listening and aware of their plaint; to signal to potentially countervailing groups the beginning of a debate on an issue which could affect them adversely; to indicate to a foreign government that the U.S. intends to pursue its interests more forcefully in international negotiations; and most importantly, to signal to the executive branch that its administrative or negotiating behavior has either not been satisfactory or not been responsive to the law's intent. A speech by a congressman, a hearing, or a committee report is just not as effective in attracting the attention of the Executive or anyone else as the introduction of a bill; the power of the Congress is therefore at its apex when it considers legislation.

The structuralist argument is not only unhelpful in explaining the development of U.S. trade policy, it is misleading. It is at the domestic, process level that one needs to seek answers to the three questions specified at the beginning of this chapter. At that level, the most useful way to visualize the process along the two critical continua of trade policy— restricted vs. discretionary authority, an open vs. closed system—is by following the interaction between the two branches of government. If this proposition is correct, then it would suggest that the contents and the contours of trade laws are less a function of the economy, of congressional behavior, of interest groups, or of bureaucratic intrigue, than the product of a legislative-executive process. Moreover, it suggests that individual actors in the policy-making process can make a difference; that there is more fluidity and free will in the process than one would think. The paradox is that the involvement of certain actors leads almost inevitably to the involvement of countervailing groups, and the resulting pattern has repeated in every trade policy cycle since 1948.

The process is as follows: suffering from declining competitiveness or severe import competition, firms, industries, and/or labor unions have petitioned the Tariff (or International Trade) Commission and the Administration for some kind of subsidy or relief. Finding these escape valves closed, and the Executive unresponsive, the groups turn to Congress and specifically to their congressman for relief. The Legislator introduces a bill which attempts to respond to the problem, and if done so in a sufficiently generalizable way, others will co-sponsor it. Hearings are held, and other groups interested in similar relief try to make the log roll. At this point, economists and free trade groups mobilize and *cry protectionism*. Foreign governments soon realize the change in the nature of the debate in the United States. They take the threat that America might close its markets more seriously. During those periods when the State Department was negotiating a readjustment of the economic policies of foreign governments, the one hand of the State Department was strengthened by the pressures of Congress, while, ironically, State's other hand was trying to keep Congress from getting involved or was slapping Congress for its irresponsibility.

At times, this is a deliberate tactic, as appears to have been the case when Secretary of Commerce Stans asked Mills to introduce a bill on textile quotas in order to demonstrate the seriousness of the U.S. negotiating position to Japan. But the strengthening of the Executive's bargaining position by congressional obduracy is a delicate tactic, for if foreign governments perceive the interaction as a part of a unified strategy, then the hand that could strengthen U.S. foreign policy becomes the hand that weakens it. In short, the Stans-Mills strategy is a risky one, particularly in the current era of public diplomacy and in issues of foreign economic policy which directly affect domestic political groups.

As the debate proceeds, and restrictive pressures become more threatening, several new developments occur. The Administration opens its escape valves; foreign governments search for ways to demonstrate their interest in maintaining a normal trading relationship with the United States; the Executive shows, in various ways, that it is listening to the Congress; some of the interest groups are satisfied, and the others, which aren't, can at least take satisfaction that the issue they raised was addressed, though at a more general level than they would have preferred. In short, the signals from Congress are received, and upon recognizing this, the congressional frustration quotient drops, and a liberal trade law is passed, or at the least, a restrictive bill fails. *A sigh of relief is heard.*

Sometimes, as in the case of the Trade Act of 1974, the bill which passes is considered "neutral" or "ambiguous" in the sense that it contains provisions, for example, on countervailing duties or the escape clause, which could be used in a protectionist manner. Still, one needs to distinguish between legislated protectionism and discretionary protectionism; the latter permits the flexibility in the administrative escape valves which could preclude the former.

This is the pattern when the system works; and that has been the case for every *major* trade law passed since 1934. The closest the system has come to breaking down in the postwar period was probably in the period following the successful conclusion of the Kennedy Round in 1967. The difficulty then was the number and complexity of international economic problems, and the doggedness of an obsolete economic system in which the U.S. was intended to play a role which no longer corresponded to economic reality. Adjustments by all the principal governments were required, but none were willing to make them. The Mills bill in 1969–70 and the Burke-Hartke bill in 1971 were clear signs of congressional frustration with this situation; at the same time, these bills were signals. The time had come, the

Congress said, for the Japanese and the Europeans to play by the same rules and acquire the same responsibilities as the United States. Given the sorry state of the American domestic economy and external balance, Congress, in short, underscored its determination to cease tolerating the exceptions granted to our trading partners. This was an interesting and instructive twist on the theory of passing hegemony, and it augers well, not poorly, for a world in which the trilateral countries become more nearly equal. The Congress was not asking for special treatment for the United States, only equal treatment; this is what I referred to earlier as the "internationalist standard."

Neither the Mills bill nor the Burke-Hartke bill passed, but they came close enough to frighten liberal traders—in the United States and in the world. In short, they functioned as motors in the governmental process, attracting attention to a problem by both sides, and forcing both sides to recognize that the status quo was no longer an acceptable option. It then encouraged the movement toward a new policy which took into account the old grievances and the new realities.

There are analogues in the administrative process to this pattern of the legislative process by which trade concerns become trade law. A recent example will illustrate the point. From 1973 to 1975, the auto industry was suffering from a glut of foreign competition, and one important cause was the reluctance of foreign auto companies to adjust their prices to the changed exchange rate and risk losing their share of the market. The result was that almost every foreign exporter was selling its cars to the United States at prices which were much lower than prices in both their home and their host markets. This was a classic case of "dumping," and the labor unions were the first American groups to express frustration at the failure of the U.S. Government to take action required by the law.

Finally, Representative John Dent of Pennsylvania, Chairman of the Subcommittee on Labor Standards, held hearings on the subject, and then on July 20, 1975, filed an antidumping petition with the Treasury Department accusing virtually every foreign auto manufacturer from almost every friendly industrialized government of dumping in the U.S. market.[2] Dent's senior staff insists that Dent was not approached by the labor unions; that, in fact, he generally acts on his own initiative, before the labor unions even think of taking action. Had Treasury found the charges to be correct, they could have assessed damages of as much as $400 to $800 per vehicle. The reaction abroad as well as among the liberal community in the United States, including the *New York Times* and the *Washington Post*, was one of sheer horror, one which increased as it appeared that Dent had a point and a

[2]U.S. House of Representatives, Subcommittee on Labor Standards of the Committee on Education and Labor, *Hearings: Impact of Motor Vehicle Imports on Employment in the United States*, 94th Congress, 1st sess., March 4, 5 and April 15, 1975, p. 118. (Hereafter Dent Hearings)

case.[3] Because of exchange rate problems and the cost of new pollution and safety equipment, which was not reflected in the price of the foreign cars, the charges were largely correct, and Dent as well as Treasury officials and the foreign auto manufacturers were aware of it.

Low-level Treasury officials had been unresponsive in supplying information to Dent before the petition was filed, but afterwards, Secretary of the Treasury William Simon personally interceded and cooperated with Dent to the fullest. "They were very responsive. The law was well enforced," said Dent's senior staff, Julie Domenick. Because no one questioned Dent's desire or ability to push the case to its legal conclusion, Treasury's bargaining power vis-a-vis the foreign auto manufacturers was enhanced, and the result was an agreement with the foreign auto manufacturers, which not only stopped the dumping, and realigned the prices, but assured the U.S. Government that these companies would seriously consider establishing production facilities in the United States. This last decision would probably have been postponed indefinitely; Volkswagen had been considering it for a decade. A shock or a prod of some sort was required for these companies to make the decision to readjust to changed economic conditions. The Congress was perfectly suited to do the prodding.

As a postscript to this case, Volkswagen, which was one of the principal manufacturers charged with dumping, decided to establish its first major plant in the United States in New Stanton, Pennsylvania. The new plant is expected to generate five thousand jobs directly and fifteen thousand to twenty thousand jobs indirectly, increasing payrolls by $160 million annually and increasing the state's yearly tax take by $14 million. It is not entirely coincidental that Volkswagen chose New Stanton, which is located in the district of Rep. John Dent. Faced with almost equal offers from Ohio and New Stanton, Pennsylvania, Volkswagen chose Dent's district,[4] for fear that if they moved to Ohio, and then decided, for example, to import engines from Germany or Mexico, that Dent would be the first one in Congress to urge legislating quotas on engines. Their respect for Dent's political influence had grown during the antidumping and trade bill struggles. The result, in the words of Dent's staff, was "a positive interplay of forces between Congress and the Treasury Department."[5]

[3]Dent Hearings, see pp. 118–119 for news articles.

[4]For these statistics, see *Newsweek*, 13 May 1976, p. 66; and George Will, "Volkswagen and Inroad of the Corporate State," *Washington Post*, 26 September 1976. Will argues that Gov. Shapp of Pennsylvania lured Volkswagen with more than $70 million of State-financed subsidies.

[5]Julie Domenick, Research Assistant to Subcommittee on Labor Standards, interview, 10 June 1976. Several other staffers argue that the Dent-factor was not decisive in Volkswagen's decision to go to Pennsylvania, but faced with a similar offer from Ohio, they admit the Dent-factor may have tipped the balance. There is little question, however, that the antidumping case was the decisive factor in finally pushing VW to make the decision to establish a plant in the United States, a decision it had been contemplating but postponing for almost a decade.

While recognizing the importance of the process by which Congress signals the Executive and others, one should not overlook several other important reasons why trade policy has been predominantly liberal and why the cry-and-sigh paradox repeats so often. When Mills introduced his bill in 1970, his intention was primarily to affect both the restrictive import policies of Japan and Europe and the Administration's escape valves, which were stuck by decision, or rather lack of decision; he was much less interested in the bill's passage. That partially explains why he and Senator Long pushed the bill right up to the end of the session, but unlike the Trade Act of 1974, which was passed in large part because of their efforts on the very last day of the Congressional session, the Mills bill of 1970 was allowed to die. The force of congressional leadership is only one of three factors which explains this policy and process. Also important are Presidential leadership and the free trade ideology.

In the legislative process, Presidential leadership is hardly confined, as constitutionalists once maintained, to State of the Union messages and to vetoes. The President resists restrictive congressional bills; he drafts and monitors the major trade messages and bills; he cajoles and pressures Congress to accept his trade policies. As Lawrence Chamberlain observed: "When the President takes a strong stand and is willing to use the weapons of persuasion at his disposal, he can compete with the most powerful economic combines on more than equal terms."[6] The President's power and influence is brought to bear on the legislative process through the various liaison offices of the executive branch; and the way in which the liaison staff relate to the two committees and to the Congress as a whole has an important bearing on the specifics and the tone of the trade policy.

Perhaps of greatest importance, however, in determining U.S. trade policy and in explaining the cry-and-sigh paradox, is the ideological underpinning of the debate: that is, the almost universal belief in the importance and the benefits of freer trade to the domestic and global political economy. In the last stage of Smoot-Hawley, 1028 professional economists sent Hoover a letter urging him to veto the bill. Instead, Hoover ridiculed the message, saying that it "was organized behind the scenes by a New York agency interested in promoting free trade."[7] He signed the bill into law.

No President after Hoover would so ignore advice from professional economists in those few instances when there was complete unanimity on a particular issue. The reason Hoover could, in good conscience, mock the economists was because he thought they were wrong. As Joan Hoff Wilson

---

[6]Lawrence Chamberlain, *The President, Congress, and Legislation*, (N.Y.: Columbia University Press, 1946) 461.

[7]Quoted in Myers and Newton, *The Hoover Administration: A Documented Narrative*, (N.Y.: Charles Scribner's Sons, 1936), 432.

pointed out in her book, Hoover thought he was signing a bill that would protect the small-businessman in America from cheap imports from Europe and elsewhere. He didn't think it would harm American exporters or world trade, and he just didn't take the threats or protests from foreign countries seriously.[8]

Since then, America's Presidents and most of her congressional leaders have made the conceptual connection between U.S. tariff barriers and U.S. exports and between economic progress and freer trade; and the unanimity on this issue is reflected in the final votes on the major trade bills, which are overwhelmingly positive. (See table 10 below.) Few Legislators can afford to be against freer trade because few disagree with the fundamental premise

TABLE 10   Congressional Votes on Major Trade Laws, 1934–74

Year	Senate		House of Representatives	
	For	Against	For	Against
1934	56	33	271	110
1937	56	23	281	99
1940	41	35	212	166
1943	59	22	340	63
1945	53	21	238	152
1948	70	18	234	147
1949	59	19	(Votes on Con-	318	69
1951	72	2	ference Bill) (voice vote)	voice vote	
1953	voice vote	(voice vote)	363	34
1954	71	3	(voice vote)	281	53
1955	75	13	(voice vote)	295	110
1958	72	16	(72–18/161–56)	317	98
1962	78	8	(voice/256–91)	298	125
1974	77	4	(72–4/323–36)	272	140

SOURCES: 1934–49, *Congressional Quarterly Almanac*, 1951, pp. 215, 259; *CQ Almanac* 1953, p. 252; *CQ Almanac* 1954, pp. 292, 296; *CQ Almanac*, 1955, pp. 123, 138; *CQ Almanac*, 1958, pp. 388, 448; 1951-62, also in *Congressional Quarterly, Congress and the Nation, 1945-64*, pp. 187-207.

[8]Joan Hoff Wilson, *American Business and Foreign Policy, 1920–33*, (Lexington, Ky.: University of Kentucky Press, 1971), pp. 87–91.

that freer trade means greater domestic and international prosperity. Because Congress accepts the main thrust of trade policy, the toughest fights and the closest votes are on specific provisions.

Economists are the reigning priests of this freer trade ideology, and at the slightest threat that the gates of their hallowed temple might be closed, they respond with great vigor and not a little exaggeration. Harald Malmgren warned of approaching trade wars in 1971;[9] Bergsten of a "crisis." But it is the force of exaggeration which makes these prophecies self-denying. To survey trade policy over the last forty years is to be surprised and somewhat awed by the number of times this cry-and-sigh cycle has been successfully repeated.

ALTERNATIVE THEORIES

In his study of the Ways and Means and Finance Committees, John Manley examined the way in which they handled trade policy since 1934, and failed to find any discernable pattern.[10] "The striking thing about Congressional trade decisions," he wrote, "is their diversity."[11] Given the decision-making patterns described in the previous sections, Manley's conclusion only demonstrates the inadequacy of congressional theories in explaining trade policy. In the course of the analysis on trade policy undertaken in the last four chapters, the interest group lens, the bureaucratic political lens, and the structuralist lens proved much more helpful in providing us with questions than with answers. Including the congressional lens, all four contributed to a richer narrative and to a more detailed understanding of the particulars of the development of each trade policy. But the overall policy, the swings from ostensible protectionism to freer trade, the opening and closing of the escape valves of the administrative processes—this could not be adequately explained by any of these three lenses. All four explain the parochialness in policy, but not the liberalness, nor the swings between both. In short, all four—bureaucratic politics, congressional behavior, interest groups, structuralism—explain one part of the whole picture very well, but only at the cost of overlooking or distorting the overall policy.

As for the particular content of U.S. trade policy, the interbranch politics lens provides substance to the process-explanation, and is helpful in explaining why certain provisions, for example, adjustment assistance or

---

[9]Harald Malmgren, "Coming Trade Wars?" Richard N. Cooper, (ed.), *Reordered World* (Washington, D.C.: Potomac Associates, 1973)., p. 45.

[10]John Manley, *The Politics of Finance*, (Boston: Little, Brown, and Co., 1970), pp. 281-91.

[11]Ibid., p. 287.

negotiating authority, were changed by the Congress and how they were changed. Over time, we noted a definite pattern and consistency to the changes recommended and pressed by the Congress, as well as those introduced by the executive. The bolder and more insensitive the Executive (i.e., if the Executive acts unilaterally, failing to consult or to anticipate congressional behavior), the more likely it will face an uncompromising or at least an aggressive Congress.

The variables and the lens which were considered most important in determining both trade policy and the policy-making process have been explained, explored, and analyzed. I have devoted perhaps a disproportionate share of space to trade policy because, with Jacob Viner, I believe that "the most important element in our economic foreign policy is our commercial policy."[12] Nonetheless, the time has come to test these hypotheses in the fields of foreign investment and foreign assistance.

[12]Jacob Viner, "Economic Foreign Policy on the New Frontier," *Foreign Affairs* 39 (July 1961): 564.

III

U.S. POLICIES ON FOREIGN INVESTMENT AND FOREIGN ASSISTANCE

7

U.S. POLICY ON FOREIGN INVESTMENT, 1960-76:

A Conceptual Overview of Host and Parent Government Policies

In the period 1960–76, U.S. policy on foreign investment, like foreign economic policy in general, did not suffer from inadequate attention. By his own admission, President Kennedy was obsessed with the flight of American capital overseas and its implications for the dollar and the prestige of the United States.[1] One of his first messages to the Congress was devoted to this issue.[2] At the same time, however, that he asked the Congress to pass on Interest Equalization Tax (IET) to stem this flight, he urged U.S. business to join with the government in channelling $20 billion to Latin America in the 1960s.

While not as preoccupied with the subject as Kennedy, Lyndon Johnson nonetheless devoted two special messages to the Congress on the issue of U.S. investment abroad, announcing first voluntary restraints on the export of capital and then mandatory controls. Similarly, the problems of foreign investment continued to concern the Nixon Administration, and his statement on U.S. policy on expropriations on January 19, 1972, is one example.

While it may not have suffered from lack of attention, U.S. policy on foreign investment, as suggested by the few examples above, did suffer from lack of definition and consistency. The inconsistency was in part due to a conceptual failure, an inability to understand the relationship between the various dimensions of U.S. investment policy.

---

[1]Theodore Sorenson, *Kennedy* (New York: Harper and Row, 1965), 454–458. Kennedy once admitted to Sorensen: "I know everyone thinks I worry about this [balance of payments problem] too much." (p. 458)

[2]"Special Message to the Congress on Gold and the Balance of Payments Deficit," 6 February 1961, in John F. Kennedy, *Public Papers of the President, 1961*, pp. 57–66.

In the early 1960s, for example, foreign investment policy was quite correctly viewed as either an adjunct or an instrument of balance of payments policy. At the same time, foreign investment policy was often viewed as a part of foreign assistance when public sources were viewed as inadequate. Later, it was attached to foreign trade policy when labor unions evinced concern about rising imports from subsidiaries of U.S. corporations that relocated and produced abroad. Only recently has it been seen as a distinct policy in itself; or more accurately, two policies.

Of course, foreign investment policy reaches back historically as far as foreign investment. This chapter and the next, however, will deal only with the period since 1960 when the issue engaged the active and ongoing attention of the Congress and the public, and the various fragments of a coherent policy began to congeal.

In this chapter, the phenomenon of foreign direct investment and its principal conveyor, the Multinational Corporation, will be defined and identified. In addition to describing the physical dimension—the growth, source, and destination—of foreign investment, there will be a discussion of the various fragments which together can be said to make up foreign investment policy. A brief review of U.S. parent or outward investment policy from 1961–72 will be the subject of the remainder of this chapter. Using the various theories described in chapter two, a more detailed analysis of the process by which foreign investment policy has been made will be undertaken in the next chapter. Specifically, the formulation of U.S. host government investment policy from 1973 to 1976 will be analyzed.

PHYSICAL DIMENSIONS

Foreign direct investment (FDI) exists when at least 10 percent of the stock of a domestic corporation is held by a foreign person or organization. If the investment is less than 10 percent, it is called foreign portfolio investment (FPI). The 10 percent threshold is an arbitrary distinction determined for statistical purposes; the important point is that FPI does not imply sufficient voting stock to have control of an organization whereas FDI does. Like the trade in goods, the transfer of long-term investment moves in both directions. Since our perspective is American policy, American investment abroad will be referred to as *outward* investment, and the foreign investment in the U.S. as *inward* investment. U.S. policy on foreign investment consists of all those measures, statements, or actions which affect the direction, flow, or composition of international investment. It consists of parent government investment policy for outward investment and host government investment policy for inward investment.

TABLE 11   Growth of U.S. Foreign Direct Investment, 1945–75
              (in billions of dollars)

Year	USFDI
1945	8.4
1950	11.8
1955	19.3
1960	32.7
1965	49.5
1970	78.2
1975	133.2

Robert Heilbroner has written that "the internationalization of production" in the postwar period due to the spectacular growth of foreign
direct investment is the most significant new development in international
economic relations.[3] As table 11 shows, the expansion of U.S. foreign direct
investment in this period, from $7.2 billion in 1946 to $33 billion in 1960 to
$133 billion in 1975, certainly justifies Heilbroner's description.

And the stock of U.S. FDI represents approximately one-half of the
world stock.[4] Since 1961, FDI has grown at a faster rate than the gross
national product of the United States or any other country, and faster still
than world trade.[5] Although U.S. exports doubled from $49.2 billion in 1972
to $97.9 billion in 1974, the latter figure represented less than a quarter of
the sales of goods produced by U.S. Multinational Corporations abroad.[6]

Fred Bergsten wrote in October 1974 that "foreign direct investment
and multinational enterprises have now replaced traditional, arms-length
trade as the primary source of economic exchange."[7] And Lawrence Krause
queried whether trade was becoming obsolete or perhaps irrelevant.[8]

The principal conveyor of U.S. foreign direct investment, accounting
for 80 percent of it, is the multinational corporation (MNC), which has been

[3]Robert Heilbroner, "The Multinational Corporation and the Nation-State," *New York
Review of Books* (11 February 1971).

[4]United Nations, *Multinational Corporations in World Development* (N.Y.: United
Nations, 1973), p. 159.

[5]Ibid., p. 14, no. 17.

[6]Chicago *International Letter*, 28 May 1976. Sales were estimated at $438 billion.

[7]C. Fred Bergsten, "Coming Investment Wars?" *Foreign Affairs* 53 (October 1974): 149.

[8]Lawrence B. Krause, "Why Exports Are Becoming Irrelevant," in Cooper (ed.), *A
Reordered World* (Washington, D.C.: Potomac Associates, 1973), 92–99.

defined in many ways.[9] A widely-accepted definition of the MNC is that of a corporation which owns or controls production or service facilities in other countries, though all the subsidiary corporations have access to a common financial, managerial, and technological resource poll and pursue a common strategy.[10]

A Senate study listed 300 corporations, which according to its definition qualified as multinational, and 200 were American-based.[11] With very few exceptions, like Shell or Lever Brothers, however, most MNC's obtain their multinationality from the many destinations of the investment rather than from their source, which are typically uni-national. Even in the European Community, for example, the 1960s saw an unprecedented number of corporate mergers to increase competitiveness and productivity, but the vast majority of these mergers involved corporations from the same country.[12]

Though MNC's have been active throughout the postwar period, they have only recently been discovered by scholars and policy-makers. The Harvard MNC project got underway in 1965; *The American Challenge* was published in 1967; and then, as if in a frenzied attempt to catch up to the phenomenon, conceptually and politically, academics, business organizations, the Congress, and the United Nations all began publishing books, organizing study groups, and delving into the policy-related questions.[13]

The first questions asked by American students of the MNC related naturally to the central concern of the American government's outward investment policy: the implications of FDI for the balance of payments. One answer to the question whether FDI hurt or helped the U.S. balance of payments was suggested by Raymond Vernon who showed with his "product cycle model" that U.S. MNC's invested abroad when the competitive edge of their exports was eroding. The choice for the MNC at that point in time was to invest or lose its market.[14] The implication was that FDI had an export-inducing effect, and thus a favorable impact on U.S. balance of payments.[15] When the AFL-CIO lead a new wave of questioners to ask about

---

[9]U.N., *Multinational Corporations in World Development*, for a selected list of definitions, pp. 118–19.

[10]Raymond Vernon, *Sovereignty At Bay* (N.Y.: Basic Books, 1971).

[11]U.S. Senate, Committee on Finance, *Implications of Multinational Firms for World Trade and Investment and for U.S. Trade and Labor*, February 1973, p. 94.

[12]Christopher Tugendhat, *The Multinationals* (London: Eyre and Spottiswoode 1971), p. 78.

[13]For a list of the congressional studies, see *National Journal*, January 17, 1971, p. 1491; for a list of international negotiations, see International Economic Report of the President, 1976, pp. 80–84.

[14]Raymond Vernon, "International Investment and International Trade in the Product Cycle," *Quarterly Journal of Economics* 80 (May 1966).

[15]See also G. C. Hufbauer and M. Adler, *Overseas Manufacturing and the Balance of Payments*, U.S. Treasury Department Tax Policy Research Study No. 1 (Washington, D.C., 1968).

the implications of FDI on employment, those who found the "product cycle model" persuasive used it to show that there would be a net gain in employment. Others, however, looked more closely at the distributional effect of foreign earned income and concluded that labor was adversely affected by FDI.[16]

This concern with the balance of payments and employment effects of U.S. direct investment abroad has contrasted with the kinds of issues which have concerned investment-receiving countries. From the host government's perspective, questions of sovereignty, control, technology, profit remittances, and productivity were of greater importance. Answers, of course, varied, but in general the most important variable was the amount of bargaining power which the host government could bring to the bargaining table. Few were prepared to argue that MNC's could do all good or no good; the extent to which they could contribute to the growth or development of the host government was a consequence of its bargaining strength and was a factor in answering these questions.[17]

The growth of foreign direct investment in the postwar period has passed through three phases. The first phase, from 1945–57, was characterized by large-scale investments in petroleum and raw materials in Latin America, the Middle East, and Canada by the U.S. and to a lesser extent by the Europeans. The second phase commenced with the beginning of the European Economic Community in 1958. Confronted by the problem of a high and uniform tariff wall around almost all of Western Europe and the opportunity of a single market, American corporations leaped the wall and invested on an unprecedented scale and volume. From 1958 to 1968, American foreign direct investment in Europe increased from $2 billion to $13 billion. By 1968, American subsidiaries in Europe were selling $14 billion worth of goods a year, or two and one-half times the value of U.S. exports to the Community.[18]

The recognition of *The American Challenge* by Jean-Jacques Servan-Schreiber ironically occurred not at the beginning but at the end of the second, predominantly American phase, and at the beginning of the European and Japanese challenge.[19] From 1966 to 1970, the rate of growth of European foreign direct investment in the U.S. exceeded that of the U.S. in Europe for the first time since World War I.[20] Between 1968 and 1970, nearly half of all

---

[16]Peggy Musgrave, "Direct Investment Abroad and the Multinationals: Effects on the United States Economy," prepared for the use of the Subcommittee on Multinational Corporations of the Committee on Foreign Relations, U.S. Senate (Washington, D.C., 1975).

[17]The report of the U.N. Group of Eminent Persons addresses itself to these questions. See U.N. Group of Eminent Persons, *The Impact of Multinational Corporations on Development and on International Relations* (N.Y., 1974).

[18]E. E. Ekblom, "European Direct Investments in the United States," *Harvard Business Review* (July–August, 1973), p. 17.

[19]J. J. Servan Schreiber, *The American Challenge* (New York: Atheneum 1968).

[20]E. E. Ekblom, "European Direct Investments", p. 17.

French MNC's were created; the comparable figures for new British and German MNC's were 29 percent and 39 percent.[21]

After two decades of what one writer described as "the almost unimpeded expansion" of U.S. MNC's, "a counter-movement" began.[22] European and Japanese MNC's searched for investment opportunities abroad, as did a number of third world corporations like National Iranian Oil Corporation of Iran and Petrobras of Brazil. The cross-cutting pattern of foreign direct investment unveiled new implications for those concerned with foreign investment policy.

CONCEPTUAL DIMENSIONS: A TAXONOMY OF FOREIGN INVESTMENT POLICY

Like foreign trade policy, foreign investment policy often appears inconsistent because it in fact represents a multitude of different policies, each pursuing quite different objectives, using different instruments on behalf of different slices of the national interest. Even though Americans have been the preeminent foreign investors in the world since World War II, the first comprehensive attempt by the government to formulate a foreign investment policy began in the summer of 1973, and the object of the study was an inward or host government investment policy rather than an outward or a general and comprehensive foreign investment policy.[23] Similarly, the OECD countries began discussions in 1973 on ways "to eliminate the distorting effects of governmental policies" on foreign investment, but it too failed to make the most preliminary distinction between host and parent government policy on foreign investment.[24]

The distinction between parent and host government investment policy is quite real and important, for policy as well as for analytic purposes; but the simple reason why it has seldom been made is that until 1973 neither was perceived by policy-makers as a conceptual unit. It is also quite understandable why a host government investment policy would be per-

[21]See James Vaupel and Joan Curhan, The World's Multinational Enterprises (Boston Graduate School of Business, Harvard University, 1973). A short article interpreting some of the data can be found in "Europe's Got Its Tentacles Too," Vision, October 1973, pp. 85–86.

[22]Rainer Hellman, The Challenge to U.S. Dominance of the International Corporation (N.Y.: Dunellen, 1970), p. xii.

[23]The CIEP study, of course, was not the first governmental study ever to deal with foreign investment, but the others, like the Straus Committee of 1959 and the Watson Committee of 1964, which will be discussed in chapters 10 and 11, dealt with foreign investment as a tool or an instrument for other purposes, generally developmental.

[24]See Business International, 12 October 1973, 323; William J. Casey, "The Rule of Law in International Economic Affairs," Department of State Bulletin, 3 September 1973, pp. 321–326.

ceived and would generate a comprehensive policy study before a parent investment policy. Compare, for example, the public reaction to the interest equalization tax with the reaction to the prospect of large investments in the U.S. by OPEC governments. Like many foreign policy-related issues, foreign investment becomes important only when it has an immediate impact at home—either in buying out American producers or in displacing American workers. Since the U.S. has been much more of a source than a recipient of foreign investment, the U.S. had much less need to formulate a host investment policy.

Probably the most important reason why host investment policy did not materialize until quite recently and parent investment policy has yet to materialize is because foreign investment has been viewed as almost exlusively a private, not a public, decision. The U.S. Government considered its role in foreign investment as completed after ratification of Friendship, Commerce and Navigation (FCN) treaties, which promise fair and nondiscriminatory treatment of foreign businesses in the signatory's country.[25] Unlike the French, whose Sixth Plan (1971–75) allocated resources for "creating multinational enterprises of French origin,"[26] the United States never deliberately formulated a parent investment policy. (Even in those cases where the U.S. government has adopted programs which promote the expansion of U.S. FDI in the developing world, such a program was more an instrument for development purposes than a comprehensive investment policy which screens investments and channels them in certain directions.)

As a result, U.S. parent investment policy was so fragmented that it is more accurate to describe it as a number of distinct policies, which sometimes touched or became entangled, but never quite meshed into a single systematic and coherent policy. These distinct policies include the following: (1) a balance of payments policy, which entailed the discouragement of an outward flow of U.S. capital; (2) a policy to the developing world which relied on private foreign investment as a supplementary tool for development assistance, but also provided guarantees, protection, and diplomatic assistance to the U.S. investor should problems arise with the host government; (3) a third country policy (The Trading with the Enemy Act) which discouraged trade with Communist countries by prohibiting exports from the subsidiaries of American MNC's; (4) a tax policy on U.S.

---

[25]Robert Gilpin argues that the postwar "Pax Americana," which provided a relatively secure and open political environment in Western Europe and most of the developing world, was a necessary condition for the expansion of multinational corporations. (Robert Gilpin, *U.S. Power and the Multinational Corporation: The Political Economy of Foreign Direct Investment* [N.Y.: Basic Books, Inc., 1975], chap. 5.)

[26]See "France Enters the 1970s," *Business International,* (Paris, Business International Co. 1970), p. 13; Charles-Albert Michalet, "France," in Raymond Vernon (ed.), *Big Business and the State* (Cambridge, Mass.: Harvard University Press, 1974), pp. 121–22.

MNC's which sometimes served to encourage, sometimes to discourage foreign investment, and sometimes was neutral; and (5) the extraterritorial application of domestic law like antitrust and securities disclosure; and (6) the use of foreign investors as overt and covert instruments of American diplomacy.

However, compared to *inward investment policy* prior to 1973, U.S. outward investment policy was coherent and consistent. While defining U.S. policy on inward investment as the "open door" and as "a welcome mat," the government has pursued a wide range of policies which include discrimination against foreign investors and sometimes outright exclusion; and these policies are administered at the state level even more than at the Federal level. While the Congress was considering more than a dozen bills to monitor, restrict, or exclude FDI in the United States, the Commerce Department in cooperation with the National Association of State Development Agencies undertook a vast program in Europe to promote investment in the United States.[27] In short, it would be just as difficult to identify a coherent host investment policy as a parent one.

While one would expect that both parent and host investment policies would naturally gravitate towards the other and toward a single standard based on "national treatment," this has not yet occurred. Indeed, after a year of holding hearings on the subject, Congress learned that the Commerce Department used different statistical criteria for defining inward than it did for outward investment.

The remainder of this chapter will provide a brief survey of those policies which could be included within a hypothetical parent investment policy in the period 1961–72. Then, I shall identify the issue of host investment policy and describe its characteristics. The policy and the process by which it has been formulated will be the subject of a more detailed analysis in the next chapter.

U.S. OUTWARD (PARENT) INVESTMENT POLICY, 1961–72

Of the six components of the outward investment policy listed above, the most controversial and influential in this period were the policy on *balance of payments* and the policy on the promotion and protection of private *foreign investment* in the developing countries.

In 1961, the governments of the Organization of Economic Cooperation and Development (OECD) agreed to a Code of Liberalization of Capital Movements. Though not binding, and subsequently criticized as "nothing

[27]*National Journal*, 10 January 1976, p. 35.

more than a general statement of intent,"[28] the code set rules for the flow of transnational investment and established a mechanism for consultation when restrictions on capital movements were felt necessary by a government. In those cases, a government was required to justify the exception and request a right of derogation before a Committee on Invisible Transactions. Much of the criticism of the code has derived from the fact that no such request has ever been denied.

In the same year, President Kennedy sent a special message to the Congress on the balance of payments and the gold problem, announcing a series of measures to stem the outflow of capital. Two years later, he urged the passage of an Interest Equalization Tax (IET) on the purchase of foreign stock by U.S. citizens. There was an obvious but unspoken irony in signing a code on the free flow of capital and passing a law which denied the margin of profit on the purchase of foreign securities, thus rendering the flow of capital theoretically unnecessary.

While fixed exchange rates prevailed, the balance of payments problem remained the envelope within which all U.S. parent investment policy was made.[29] Though not as stringent as the comparable programs of exchange restrictions undertaken by the Europeans in the early postwar period, the U.S. policy nonetheless did have a distorting influence on the flow of U.S. investment. Unlike most unilateral restrictions, however, those of the United States were not only acceptable to our trading partners; it was said to have been requested by them as a means of retaining confidence in a convertible dollar.[30] But the IET coupled with exhortations from the President was not sufficient to stem the flow of capital. Indeed, as was mentioned above, the early 1960s saw an unprecedented wave of U.S. foreign investment in Europe. One would expect, as Theodore Sorenson observed somewhat sardonically, that the sensitivity by Europeans to American investment would coincide with the interest of the United States in inhibiting the flow of U.S. capital overseas: "Every time General De Gaulle and his aides talked menacingly about keeping American investment out of Europe, Kennedy secretly wished they would."[31] But, of course, Kennedy's secret wish didn't come true.

[28]Marina von Neumann Whitman, "Leadership Without Hegemony," *Foreign Policy* 20 (Fall 1975): 149. The code was also criticized by John Culver as "lacking enforceability" and "riddled with reservations and exemptions." John Culver, "Foreign Direct Investment in the U.S.," *Foreign Policy* 16 (Fall 1974): 161.

[29]"In recent years, policy decisions in a variety of fields—credit and interest rates, price and wage guideposts, the use of aid funds, military procurement and expenditure, to name just a few—have been determined to an important extent by balance of payments considerations." In the Review Committee for the Balance of Payments Statistics to the Bureau of the Budget, *The Balance of Payments Statistics of the United States: A Review and Appraisal* (Washington, D.C.: G.P.O., April 1965).

[30]See Marina von Neumann Whitman, "Leadership Without Hegemony."

[31]Theodore Sorenson, *Kennedy*, p. 459.

In 1965, therefore, President Johnson announced a Voluntary Foreign Credit Restraint Program (VFCR) to curb bank lending and to urge business-men to reduce their foreign investment. Unlike the IET, the VFCR did not require legislative action, but similar to the IET, there was considerable congressional support and understanding of the program. Since the alterna-tive seemed to be a stringent deflationary policy, the AFL-CIO was also quite supportive. Their position in 1965 was that " . . . supervision of private capital outflows is an essential mechanism to curb balance of payments pressures without inflicting dangerous deflationary pressures on the domes-tic economy."[32]

Like the IET, the VFCR wasn't effective. The situation grew even worse as American deficits grew larger because of the Vietnam War. In 1968, President Johnson issued an Executive Order setting mandatory ceilings on foreign investment. The program was supported by the principal congres-sional leaders on international monetary policy, including Rep. Henry Reuss, Sen. William Proxmire, Rep. Wilbur Mills, and Sen. Mike Mansfield.[33]

Congress played only an indirect role in the development of this policy.The President was quite aware that the Congress would have great difficulty with the alternative to mandatory controls, which was a deflation-ary policy, and thus he narrowed his choice in anticipation of congressional reaction.

The controls were not effective in halting the growth of foreign direct investment abroad, and indeed, S. Stanley Katz, Deputy Director of the Commerce Department's Bureau of International Commerce, remarked that one misunderstood the program if one thought that was its purpose: "The program [controls on FDI] was really not designed to stop U.S. investment abroad, but to shift the source of financing for such investment from the United States to other countries—to keep the dollars from flowing from the United States."[34] But as table 12 shows quite clearly, neither the professed nor the implicit objective was achieved. In the period 1968–74 when controls were mandatory, both U.S. foreign direct investment and net capital outflows increased in absolute numbers at a much higher rate than during the previous eight years when there weren't controls.

[32]Statement of Nat Goldfinger, U.S. Congress, Joint Economic Committee, *Guidelines for International Monetary Reform*, Hearings Before the Subcommittee on International Exchange and Payments, 89th Congress, 1st sess., 1965, p. 187. I am indebted to John Conybeare and John Odell for their description and analysis of the various programs to stem the flow of capital in the 1960s.

[33]President Johnson invoked the Trading With The Enemy Act, but a Federal court found in 1973 that his action was illegal. *New York Times*, 3 March 1973.

[34]Richard S. Frank, "Improved Balance of Payments Prospect Prompts End to Controls on Foreign Investment," *National Journal*, 2 June 1973, p. 810. See also Frank V. Fowlkes, "Administration Plans Cutback in Foreign Investment Quotas," *National Journal*, 6 December 1969, pp. 268–70.

TABLE 12   Changes in U.S. Private Long-Term Investment Abroad, 1960–74
            (in billions of U.S. dollars)

	1960	1962	1964	1966	1968	1970	1972	1974
Direct investment	2.0	2.6	3.7	5.6	5.4	7.3	7.4	14.9
Net capital outflows	1.7	1.7	2.3	3.6	2.9	4.3	3.5	7.5
Reinvested earnings	1.3	1.2	1.4	1.8	2.4	3.2	4.5	7.5
Other adjustments	-.9	-.3	neg.	-.2	.1	-.2	-.6	neg.
TOTAL (including Portfolio)	3.2	3.7	6.7	5.3	7.7	8.8	13.1	17.4

SOURCE: *International Economic Report of the President*, March 1976, p. 162.

The controls had exempted Canada and established a four-tiered schedule for Americans investing abroad. One of the reasons for the multitiered schedule was to permit the flow of private capital to the developing countries. Beginning with the Marshall Plan, the U.S. Government had always encouraged U.S. businesses to invest abroad in order to supplement the flow of public capital to areas deemed important for foreign policy reasons. To promote such investment, it was felt necessary to provide political-risk insurance, and these programs were built into the International Cooperation Administration in 1948, the Agency for International Development in 1961, and since 1969, through the quasi-public Overseas Private Investment Corporation (OPIC). OPIC administers this insurance program and also guarantees loans made by commercial creditors to U.S. investors.

But there was another side to the policy of promoting foreign investment. In cases where U.S. investments were subject to nationalization or expropriation "without adequate, effective, and prompt compensation," the U.S. Government made clear its intention to assist the investor by denying the country bilateral assistance, by voting against loans in multilateral development institutions, and by threatening and often instituting harsher action. The process by which this dual policy of promotion and protection evolved was very much a legislative-executive process, but since it relates more to foreign assistance policy than to foreign investment policy, it will be dealt with in a later chapter. Just a few comments here are necessary.

Senator Wayne Morse of Oregon was not only prescient in his opposition to the Tonkin Gulf Resolution in 1964, but he also saw the problems inherent in supporting our investors overseas long before anyone else. In 1957, he remarked in hearings before the Senate Foreign Relations Committee:

> . . . I am concerned about the difficulties we seem to get into
> frequently as a result of American investments abroad, where

American companies seem to develop domestic policies in a foreign country that are embarrassing, that cause great trouble. Then after they get into trouble they come running to the American people and say, "Protect us." And too frequently, I fear, when one gets into an examination of what has happened in that country, we find that if we were a native of that country we would probably be picking on these American companies too, because of bad policies.[35]

At the same time, however, Morse recognized that the government had an obligation to its citizens abroad, to international law, and to concepts of fair play: "We must make it clear to American investors that if there is a seizure of their property they will get fair compensation. If they do not . . . we do not propose to take American tax dollars and pour them into any country."[36]

As the developing countries increased and widened their control over their national economies, particularly over those sectors like natural resources, communications, and utilities, which were often controlled by foreign corporations, the number of investment disputes increased proportionately. (The irony was that the United States and most industrialized countries traditionally reserved these sectors in their countries for their own citizens or for the government.) The problem of supporting our investors and at the same time encouraging a development process which increasingly impinged upon those very same investors was a contradiction which U.S. policy-makers never resolved, and it lead to a continuous and almost inevitable deterioration in relations between the United States and several developing countries.

On January 19, 1972, President Nixon issued a policy statement entitled "Economic Assistance and Investment Security" which boldly and aggressively stated that U.S. assistance to a government which expropriates a significant U.S. investment without making reasonable provisions for compensation will be presumed terminated "unless and until it is determined that the [expropriating] country is taking reasonable steps to provide adequate compensation or there are major factors affecting U.S. interests which require continuance of all or part of these benefits."[37]

This statement was issued after a series of expropriations and nationalizations, and at the end of a long and difficult bargaining process within the Administration on how to cope with these developments.[38] The result,

---

[35]U.S. Senate, Hearings before the Committee on Foreign Relations, *Nomination of Roy R. Rubottom, Jr.*, 85th Congress, 1st sess., May–June, 1957, p. 22.

[36]Cited in David Horowitz, *From Yalta to Vietnam* (Middlesex, England: Penguin Books, 1967), p. 224.

[37]International Economic Report of the President, 1973, p. 61.

[38]Jessica Einhorn's *Expropriation Politics* provides a case study of the bureaucratic political debate which led up to this Presidential statement.

however, was basically a restatement of the intent of the Hickenlooper amendment of 1962 on bilateral assistance and the Gonzalez amendment of 1972 on multilateral assistance. This Congressional intent was written into virtually every U.S. law, including the Fisheries Act, the Sugar Act, the generalized system of tariff preferences, and food aid (PL 480): any law which in any way could be construed as transferring resources to another country.

There is another important element in U.S. parent investment policy: the covert use of MNC's for foreign policy purposes, ranging from intelligence-gathering to political "de-stabilization." The interaction of the U.S. government and U.S. MNC's abroad is similar in many ways to the interaction of two independent actors, each trying to use the other for its own purposes. In the 1950s and 1960s, the cold war ideology, which guided U.S. policy-makers, melded neatly with the private enterprise ideology, and the MNC's could seek diplomatic assistance more openly on behalf of the "national interest" than was the case in the 1970s. Nonetheless, their strategy in the 1970s remained the same as before: to seek enough diplomatic assistance to improve the MNC's bargaining power but not too much to impinge on its bargaining autonomy. Since the government's policy was to protect the investor, the State Department often found itself acting as a lawyer on behalf of a corporate client rather than as a judge sifting the evidence and weighing the arguments of both sides on the scales of truth. Rather than interpret the MNC's case in the light of the overall national interest, as the State Department did in the period 1880–1930,[39] the department and the government in general in the postwar period often defined the national interest in terms of the grievances of the MNC.

The government also turned occasionally to the MNC for assistance in furthering a diplomatic objective, whether that be helping to "squeeze" an unfriendly regime, as in Guatemala in 1954 or Chile, 1970–73, or in securing access to important raw materials, as in Iran in 1953.

The problem of expropriation as well as the other elements of United States parent investment policy have gradually declined in importance. The foreign investment controls were gradually lifted under the Nixon Administration, beginning in 1969 and terminating in 1974, by which time balance of payments considerations had become, with flexible exchange rates, relatively unimportant. The extraterritorial application of antitrust law and the Trading with the Enemy Act were both diplomatically defused—the first by prior consultations with governments, the strengthening of the antitrust laws of other industrialized governments, and multilateral negotiations within the OECD for a harmonization of such policies. The second, the Trading with the Enemy Act, had become less contentious in the 1960s with

---

[39]See Eugene Staley, *War and the Private Investor: A Study in the Relations of International Politics and International Private Investment* (Garden City, N.Y.: Doubleday, Doran and Company, 1935).

the single exception of those foreign subsidiaries of U.S. MNC's which were required by host governments to trade with Cuba. Gradually, the State Department loosened its criteria for applying third country sanctions and allowed for exceptions for those governments which made strong cases on the basis of offended sovereignty.[40] Finally, in August 1975, the Commerce Department, which has primary responsibility for the program, announced relaxation of U.S. policies on third-country trade with Cuba.[41]

The issue of taxation of Multinational Corporations (MNC's) increased in importance in the 1970s as the labor movement made that one of its central concerns. As related in chapter 6, the AFL-CIO's ineffectiveness in its lobbying campaign against the Trade Act of 1974 coupled with its decision not to press for the strengthening of the tax provisions in the bill contributed to the decision by the Ways and Means Committee to drop the entire issue from the Trade Act. Since then, the issue re-emerged in the Tax Reform Act of 1976, though the question then was not whether all U.S. MNC's should be denied the foreign tax deferral and credit, but whether those corporations which bribed or participated in the Arab boycott should receive the tax deferral. Congress's answer was "no." The Tax Act examined foreign source income in greater detail than ever before. The taxation of income earned abroad by individuals was altered, the double tax allowance for corporations investing in developing countries was terminated, and the preferential tax treatment for American investments in the Western hemisphere was phased out.[42]

Interestingly, all sides—the Administration, the labor movement, and the MNC's—argue on behalf of the principle of neutrality of tax treatment, that MNC's should not be given special privileges nor should they be double-taxed or subject to discriminatory treatment. However, the three parties differed on whether in fact the current tax treatment, which permits deferral of taxation until earnings are remitted and permits credits on foreign taxation, represents neutral treatment. The Ford administration and the MNC's believed that it did; whereas labor believed it offers special benefits to MNC's which are not offered to domestic corporations and thus, in effect, subsidizes and encourages foreign investment.[43]

[40]See U.S. House of Representatives, Committee on International Relations, Hearings before the Subcommittee on International Trade and Commerce on H.R. 6382: *U.S. Trade Embargo of Cuba*, 94th Congress, 1st sess., May–September 1975, pp. 199–200.

[41]International Economic Report of the President, 1976, p. 41.

[42]"Tax Bill Cleared," Congressional Quarterly, *Weekly Report*, 18 September 1976, pp. 2499–2501, 2508–2511. The Tax Reform Act (H.R. 10612) was signed into law on 4 October 1976.

[43]Peggy Musgrave, "Direct Investment Abroad and the Multinationals." For a good discussion of the pro's and con's of different kinds of taxes on MNC's, see U.S. House of Representatives, Committee on Ways and Means, *Multinationals: Perspective on Trade and Taxes*, prepared for the use of the Committee by the Congressional Research Service, July 1973.

In summary, U.S. parent government investment policy remained fragmented in the period 1960–73, but even "fragmentation" is too generous an adjective for a policy which for all intents and purposes was no policy at all. It was in actual fact merely an instrument to contribute to the accomplishment of three other policy objectives: to balance our external payments; to ensure the fair, equitable, and nondiscriminatory treatment of U.S. citizens (whether as individuals or corporations) abroad; and to promote development in the poorer countries of the world. For each of these policy categories, the specific policy on foreign investment was but one of many very diverse policies. For example, in 1968, to deal with the worsening balance of payments problem, President Johnson announced a number of programs, including taxes on U.S. citizens travelling abroad, a tax on airline tickets for foreign travel, and new negotiating authority for nontariff barriers. There were many other programs, only one of which involved mandatory controls of U.S. private investment abroad.[44] Similarly, the U.S. Government has a large number of programs and strategies to ensure the fair treatment of U.S. citizens abroad; and it also has many programs to assist in the development process in poorer countries. Policies on foreign investment are just one item in these packages.

U.S. INWARD INVESTMENT POLICY

Until 1973, a host government investment policy was something other governments had; America's problem was not in formulating one for itself but in adjusting to or contending with those of other governments. Writers like Charles Kindleberger and Raymond Vernon contended that the "mercantilist instinct" or a nonrational, emotional nationalism were the explanations for governments adopting restrictive policies on foreign direct investment when economic rationality would have argued for more open policies.[45]

To be sure, industrialized governments did not unfairly nationalize or expropriate U.S. MNC's like the developing countries did; but countries as wealthy and secure as Canada, France, and Australia risked discouraging investment by legislating increasingly stringent policies which screened all foreign investments and rejected those which it deemed injurious or merely not advantageous to their national interest. And in 1973, the United States showed that it too was not immune to this nationalistic infection when a

---

[44]"Congress Rejects Most Balance of Payments Request," Congressional Quarterly, Almanac, 1968, pp. 717–719.

[45]Charles Kindleberger, International Economics, 5th ed. (Homewood, Ill.: Richard D. Irwin, 1973), chap. 7. Also see Raymond Vernon, Sovereignty At Bay: The Multinational Spread of U.S. Enterprises (N.Y.: Basic books, 1971).

slew of legislation was introduced in the U.S. Congress to screen, restrict, and in certain cases, exclude foreign investors.

The issue of inward investment is more nearly an issue of economic interdependence than that of outward investment, in the sense that the former affects a greater number of people more intensely, and therefore has a much more immediate and pervasive impact on the domestic political system. Decisions on inward investment policy require all of those trade-offs referred to in the discussion of interdependence issues in an earlier chapter: between short-term and long-term interests, domestic and foreign, economic and political, and in this case, a new dimension: State vs. Federal Government. In the course of formulating a host government investment policy, a government can view it broadly as an opportunity to adopt a policy consistent with those of other governments, or it can view it entirely as a domestic issue and adopt a policy which maximizes the short-term benefits of foreign investment to the local economy. The issue also involves questions related to the boundaries of national security in an age of growing interconnectedness: which sectors or industries should be protected from foreign investment in order to ensure national control in a period of crisis? This question is fundamental to all interdependence issues which have as their goal the freer flow of goods, capital, or people. Given that interdependence implies greater vulnerability, *at what point* does interdependence become too risky to be worth the economic benefits?

In the next chapter, we shall examine this issue in greater depth, and look more intensively at the legislative-executive decision-making process from 1973–76.

8

A POLICY ON FOREIGN INVESTMENT IN THE UNITED STATES OR AN INWARD POLICY ON INVESTMENT?

It is not impossible that there may be persons disposed to look with a jealous eye on the introduction of foreign capital, as if it were an instrument to deprive our own citizens of the profits of our own industry; but, perhaps, there never could be a more unreasonable jealousy. Instead of being viewed as a rival, it ought to be considered as a most valuable auxiliary, conducing to put in motion a greater quantity of productive labor, and a greater portion of useful enterprise, then could exist without it.[1]

—*Alexander Hamilton*

While multinational corporations are a proper focus, the behavior of nations is also a genuine part of the problem: the internationalization of production in a world of intensified national feelings.[2]

—*J. Irwin Miller, Chairman*
Cummins Engine Company

. . . the Arabs have learned a lot from us, including from the Harvard Business School. If I am still around, I will learn a lot from them. There is such a thing as expropriation.[3]

—*Rep. Wayne Hays, 1974*

[1]Cited in Detlev Vagts, "The Corporate Alien," *Harvard Law Review* 74 (1961): 1492.

[2]Comments by J. Irwin Miller, Member of the Group of Eminent Persons in U.N. Department of Economic and Social Affairs, *The Impact of Multinational Corporations on Development and International Relations* (N.Y., 1974), p. 139.

[3]Remarks by Rep. Wayne Hays in House debate and passage of Foreign Investment Study Act of 1974, *Congressional Record*, 21 August 1974, H8850.

HISTORY

"The United States has always had a policy of welcoming foreign investment," wrote the White House Council on International Economic Policy (CIEP) in 1973,[4] but history suggests a more equivocal conclusion. Two-thirds of the shares of the National Bank, which Secretary of the Treasury Alexander Hamilton successfully lobbied the Congress to accept, was owned by foreigners. Most of the Louisiana Purchase, the canals, the roads, bridges, and later the intercontinental railroad were financed with foreign capital. In the latter half of the nineteenth century, foreign corporations invested in real estate, petroleum and mineral extraction, insurance and banking, and milling and textiles. By 1914, total long-term investment in the United States had risen to $7.2 billion, or nearly 20 percent of the U.S. gross national product.[5]

The United States has not always been hospitable to foreign investors. In 1832, Americans attacked the National Banks as outposts of British imperialism. In 1887, fears were widespread that unless the government did something, the Europeans would become America's absentee landlords. The result was a proliferation of State and Federal legislation prohibiting alien ownership of land. The last xenophobic phase occurred from 1916 to 1930.[6]

Each antiforeign wave washed ashore a flotsam of restrictive and exclusionary legislation which receded slightly or became buried and forgotten in the sand, only to advance again with a new wave. The cumulative impact of successive waves is that inward investment is presently excluded or severely restricted in the following areas and industries: merchant shipping; banking and fiduciary activities; lands and minerals; electrical communications; air commerce; public utilities and the utilization of hydroelectric and atomic power.[7]

The depression and the demands of two world wars forced most European governments to liquidate much of their investment in the United States. By 1950, the stock of foreign investment in the U.S. had declined to $3.4 billion, and a dollar-short Europe was not capable from either an economic, technological, or a managerial perspective to undertake new investments. The expansion of the U.S. economy and the reinvestment of earnings of these investments rather than new capital inflows were responsible for a doubling of the stock by 1960, to approximately $6.9 billion.

[4]International Economic Report of the President, 1973, p. 62.

[5]S. Stanley Katz, "Foreign Direct Investment in the United States," in Williams Commission Report, vol. 1, p. 966. Only $1.3 billion of the $7.2 billion was in the form of foreign direct investment; the rest being in portfolio investments. U. S. Gross National Product in 1914 was estimated at $38.6 billion.

[6]For the history, see Vagts, "Corporate Alien."

[7]See Foreign Direct Investment in the United States, Report to the Congress of the Secretary of Commerce, April 1976, chap. 10. [Hereafter Commerce Report, April 1976]

In 1961, President Kennedy launched an "Invest in the U.S.A." program as a component of his balance of payments policy in order to encourage the inflow of long-term capital. The program was assigned to the Office of International Finance and Investment (later the Office of Foreign Direct Investment) of the Bureau of International Commerce of the Commerce Department, and its mission was to supply information on markets, financing, and legal matters to prospective foreign investors. The program was relatively small with a staff of only five professionals—three in Washington, one in Paris, and one in Brussels.[8]

The program didn't have much of an impact on the flow of inward investment, and in 1963, President Kennedy appointed a Task Force to be chaired by then Undersecretary of the Treasury, Henry Fowler, and including representatives of State and Treasury and from the business and financial community to "design a new and positive program . . . to promote overseas sales of securities of U.S. companies."[9] By mid-1964, the Task Force had issued its report, and Treasury used it as the basis for a bill it began to draft for the President. In his State of the Union message of 1965, President Johnson mentioned the various proposals, and on March 8, 1965, he sent the draft bill to the House of Representatives.

From the perspective of Chairman Mills and Ranking Minority Member Byrnes, the Foreign Investors Tax bill bent over so far to encourage foreign direct and portfolio investment in the U.S. as to place U.S. corporations and banks at a disadvantage. Mills said it would make the U.S. into a "foreign tax haven." Nonetheless, the Ways and Means Committee devoted two sets of hearings to the bill, and redrafted it no less than three times. On April 26, 1966, after working closely with the staff of the Joint Committee on Internal Revenue Taxation, Ways and Means Committee reported a bill which made a number of important changes from the Administration's draft. While demanding equity between foreign and domestic investment, the bill accepted certain inducements, such as broadening exemptions for foreigners from capital gains taxes and exempting certain foreign corporations from income tax rates of over 30 percent. But it also tightened some loopholes. For example, it terminated the exemption foreigners enjoyed from paying income taxes on the interest from their bank deposits. The National Foreign Trade Council opposed the changes, arguing that they might invite retaliation from other governments, but the Treasury Department had worked closely with Ways and Means Committee and accepted the changes. The bill passed the House without debate on June 5, 1966.

Senator Russell Long complained that the House had written a different bill than was originally intended: "Rather than having its purpose

[8]*National Journal,* 24 November 1973, p. 1755.

[9]For a case study of the Foreign Investors Tax Act, see David Price, *Who Makes the Laws?* Cambridge, Mass.: Schenkman Pub. Co., 1972., pp. 151–65.

the encouragement of foreign investment in the United States . . . the bill passed by the House is concerned with providing taxation of nonresident aliens and foreign corporations comparable to that of U.S. individuals and corporations.[10] Long transformed the bill into a grab-bag of unrelated provisions on medicare, campaign finance, and tax depletion amendments (on clams and oyster shells). No one thought it would pass, but perhaps because many had a stake in it, and perhaps to send signals to the House, it did. In conference, however, the Foreign Investors Tax Act which emerged in October 1966 was much closer to the Ways and Means bill.[11]

The law's impact on the inward flow of investment was not discernable. From 1966 through 1972, the average annual net capital inflow was $350 million, which was less than 10 percent of the average annual net capital outflow in the same period.[12] A policy of promoting investment by tax inducements or governmental assistance was not sufficient to overcome the disadvantage of an over-valued currency.

With the exceptions of the "Invest in the U.S.A." program and the Foreign Investors Tax Act, between 1961 and 1972 neither the Congress nor the Executive displayed any interest in the issue of inward investment. Rep. John Culver, the chairman of the Subcommittee on Foreign Economic Policy of the House Foreign Affairs Committee, held hearings in 1972 on the adjustment assistance program, which he believed could, if properly administered, help to stem the protectionist pressures. In the course of the hearings, no one even mentioned the possibility of encouraging foreign investors as a way to increase domestic employment. "It was not even a potential issue," Culver later wrote.[13] And in the executive branch, S. Stanley Katz, director of the Commerce Department's Office of Foreign Direct Investment, prepared a memo for Secretary of Commerce Peter Peterson on how to make the "Invest in the U.S.A." program more effective, but the memo was ignored. Peterson's priorities were elsewhere, and he evidently didn't believe that the issue justified a departmental let alone an interagency review.[14]

1973: TURNING INWARD FOR A NEW INVESTMENT POLICY?

If 1971 was the watershed year for U.S. monetary policy, then 1973 played a similar role for U.S. host government investment policy. It was then that the

[10]Ibid., p. 154.

[11]Ibid., pp. 151–55, 160–65.

[12]Average Annual Net Capital outflow was over $3.6 billion. (See table 47, International Economic Report of the President, 1976, 162.)

[13]John Culver, "Foreign Investment in the U.S.," Foreign Policy 16 (Fall 1974): 157.

[14]John Maffre, "Foreign Investment in U.S. Grows Slowly as Commerce Gives Priority to Commerce," National Journal, 26 August 1972, pp. 1367–72.

U.S. economy was first beginning to feel the effects of the 1971 devaluation, and in February 1973, the dollar was devalued a second time. Once competitive, European and Japanese exports were being priced out of the American market by the exchange rate changes, and foreign corporations began to consider the direct investment option. The Japanese government decided to use the $4.2 billion trade surplus, which it had accumulated in 1972, to encourage its corporations to establish production and service facilities overseas, especially in the United States.[15] Most Japanese investors looked to Hawaii and California first, but some went as far as the American Middle West in search of farm land as well as manufacturing facilities.

The devaluations also meant a relative decline in the costs of American labor, raw materials, and production. Between 1968 and 1973, the price-earnings ratio, according to Lehman Brothers, of common stocks in the United States fell an average of 37 percent. This coupled with the currency realignments made many U.S. corporations exceedingly vulnerable to foreign takeovers, and dramatic fights occurred, e.g., in 1973 for the control of the Ronson Corporation, Texasgulf, and Signal Oil and Gas Company.[16] After a decade of intranational mergers, many more European and Japanese corporations had the capability and the confidence to enter the U.S. market.[17] And enter they did. In 1972, foreign direct investment in the United States increased by $1 billion, but in 1973 and 1974, it increased by an annual average of nearly $3.5 billion.

The new investors were not exactly welcomed with open arms. While aggregate Japanese investment was insignificant—less than 1 percent of all foreign investment in the United States in 1974; before that, it was too small to be listed—the Japanese unfortunately chose to invest in the most visible enterprises, such as motels in tourist areas. Ironically, the strongest reaction to the "Japanese invasion" came in Hawaii, where they were reported to have purchased as much as 4-5 percent of the state economy.[18] A letter sent April 26, 1973 from a state representative to U.S. Senator Hiram Fong included the following passage:

> As more and more local businesses are sold to 'outsiders,' and the
> public is reacting with increased unease and isolationistic
> tendencies. . . . The intensity of feeling among Hawaii's citizens is
> such that even the possibility of increased employment and other
> economic benefits that are derived from outside investment are no

[15]*National Journal*, 24 November 1973, pp. 1753–54.

[16]Ibid.

[17]"The New Competition From Foreign-Based Multinationals," *Business Week*, 7 July 1973, pp. 56–65.

[18]See Hearings on the Impact of Foreign Investment in the United States Before the Subcommittee on Commerce and Tourism of the Senate Committee on Commerce 93d Congress, 1st sess., 1973. (Hereafter Inouye Hearings)

longer enough to quell public disenchantment. We believe this matter is of great and growing urgency.[19]

On June 25, 1973, U.S. Representatives John Dent and Joseph Gaydos introduced H.R. 8951, which was the first of many restrictionist bills designed to respond to the increased unease and to the increased vulnerability to outside pressures which Americans felt, perhaps as a result of the devaluations, perhaps due to a sluggish economy. An amendment to the Securities Exchange Act, H.R. 8951 would "protect American corporations and workers from foreign control" by prohibiting foreigners "from acquiring, directly or indirectly, more than 5 percent of the voting securities, or more than 35 percent of the non-voting securities" of any American corporation whose securities are registered with the Securities Exchange Commission. The bill was not intended to be retroactive though it would prohibit any foreigner who already owns more than 5 percent of voting stock to acquire any more. Later, Rep. Dent would speak on the House floor: "Perhaps all the Members have not paid attention to what is going on, but I have foreigners travelling all over my coal fields, buying up all the coal they can get."[20] The Dent-Gaydos bill was subsequently reintroduced with twelve cosponsors on November 6 as the Foreign Investors Limitation Act (H.R. 11265), and it was the first of many bills to bar or restrict foreign investment from various sectors of the economy.[21]

In June 1973, Peter Flanigan, Executive Director of the Council on International Economic Policy, and David Gunning, his Assistant Director, decided that the inward investment issue was one "which you could see looming on the horizon" and although "there weren't any clouds yet," they decided to organize an Interagency Task Force to study the problem and recommend policy alternatives to the President.[22] Those government departments invited to participate in the Task Force were assigned specific topics to describe current policy and make recommendations for policy improvements. The State Department was assigned visas, immigration, technological transfers, psychological impediments to investment, and implications

[19]Letter from a State Representative to U. S. Senator Hiram Fong, unpublished correspondence, Council on International Economic Policy.

[20]*Congressional Record,* 21 August 1974, H8847.

[21]For a list, description, and analysis of this legislation, see Mina Gerowin, "U. S. Regulation of Foreign Direct Investment: Current Developments and the Congressional Response," *Virginia Journal of International Law* 15 (Spring 1975), pp. 634–46.

[22]Interview with John Niehuss, then Assistant Director of the Council on International Economic Policy, October 1974; June 1976. This case study was compiled from interviews with officials and staff in CIEP, Treasury, and on Capitol Hill. For two studies on the issue, which are published, see Gerowin, "U.S. Regulation", and John Niehuss, "Foreign Investment in the United States: A Review of Government Policy," *Virginia Journal of International Law* 16 (Fall 1975): 65–102.

for multinational negotiations. Treasury was responsible for balance of payments considerations and effects of monetary changes on FDI. Other agencies participating included the Commerce Department, the Labor Department, Justice, S.E.C., and the Federal Reserve Board. The papers that were returned in August and September 1973 were of varying quality,[23] though most were little more than descriptions of the agencies' mandate for the particular issue. The Task Force slowly but inexorably moved toward acceptance of the existing policy defined as "minimal regulation of foreign investment applied on a non-discriminatory basis."[24]

Quite independent and initially unaware of the executive's interagency study, three Legislators, Rep. John Culver, Senator Daniel Inouye, and Senator Adlai Stevenson III, became interested in this issue, and began preparing their subcommittees to hold hearings on the subject either in late 1973 or early 1974. Interestingly, all three were internationalists and chaired important subcommittees dealing with some aspect of foreign economic policy.[25] All were also motivated in part by the desire to help stem any possible slide toward protectionism, or more accurately, exclusionary-ism (legislation which would exclude foreigners from certain kinds of investment). Although Sen. Inouye had "local pressures" to do something on this issue, he also adopted a very long-term, cautious approach. Culver was an ambitious young congressman with one eye on a Senate seat and the other on an issue that could attract some attention in his home state. As he explained in hearings, his constituents were not disinterested in the issue: "Citizens of my own state of Iowa have been aroused by widespread rumors of foreign interest in acquiring large tracts of farmland as well as agricultural processing facilities."[26] The staff of each Legislator contacted each other in the hope of avoiding unnecessary duplication for all three hearings, but such efforts were not productive.

An important preliminary question about a "new" issue like inward investment, which overlaps many committee jurisdictions, is which committee will be responsible for developing the policy. In such situations, the criterion seems to be interest, or in the words of one Congressional Staff, "whoever gets their teeth into the issue first." In the House, Culver

[23]See Hearings Before the Subcommittee on Foreign Economic Policy of the Committee on Foreign Affairs of the House of Representatives, *Foreign Investment in the United States,* 93rd Congress, 2d sess., January–February, 1974, pp. 201 ff. (Hereafter Culver Hearings)

[24]Internal Memorandum of the Council on International Economic Policy, 19 October 1973.

[25]Culver was Chairman of the Subcommittee on Foreign Economic Policy of the House Foreign Affairs Committee; Stevenson was Chairman of the Subcommittee on International Finance of the Senate Committee on Banking, House, and Urban Affairs; and Inouye was Chairman of the Subcommittee on Foreign Commerce and Tourism of the Senate Commerce Committee.

[26]Culver Hearings, p. 75.

scheduled hearings in his subcommittee first. The House Interstate and Foreign Commerce Committee or the Banking and Currency Committee could have challenged Culver on jurisdiction and probably won, but they didn't.

Why didn't Dent or Gaydos press these other committees to hold hearings first? Besides his concern, which was to prove unwarranted, that foreigners might buy "his" coal fields, Dent was also concerned about the Administraton's indiscriminant promotion of foreign investment at home and abroad, about the various American corporations like Ronson and Gimbel Brothers which were trying to resist foreign take-overs, and in the fall of 1973, by the energy crisis. There was apparently no legislative authority to prevent foreign acquisitions of American corporations, and with Japan's great surplus and OPEC's new wealth, there was for the first time a prospect of such a threat. According to John Culver, many of his colleagues began to ask: "Will we put a camel instead of a tiger in our gas tanks?"[27] More disturbing to Dent was that no one seemed to know anything about the issue or seemed to be studying the problem.

Dent's interest from the start, according to his staff, was simply to focus attention on the issue and obtain authorization for a complete and comprehensive study of foreign investment in the U.S. As in the trade bill and antidumping cases, his style was to stake out an extreme position as a spur to the legislative process. "How do you get attention?" was the question he put to himself and his staff, Julie Domenick, the research assistant on the Subcommittee on Labor Standards, which he chaired. Their answer: introduce an extreme bill. He would have pressed for hearings if no one else had, but that was not necessary.

Not only did his bill mobilize the Executive to speed up their schedule, but it motivated all three Legislators to hasten preparations for hearings.

The first set of hearings was held in Hawaii by Senator Inouye's Subcommittee on Foreign Commerce and Tourism to consider his bill S. 2840 which would authorize a three-year, $2 million study project of foreign investment in the U.S.

Other hearings were being prepared by Culver's and Stevenson's subcommittees for late 1973. Because the Council on International Economic Policy (CIEP) was expected to testify and present the Administration's position on the legislation, the Inter-Agency Task Force had their deadline set for them.

In December 1973, the Cabinet-level Executive Committee of CIEP met and considered the recommendations of the Task Force on inward investment. Three conclusions emerged from the discussion. First, the "open door" policy on foreign investment, subject to certain internationally-

---

[27]John Culver, "Foreign Investment in the U.S., *Foreign Policy* 16 (Fall 1978): 157.

accepted exceptions, should continue to be the policy of the U.S. This policy was also referred to as "national treatment," treating foreign investors on the basis of equality with domestic investors. Secondly, the Administration decided to oppose any congressional efforts at legislating new restrictions on inward investment for three reasons: it would conflict with the OECD Capital Movements Code; it would deny the U.S. the economic benefits of new investment; and "there is no sound economic or national security ground for additional restrictions on such investment at this time."[28] The third conclusion of the Cabinet committee was the recognition of the need for a "better system of data collection so that we can follow more closely the current amount and pattern of foreign investment in the United States."[29]

Because the committee obtained an easy consensus, the options paper was not sent to the President. Essentially, the Cabinet committee reaffirmed the status quo. They deliberately shied away from a monitoring system for fear that it might eventually lead to a screening process in which some investments would be prohibited. Many felt that just as the government had helplessly slid from a voluntary foreign credit restraint program to one of mandatory controls, the acceptance of any kind of monitoring mechanism would inevitably lead toward a restrictive and exclusionary policy.

The committee opted to improve the data collection system by way of an executive decision rather than by seeking authority from the Congress, even though it wasn't clear whether the Executive had the necessary authority to make that kind of decision. The existing authority, which CIEP Assistant Director John Niehuss wrote "would probably have been sufficient,"[30] was the Bretton Woods Agreement Act of 1945, which permitted the collection of data in response to questions posed by the International Monetary Fund. Other sources of authority, which the Executive might rely on, include the Trading with the Enemy Act or the Emergency Banking Act of 1933, both of which gave vague grants of authority to the Executive and relied on a Declaration of National Emergency, the most recent being 1950, for the Executive to be technically permitted to use it. While the CIEP Committee decided to support the Inouye bill for a comprehensive study, it recommended to the Commerce Department that it begin sending questionnaires for a new benchmark study before the passage of the legislation.

The Commerce Department was agreeable in principle. In fact, the department had planned a major new study on U.S. investment abroad, but then it cancelled it, ironically because of lack of authority. (It chose, however, not to ask the Congress for such authority, or even to request an

[28]International Economic Report of the President, 1974, 65.

[29]Ibid., 65.

[30]John M. Niehuss "Foreign Investment in the U.S." pp. 79–81.

amendment to the Inouye bill which would have permitted the study.)[31] Commerce's problem was that it didn't have the time or the manpower, but that problem was solved by the Secretary after the Cabinet committee's decision. As for the Treasury Department, they sent out questionnaires on January 1, 1974 for a new benchmark study of foreign portfolio investment.

Both studies were therefore undertaken prior to obtaining legislative authority. The Commerce Department went so far as to request in June of 1974 additional appropriations from the Senate Appropriations Committee before an authorization had passed; indeed before the various committees had even reported the Inouye bill.[32]

THE FOREIGN INVESTMENT STUDY ACT: PHASE I OF AN INWARD INVESTMENT POLICY

The decisions made by the CIEP Executive Committee were conveyed to the Congress in the testimony of the CIEP Executive Director, Peter Flanigan, to Stevenson's Subcommittee on International Finance on January 23, 1974 and to Culver's Subcommittee on Foreign Economic Policy on January 29, 1974. Flanigan said that he felt the "recent concern over direct investment is largely unjustified," although he did acknowledge that more studies were necessary and therefore "welcomed" Inouye's bill.[33]

In his remarks, Stevenson effectively set the tone for the hearings and outlined the perspective he hoped Congress would adopt as it approached the issue of inward investment:

> I, and I think all· of the members of this committee, approach trade and investment with your bias toward free exchange of goods, money, and investment. But, as you acknowledge, the world is changing very rapidly, and anytime we dig in and say the world is changing but our policy isn't changing, I think it is time we take a look.[34]

Stevenson followed up his introductory remarks with a series of very incisive questions. Why, he asked, couldn't we use our investment policy as

---

[31]Interview with John M. Niehuss.

[32]U. S. Senate, State, Justice, Commerce, the Judiciary and Related Agencies Subcommittee on Appropriations on H. R. 15404 for Appropriations for FY 1975, May 29, June 4–6, 11, 12, 1974., p. 632.

[33]Hearings on Foreign Investment in the United States before the Subcommittee on International Finance of the Senate Committee on Banking, Housing, and Urban Affairs, 93rd Congress, 2d sess., January 1974, pp. 10–11. (Hereafter Stevenson Hearings)

[34]Ibid., p. 11.

a lever to get other industrialized governments to lower their barriers and restrictions to U.S. investment? Flanigan answered that the administration was trying to accomplish this objective in the OECD discussions.

Perhaps, Stevenson said, the United States should adopt "a screening device," which several other governments had, and which, at the least, held "out the possibility of exercising some control." Flanigan said that such a device would discourage foreign investment and might lead other governments to believe "that we are moving towards some kind of restrictions." What about an overall investment policy which encouraged the flow of Arab and other money and channelled it into areas and sectors where it would be most beneficial to the American economy? Flanigan again responded that he thought this would discourage investment and that "the operation of free market forces in determining the direction of world-wide investment flows will maximize the efficient use and allocation of capital resources in the international economy."[35]

Stevenson asked whether the U.S. Government could stop investment which might not be in the national interest. Flanigan said that there was sufficient authority, and that it was "unrealistic" to think that the Arabs, for example, could undertake such investments. Senator J. Bennett Johnston of Louisiana, however, pursued that point, saying that "we ought to take steps to guard against the manipulation of U.S. markets,"[36] and that "we need to anticipate all these things . . . "[37] While Flanigan agreed that "we have to hope for the best and prepare for the worst," he insisted that " . . . on the basis of the facts as they exist today, we don't think that it would be appropriate to put in a restrictive mechanism . . . "[38] Stevenson decried the "tendency . . . to treat disclosure as a restriction."[39] But Flanigan clarified his remarks by saying that he was in favor of more information, but he opposed "a screening device."[40]

At the most basic level, what the Congress did was ask questions publicly which the Executive had asked privately. The issues remained the same, but the answers, or rather the inferences, which the two institutions drew from the facts of the situation were somewhat different; and thus the policy prescriptions were also somewhat different.

The hearings conducted by Culver and his subcommittee were not, however, very different from those of Stevenson's subcommittee or those of Inouye's Subcommittee on Foreign Commerce and Tourism, which held

[35]Ibid., p. 4.
[36]Ibid., p. 19.
[37]Ibid., p. 22.
[38]Ibid., p. 20.
[39]Ibid., p. 22.
[40]Ibid., p. 23.

hearings in March 1974 and reported the Foreign Investment Study Act of 1974 to the full Senate. The first question was the simple, factual one: how much foreign direct investment was there in the United States? The Department of Commerce computed $14.4 billion, but that was based on a benchmark study originally done in 1959, which required reports from only 450 foreign corporations. And the criterion for determining FDI in the United States was that a foreigner must own 25 percent of a firm's equity. (The Commerce Department promised Congress that it would promptly harmonize the criterion used for determining both inward and outward foreign investment so that both were 10 percent.)[41] Culver's subcommittee had commissioned a study by Jeffrey Arpan of Georgia State University and David Ricks of Ohio State University, and that study had estimated that the amount of inward investment (i.e., foreign direct investment in the United States) was closer to $38 billion.[42] Even by Commerce Department admission, the government's data was hopelessly "out of date" and "subject to a significant margin of error."[43] Similarly, the benchmark study for foreign portfolio investment in the U.S. had not been updated since 1941, and both Inouye and Culver agreed after independently consulting with CIEP's staff that it might be appropriate to have the two studies done separately, on FPI by Treasury and on FDI by Commerce. In brief, the simple factual question did not yield a similarly simple or factual answer.

After asking about the facts of inward investment, congressmen were naturally curious about the policy. They were surprised to find that it was not only incoherent, but that the best one could call it would be a "patchwork."[44] U.S. policy ranges from one of "affirmative" inducements to outright discrimination and prohibition, and is administered by dozens of offices at the federal, state, and local levels. Let me briefly review these policies, distinguishing between those statutes and policies which exclude, restrict, and impede inward investment and those which encourage and promote it.[45]

---

[41]On 5 February 1974, Flanigan first told Culver that the Commerce Department wanted to change the criterion to 20 percent in both directions. Finally, the Inouye-Culver bill mandated the 10 percent criterion for both directions, and that was implemented in January 1975.

The problem with several categories of foreign investment, for example real estate, is that individual states often keep the data, and their criterion for defining foreign investment sometimes approaches the amusing. For example, Iowa defines a foreign investor as any citizen or corporation who owns land or property in Iowa but is not from Iowa. (See Culver Hearings, pp. 117–118.)

[42]Ibid., pp. 2–4.

[43]*Survey of Current Business*, U.S. Department of Commerce, Office of Business Economics, February 1973, p. 29.

[44]Culver, "Foreign Investment in the U.S.", p. 160.

[45]See Commerce Report, April 1976, vol. 1, pp. 141–68.

Restrictions

Most OECD governments have signed Friendship, Commerce, and Navigation Treaties (FCN) with the United States which set forth the rights of citizens to do business in both countries on the basis of "national treatment," that is treatment no less favorable than that accorded nationals and firms of the host country. Nonetheless, most of the governments accept that there are certain sectors which are appropriately excluded from this national treatment. These include merchant shipping, banking and fiduciary activities, natural resources, radio and electrical communications, nuclear energy, hydroelectric power, mining on federal lands, domestic air transport, and defense-related industries. Foreigners are permitted to own stock in firms which engage in some of these activities, providing they don't have control. In other sectors, such as natural resources, aliens are permitted to own the corporation providing that it is chartered in the United States. In radio and electrical communications, firms can only obtain licenses from the Federal Communications Commission if Americans own at least 80 percent of the firm, control it, and exclude all foreigners from their Boards of Directors.

Banking and fiduciary activities have been considered a "sensitive" sector since Alexander Hamilton drafted the first National Bank Act in 1791. Hamilton astutely balanced America's need for foreign capital with her demand for domestic control by permitting foreign ownership of stock but forbidding foreign management and voting rights. Attitudes towards foreign banking have always been subject to the most extreme changes. In the 1920s, virtually all foreigners were driven out of banking, and it was only in the postwar period, when Europeans began applying pressure on America's international banks, that several large states like California, New York, and Illinois relaxed their laws to permit foreign banking subject to special provisions, including reciprocity.[46]

Though barred from many states, foreign banks were permitted to establish branches in more than one state and were not subject to the jurisdiction of the Federal Reserve System, and as such, they had an advantage which domestic banks didn't have. In addition, they were permitted to combine commercial banking with investment banking, which was not permitted to Americans.[47]

---

[46]For a good history of foreign banking in this country, see Joint Economic Committee, "Foreign banking in the U. S.," Paper No. 9, 89th Congress, 2nd sess., 1966; and Fred Klopstock, Foreign Banks in the U. S.: Size, Scope, and Growth in Operations (N.Y.: Federal Reserve Bank, 1973).

[47]When the Congress began to consider the International Banking Act of 1976 which would harmonize U. S. domestic laws as they apply to both domestic and foreign banks, German banks were so disturbed that they threatened to retaliate on American banks in Germany. See New York Times, 31 August 1976, p. 37.

The Defense Industrial Security Program (DISP) scrutinizes foreign ownership, control, or influence over firms which are engaged in U.S. Government contracts involving classified information, and can deny a "facility security clearance" if it believes that classified information can be compromised. But this is the extent of controls over the defense industry; there is no federal legislation which directly prohibits alien investment.[48]

Impediments

Though not discriminatory, there is a body of law on antitrust, securities regulations, and taxes, which by being more vigorous, constraining, or stringent than most foreign laws is viewed as an impediment to foreign investment. The Securities Exchange Act of 1934, for example, requires an investor acquiring more than 5 percent of the stock of a public corporation to file a report with the Securities Exchange Commission.

State Laws

There are many state laws which prohibit foreign ownership from various businesses or sectors. The judicial conflict in 1973 between Texasgulf and the Canadian Development Corporation, for example, was based on a Texas law which required the dissolution of a Texas corporation when foreign ownership exceeds a certain level. More than half of the states have restrictions on alien land ownership.[49]

Other state restrictions have not been subject to any comprehensive codification or analysis, and so it is difficult to judge their extensiveness. The question of the constitutionality of such statutes is an important one, though it hasn't yet been adequately addressed. Detlev Vagts, in an important article on inward investment, inferred from previous court decisions that the Supreme Court would invalidate state legislation which discriminates against foreign investors unless the state has a valid case that its restriction is connected directly with the "legitimate national interest."[50]

Incentives to Investment

Though the Federal Government has maintained an "Invest in the U.S.A." program since 1961, the principal promotional efforts and the principal material inducements emanate from the states. Many states offer packages for foreign investors, which include low-interest loans, tax exemptions, state subsidization for research and development, free technical advice, and University-sponsored feasibility studies.

[48]Commerce Report, April 1976, vol. 1, p. 151.
[49]Ibid., p. 183.
[50]Vagts, "Corporate Alien", p. 1486.

Restatement of Policy

In the light of the wide range of policies bearing on inward investment, the simplistic statement that foreign investment is welcomed and treated equally is clearly inadequate. Foreign investment is subject to deliberate, discriminatory exclusion from certain sectors and industries. However, many of the impediments and regulations which annoy foreign investors, such as antitrust, securities disclosure, and environmental standards, are not intended and do not in fact discriminate against them. The rules apply equally to domestic business. On the other hand, the Federal Government as well as most State governments devote a good deal of time, money, and effort to attract foreign investment for the purposes of generating income, employment, capital inflow, increased competition, and transfer of technological and managerial skills.

Short of using the Trading with the Enemy Act, however, the President doesn't have the authority to prohibit an investment. And local incorporation is only one of many paths a foreign investor could follow to circumvent most of the exclusionary laws.

During the hearings, Congress in its committees discussed and discovered these policies, although the learning process was hardly comprehensive or systematic. In fact, Congress necessarily relied on the Executive to point out the various holes in existing policies; but their reliance was misplaced. When the Executive found such holes, which was rare, they were more apt to ignore them, paper over them, or patch them up by bureaucratic decision than by informing Congress or seeking a legislative mandate. As a supplement but hardly a substitute to the executive's information, Culver's Subcommittee on Foreign Economic Policy requested and received from the Foreign Affairs Division of the Congressional Research Service a study of the host government investment policies of several other industrialized countries for comparative purposes.[51]

What was the role of interest groups in the legislative process? Basically, interest groups were not very interested in the issue of inward investment. With a few exceptions, the congressional staff found themselves pushing interest groups more than they were being pushed. The AFL-CIO didn't have a position on the issue until February 1975, four months after the President signed the legislation. The U.S. Chamber of Commerce, however, organized a Task Force on the issue in August, 1973 and within three months, their report was issued and accepted by their Board of Directors. Their position was stated in testimony before the Stevenson

[51]*International Trends in the Regulation of Foreign Investment, a Report prepared for the Subcommittee on Foreign Economic Policy* by the Foreign Affairs Division of the Congressional Research Service, Library of Congress, reprinted in Culver Hearings, pp. 375–468.

Hearings: "We welcome the recent increase in the flow of capital and technology into the United States from foreign sources. These inflows promise to be of great benefit to the American economy. They should be encouraged by the business community and the Government and kept free of new Government controls or other restrictive policies, save in exceptional cases where there is a clearly established overriding national interest consideration."[52] The National Farmers Organization opposed FDI in agriculture, but they did so because they favored family farms and opposed all absentee corporate ownership.[53]

Culver discovered that, contrary to press reports, the Japanese had not invested in farm land in Iowa or anywhere else. Several Japanese corporate representatives had visited the Midwest, but had chosen not to invest because they weren't certain they had the necessary expertise, and they were very sensitive to the U.S. reaction to their investment.[54]

While the three internationalist-oriented committees were holding hearings, the congressional docket was being filled with a great number of restrictionist bills. Representative Robert Roe (D-N.J.) with twenty-five cosponsors introduced two bills, H.R. 13897 and 13898, to establish a Foreign Investment Control Commission to bar alien ownership in areas deemed vital to U.S. economic or military security, and to provide for a Joint Committee of Congress to oversee executive action on this issue. Senator Harrison Williams introduced a bill which would give the President a veto over undesirable investments. Rep. Henry Helstoski's bill would prevent OPEC from gaining control over the U.S. energy industry, and there were many other bills which called for stricter supervision and potential veto power over investments in energy and defense-related industries.[55]

With the added pressure of the restrictionist bills and the added knowledge of the Hearings, the Subcommittee on Foreign Economic Policy voted unanimously to send H.R. 15487, the Foreign Investment Study Act, to the full Committee on Foreign Affairs, which reported it out favorably on July 9, 1974. The report briefly reviewed the information compiled in the hearings, and concluded: "Given the existing data base and in the context of the implications for the overall U.S. economy, the administration's policy is probably appropriate, as there is no existing information indicating serious adverse effects."[56] But the Committee also insisted that the policy should "be kept flexible" until "the hard questions" which the "administration's policy fails to answer" are addressed satisfactorily. These questions, which

[52]Stevenson Hearings, p. 129.
[53]Culver Hearings, pp. 59–63.
[54]Ibid., pp. 41–45, 71.
[55]Gerowin, "U.S. Regulation", pp. 634–646.
[56]House Foreign Affairs Committee, House Report pp. 93–1183, 9.

were listed in the report, were largely empirical questions, like "how much of the timberland on the west coast is owned by foreign interests? Are foreigners buying up large stocks of land?" There were also a few judgmental questions, which the Committee urged the Administration to address.[57]

The bill was a virtual copy of the Inouye bill calling for a $3 million, 2½ year benchmark study of Foreign Direct Investment by the Commerce Department and Foreign Portfolio Investment by the Treasury Department.

The companion bill in the Senate, Inouye's S. 2840, had been favorably reported by the Senate Commerce Committee on May 8, 1974. It too stressed the inadequacy of existing information. On June 13, the bill was considered and passed the Senate by voice vote.

Many more voices were raised in the House. The Rules Committee allocated one hour for debate, giving thirty minutes to Culver, the bill's primary sponsor, and thirty minutes to James A. Burke, who was in favor of a more restrictive bill. Culver began by explaining the bill. Its purpose was simply "to develop a firm and reliable data base from which both the Congress and the Executive can derive responsive and responsible policy recommendations." He expressed some fear of the giant "overhanging oil surpluses" and some hope that a future screening process, which almost all industrailized countries other than the United States had, would help guide these funds to make a more positive contribution.[58]

During the debate, mention was made of a number of other bills, which involved foreign investment in certain sectors. For example, the House Banking and Currency Committee had begun work on the International Banking Act which would, among other things, eliminate the advantages which foreign banks had over domestic banks. Mention was also made of the Deepwater Ports Act, which would have excluded foreigners from any ownership or control over the new deepwater ports which the government would finance. These various bills did not have a coordinating focus in Congress. Indeed, neither Culver in the House nor Stevenson or Inouye in the Senate were aware of the many bills which had a direct bearing on the issue. The coordinating focus for the diverse legislation on the subject was not in Congress but in the Executive. CIEP followed the bills and tried, to the extent that a small staff could, to ensure that an overall consistency was preserved. CIEP's strategy, however, was not to build a congressional consensus or even a coalition for a new policy, but rather to specifically address each bill solely within the context of the committee that was handling it.

There were many who favored much more stringent legislation but acknowledged that a study which provides essential data was preliminary to

[57]Ibid., pp. 9–10.

[58]For the House debate and passage of the Foreign Investment Study Act of 1974, see *Congressional Record*, 21 August 1974, H8839–54.

consideration of such bills. For example, Rep. Young of Florida called the
Act "imperative . . . because it will tell us exactly what is going on and
enable us to make a decision as to how much of America has been sold to
foreign interests. We must have this information and fast if we are to protect
the independence and security of our economy. We must not allow America
to be sold to foreign investors, and we must not allow a controlling interest
to pass into foreign hands. I only wish we had the necessary information
today, so that we could take more direct action now against heavy foreign
investment."[59]

Thus, when Rep. Dent introduced an amendment which would reduce
the time for the study from thirty months to eighteen, it was easily adopted
over the objections of both Rep. Dante Fascell of the House Foreign Affairs
Committee and Culver who insisted that Commerce and Treasury had
originally asked for three years, but they had reduced it to two and one-half.
Said Dent: " . . . unless we cut the time down [for doing the study], by the
time this report comes in we will have lost the greater portion of whatever
amount of minerals and mineral lands that can be bought by foreign
countries."[60] But even Dent made clear that his purpose was not to bar the
American door to foreign investment, but to provide the same treatment
that other nations provide U.S. investors. "No other nation," he said,
"allows the purchase . . . of their minerals" to the extent that the U.S.
does.[61]

There was growing concern about Arab investors. One congressman
inserted a newspaper article entitled "Arab Investors: As Oil Money Pours
in, Mideast Lands Search for Places to Put It." But Rep. Wayne Hays, not one
to be outwitted by Arabs, commented on this issue: " . . . the Arabs have
learned a lot from us, including from the Harvard Business School. If I am
still around, I will learn a lot from them. There is such a thing as
expropriation."[62]

There was an interesting consensus among those who debated the act.
All agreed that some restrictions might be necessary, but all also agreed that
such decisions should await the outcome of a comprehensive study. It was
"interesting" because there was already enough data and enough information
on present policies to permit rational and responsible decisions on altering
present policies. For example, the points which Stevenson had made in his
exchange with Flanigan were equally valid whatever the dimensions of the
investment. One could predict that the new benchmark study would find a
greater volume of FDI and Foreign Portfolio Investment (FPI) than present
estimates; why not, therefore, make some decisions about screening and

[59]Ibid., p. H8843.
[60]Ibid., p. H8847.
[61]Ibid.
[62]Ibid., p. H8850.

monitoring based on the lower estimates? The explanation lies in the Congress and in the legislative-executive process.

There were only about four or five Congressional Staff who were responsible for conducting the hearings, for generating the data and information on the subject, and for explaining it to the staff of other Legislators. As the issue attracted increasing attention, and it became known that of all the bills on the issue, the Inouye-Culver bill was the most likely to pass,[63] these core staff found their time increasingly filled explaining the bill to the press and to other staff and criticizing other bills. They found less and less time to look into other questions or probe deeper into those questions which had concerned them in the beginning. In short, their public relations role had overtaken their role as public policy thinkers and makers.

This significant constraint on their time had an immediate impact in the way in which they related to the executive branch. Since, as Stevenson put it, both sides were internationalists, there was always a harmonious relationship, and the Executive did provide some useful and important information. For example, the idea that the study should be divided between the Treasury, which would have responsibility for FPI, and the Commerce Department with responsibility for FDI came from the Executive and was readily accepted by Inouye's staff. But as the exchange during the hearings indicated, the Congress was more interested in improving on the existing laws and policies so as to maximize the beneficial impact of foreign investment, and the Executive was primarily interested in keeping the Congress from doing anything more than authorizing a study bill. Without an alternative source of information and research and with inadequate amounts of time to lobby the Legislators on the importance of major additional changes (assuming they found such changes necessary), the staff found themselves fully occupied trying to get the bill passed, with no time to push the bill forward an additional step, for example, toward setting up a more permanent reporting or monitoring system.

Also, the Legislators were reluctant to fight the executive on the issue of where to lodge responsibility for the study. In the hearings before the Stevenson Committee, C. Fred Bergsten from the Brookings Institution recommended that the study be undertaken by a nongovernmental organization.[64] And Rep. Joseph Gaydos queried on the floor of the House: "Does anyone here expect the Department of Commerce to come up with any other conclusion than that foreign investment in the U.S. is all to the good?" He urged the Congress to undertake the study or give it to an organization that would report directly to the Congress.[65] But the Executive had already begun the studies and had even obtained funding from the Appropriations

---

[63]Interviews.

[64]Stevenson Hearings, pp. 77–84.

[65]*Congressional Record*, 21 August 1974, p. H8850.

Committees, although this was not widely known in the Congress. Treasury and Commerce, after all, had the resources and facilities, had done these studies in the past, and would most likely be responsible for doing the studies in the future. The Executive argued successfully for continued control.

The House adopted the Senate bill and added its changes in the form of amendments. These changes gave the Executive more statutory authority to obtain information from investors while at the same time permitting more confidentiality. The final report would be due eighteen months after signing the act, but an interim report would be due in twelve months. The House then passed the bill 324 to 29, and sent it back to the Senate, which concurred in the House amendments on October 9, 1974.

President Ford signed the Foreign Investment Study act (PL 93-479; 88 Stat 1450) on October 28, 1974 and issued the following statement:

> As I sign this act, I reaffirm that it is intended to gather information only. It is not in any sense a sign of a change in America's traditional open door policy toward foreign investment. We continue to believe that the operation of free market forces will direct worldwide investment flows in the most productive way. Therefore my administration will oppose any new restriction on foreign investment in the United States except where absolutely necessary on national security grounds or to protect an essential national interest.[66]

PHASE II: THE OPEC THREAT AND OPPORTUNITY

As the implications of the quadrupling in the price of petroleum became more widely understood, concern over Arab investment in the United States increased. Early studies by the World Bank estimated that OPEC would amass as much as $650 billion in surplus by 1980,[67] and as Senator Howard Metzenbaum pointed out, the Arabs could then "buy 100 percent of all of the stock of all of the companies listed on the New York Stock Exchange."[68] Another World Bank study released in the summer of 1974 estimated that the Arab governments would have accumulated $1.2 trillion by 1985.[69]

[66]International Economic Report of the President, 1975, 47.

[67]Paul Lewis, "Welcome Mat for Foreign Investment," National Journal, 10 January 1976, p. 36.

[68]Hearings before the Subcommittee on Securities of the Committee on Banking, Housing, and Urban Affairs, U. S. Senate, Foreign Investment Act of 1975, 94th Congress, 1st sess., on S. 425, March 1975, p. 58. (Hereafter Williams Hearings)

[69]National Journal, 31 August 1974, p. 1310. These estimates were revised downward significantly by early 1975 to $200–250 billion by 1980, less than half of the original estimate. See Gerowin, "U.S. Regulation", p. 624.

Moved by this dramatic shift in the economic balance of power, several Senators pushed the debate on foreign direct investment in the United States into a second phase even before the first, symbolized by the Foreign Investment Study Act, was completed.[70] On August 22, 1974, the day after the House passed the benchmark Study Act, Senator Metzenbaum sponsored with Senators Inouye, Stevens, Allen, Cranston, Huddleston, Humphrey, Metcalf (Mont.), and Nunn a bill, S. 3955, which would establish within the Department of Commerce a Foreign Investment Review Administration to conduct a continuing review and analysis of foreign investment in the United States (rather than the one-shot benchmark study) and to require a series of reports, which would contain specified information mandated by the Congress and would be published periodically.

While the Administration publicly opposed the Metzenbaum bill for the same reasons it opposed any legislation stronger than a study act,[71] CIEP privately responded to the congressional concern by organizing two new study groups. The first was jointly organized with the Office of Management and Budget (OMB) to survey all the agencies which collected data on foreign investors and to review the existing reporting requirements with the purpose of determining whether these requirements were adequate.[72] Using the data and the report written by this OMB/CIEP survey, a second high-level policy review was conducted beginning in late 1974 and continuing into the spring of 1975. Unlike the first review, which was completed in December 1973 and had addressed the more general questions about inward investment, the second one was more concerned with the question of private and government investment from the OPEC countries, and whether the U.S. government had adequate safeguards to defend against investment which might jeopardize the national interest.

The conclusions of this policy review were not much different than those agreed to one year earlier. First, existing safeguards were deemed sufficient. Second, there was no need for restrictive legislation, but there was a need for legislation which would reveal the true or "beneficial" owners of securities, so that accurate data could be collected on the magnitude of inward portfolio investment. This requirement, however, would have to be written and implemented in a nondiscriminatory manner so that it applied equally to domestic and foreign investors. Thirdly, the

[70]It should be noted that the fear of being purchased by the Arabs was hardly unique to the United States. Most of the industrialized countries, which had considered their policies basically liberal and nondiscriminatory, began concerted reviews of these policies in the light of OPEC's new wealth. (See U. S. Commerce Department, Interim Report on Foreign Direct Investment in the U. S., October 1975, vol. 1, pp. 86–89.)

[71]Williams Hearings, p. 58. See also Niehuss, "Foreign Investment in the U.S."

[72]Joint Report of the Council on International Economic Policy and the Office of Management and Budget, *United States Government Data Collection Activities with Respect to Foreign Investment in the United States* (1975).

committee decided that several minor administrative actions to implement these decisions would be necessary.

The conclusions and the administrative actions were announced in testimony given by Undersecretary of the Treasury Jack F. Bennett before Senator Harrison Williams's Subcommittee on Securities of the Senate Committee on Banking, Housing, and Urban Affairs. The Williams Hearings were held to consider a bill, S. 425, the Foreign Investment Act of 1975, which Senator Williams introduced on January 27, 1975 with seven co-sponsors to address the same issues which the Executive had just reviewed. The legislative answer also came in three parts: the bill required the disclosure of the beneficial ownership of all equity securities in order to assure effective reporting of all inward investment; it required all foreign investors to notify the SEC and the President *before* acquiring 5 percent or more of the securities of a corporation; and it established a straightforward and usable procedure by which the President could prohibit such a transaction if "he deems it appropriate for the national security, to further the foreign policy, or to protect the domestic economy of the United States."[73]

Bennett opposed the bill because he felt administrative monitoring was sufficient, and that "new legislation would not provide any significant additional safeguards, but would, in practice, be likely to deter a substantial amount of beneficial investment in the United States."[74] The monitoring system which he sketched in his testimony was implemented by Executive Order 11858 on May 7, 1975, establishing a high-level Committee on Foreign Investment in the United States (CFIUS). This committee would serve as the watchdog over new investments, as a focal point for policy-making on the issue, and as a consultative mechanism with foreign governments on major investments. Chaired by Edwin Yeo, Undersecretary of the Treasury (replacing Bennett), the CFIUS included the Assistant Secretary of State for Economic Affairs, the Deputy Secretary of Defense, the Undersecretary of Commerce, the Executive Director of CIEP, and the Assistant to the President for Economic Affairs, L. William Seidman.

The committee didn't have the power to reverse an investment, but Bennett felt that the power of review and publicity would be sufficient, and if it weren't, the President could invoke the Trading with the Enemy Act to prevent an investment. Since the government had already begun consultative procedures with various OPEC countries, including Iran and Saudi Arabia, and gained their assurance that they would "consult in advance of major direct investments," they felt that "legislation to deal with foreign investment is not necessary at this time."[75] The same Executive Order also

---

[73]Williams Hearings, p. 1.

[74]*Ibid.*, p. 26.

[75]Niehuss, *Foreign Investment in the U.S.*, pp. 94–95.

established the Office of Foreign Investment in the U.S. to be located in the Domestic and International Business Administration of the Department of Commerce to work with the OMB/CIEP Review to devise an improved data collection system on inward investment and then report periodically on the number and nature of foreign investments.

Many of the Senators found themselves frustrated by the comments of administration officials. Senator Williams, upon opening the hearing, said:

> In light of the Arab boycott, I find it just short of incredible that Secretary Simon and his assistant, Mr. Parsky, have been so myopic as to claim there is no danger of Arab investors using their U.S. investment for political purposes or in a way detrimental to fundamental national commitments.

> Surely among the most naive statements of recent times was Mr. Parsky's pronouncement that based on personal assurances from Arab leaders he had every reason to believe they intend to be responsible investors in our economy. It preceded by less than one month the Arab attempt to force Lazard Freres out of a U.S. underwriting syndicate.

> I am afraid I simply cannot share the administration's complacency. The Arab boycott of firms such as Ford, Coca-Cola, Kaiser, Motorola and NBC has chilling implications . . . [76]

The Administration's new review mechanism obviously didn't have the power to do what Senator Williams and many others believed was necessary, but the Administration clearly chose this mechanism as a compromise between doing what it preferred, which was nothing, and getting the congressional bill, which would grant the President the power to veto new investments. The Administration accurately believed that the establishment of the committee would be viewed by many Legislators as sufficiently accommodating to defuse enough of the congressional criticism to either impede or halt the movement toward a legislative answer.

The Administration's laissez-faire approach found some support among business groups like the National Foreign Trade Council, Inc. and the U.S.

---

[76]Williams Hearings, p. 3. Parsky's Deputy Assistant Secretary John Niehuss, who had formerly chaired the CIEP Interagency Task Force, also wrote, "General experience to date with OPEC government investment behavior suggests that they are not motivated primarily by political purposes . . . " (p. 100) He was, of course, referring to the experience of OPEC short-term investment in the U.S. for the two years following the quadrupling in the price of petroleum, but the inference that the future would imitate the past largely ignored the oil embargo of 1973–74 whose purpose was explicitly stated by the Arab member of OPEC to be political and diplomatic; it also overlooks the boycott against American firms doing business with Israel. For an article about Parsky's press conference, see Paul Lewis, "Foreign Investors Taking Bigger Slice of the American Pie," *National Journal*, 8 May 1976, p. 626.

Chamber of Commerce. But the congressional proponents for legislative safeguards were also gaining some important outside support. In February 1975, the AFL-CIO called for "the full identification of all significant foreign investments" and stated that additional safeguards were necessary "to prevent a foreign takeover of major and sensitive facilities."[77] In October 1975, the AFL-CIO convention, in a statement intended to prod the congressional hearings further, condemned the "unregulated takeover of U.S. firms by foreign interests."[78]

Two quite distinct positions were emerging, and although one was resident in the administration and the other in Congress, the policy positions were general and could have divided people whose stands were not determined by where they sat. For example, in February 1974, before Stevenson's Subcommittee, C. Fred Bergsten and George Ball discussed Bergsten's proposal for an escape clause mechanism for screening out some kinds of foreign investment, including some takeovers. Ball found Bergsten's proposals "quite appalling." To Ball, the proposals would not only discourage future investment but would invite foreign retaliation of U.S. investment abroad. Bergsten responded by saying that the only way to head off investment wars like the trade wars of the 1930s was not to call for a laissez-faire system as Ball was doing, but to selectively monitor and control foreign investment and to seek international harmonization of regulations. Stevenson suggested that the United States use Bergsten's idea as a tactic to bargain for the reduction of investment barriers.[79]

Though the Commerce and Treasury Departments had argued in the summer of 1974 that they needed three years to do an adequate study, they completed their studies within the eighteen months allotted in the act. The Interim Reports were filed in October 1975, and the Final Report in nine monstrous volumes with eighteen appendices was delivered to the Congress in April 1976. Not surprisingly, the report concludes "that there is no need to change the basic U.S. policy toward investment from abroad . . ."[80]

The new benchmark study was based on 7200 reports covering some 10,200 businesses in the United States (as compared with 450 reports in the 1959 benchmark study), and its new estimate of FDI in the United States at the end of 1974 was $26.5 billion, which represented an increase of $5.1 billion from the year before. (In comparison to this total of all FDI in the United States, Americans alone had $28.4 billion in Canada.)[81] Using the 25

[77]*National Journal,* 10 January 1976, p. 32.

[78]Louis Kohlmeier, "Concern Over Corporate Takeovers," *National Journal,* 21 September 1974, p. 1431.

[79]Stevenson Hearings, February 1974, pp. 96–111. Needless to say, Stevenson's idea was not adopted by U. S. negotiators.

[80]Commerce Report, April 1976, p. xiii.

[81]International Economic Report of the President, March 1976, p. 66.

percent criterion and the 1959 benchmark, Commerce would have estimated the total FDI in the United States in 1974 at $21.7 billion, or $4.8 billion less than the newer estimate. Using a 25 percent instead of a 10 percent criterion the 1974 benchmark would have estimated $25.3 billion.[82]

The United Kingdom, Canada, and the Netherlands had the greatest investment, as has been the case for quite a long time. Each accounted for about 20 percent of total investment, while Germany accounted for 6 percent and Japan for 1 percent. Manufacturing continued to account for the largest share of the direct investment (31 percent), although this had declined from a high of 49 percent in 1971. Investments in petroleum increased to 24 percent of the total (from 19 percent in 1962 and 23 percent in 1971). Putting it in perspective, foreign investment accounted for six percent of the nation's output in any broad industry category. Of greater interest is the importance of foreign investment in foreign trade. U.S. affiliates of foreign MNC's accounted for $24.2 billion or 24 percent of total U.S. exports in 1974 and about 30 percent of U.S. imports.[83]

Legislators continued to introduce, revise, and refine their bills, but the Commerce Department's Report was taken by several more restrictionist-oriented congressmen as grounds for less concern and less urgency. As one Congressional Staff said: "Because of the Report, you're not likely to get legislative authority to monitor and to regulate foreign investment unless there's a crisis of some sort."[84]

THE LEGISLATIVE-EXECUTIVE PROCESS AND INWARD INVESTMENT POLICY: SOME PRELIMINARY OBSERVATIONS

Bureaucracies, unmolested, are not famed for their creativity.[85]
—Kenneth Waltz

Prior to 1973, U.S. inward investment policy was little more than an afterthought of a policy whose principal objective was to mitigate the effects of our balance of payments deficit. But after more than a decade of

[82]Commerce Report, April 1976, pp. 11, 55—58. For a reasonable summary of the report, see Paul Lewis, "Foreign Investors Taking Bigger Slice of the American Pie," *National Journal*, 8 May 1976, 626—8.

To put it another way, only $1.2 billion worth of foreign investment or about 4 percent of total foreign direct investment in the U. S. was in corporations in which less than 25 percent of the stock was owned by foreigners. The 25 percent criterion was a pretty accurate one.

[83]Commerce Report, April 1976, pp. 19, 35ff.

[84]Julie Domenick, interview.

[85]Kenneth Waltz, *Foreign Policy and Democratic Politics: The American and British Experience* (Boston: Little Brown and Co., 1967), p. 104.

unprecedented economic growth by Japan and Europe, and after two devaluations, the United States became an exceedingly attractive market for foreign investment, and American policy makers began to re-examine the issue. Reports of Japanese businessmen seeking investments in highly visible tourist and sensitive natural resource industries first attracted the attention of the national press, and headlines attracted the Congress. Many members responded reflexively and introduced bills which mandated strict prohibitions on foreign investment.

Three years later, the U.S. Government completed a comprehensive benchmark study of foreign direct and portfolio investment in the U.S. and a massive, wide-ranging study of the implications and the effects of such investment. In addition, data collection activities have been surveyed, catalogued, and improved. A bureau has been established in the Commerce Department to monitor direct investment flows, and a high-level committee has been established by Executive Order to review major new investments, particularly those undertaken by foreign governments, and to discourage those which could be considered harmful to the national interest. In addition, the government is moving, though haltingly, toward a system which provides for greater disclosure and reporting requirements from foreign as well as domestic investors and a screening mechanism with the legislative authority to prohibit certain investments. In addition to this new post-1973 layer, there still remains a veritable "patchwork" of local, state, and national policies which promote, regulate, and in some cases prohibit some forms of foreign investment. This, in short, is the U.S. inward investment policy. How can we explain its development sine 1973?

The Bureaucratic Debate and Theory

While each department had a different reason for opposing restrictive or regulative legislation on inward investment, there was a consensus within the executive branch that all such congressional initiatives should be discouraged. Commerce, of course, had a vested interest in encouraging more direct investment. Treasury wanted the corporations to be free to make the investment decision according to economic criteria, free from governmental interference. And the State Department was interested in reducing economic impediments between nations, not increasing them. Aware of the fact that U.S. FDI abroad was six times inward investment, the State Department wanted to avoid new restrictions in the U.S. for fear it might lead to retaliation abroad. The result was that the Executive chose to oppose any and all restrictionist or regulative legislation, a category which they interpreted very broadly.

This is as far as the bureaucratic lens will take you. It cannot explain the depth or the intensity of the Executive's position vis-a-vis Congress; for example, why the Executive initially opposed every effort by Congress to do anything more than study the issue. Nor does it explain the feeling of one staff who worked for an internationalist congressman and had repeated communications with the Executive: "Overall, you got the feeling that the Administration would just as soon wish the issue would go away." And, of course, it doesn't explain the changes made by the Congress or caused by the Congress.

After learning that the last benchmark study of foreign direct investment had been undertaken in 1959, and on portfolio in 1941, the Executive recommended that the Commerce Department and the Treasury Department undertake studies in early 1974. It is debatable whether the Executive would have made that decision had they not felt the "hot breath" of Congress; it is ironic that they should have decided to go ahead with the study without awaiting formal and legal authorization by the Congress.

The study recommended by the Executive was much simpler and less comprehensive than Congress mandated, and to explain this, one must turn to a broader theory than bureaucratic politics. Indeed, it is by no means clear whether even the modest study originally envisaged by the Executive would have been undertaken without a prod from Congress. One participant in the administration debate conceded that Congress served a "catalytic and constructive" role in this first phase, and that "there is no question that the pace was hurried up because of the Congressional hearings." The recommendation from the CIEP Committee, in fact, had landed in mud in Commerce and would probably have remained there had it not been for high-level attention which itself was due to the Congress.

Congressional Behavior and Interest Groups

Theories of congressional behavior also don't contribute very much to an understanding of either the process or the final policy. Constituent interest did prod several Legislators much as Congress prodded the Executive, but congressional attention was stimulated more by headlines than by letters, and Legislators pushed interest groups more than they were pushed.

Even those Legislators responsible for the first flurry of restrictionist bills did so more for purposes of shedding light on a subject, which the Executive would rather have kept in the shadow, than to score points back home with their constituents. Indeed, the issue was so esoteric, and so few people even knew that the Study Act passed, let alone what it contained, that few constituents could have known that their Legislators were involved.

Theories of committee behavior are useful in helping to understand why the congressional product was more internationalist than it would have been had a domestically-oriented committee handled the legislation. But, again, these theories are more useful in the questions which they have suggested than in the answers they have provided. As a "new" issue, inward investment policy could have been handled in any of a dozen different committees. In spite of the weight of restrictionist bills which had been introduced, not one of the sponsors of these bills quarrelled with the fact that the congressional policy would be developed in admittedly internationalist-oriented committees. So the most important questions are not what policy emerged from a particular committee, but why these committees and not others, and why weren't there countervailing efforts to handle the policy in more domestically-oriented committees? And why was there so much disagreement between internationalist committees of Congress and internationalist agencies of the Executive?

These questions suggest that what is particularly interesting about inward investment policy is not constituent-oriented congressional behavior nor committee behavior, but the dynamics of the interaction within the Congress and between the Congress and the Executive.

Rep. Dent's contribution to the Study Act and subsequent developments should not be understated, and other staff and officials involved in the process are quite open and candid about the effect of his restrictionist bill on the debate. "His impact was to swing support for more moderate legislation," said one Senate staff. Another said that the "administration wanted the Study Act because they were afraid of what was going to happen in the House if they didn't get it, and this attitude was shared by the Chamber of Commerce, the National Associations of Manufacturers, and others." One writer similarly concluded that "the Administration seized on the Inouye-Culver bill as the least objectionable, least restrictive FDI proposal and endorsed it in order to head off more extreme measures whose passage suddenly seemed less unlikely than before."

Julie Domenick, Dent's staff on this issue, said that "the Executive couldn't speak to me often enough after Dent introduced the bill."[86] This stands in sharp contrast to the fact that the staff of Culver, Stevenson, and Inouye first contacted the Executive rather than the other way around, and found that with the exception of the CIEP staff, other administration officials were quite unresponsive. Not to be overlooked is the fact that Dent, the congressman who introduced the first and one of the most restrictive of the bills, should have reaped for his district one of the most lucrative new foreign investments ever made in the U.S. at one time.

As the hearings and the congressional debate indicated, however, even the internationalists, who quickly took control of the issue, were interested in much more regulation, supervision, and screening of foreign investment than was incorporated in the final policy. How then do we explain that final policy?

[86]Gerowin, "U.S. Regulation", p. 632.

Legislative-Executive Process: Branch Biases

Clearly, Congress made a difference in the development and outcome of inward investment policy. Without congressional prodding, there would not have been the following: a major benchmark study which would identify the magnitude and nature of all foreign direct and foreign portfolio investments in the U.S.; the power to subpoena relevant records from foreign corporations in the U.S., and the promise of confidentiality; a massive study of the entire issue and its implications; a new criterion for defining inward investment which was the same as the definition of outward investment; a policy-level committee in the executive branch which reviews major foreign investment decisions and which consults with governments which intend to invest; a permanent office in the Department of Commerce charged with collecting data on foreign investment and monitoring the flows; new disclosure and reporting requirements to be implemented by the SEC; a tighter set of regulations governing investment in defense-related activities;[87] an educational campaign which reviewed existing policy and examined the rationale of this policy; and taking into account the changes which had occurred in the U.S. and in international economic relations since the first development of this policy, Congress chose among several alternatives, that policy which seemed more appropriate and suited to the contemporary situation.

These represented the components of a binding U.S. policy on foreign investment in the U.S. On the journey to the final policy, there was good reason to be uncertain whether the ultimate policy would be exclusionary, liberal and pragmatic, or laissez-faire. To the Europeans, the attempts by the U.S. to get them to treat U.S. MNC's in a nondiscriminatory manner at the same time that various bills introduced in the U.S. Congress threatened discrimination against their MNC's was not easily explained. The best the Europeans could say about this seemingly contradictory and short-sighted policy was that it represented what the *Economist* called "sincere hypocrisy." Such a conclusion is appropriate only if one assumes a monolithic executive decision-making structure in the U.S., or if one assumes that the introduction of a bill is as important as its passage. None of these assumptions is correct. For the foreign investment issue, it is useful to distinguish between two decision-making arenas—the Congress and the Executive—with different priorities on this issue, struggling to integrate them in an coherent a manner as possible.

[87]Sen. Inouye's staff pursued this area with the Defense Department and after finding a number of holes in the Defense Department's regulations, brought it to their attention, and then quietly worked out new regulations.

Representative John Culver tried to put his finger on the differences between the questions which the congressmen in his subcommittee asked and the kinds of responses of the Executive: "I don't sense in here [in the Executive response] an appreciation of the impact in political and social terms of the accelerated rates of foreign investment on the consciousness of the American people."[88] To the congressmen, the Executive did not recognize that a public policy problem existed and required some thinking, some talking, some educating, and some responses from public officials. To the Executive, however, the problem was not so serious that it couldn't be handled quietly and "administratively." In fact, the interagency study had found that existing policy and existing safeguards were adequate, and although a new benchmark study would be useful, it didn't require the congressional attention it was getting.

The Executive's arguments were not entirely unpersuasive as is evident by the policy outcome, which clearly represented a compromise between the Executive's desire to do nothing and the Congress's desire to begin screening and regulating foreign investment. In a sense, the traditional foreign policy roles which scholars have attached to the Congress—to delay, impede, amend, or halt the policy thrusts of the Executive—were more applicable in this case to the Executive. With each major policy suggestion by the Congress, the Executive dug in its heels and slowed and fragmented it.

On the basis of this analysis, one would predict that eventually the U.S. will have a screening process, and the Executive will have the legislative authority to prohibit certain kinds of foreign investments; but because of the Executive, and because of the legislative-executive process, there will be a half dozen steps, which will be tried and tested, before policy arrives at that point. That explains why the positions of the activist international Legislators were modified, but why did the restrictionists fail so completely?

One reason is that some of them, like Rep. Dent, never intended to succeed. Their goals were to hasten the process and gain some exposure for the issue (and themselves). All of the preliminary furor was actually just part of a long process which led to a policy which proved quite tame, methodical, and cautious. Others, like Rep. Robert Roe of New Jersey, claimed that they "weren't against foreign investment per se," but rather were concerned with the safety of defense-related and energy industries.[89]

The argument that foreign investment, in general, is beneficial to a host economy was widely accepted, and there was never any serious argument that it should be prohibited across-the-board. The real question

[88]Culver Hearings, p. 93.
[89]Interview with Peter Blake, Assistant to Rep. Robert Roe, 14 June 1976.

was: on what terms, and how can we maximize its positive effects? This, unfortunately, was a question that the Executive was not interested in joining for three reasons: institutional prerogative—the preference that the answer not be legislative and thus "congressional," in an institutionally competitive sense; the fear that any action might be interpreted by foreigners as restrictive and might induce retaliatory actions;[90] and a Republican belief in limited government.

That the protectionist argument was seen as so virile and dangerous was partly due to a determined and sensitive internationalist bias in the national press, and the hope that the self-denying prophecy which has been so successful in many international trade issues would work for the inward investment issue. Of course, the fact that every single committee or subcommittee which handled this issue had "international" or "foreign" in its title and in its orientation didn't hurt. What it meant was that the international implications of the legislation on inward investment would not be overlooked; indeed, they would be important factors in their deliberations.

Another significant brake on congressional decision making was the internationalist standard. Legislators showed a deep interest in what other governments' host investment policies were. Had these policies proven less restrictive than America's, one gets the impression from reading the hearings and the debates that Legislators would not have made U.S. policy more restrictive. But because others' were more restrictive, Congress felt justified in asking for a similar amount of regulation.[91] One congressional staff comments on this tacit adherence to an internationalist standard: "It is much easier to get something accepted by Congress if you can tell them that all the other nations are doing the same thing."[92] And conversely, it is easier to get Congress to reject a bill if it can be shown that no other nation is doing it, and that some nations might take offense. In short, Congress is sensitive without being slavish to the policies and attitudes of other governments.

Inward investment policy was a routine issue, yet it was a new, one which exhibited the basic characteristics of issues of interdependence. In examining the development of this new policy, we are in the happy position of trying to explain why the system worked, when at several points in time, the protectionists or the restrictionists seemed to be taking charge. In this sense, inward investment policy is quite similar to trade policy as described in Chapters 3–6, and like trade policy, the interaction of two branches, the Congress and the Executive, was the best lens with which to see the policy develop, both in its content and its contours.

[90]Foreigners can also "signal" by over-reacting as was the case with the Germans and the International Banking Act. *infra* no. 47.

[91]Williams Hearings, p. 33.

[92]Interview with George Ingram, Staff Consultant to Rep. John Culver, May 14, 17, 1976.

The interbranch politics lens also helps us to see a trend, which was more evident in the new issue of inward investment policy than in trade policy; it is the tendency toward making policy by circumventing the legislative process. Throughout the legislative-executive debate, the main question which the Executive repeatedly asked itself seemed not to be what is the best policy, or how can we devise a cooperative strategy with the Congress to formulate the best policy, but simply: how can we exclude the Congress from making policy on this issue? In those areas, where policy was necessary or unavoidable, the Executive either went ahead unilaterally—as when the Commerce Department was instructed to begin a new benchmark study in early 1974—or announced it by Executive Order, as in May 1975 when the Committee on Foreign Investment in the U.S. was established. In both these cases, and others, the Congress had in fact introduced bills suggesting the same policy; but the Executive chose to implement the proposals by Executive fiat rather than legislation.

The Congress is instructed by the Constitution to make laws, but for the reasons described in the first chapter, the Executive in the twentieth century has in fact if not in law become the chief legislator. This is not inherently dangerous; what is unsettling, however, is the possibility that the Executive could become the exclusive legislator. One can see this danger clearest in routine issues like inward investment policy. At any point in the development of the policy, the Congress could have halted the Executive's attempt to usurp the legislative prerogative, but the Congress did not do that, and, as a rule, it does not halt or reverse this "imperial drift" unless the beacon of publicity or controversy shines on a particular issue. When that beacon fails to shine, the Congress frequently fails to take heed. And once Executive policy is implemented, or in those cases when the Executive is particularly intransigent on a routine issue, the Congress just doesn't have the time or the resources to follow through.

9

U.S. FOREIGN ASSISTANCE POLICY, 1945–76: WHAT DIFFERENCE DOES CONGRESS MAKE?

> . . . it is folly in one nation to look for disinterested favors from
> another; . . . it must pay with a portion of its independence for
> whatever it may accept under that character . . . [1]

> —George Washington
> Farewell Address
> September 17, 1796

In his book, *The House of Representatives and Foreign Affairs*, Holbert
Carroll cogently argues that 1945 is the real watershed year in U.S. foreign
policy not because the United States had emerged from the war as the sole
superpower, but because 1945 represents the first year in peacetime that the
U.S. began what has become an unbroken, continuous history of unilaterally
transferring resources to other countries.[2] To a considerable extent, U.S.
foreign assistance policy in the post-war period became so identified in both
means and ends with U.S. foreign policy, and particularly with U.S. foreign
economic policy, that writers often used the words interchangeably.[3]

In 1934, Congress appropriated $102,000 for foreign affairs; two decades
later, the House Foreign Affairs Committee considered bills which involved

---

[1]George Washington, "The Decision to Avoid Foreign Entanglements: Washington's
Farewell Address," in Richard B. Morris (ed.), *Great Presidential Decisions: State Papers that
Changed the Course of History* (N.Y.: Harper and Row, 1973), p. 46.

[2]Holbert Carroll, *The House of Representatives and Foreign Affairs* (Boston: Little,
Brown and Co., 1966); see especially chaps. 1 and 2.

[3]For example, see Benjamin Higgins, *The United Nations and U. S. Foreign Economic
Policy.* His book is actually about U. S. foreign assistance policy with particular stress given to
the United Nations, but he almost always refers to the relevant U. S. policy as "foreign
economic policy."

more than $8 billion.[4] Not only did this vast transfer of wealth imply a new source of influence and a new role for the United States in the world, but it also meant a new role for the Congress and a new relationship between the Congress and the Executive. And within Congress, by dint of the authorization and appropriations process, the House suddenly found itself for the first time playing a vital role, almost co-equal to the Senate, in the formulation of U.S. foreign policy.[5]

Congress found that its traditional function of setting the limits and conditions on the allocation of public money for domestic policy was easily transferrable to foreign policy.[6] Considered a "political graveyard" before World War II,[7] the House Foreign Affairs Committee suddenly acquired prestige, and foreign aid became its top priority. In the words of one member who was interviewed in the 1960s: "Really, we are sort of a committee on foreign aid. We have other bills, and I don't mean to downgrade the importance of the Arms Control and Disarmament Agency or the Peace Corps. But they aren't the kind of bills you spend six months on."[8]

In the compelling years of the Cold War, the very idea of having debates on foreign aid and policy "in full public view" each year was disquieting to many, particularly those who believed foreign policy is best made with secrecy and dispatch.[9] One writer commented that the aid bill was "tied in knots" by Congress, which wasted too much time on it.[10] Traditionally, the bill was drafted in an executive agency, and then debated and amended by both the House and the Senate Foreign Affairs Committes, the Appropriations Committees, and on the floor of both chambers. John Montgomery called it "the fourfold Congressional obstacle course,"[11] while Harold K. Jacobson wrote that "the process is ungainly. It is dismaying not only to the proponents of foreign aid but also to its opponents, albeit for

[4]Holbert Carroll, *House of Representatives*, p. 20.

[5]Carroll notes, however, that the order of relative importance with regard to the formulation of U. S. foreign policy still remains as before—President, Senate, and the House of Representatives, but that the power of the House increased the most dramatically, primarily because its role before the war was minimal.

[6]Carroll shows that the "power of the purse served as the opening wedge" back as early as 1796, when the House had to consider the appropriations of funds for the implementation of the unpopular Jay Treaty. (pp. 7–10)

[7]Ibid., p. 91.

[8]Quoted in Richard F. Fenno, *Congressmen in Committees* (Boston: Little, Brown and Co., 1973), p. 69.

[9]Harold K. Jacobson, "Foreword," to Michael K. O'Leary, *The Politics of American Foreign Aid* (N.Y.: Atherton Press, 1967), p. ix.

[10]Francis O. Wilcox, *The Congress, the Executive, and Foreign Policy* (N.Y.: Harper and Row, 1971), p. 83.

[11]John D. Montgomery, *The Politics of Foreign Aid: American Experience in Southeast Asia* (N.Y.: Praeger, 1962), p. 237.

different reasons and to a lesser extent."[12] To the executive branch, the bill often emerged from Congress as "a Christmas tree of restrictions,"[13] laden with ornaments which Montgomery called "crippling amendments."[14] From the congressional perspective, however, the foreign aid bill can be considered the principal vehicle by which it attempts to influence and make U.S. foreign policy.[15]

FOREIGN ASSISTANCE POLICY: DEFINITIONS, PURPOSES, PRELIMINARY QUESTIONS

Foreign aid can be defined narrowly as economic assistance or broadly as the unilateral transfer of capital, technical, technological, and managerial resources from one government to another. Since we are concerned primarily with the transfer of influence which accompanies these resources abroad as well as between the two branches of government, the broader definition will be used.[16]

Too often, scholars and critics of foreign aid take policy-makers at their word when they state that the sole purpose of foreign assistance is to promote and assist the development process in the recipient nations. Upon discovering other purposes, these critics often leap to the opposite conclusion, arguing that foreign aid has either nothing to do with development or is intended to inhibit it.[17] Other purposes of foreign aid identified by critics include assuring that a recipient country has a foreign policy which is compatible with that of the United States, maintaining or increasing the

[12]Harold K. Jacobson, "Foreword to *Politics of American Foreign Aid*, pp. ix–x.

[13]Allan Furman, "Foreign Aid: New Directions or the End of an Era," unpublished paper for the Center for International Affairs, Harvard University, May 1974.

[14]John D. Montgomery, *Politics of Foreign Aid*, 204.

[15]See my "Congress's Impact on Latin America: Is There a Madness in the Method?", pp. 259–272, in Abraham F. Lowenthal, (ed.), *The Conduct of Routine Economic Relations: U. S. Foreign Policy-Making to Latin America*, vol. 3, app. 1, Commission on the Organization of the Government for the Conduct of Foreign Policy (Murphy Commission) (Washington: G.P.O., 1975). Hereafter "Congress' Impact." A foreign observer finds the process not only appealing but productive, leading to a program and a rationale which "is a good deal richer than in most other countries." See Goran Ohlin, "The Evolution of United States Aid Doctrine," in B. J. Cohen (ed.) *American Foreign Economic Policy: Essays and Comments* (New York: Harper and Row, 1968), p. 347.

[16]For a variety of definitions, see app. in Robert A. Packenham, *Liberal America and the Third World: Political Development Ideas in Foreign Aid and Social Science* (Princeton: Princeton University Press, 1973).

[17]For example, John Gerassi writes: "It seems inescapably clear that the Alliance for Progress was not aimed . . . at his [Kennedy's] 'voiceless ones,' but at fostering 'anti-Kommunism' in Latin America." *The Great Fear in Latin America*, rev. ed. (N.Y.: Collier books, 1965), p. 279.

dependency of the recipient country,[18] promoting or protecting U.S. foreign investors,[19] "dumping" farm surpluses abroad, punishing left-leaning regimes and supporting right-leaning regimes, or promoting U.S. exports. These "ulterior" purposes do, in fact, represent the range and the diversity of the goals of foreign aid.[20] As George Ball testified to the Senate Foreign Relations Committee: "Foreign assistance is a deceptive phrase that comprehends programs and policies dissimilar in motive and effect."[21]

Since all of these goals can rarely be accomplished simultaneously, policy-makers are forced to weigh the relative value of each goal and rank them in a hierarchy of priorities. In the decision-making process by which priorities are ordered, the struggle between the President and the Congress is most profound and most important. "In many countries," Joan Nelson has written, foreign aid "is the primary instrument relied upon to protect and promote central U.S. interests."[22] As such, it represents the cutting edge of U.S. foreign policy.

While foreign aid as a foreign policy instrument is likely to be of lesser importance in the future than it was in the past,[23] the process by which the two Branches develop foreign aid policy contains lessons of more lasting significance for the entire range of foreign policy-making. Moreover, many of the issues of interdependence have significant components, like the GSP in the Trade Act, which are viewed in the same light as traditional foreign aid issues, i.e., as resource transfers or, more crudely, as "give-aways." And as Legislators are wont to point out, on those issues, "the Congress has the

[18]For a survey of the dependency literature, see Susanne Bodenheimer, "Dependency and Imperialism: The Roots of Latin American Underdevelopment," in K. T. Fann and Donald C. Hodges (eds.), *Readings in U. S. Imperialism* (Boston: Porter Sargent Publishers, 1971), pp. 162–65. Also see Harry Magdoff, *The Age of Imperialism: The Economics of U. S. Foreign Policy* (N.Y.: Monthly Review Press, 1969), p. 173.

[19]J. P. Morray, "The United States and Latin America," in Gustav Ranis (ed.), *The U. S. and the Developing Economies* (N.Y.: W. W. Norton and Co., 1973), pp. 295–306. Also see Robert H. Swansbrough, *The Embattled Colossus: Economic Nationalism and United States Investors in Latin America* (Gainesville, Florida: University Presses of Florida, 1976).

[20]Both Packenham and Joan Nelson make this point.

[21]Statement of George Ball before the Senate Foreign Relations Committee, June 3, 1975, cited in Congressional Quarterly, *Almanac*, 1975, p. 336.

[22]Joan Nelson, *Aid, Influence, and Foreign Policy* (N.Y.: MacMillan, 1968), p. 1.

[23]Since the Seventh Special Session of the United Nations General Assembly in September 1975, the issues of concern in U.S.-developing country relations and more generally North-South relations have proliferated, particularly with regard to the areas of trade, commodities, investment, and debt; and the issues of foreign assistance in its conventional, bilateral form have diminished proportionately. In a 1976 report, a private Commission on U.S.-Latin American Relations recommended a sympathetic approach to the problems of the developing world, but explicitly called for the termination of bilateral assistance to all middle-income developing countries (in Latin America). (See Commission on U. S.-Latin American Relations, *The United States and Latin America: Next Steps* (N.Y.: Center for Inter-American Relations, December 1976).

responsibility and the right to determine the conditions under which U.S. assistance is to be given."[24]

Political analyses of foreign aid have generally focused on the funding levels and the importance of Congress as "the major wielder of the axe."[25] Although the reduction in the foreign aid budget is no doubt important, the process is more complicated than is suggested by a simple chart which juxtaposes administration request and congressional appropriation. Aaron Wildavsky has shown that the budgetary process by which the Executive makes decisions on appropriations is just as nonrational as the congressional budgetary process, though it is much more private.[26] More interesting than this budget-cutting exercise is the tug-of-war between the executive and Congress on where to spend the money.

In this chapter, I will briefly review and explain U.S. foreign assistance policy and the institutions responsible for administering this policy in the post-war period. Foreign aid policy is viewed as an instrument for contributing to the economic and military reconstruction, the military security, and the economic development of foreign countries or regions. In this chapter, I will explore the extent and the ways Congress shaped the policy and the institutions.

In the next chapter, I will examine the foreign aid bill as a vehicle which Congress uses to make *specific* foreign policies on issues not directly related to the long-term goals of reconstruction or development. The process by which Congress and the Executive interact to make "foreign policy by amendment" will be examined in two cases in which the sparring between the branches has been particularly heated: U.S. policies on expropriation and on human rights.

[24]Remarks by Senator James Abourezk, *Congressional Record*, 5 December 1975, p. S21276.

[25]See Gustav Ranis, *U.S. and the Developing Economies*, p. xxi. See also Montgomery, *Politics of Foreign Aid*, 212.

[26]Aaron Wildavsky, *The Politics of the Budgetary Process* (Boston: Little, Brown and Co., 1974). Perhaps the most important difference in the budgetary processes of the Executive and the Congress was the lack of a coordinating center in the latter, but the passage of the Budgetary and Impoundment Act of 1974 helped to correct that imbalance.

For a sample of the degree to which the congressional "axe" was wielded, see the table below:

Foreign Aid Cuts, 1948–1969

Fiscal Year	Request	Author- ization	Appropri- ation	Per Cent Cut[1]
1948–49	$7.37	$6.91	$6.45	12.5%
1950	5.68	5.59	4.94	13.0
1952	8.50	7.58	7.28	14.4

A HISTORY OF FOREIGN AID POLICY

Since World War II, U.S. foreign assistance policy has passed through three stages which have, to a certain extent, overlapped, but which have been aimed at different goals and recipients. In the first stage, from 1945–52, the principal objective of U.S. foreign assistance policy was the relief, reconstruction, and recovery of Western Europe. Over $34 billion was appropriated for that purpose, of which more than $22 billion were grants for economic assistance; the rest being loans, and a relatively small amount for military assistance.

The passage of the Mutual Security Act in 1951 ushered in a new era for U.S. foreign assistance policy, one directed at building up the military capabilities of our allies on the rim of the Soviet Union. Between 1951 and 1961, over $48 billion was dispersed, the vast majority being grants, and the slight majority was for military assistance. The principal countries receiving aid were South Korea, Taiwan, the Philippines, Indo-China, Iran, Turkey, and Greece. In many ways, the shift in priorities is the most clear-cut in 1950 when military assistance as a ratio of economic assistance changed from 1:4 to 4:1.[27]

In 1961, with the passage of the first Foreign Assistance Act, the U.S. once again altered the geographical direction of its foreign assistance policy, this time to the developing world, with special interest in Latin America. From 1962 to 1975, nearly $103 billion was authorized under that act, with a

Fiscal Year	Request	Author- ization	Appropri- ation	Per Cent Cut[1]
1954	5.83	5.16	4.53	22.3
1956	3.53	3.42	2.70	23.5
1958	3.86	3.39	2.77	28.2
1960	3.93	3.58	3.23	17.8
1962	4.77	4.26	3.91	18.0
1964	4.53	3.60	3.00	33.8
1966	3.46	3.36	3.22	6.9
1968	3.23	2.68	2.30	28.8
1969	2.92	1.97	1.76	39.7

[1]Appropriation below request

[Source: Congressional Quarterly, *Congress and the Nation*, vol. 2, 1965–68, p. 50.]

[27]Congressional Quarterly, *Congress and the Nation*, 1945–64, p. 167; Packenham, *Liberal America*,.p. 49.

slightly higher amount for economic than for military assistance. Nearly 90 percent of the military assistance was in the form of grants, as contrasted with less than 60 percent of the economic assistance.[28] During this third phase, an important initiative occurred in 1973 which significantly redirected the aid program toward assisting the poorest people in the poorest countries by investing in "basic human needs" projects.

The relative distribution between economic and military aid, the geographical focus, and the purposes of aid—all changed in each phase. The goals changed from the reconstruction of European countries, to the strengthening of the defense of U.S. allies sharing borders with the Soviet Union, to promoting the development of the poorer countries of the world, but the thread which tied each phase together was the desire to help and maintain those countries which were threatened, however indirectly, by the menace of the Soviet Union or the "infection" of Communism. On this fundamental security-oriented goal, there was a complete consensus between the Executive and Congress until the late 1960s when a number of Senators led by J. William Fulbright and Frank Church began to question the wisdom of a foreign policy rooted in a single-minded commitment to anti-Communism.

Yet other goals—humanitarian, economic, and political—were also professed and had their constituencies in Congress, in the Executive, and among the general public. The dilemma of choosing between the various goals was posed starkly by President Kennedy as he examined U.S. interests in the Dominican Republic after the assassination of Rafael Trujillo in 1962. He said that there were "three possibilities in descending order of preference: a decent democratic regime, a continuation of the Trujillo regime, or a Castro regime. We ought to aim at the first, but we really can't renounce the second until we are sure that we can avoid the third."[29] Until quite recently, one would have been hard pressed to find a Legislator who disagreed with the order of priorities reflected in Kennedy's statement.

Europe First: The Marshall Plan

The passage of the European Recovery Program, better known as the Marshall Plan, in March 1948 by Congress can be considered the beginning of the foreign aid program, though it was not the beginning of U.S. aid to Europe. From 1940 to August 17, 1945, the United States transferred more

[28]All of these statistics are from Statistics and Reports Division, Office of Financial Management, Agency for International Development, *U. S. Overseas Loans and Grants, Obligations and Loan Authorizations*, 1 July 1945–30 June 1975 [Hereafter Overseas Loans]. When there is some discrepancy between these statistics and those cited in less authoritative books, I use these.

[29]Arthur M. Schlessinger, Jr., *A Thousand Days: John F. Kennedy in the White House* (N.Y.: Fawcett World Library, 1965), pp. 704–05.

than $41 billion of resources, mostly war materiel, to Europe, and for the three postwar years prior to the Marshall Plan, the United States gave $6 billion in grants and $8.5 billion in credits.[30]

Throughout the history of U.S. foreign aid, it was unusual when American largesse was offered without strings. Even during World War II, the United States pressed its allies to accept certain conditions on their internal or external policies as "compensation" for the aid. Sometimes, the exigencies of war forced the United States to offer aid even when the conditions were rejected. For example, in the long and arduous negotiations between the United States and Great Britain on the terms of lend-lease, the U.S. negotiators, prodded by Congress, demanded that Britain agree to a postwar economic system based on open market access, implying the end of the Imperial Preference System. British negotiators believed that the Imperial Preference System was too important to be bartered away, and that the major problem of the postwar period would be U.S. tariffs, not British preferences. This was the most difficult and one of the only problems in U.S.-British relations during the war that proved incapable of resolution. It was only because of the personal intercession of FDR that the differences were papered over, and an ambiguous statement of intent was substituted for an explicit commitment.[31]

Congress was more willing to compromise during the war than after. One example of this was an amendment to the 1944 authorization for lend-lease mandating the abrupt termination of lend-lease with the ending of the war.[32] On the British loan agreement negotiated in 1945–46, congressional involvement was very great. As Richard Gardner wrote: "There was never any detailed consideration at a high-level in the American government of just how much assistance Britain required. The question was how much assistance could safely be asked of Congress. The politically cautious Vinson [former Representative from Kentucky; appointed Secretary of the Treasury by Truman in 1945] proposed $3.5 billion; [Undersecretary of State for Economic Affairs, William] Clayton and the State Department, $4 billion. The disagreement was eventually settled by Truman himself, who split the difference at $3.75 billion."[33]

Congress spent six months debating the agreement. Amendments were introduced demanding more bases and aviation rights for the United States, special guarantees for U.S. investors in Great Britain, and better treatment of Ireland and Palestine by the British. Perhaps the greatest concern was that

[30]Congressional Quarterly, *Congress and the Nation* vol. 1, 1945–64, p. 167.

[31]Richard N. Gardner, *Sterling-Dollar Diplomacy: Anglo-American Collaboration in the Reconstruction of Multilateral Trade* (Oxford, England: Clarendon Press, 1956), chap. 8.

[32]Ibid., p. 176.

[33]Ibid., p. 202.

the money would be used by the Labor Party to "socialize" Britain, but the fear of Communism and Winston Churchill's famous "Iron Curtain" speech in Fulton, Missouri on March 5, 1946, took the wind out of the amendments, and the agreement was passed in July virtually unchanged from the draft introduced by the Executive.[34]

When in February 1947, the British government informed the Americans of their inability to continue supporting the Greek government against a Communist insurrection, Congress and the American public believed that the U.S. had already fulfilled most of its postwar burden. In the fall election of 1946, the Republicans had won control of the Congress for the first time since 1930, and Senator Arthur Vandenberg, a newly-converted Republican internationalist and Chairman of the Senate Foreign Relations Committee, warned Truman that if he expected to get congressional approval for a significant new American initiative, he would have to "scare hell out of the American people."[35] Truman followed his advice.

On March 12, 1947, President Truman addressed a joint session of Congress and requested $400 million to assist the government of Greece and Turkey. He painted a bleak and manichaean picture of two ways of life facing the people of the world. "One way of life is based upon the will of the majority, and is distinguished by free institutions. . . . The second way of life is based upon the will of a minority forcibly imposed upon the majority. It relies upon terror and oppression . . . "[36] If the United States didn't assist Greece, Turkey, and other free world nations, the world, in Truman's vision, would gradually come to be dominated by the second system. Even Joseph M. Jones, who drafted the speech, recognized it for its hyperbole,[37] and George F. Kennan, whose famous telegram of January 1946 from the U. S. Embassy in Moscow provided the intellectual and historical underpinning for the Truman Doctrine, objected bitterly to the language of the speech and considered the policy of sending military aid to countries like Turkey which bordered the Soviet Union as needlessly provocative.[38] But, in the short-term at least, the tactic worked. Vandenberg guided the bill through Congress, deflecting amendments. On May 15, Congress voted the funds, and one week later, the bill was signed into law.

[34]Ibid., chap. 12; Congressional Quarterly, *Congress and the Nation, 1945–64*, p. 160; William A. Brown, Jr. and Redvers Opie, *American Foreign Assistance* (Washington, D.C.: Brookings Institution, 1953), pp. 104–105; Congressional Quarterly *Almanac, 1946*, pp. 73–76, 271.

[35]Walter La Feber, *America, Russia, and the Cold War, 1945–1971*, (N.Y.: John Wiley and Sons, Inc. 1972), p. 45.

[36]"The Truman Doctrine: Message of the President to Congress, March 12, 1947," reprinted in H. L. Trefousse (ed.), *The Cold War: A Book of Documents* (N.Y.: Capricorn Books, 1966), p. 100.

[37]Joseph M. Jones, *Fifteen Weeks* (N.Y.: The Viking Press, 1955).

[38]Walter LaFeber, *America, Russia, and the Cold War*, p. 45.

On June 5, 1947, fifteen weeks after the message arrived from Britain, Secretary of State George C. Marshall addressed the Harvard Commencement, and in explaining the economic plight of Europe, urged Americans to respond not "on a piecemeal basis; . . . not against any country or doctrine but against hunger, poverty, desperation, and chaos."[39] Instead of the Cold War rhetoric of Truman's speech, Marshall concretely suggested that the Europeans confer and agree on a general plan of economic reconstruction, and the U.S. would respond to their initiative and assist in their effort.

U.S. officials feared that the Russians might accept the invitation, but the U.S. was saved that embarrassment. At a European Conference in Paris in July, the Russians rejected the conditions set by the European governments for receiving assistance and walked out of the Conference. Their absence from a general program facilitated its acceptance by Congress. Shortly after Marshall's speech and Truman's endorsement, both leaders met with a bipartisan group of congressional leaders to discuss the program. After that initial meeting, Marshall met with Vandenberg frequently, sometimes as often as twice a week at the Blair House.[40] On July 29, 1948, the House adopted H. Res. 296 creating a special Select Committee to study the Marshall proposal. Formally chaired by Charles A. Eaton, who was also Chairman of the House Foreign Affairs Committee, this Select Committee was composed of nineteen members representing a geographical and political cross-section of the House. The committee soon became known as the Herter Committee, after Rep. Christian A. Herter of Massachusetts, who lead the group on an extended investigation of the economic problems of Western Europe. The group travelled widely, and transmitted its findings to the House Foreign Affairs Committee in an 833-page report in November 1947. Most of the members had been converted into committed supporters of the Marshall Plan by the experiences gained in their travels. On their return, however, their commitment was severely tested by the skepticism of a people tired of foreign involvements. But the choice, in the view of several of the members, was indeed stark. Rep. Everett M. Dirksen of Illinois posed three options for Congress and his constituents. The first was to withdraw from Europe; the second was to give "niggardly aid." "There is a third choice," he said, "and that is the choice we must make."

> I want to make it. I have been back home. People have talked to me about giving away my country, and I have talked to them. . . . And I have said, 'Look, let us examine this whole picture.' And it is amazing

[39]"The Marshall Plan: Remarks by Secretary of State George C. Marshall, June 5, 1947, at Harvard University," reprinted in Trefousse, Cold War, p. 105.

[40]Harry B. Price, The Marshall Plan and Its Meaning (Ithaca, N.Y.: Cornell University Press, 1955), pp. 50–52.

to me to see how the people back home have changed their minds on the basis of such facts as you disclose them. I am not afraid of the reaction in this country. I am confident that in proportion as we do our jobs as representatives to bring them the story—that they will go along with the third choice, and the third choice in my book is immediate-adequate-aggressive aid. My formula, Mr. Chairman, is very, very brief. Do it—do it now—and do it right.[41]

In a superb analysis of the government's decision-making process in framing the Marshall Plan legislation, Hadley Arkes argues that because of the degree of administrative discretion required to administer the program, the central issue was the structure and mission of the agency which would be responsible for implementing it.[42] Marshall later said that Vandenberg had served as "a full partner in the adventure" of drafting the bill. "At times," Marshall said in an interview, "I was his right-hand man, and at times, he was mine."[43] An analysis of the bureaucratic debates by Arkes shows that relatively little of this exchange penetrated the legislative process in the State Department, which was the lead agency for drafting the proposal sent to Congress. That is not to say that congressional sentiment was not a consideration; in fact, as Arkes discovered, the opposite was more nearly the truth: "State appeared to become almost slavish in its anxiety to anticipate the whims of Congress. It seemed determined to satisfy and, indeed, overfulfill those Congressional demands even before they were explicitly raised."[44] However much State wanted to administer the program, it realized that the program's functions touched those of the Commerce, Agriculture, and Treasury Departments, and after several interagency drafts of the proposal, Secretary of State Marshall appeared willing to accept the idea of an independent agency, provided that State would continue to be able to exercise control over the agency.[45]

On December 9, 1947, Truman sent the proposal requesting $17 billion over a four-year period to Congress. Vandenberg immediately recognized that the central issue was the structure of the administering agency, and he commissioned the Brookings Institution to do a study of it. When the Brookings report was submitted to the Committee on January 22, 1948, it became clear that Vandenberg intended to use it to justify alternatives to the Administration's proposal. The Committee agreed with the State Depart-

[41]Ibid., p. 53.

[42]Hadley Arkes, *Bureaucracy, The Marshall Plan, and the National Interest* (Princeton: Princeton University Press, 1972).

[43]Price, *Marshall Plan*, p. 65.

[44]Ibid., p. 73.

[45]Arkes, *Bureaucracy*, chap. 4, pp. 64–83.

ment that "it would be unwise to place the agency in the Department of State," but it agreed on little else.[46] In hearings, Vandenberg repeatedly stated that the American people had lost confidence in the foreign policy conducted by the State Department, and they wanted another approach:

> [The American people] have a general feeling that the administration of our foreign grants and loans and aids since the war has been pretty sterile of results. . . . Therefore, they come up, in my opinion, with the new view that if they are to be happy about hopefully anticipating that this is going to be a success where other things have failed, they want a new element of business responsibility injected into this formula which will give them a feeling of reliance that as a business operation this is to be conducted in a business way.[47]

The formula which the Senate Committee devised and the Congress accepted was that the independent agency, the Economic Cooperation Administration (ECA), would be directed by an Administrator who would have equal status with other Cabinet officers, and like the others be appointed by the President with the advice and consent of the Senate. He would therefore not be subordinate to the Secretary of State, but he should keep the Secretary "fully and currently informed on matters, including prospective action . . . pertinent to the duties of the other." The Secretary of State was expected to do the same, and any differences should be decided by the President, not as in the Administration's proposal, by the Secretary of State.[48]

It was logical, therefore, that the Senate would want a businessman to administer the program. When the *Washington Post* reported that Truman was considering the appointment of Will Clayton, former Undersecretary of State and a businessman, Vandenberg immediately wrote to Secretary of State Marshall calling attention to "the overriding Congressional desire that the ERP Administrator shall come from the outside business world with strong industrial credentials and not via the State Department. . . . This job as ERP Administrator stands out by itself . . . as requiring particularly persuasive economic credentials unrelated to diplomacy."[49] Truman then tried to convince Vandenberg to accept Dean Acheson as administrator, but Vandenberg instead insisted on Paul Hoffman, the president of Studebaker

[46]U. S. Senate, European Recovery Program, Report of the Committee on Foreign Relations on S.2202, 80th Congress, 2d sess., 26 February 1948, p. 14.

[47]U. S. Senate, Committee on Foreign Relations, *Hearings on the European Recovery Program, 1948*, p. 150, cited in Arkes, *Bureaucracy*, pp. 99–100.

[48]Price, *Marshall Plan*, p. 69. European Recovery Program, sec. 105(b).

[49]Arkes, *Bureaucracy*, p. 100.

and a member of the Harriman Committee established in June 1947 by the President to make specific recommendations on ways to implement the Marshall Plan.[50] Truman acceded to Vandenberg's suggestion.

The establishment by congressional initiative of a genuinely independent ECA had implications not only for the ECA's relationship with the other departments but for its relationship with Congress. Holbert Carroll stated the fundamental principle of public administration which would shape the relationship between the congressional creator and the administrative offspring: "The department or agency receiving power from another unit of government at the behest of a committee [or Congress as a whole], it should be noted, rarely resists the congressional vote of confidence. The department or agency knows that it is easier to cope with a frustrated President than with an unhappy congressional committee."[51]

While the structure of the ECA and the professional background of its Administrator may have been the most important issues decided by Congress, there were other changes made in the Administration's bill which had an important impact on the direction of the aid program. The Herter Committee's Report included a series of recommendations on the utilization of (U.S.) resources, local currency counterpart funds, and program management, which were incorporated in the bill.[52] The Senate successfully overcame House objections and inserted a provision which established a watchdog Joint Committee on Foreign Economic Cooperation composed of ten members of both Houses and parties. The standing committees, however, sharply curtailed the range of the new committee's power, and in retrospect, perhaps its only real contribution was the publication of several very good reports and histories of the ECA.[53]

While Congress accepted that the major proportion of ERP would be in the form of grants, it deliberately included a provision which mandated at least $1 billion of the total to be in the form of loans. Apparently, this was done to make the program more "businesslike" and partly to function as a source of funding investment guarantees for U.S. investors in Europe.[54]

Congress also objected to the Administration's request for a four-year appropriations bill. After negotiations with the Executive, the Senate Foreign Relations Committee reported a bill which provided for annual

[50]Acheson saw this event differently. In his memoirs, he wrote that Truman had asked him on 4 April 1948 to take the job, but that he warned Truman that since only the authorization and not the appropriations had passed, that he should consult with Vandenberg first. Dean Acheson, *Present At the Creation: My Years in the State Department* (N.Y.: New American Library, 1969), p. 322.

[51]Holbert Carroll, *House of Representatives*, p. 63.

[52]Price, *Marshall Plan*, p. 54.

[53]Arkes, *Bureaucracy*, pp. 129–31.

[54]Ibid., pp. 205–6.

appropriations and authorization, but it did include a terminal date of June 30, 1952 for the program.[55]

Rep. J. William Fulbright introduced an amendment which would have urged the European governments to move towards political unification, but this amendment was defeated largely because it was feared—primarily by the State Department—that it would be viewed by Europeans as interference in their domestic affairs.[56] For the same reason, the Conference Committee dropped a Senate provision which would have added Spain to the ERP; instead the new provision left the matter of membership to the Europeans themselves.[57]

In addition to these general foreign policy items, Congress added a couple of "special interest" provisions. One stipulated that 50 percent of all assistance goods be transported in American ships; and the other stated that not less than 25 percent of all wheat shipments from the U.S. be flour.[58] But there were many other product provisions, for example, on corn, canned goods, and fish, which were eliminated in Conference.[59]

On April 3, 1948, the European Recovery Program passed Congress by overwhelming votes, and was signed the next day by President Truman. The Marshall Plan has been called by one writer "the most successful program in the history of American foreign aid."[60] It not only achieved its stated objectives of the industrial recovery of Europe, but it did so before the projected four-year time span and at a cost of $4 billion below the original appropriations of $17 billion.[61]

The Plan had not involved the kind of "collaboration" between branches which had characterized the drafting of the U.N. Charter or the Bretton Woods Agreement, but the atmosphere of interaction was generally cooperative and the changes made by Congress were generally constructive.[62]

On the other hand, there were several congressional leaders involved in the early stages of shaping the Truman Doctrine and military assistance to

---

[55]Brown and Opie, *American Foreign Assistance*, p. 149.

[56]Arkes, *Bureaucracy* 203. In the authorization act of 1949, the problem of reconciling the sentiment for noninterference with the equally-strongly-held sentiment for European unification was resolved by inserting a statement in the "purposes" section of the act rather than in a binding section, stating it as U.S. policy to encourage European unification. The 1950 Act took an additional step by urging "further" unification. (Brown and Opie, *American Foreign Assistance*, pp. 161–62).

[57]Arkes, *Bureaucracy*, p. 203.

[58]Price, *Marshall Plan*, p. 67. The Merchant Marine, it will be recalled, has been the recipient of subsidies since the first Congress.

[59]Arkes, *Bureaucracy*, pp. 170–71.

[60]Robert Packenham, *Liberal America*, p. 34.

[61]Ibid., p. 34.

[62]Holbert Carroll compares the interaction between Congress and the Executive on all three cases. *House of Representatives*, pp. 326–29

Greece and Turkey, and, if anything, this had a chilling impact on the first years of the Cold War. Lowi has argued that the legislative-executive process requires that the President "oversell" major foreign policy initiatives in order to obtain congressional approval, and that there is almost a self-destructive aspect to this process. Certainly, the duration and the intensity of the Cold War testifies to the difficulty of trying to extract U.S. foreign policy from this rigid and oversold initiative.[63]

From Economic Recovery to Military Security: The Mutual Security Act, 1951–61

With the passage of the Mutual Security Act in 1951, U.S. foreign aid policy shifted direction. Like the previous initiative, this had numerous antecedents. The Philippines Military Assistance Act of 1946 was the first comprehensive postwar military assistance package developed by the U.S., and many of the elements included in the package—materiel, training, rearmament—were incorporated on a larger scale in the programs to Greece and Turkey in 1947. While the Congress was rewriting the European Recovery Program, the Executive was already planning the North Atlantic Treaty Organization (NATO). In June of 1948, Senator Arthur Vandenberg and the Administration concurrently announced a new position on the need for a regional security organization for the North Atlantic governments under the charter of the United Nations. Intergovernmental negotiations in 1948 and 1949 led to NATO and to the Mutual Defense Assistance Act (MDAA) of 1949.

On July 25, 1949, the Administration sent a draft of that bill to the Senate. The bill called for unprecedented discretionary authority for the President to furnish military assistance in any amounts to virtually any government. The Senate found the draft totally unacceptable and refused to hold hearings on it. A second draft was sent on August 5th, and that became the nucleus of the MDAA.[64] The Act authorized $1.45 billion in arms aid, two-thirds of which was to be given to European governments.

The entire foreign aid program, however, continued to emphasize economic recovery until the Korean War, which was viewed by Gen. George Marshall and others in the Administration as "an incident in the world picture," and therefore requiring both a specific and a global response.[65] On May 24, 1951, President Truman asked Congress to approve an $8.5 billion Mutual Security Program to support the rearmament of our European allies

[63]Theodore Lowi, *The End of Liberalism*, chap. 6; Richard M. Freeland, *The Truman Doctrine and the Origins of McCarthyism* (N.Y.: Knopf, 1972).

[64]Brown and Opie, *American Foreign Assistance*, pp. 457–61.

[65]Congressional Quarterly, *Almanac*, 1951, p. 205.

and to assist in the development of the defense capabilities of other allies in the Far East, the Near East, and Latin America. The request included $6.3 billion for military assistance and $2.2 billion for economic aid. Though he asked for a unified program, Truman insisted that for reasons of efficiency, the new funds be channelled to the three existing organizations, the ECA, the Mutual Defense Assistance Program, and the Technical Assistance Program established in 1950.[66]

Though the House and the Senate had different ideas on the kind of organization which would best suit the program, both chambers agreed that the President's proposal was inadequate, and that a new centralized structure was necessary. On this point, congressional instincts were reinforced by three reports—The Gray Report (November 1950), Partners in Progress (March 1951), and Administration for Foreign Affairs by Brookings (June 1951)—all of which recommended a unified organizational structure to administer the foreign aid program.[67] In Conference, the two Houses decided to abolish the Economic Cooperation Administration and transfer its responsibilities to a new Mutual Security Agency which would be headed by a Director for Mutual Security, to be appointed by the President with the advice and consent of the Senate. The director would have primary responsibility under the President and in consultation with the Secretaries of State and Defense to coordinate and supervise all the military, economic, and technical assistance programs. Thus, as Congress had done with the ECA in the European Recovery Program, it once again concentrated its attention on the administrative structure of the Mutual Security Program as a way to ensure that the program would be administered in an integrated and relatively impartial manner and not be captive to a single bureaucratic perspective.

The program was organized on a geographical basis, and although the largest share of assistance was allocated to Europe, the Asian/Pacific region (exclusive of Korea) also received sizeable increases, as did the Near East/Africa (Greece, Turkey, Iran, Palestine), and the American Republics. Although Congress made a few modifications of the policy, much of the time was devoted to ways of "economizing" on the Administration's request. The entire package was scaled down from $8.5 billion to $7.5 billion with the economic assistance section pared down the most. Congressional tolerance for economic assistance had apparently run its course, whereas the security threat was being taken more seriously. Indeed, Senator Joseph McCarthy was about to accuse the administration of being inadequately concerned with military preparedness.

Congress did, however, press the Administration to encourage our allies to share the burden of defense and to enter into more formal defense

---

[66]Brown and Opie, American Foreign Assistance, pp. 507–8.
[67]Ibid., p. 506.

agreements along the lines of NATO. This concern was more readily accepted by the Administration than by some of our allies who viewed this as interference.[68] The Administration's proposals did not include either a terminal date for the new program or a requirement to report periodically to the Congress. Both of these oversights were corrected by the Congress.[69]

As it had done on virtually every foreign aid initiative, Congress once again reiterated specifically the principle that the act should be administered in a way which would encourage free enterprise in countries receiving assistance.[70]

Since the beginning of lend-lease which had been organized on a bilateral basis, there had been a gradual enlargement in the focus of the U.S. foreign aid program, from lend-lease which was bilateral, to an economic reconstruction program (ERP) which was genuinely regional in scope, to a comprehensive global scheme which was based on purely security considerations. The Mutual Security Act remained the principal foreign aid framework for a decade, when it was finally abolished and superceded by the Foreign Assistance Act of 1961. During the decade of the MSA, the program remained relatively unchanged by the Executive and the Congress, although the Mutual Security Agency, which was established with the program in 1951, was abolished by Reorganization Plan No. 7 of 1953, and its functions were transferred to the Foreign Operations Administration (FOA). Similarly, the FOA was abolished by Executive Order 10610 of June 30, 1955, and its functions were transferred to the International Cooperation Administration, a semi-autonomous agency within the Department of State.

Throughout this period, the debate over whether aid should be in the form of grants or loans was repeated with virtually every renewal. The Executive strongly resisted congressional attempts to abandon the grant program, arguing that most recipient countries could not easily repay loans. The Congress argued for loans for several reasons, the most obvious being that it would save the taxpayer money. It was also felt that the recipient country would be more likely to use the money more efficiently and responsibly if it weren't gratis, and also that it would be more in our foreign policy interest if we loaned money. As Senator Bourke Hickenlooper warned: "The givers lose the gifts and also the friend who receives."[71] Gradually, Congress wore the Executive down on this issue. The percentage of aid which was financed by loans increased from 6 percent between 1953–55 to 22 percent between 1956–58 to 36 percent between 1959–61.[72]

[68]Ibid., pp. 523–24.
[69]Ibid., pp. 524–26.
[70]Ibid., p. 509.
[71]Remarks by Sen. Bourke Hickenlooper in hearings before the Senate Foreign Relations Committee, 1954, reprinted in David A. Baldwin, *Foreign Aid and American Foreign Policy: A Documentary Analysis* (N.Y.: Praeger, 1966), 71. (Hereafter Baldwin/Documents)
[72]Ibid., p. 32.

During the decade 1951–61, interest in the MSA gradually declined; one indication of this was the lower appropriations requests by the Executive each year, a second was the fact that Congress continued to consistently cut these lower requests by an average of 20 percent. Several other trends were evident. At Congress's insistence, the aid was gradually shifted to the "Asian arc." Congress showed more eagerness in cutting economic as opposed to military assistance. Thirdly, as the aid shifted to developing countries, Congress took a greater interest in funding guarantees for American foreign investors. Largely in response to congressional concern that U.S. private enterprise was not sufficiently active in the foreign assistance program, Ralph I. Straus, who was Special Consultant to the Undersecretary of State for Economic Affairs, wrote a Report in 1959 entitled *Expanding Private Investment for Free World Economic Growth* for the Secretary of State. The report recommended a number of policies by which U.S. foreign investors "can promote the foreign policy of the United States by stimulating the growth of the private sector in less developed countries."[73] Congress, in turn, responded by increasing the appropriations for investment guarantees from $500 million to $1 billion.[74]

Aid for Development, 1949–76

The principal thrust of the U.S. foreign aid program in the third stage was to assist the development of the poorer nations of the world. Four separate phases in the development of this part of the aid program can be identified. In the first phase, 1949 to 1960, United States foreign policy priorities were focused on Europe and on the rim of the Soviet Union. Most of the developing world was still colonial possessions. Those independent governments, such as in Latin America, requesting American attention and public assistance instead received lectures that the most effective channel for economic development was private investment, and the best way Latin Americans could encourage its transfer was by creating hospitable investment climates.[75]

While the U.S. Government *did* begin to respond in the late 1950s, the kind of massive public campaign requested by these developing countries had to await the inauguration of John F. Kennedy in 1961. This second phase ended around 1967, when the foreign aid program became the scapegoat of those Legislators who were disenchanted with the Vietnam War, but were unable to force Congress to face the Vietnam issue directly. Moreover, in this period, even pro-foreign aid Legislators began to question the existing

[73]Quoted in Baldwin/Documents, p. 155. For excerpts from the report, see pp. 153–158.

[74]For a quick review of this period, 1951–61, see Congressional Quarterly, *Congress and the Nation*, 1945–64, pp. 170–180.

[75]Robert Swansbrough, *The Embattled Colossus*, chap. 2.

aid program and seek new definitions of both aims and means. When the Executive failed to provide the focus for a new initiative, Congress in the 1973 Foreign Assistance Act moved independently, ushering in the current phase of a socially-oriented, predominantly multilateral and economic assistance program. In this most recent phase, Congress has also prodded the Executive to be more forthcoming on the wide range of issues—including trade expansion, debt rescheduling, commodities, and science and technology—which have become the North-South agenda.

It is ironically appropriate that the origin of U.S. foreign aid to the world's poorer countries was the last of four points which President Truman covered in his inaugural address on January 20, 1949. Six months later, after requesting from Congress over $7 billion of foreign aid for Europe and the "rim," Truman sent a follow-up message on Point IV requesting $45 million to fund the program. Clearly, the symbol was intended to shine brighter than the reality, and it apparently has, because few remember Point IV as not only the last, but also the least.

It was the precedent, however, which mattered. In his testimony before the Senate Foreign Relations Committee, Secretary of State Dean Acheson said that the technical assistance provision of the 1950 foreign assistance bill established "economic development of underdeveloped areas for the first time as a national policy."[76]

While the request for $45 million proved that the developing world was not completely forgotten by the U.S., the meagerness of the request also demonstrated that it remained the lowest priority on the U.S. foreign policy agenda. And it remained there until the same type of security considerations which had provoked the Marshall Plan and then the Mutual Security Act, finally induced the creation of the Agency for International Development (A.I.D.) and the Alliance for Progress in 1961.[77]

Still, A.I.D. and the Alliance did not arrive totally unexpected; there were several important policy shifts which anticipated these programs. The first, the Agriculture Trade Development and Assistance Act of 1954 (PL 480) was admittedly devised less from a concern for the developing world than from a domestic problem of a growing government agricultural commodity stock, which stood at $5.8 billion in 1954.[78] Largely written by the American Farm Bureau Federation and the two congressional agricultural committees and ultimately accepted and reworked with the help of the

---

[76]Cited in David A. Baldwin, *Economic Development and American Foreign Policy, 1943–62*. (Chicago: University of Chicago Press, 1966), pp. 43–62, 72.

[77]See Robert L. Paarlberg, "United States Attention to the Third World, 1945–1974: The Logic of Foreign Policy Agenda Formation" (Ph.D. dissertation, Harvard University, July 1975).

[78]See Peter A. Toma, *The Politics of Food for Peace: Executive–Legislative Interaction* (Tuscon: University of Arizona Press, 1967), p. 23.

Administration, PL 480, or Food for Peace as it came to be known, authorized $700 million for the "sales" program (sold for inconvertible local currencies which would be used in the recipient country for development purposes) and $300 million for donations for a three-year period ending June 1957. Since then, the program has been extended and modified.

The idea of permitting loans to developing countries to be paid back in "soft" (local) currency was also incorporated in two sections of the Mutual Security Act of 1954; and the idea gradually came to be seen as a compromise between the Executive's insistence on grants and Congress's preference for loans. Added impetus for the concept came from the developing countries themselves. In desperate need of capital but unable to repay loans in dollars, they applied pressure on the U.S. and other industrialized countries in many fora, but particularly in the United Nations. As early as January 12, 1952, these countries secured the passage of Resolution 520A (VI) by the General Assembly, calling for the establishment of a special U.N. fund to make grants and soft loans. But funds to implement the proposal were not forthcoming.[79] The U.S. Government in 1957 finally responded to these pressures by establishing a Development Loan Fund under the Mutual Security Act to make soft loans repayable in local currency.

The International Bank for Reconstruction and Development (World Bank) also showed great reluctance to establish a "soft loan" window, and so Senator A. S. Mike Monroney in February 1958 decided to press the point by introducing S. Res. 264 which urged the establishment of an International Development Association in cooperation with the World Bank to make long-term loans available at a low rate of interest and repayable in local currencies. Monroney's resolution has been called the "clearest case of Congressional initiative in foreign policy in recent years."[80] The State Department opposed the idea at first, but then worked with Monroney and the Treasury Department to revise the language and the substance of the bill. After hearings in the Senate Banking and Currency Subcommittee on International Finance, the revised resolution was approved by the Committee, and then by the Senate on July 12, 1958 by a vote of 62-25.[81]

Monroney's initiative was part of a small but growing movement among Senate liberals to reverse the emphasis on military rather than

---

[79]Baldwin/Documents, pp. 74–75.

[80]James A. Robinson, *Congress and Foreign Policy-Making*, rev. ed., (Homewood, Ill.: Dorsey Press, 1967)., p. 61. See also James A. Robinson, *The Monroney Resolution: Congressional Initiative in Foreign Policy-Making* (N.Y.: Holt, Rinehart, and Winston, 1959).

[81]Robinson tends to see more executive opposition to the Monroney idea and more congressional initiative than did David A. Baldwin in "Congressional Initiative in Foreign Policy," *Journal of Politics* 28 (November 1966). John Leddy, who was Special Assistant to Under Secretary of State C. Douglas Dillon at the time, supports Baldwin's interpretation. (John M. Leddy, "Notes on the Origins of the International Development Association, 1958–60," unpublished paper presented to the Symposium on the Congress and U. S. Economic Programs for the Developing Countries, Arlie House, October 1–2, 1972. [Hereafter Arlie House papers]

economic assistance. In August 1958, eight members of the Senate Foreign Relations Committee sent a public letter to the President decrying what they considered misplaced priorities, and recommending a renewed emphasis on economic assistance to the underdeveloped world. Eisenhower responded by appointing a Committee chaired by General William Draper and including three former generals, an admiral, and a former Assistant Secretary of Defense; and their report reflected the composition of the Committee. A rearrangement of priorities would have to await the new Administration taking office in January 1961.[82]

John F. Kennedy didn't waste any time reordering priorities. In his inaugural address, he devoted special attention and emphasis to the developing world:

> To those people in the huts and villages of half the globe struggling to break the bonds of mass misery, we pledge our best efforts to help them help themselves, for whatever period is required, not because the Communists may be doing it, not because we seek their votes, but because it is right. If a free society cannot help the many who are poor, it cannot save the few who are rich.[83]

On March 22, 1961, President Kennedy asked Congress to replace the ten-year old Mutual Security Act with a new legislative mandate which separated military from economic assistance and increased both. He requested a five-year authorization for development loans, totalling $8.8 billion, of which $7.3 billion was to be financed directly by the Treasury as a public debt transaction. Kennedy was persuaded by his development economists that long-term country-by-country planning could not be undertaken if the President had to return to the Congress each year for an annual authorization. But Congress rejected Kennedy's request for multi-year authorizations, just as it had every previous such request, on the grounds that it represented "backdoor spending."[84]

Congress did authorize $7.2 billion for development loans for a five-year period, but at the same time, it insisted that the funds be appropriated annually. Inevitably, every annual appropriation, even the first one, was cut; but even with the reductions, the development loans appropriated by Congress in the Foreign Assistance Act (FAA) of 1961 were twice the dollar amount of the last year of the Eisenhower Administration.[85] And the shift in emphasis from military to economic assistance, a shift which Kennedy as a Senator had urged Eisenhower to undertake in 1958, was accomplished with

[82]Baldwin/Documents, pp. 145–52.

[83]Theodore Sorenson, Kennedy, (N.Y.: Harper and Row, 1965) p. 276.

[84]Congressional Quarterly, Almanac, 1961, pp. 293–94.

[85]Congressional Quarterly, Congress and the Nation, 1945–64, p. 180.

Kennedy as President. During the first years of FAA, economic assistance was at least twice that of military assistance.[86]

The act passed Congress on August 31, 1961, and on November 3, Kennedy abolished the International Cooperation Administration (ICA) and the Development Loan Fund (DLF) and transferred their functions to a new "streamlined" Agency for International Development.[87]

Kennedy officially unveiled his ten-point, ten-year plan for an Alliance for Progress with Latin America on March 13, 1961. He expected the program to be so popular with Congress that it would "carry other parts of the foreign aid program past hostile budget-cutters," and so he inserted it as Title VI of the Foreign Assistance Act.[88] A request for an initial three-year authorization for $3 billion, however, was treated much the same as the rest of the bill. Congress cut $600 million, and stipulated that the Administration would have to request appropriations annually.[89]

Whatever enthusiasm there had been for the foreign aid program in 1961 was dissipated by early 1963, and Kennedy turned to the old technique of appointing a President Commission to revive interest in foreign aid. Since the Report of the Gray Committee of 1950, there were four such Committees or Commissions which either specifically addressed the issue of foreign aid or dealt with it indirectly as a component of U.S. foreign economic policy.[90] The main purpose of these Committees was to offer a canopy of legitimacy to the program (or some aspect of the program) and to strengthen support for it in Congress and the American public.[91] In 1963, Kennedy decided to take "a calculated risk," appointing a conservative, General Lucius D. Clay, to be chairman of a Committee which was composed of several other conservative and military people. The gamble, in Sorenson's words, "backfired."[92] The Committee concluded: "There is a feeling that we are trying to do too much for too many too soon, that we are overextended in resources and undercompensated in results, and that no end of foreign aid is either in sight or in mind."[93] Clay therefore recommended reductions in both military and

[86]*Overseas Loans,* p. 6.

[87]For a legislative history of the Foreign Assistance Act of 1961, see U. S. Senate Committee on Foreign Relations, "The Foreign Assistance Act of 1961," in Bernard C. Cohen (ed.), *Foreign Policy in American Government* (Boston: Little, Brown and Co., 1965), pp. 158–69. Sorenson wrote that Kennedy "later regretted the new title (A.I.D.) as an unhelpful gimmick." (p. 597)

[88]Jerome Levinson and Juan de Onis, *The Alliance That Lost Its Way* (Chicago: Quadrangle Books, 1970), p. 109.

[89]Ibid., p. 114.

[90]The committees were chaired and thus named after Rockefeller (1951), Randall (1954), Fairless (1957), and Draper (1959).

[91]Baldwin/Documents, p. 235.

[92]Theodore Sorenson, *Kennedy,* p. 393.

[93]Cited in Baldwin/Documents, p. 237.

economic assistance, but in the light of "a relentless Communist imperialism," military assistance should be cut less than economic.[94]

Added to the relaxation of tensions between the U.S. and the Soviet Union, which followed the signing of the Nuclear Test Ban Treaty on September 22, the installation of the "hot line," and the approval of a sale of 150 million bushels of wheat, this particular recommendation of the Clay Committee only reinforced the congressional inclination to cut and to restrict. The President's request was reduced by one-third, and Congress mandated a number of policies which the President would have preferred to have remained discretionary and flexible, but which he accepted reluctantly. For example, the direct embargo against Cuba and the indirect embargo, which prohibited aid to countries which traded with Cuba, were both tightened considerably. A minimum interest rate for loans was set. And aid was prohibited to countries that refused to sign agreements insuring U.S. corporations against the risk of expropriation.

While Kennedy said that he considered the "neutralism" of certain developing countries as "inevitable" rather than "immoral," as John Foster Dulles had called it, many in Congress were more comfortable with Dulles's characterization. Two examples were the prohibition against assistance to Sukarno's Indonesia (except by Presidential waiver) and the disapproval of a loan for the Bokaro steel project in neutral India.[95]

From a different direction, Senator J. William Fulbright, impatient over AID's refusal to consider population growth a development problem, marshalled support in Congress to pass an amendment which specifically authorized AID to support research and technical assistance in population control. In the face of continued indifference and opposition in AID, several Senators led by Fulbright and Gruening with the support of several nongovernmental groups repeatedly enlarged the program during the 1960s and 1970s.[96]

By 1965, a more lasting and serious disenchantment with the Foreign Assistance Act of 1961 was becoming evident. Senator Fulbright, for one, believed that the U.S. was in need of a new program, one which relied on multi-year authorizations, was more multilateral than bilateral, and more economic than security-oriented, with both programs kept separate. Sen. Wayne Morse, however, took a very different tack, opposing both multilateralism and multi-year authorizations because they reduced Congress's oversight responsibilities. In 1965, however, the Senate split the difference

[94]Ibid., p. 240.

[95]Sorenson, *Kennedy*, pp. 605–6.

[96]See Phyllis T. Piotrow, "Population Assistance: A Case Study of Innovation in the United States Foreign Assistance Program," Arlie House papers. Also, George Ball, *Diplomacy in a Crowded World*, Boston: Little, Brown, 1976. p. 343, n. 16.

between the two views and passed a two-year authorization which requested the President to present new proposals the next year.

During this period, on foreign affairs matters, the House of Representatives generally questioned the President and his programs less than the Senate. This was due in large part to the man who chaired the House Foreign Affairs Committee from 1958–76, Thomas "Doc" Morgan. "Under the Constitution," Morgan said, "the President is made responsible for the conduct of our foreign relations, and the job of developing a foreign aid program rests with him."[97] As the Senate's skepticism over the conduct of the Vietnam War was gradually transformed in the late 1960s to bitter opposition, the House, to the Senate's considerable frustration, stood firmly behind the President. In 1965, Morgan said that he didn't see the necessity of dividing the economic from the military assistance programs since they served the same objective: "to prevent war and to maintain our security."[98] He therefore opposed altering the foreign assistance act, and his views prevailed not only in the House, but with the strong support of the Administration, in the Conference.

In 1966, President Johnson *did* respond to Fulbright's suggestion and sent to Congress separate bills for economic and military assistance, though both asked for a five-year authorization. The foreign aid debate in 1966 was laced with several ironies. First, although Fulbright's opposition to the war was in full flower, he not only refrained from attacking the bill on the floor, he in fact managed it for the Administration. Secondly, the House reversed its position of the previous year and supported the President's request for a five-year authorization for the Alliance for Progress and the Development Loan Fund and a two-year authorization for a combined military and economic foreign aid bill. The Senate kept the two bills separate and limited them to a one-year authorization, though it permitted a two-year authorization for the Alliance. In Conference, Congress agreed to a combined one-year bill which included a three-year authorization for the Alliance and the DLF.

More important, the attitudes of the congressional leaders of the foreign aid program were undergoing a profound change, and each year the foreign aid bill felt the effects of this transformation. 1966 was also the last year in the 1960s when the ratio of economic to security assistance was as high as 2:1.[99]

In 1967 and 1968, the advance authorization for the Alliance and the DLF was withdrawn, and the aid package was cut to its thinnest and lowest levels in ten years. The restrictions on the Executive's discretion to conduct foreign policy also increased measurably, and interestingly, it was not so

[97]Quoted in Richard Fenno, *Congressmen in Committees*, p. 71.
[98]Congressional Quarterly, *Congress and the Nation*, vol. 2, 1965–68, pp. 65–68.
[99]Robert Packenham, *Liberal America*, p. 87.

much because liberals searched for ways to manifest their opposition to the war, but because the conservatives were unleashed by a war whose goal was to contain Communism, and the liberals no longer had an interest in restraining them. The stiffest fight of the 1967 session was on an amendment by H. R. Gross which would have required the President to stop sales or purchases on defense articles to all nations (including Britain and France) that traded with North Vietnam. Administration pressure in Conference succeeded in getting the amendment deleted, but Gross narrowly missed defeating the entire bill because of this change.[100] Other Administration attempts to expand trade with the Communist bloc were similarly defeated.[101]

During these years, Congress also extended its influence to the arms sales programs. Military assistance and credits could not be used to buy "sophisticated" weapons like jet aircraft, and those developing countries whose defense spending was considered unnecessarily high would no longer be eligible for military assistance.[102]

Despite growing opposition to the war, Congress was extremely reluctant to address directly the question of cutting off funds for the war. Instead, it sought surrogates or scapegoats to vent its displeasure. For example, instead of challenging the Executive's rationale for fighting in Vietnam (although many individual Legislators did; Congress as a whole did not), Congress tried to prevent future wars by the War Powers Act of 1973 and the National Commitments Resolution of 1969, both of which demanded that the war and commitment powers of the U.S. be shared by both branches.[103] In spite of ninety-four roll-call votes on the war from the mid-1960s to the signing of the ceasefire agreement on January 27, 1973, the Congress as a whole never voted to cut off funds for the war. In 1972, the Senate voted to cut off funds, but the House deleted it in conference. And, of course, throughout the debate, the foreign aid bill was only one of many vehicles used to attack the Administration's policy on the war.

In 1969, President Nixon requested the lowest level of economic aid ($2.6 billion) in the program's twenty-year history. He urged greater reliance on technical assistance and private investment, and proposed the creation of the Overseas Private Investment Corporation (OPIC) to stimulate private investment in the developing countries through preinvestment studies and loan and political-risk insurance.

The OPIC idea had a long history. Political-risk insurance for foreign direct investment was a component of the Marshall Plan and every foreign

---

[100]The vote was 196-200. *Congress and the Nation*, vol. 2, pp. 81–84.

[101]Ibid., p. 110.

[102]Ibid., pp. 84, 86. These restrictions were repealed in the Foreign Assistance Act of 1973.

[103]*Congress and the Nation*, vol. 3, pp. 854–6.

aid package since then. In 1961, with the establishment of AID, private enterprise was given new emphasis, and in 1963, Congress added an amendment to the Foreign Assistance Act which called for the establishment of a nine-member group to "carry out studies and make recommendations for achieving the most effective utilization of the private enterprise provisions of this Act." As a result of this provision, President Kennedy appointed Arthur K. Watson, Chairman of IBM, to chair an Advisory Committee on Private Enterprise in Foreign Aid. In July 1965, the Committee issued its report, *Foreign Aid Through Private Initiative*, which included a series of recommendations on how private enterprise can help to fill the "gap" between the resources needed for development and the governmental resources available.[104]

In order to implement the program, an office (the Office of Private Resources) was established in AID, and in close collaboration with Senator Jacob Javits, who had a long-standing interest in the issue, the officials charged with implementing the program began trying to develop a new framework. Javits continually introduced legislation on the subject, but Treasury opposed it, and Senator Fulbright refused to hold hearings. In 1968, an election year, several members of the Office of Private Resources informally briefed both candidates on an OPIC-type idea, and obtained informal agreements. After the election, Nixon sent the proposal to Congress, and Javits guided it through to passage. As his Staff Assistant commented: "The influence of a committed and influential Senator in securing the Congressional passage of legislation which he considers to be 'his baby' cannot be overemphasized."[105] Another participant attributed the success of the bill to the fact that it "was made to appear to be the brainchild of all the interested power centers."[106] There were other reasons: the concept itself was viewed as a pragmatic, businesslike response to a problem of funding development; the operating officers in the administration worked directly with their congressional counterparts in framing the bill rather than letting their liaison officers take the lead; relevant interest groups, both private and congressional, were involved early in the process of translating the concept into a program; and a cohesive and active coalition continually pressed for enactment of the bill.

Thus, in the midst of an increasingly hostile debate on the war, a debate that had begun as an outgrowth of the foreign aid bill but would return to hold the bill hostage for a couple of years, the two branches exchanged ideas and developed a new program.

The Administration had much less success in the more comprehensive

---

[104]For excerpts from the report, see Baldwin/Documents, pp. 158–171.

[105]Comments of Kenneth Guenther on William Gilbert Carter's paper, "The Overseas Private Investment Corporation (OPIC): How the Legislation Got Passed," Arlie House papers.

[106]Comments of Rutherford Poats on Carter's paper, Arlie House papers.

study on foreign aid done by the Presidentially-appointed (Rudolph) Peterson Commission. Because the reasons for its failure contrast in an instructive way with the reasons for the success of OPIC, the event merits a brief review.[107]

On September 4, 1969, President Nixon asked Rudolph Peterson, Chairman of the Bank of America, to chair a Commission to review the entire development assistance program. Six months later, Peterson presented his recommendations to the President. The Commission suggested that the U.S. shift the burden of its development efforts to multilateral institutions, and that it divide the foreign assistance package into three parts: the long-term development assistance part to new institutions, the short-term political component to the State Department, and the security assistance component to the Defense Department. It also recommended that the downward trend in U.S. official development assistance, a trend which was particularly evident since 1965, be reversed.

Thirteen months later, two draft bills containing many of the recommendations were sent to Congress where they were soon the subject of a series of hearings in the House Foreign Affairs Committee. But the proposals never left the Committee, and in a discussion two years later between one of the congressional participants, Dante Fascell, and an AID official, Ernest Stern, several explanations were suggested.[108] In the winter of 1970–71, when there should have been briefings and consultations between AID officials, Commission members, and members of Congress, there weren't any. Peterson and Dr. John Hannah, the Administrator of AID, did meet with a few Legislators but these contacts, according to Fascell, were "feeble in comparison with the kind of a campaign that the White House undertakes when it wants to see an important bill passed by the Congress." Fascell concluded "that in spite of his fine-sounding pronouncements, the President was not really interested in reshaping foreign aid during his first term in office."[109]

Obviously, the officials in AID had no incentive to lobby for a bill which would probably eliminate their agency and their jobs, and the State Department was hardly enthusiastic about losing bilateral assistance as a source of influence. Stern, however, argued for a displacement of blame: "The fact of the matter is, of course, that the lack of interest in the Executive Branch in foreign aid is more than matched by the lack of interest in Congress."[110] While Fascell had argued that if the Administration had wanted to sell the

[107]See Richard L. Cohen, "Congressional Reaction is Key to Fate of Foreign Aid Report," *National Journal*, 14 March 1970, pp. 539–541. Also see Gale W. McGee, "Following Knockdown, Foreign Aid for 1972 Funded in Final Round," Arlie House papers.

[108]Hon. Dante B. Fascell, "The Congress and the Peterson Report on Foreign Aid," Arlie House papers. Ernest Stern, "Congress and the Peterson Report; A Comment," Arlie House papers.

[109]Dante Fascell, "Congress and the Peterson Report."

[110]Ernest Stern, "Congress and The Peterson Report", p. 3.

138-page report and the bills to Congress, it should have devoted more time to briefing the Legislators, Stern countered that Congress also had thirteen months to study the report, which was public, and therefore was in a poor position to blame the Executive for inadequate attention to detail.

The quick demise of the Peterson proposals was but a preview of the more serious events which befell the foreign aid bill in the fall. On October 29, 1971, the Senate for the first time voted down the bill, 27-41. Conservatives attacked it for its failure to gain any friends in the developing world for the United States, and liberals railed against its bulging security assistance provisions.[111] Four days before, the United Nations, following the logic of President Nixon's bold initiative toward the Peoples Republic of China rather than his pronouncements upon his return, expelled Taiwan, thereby prompting a hail of congressional resolutions urging American withdrawl from the U.N. and/or reduction of the U.S. contribution. This no doubt contributed to the congressional decision, as did the Mansfield amendment to end the war which the Senate accepted but the House rejected. Mansfield and other antiwar Senators held the bill hostage, hoping to secure passage of the amendment by the House. The strategy did not work, but in the period 1971—73, the bill was trapped so often, that AID usually functioned on the basis of continuing resolutions at existing levels of appropriations rather than by annual legislative mandate.[112]

The deadlock was broken in 1973 with a dramatic shift in the direction of the foreign aid program. The thrust of the bilateral development program changed from an economic strategy of maximizing gross national product and industrialization and a political strategy of providing the largest amounts of aid and food commodities to military allies to a more socially-oriented strategy of helping the poorest countries and the poorest sectors of the population in those countries. A complete reorganization of AID from an agency defined by geographical categories to one based on the three principal functions of a development process aimed at the "poorest 40 percent": food and nutrition; population planning and health; and education and human resources. The new strategy was "intended to increase substantially the participation of the poor" in the country's development.

The ideas underlying what came to be called the "new directions" program in foreign aid emerged from a community of scholars and officials in Washington, D.C. concerned with development and based at AID, the Overseas Development Council, and particularly the World Bank. Robert S. McNamara, president of the World Bank, discussed the need for a new strategy in a speech in 1972, and in his Annual Address to the Board of Governors in September 1973, he described the "basic human needs" approach to reach the "poorest 40 percent" in some detail. At about the same time, John Hannah, administrator of AID, drafted a report suggesting ways

[111]Gale McGee, "Following Knockdown".
[112]Ibid.

to adapt the strategy to the U.S. bilateral assistance program.

All executive proposals must be screened at the Legislative Division of the Office of Management and Budget, but anticipating that OMB might reject the proposals in Hannah's report, several staff from AID formed a working group with researchers from the Overseas Development Council and staff from the House Foreign Affairs Committee to consider ways to implement Hannah's report. By the time OMB had rejected them, the proposals were written and accepted by the House Foreign Affairs Committee. AID at this point disclaimed responsibility for the new Foreign Assistance Act of 1973, and was vindicated by the Senate, whose report noted: "This fundamental redirection [of the U.S. aid program] was primarily a Congressional initiative which subsequently received the support of the Administration."[113] A more accurate description would be that it was AID's initiative, congressional endorsement and redrafting with the help of the Overseas Development Council, and OMB acceptance of a fait accompli.[114]

Prior to 1973, the usual practice was for Congress to defer to the Executive in initiating a new program. After a long period of no response, Congress fashioned its own program. Yet the coalition of liberal Legislators who shaped the Foreign Assistance Act (FAA) of 1973 were increasingly disturbed by the coalition of State and conservative Legislators who insisted on joining the military and economic assistance programs in a single bill. In 1974, Representative Donald Fraser, a liberal congressman from Minnesota, issued a strongly-worded dissent to the House Report on FAA 1974:

> Every year until this year I have voted for foreign assistance bills in committee and on the floor of the House, but always with strong reservations against many of the provisions for military assistance. I continue to believe that the U.S. has a major responsibility to provide economic and humanitarian assistance to the developing countries. However, I cannot support this bill because the executive branch has made it abundantly clear that it intends to give the maximum amount of military aid no matter how cruelly repressive recipient governments might be.[115]

Fraser's dissent represented a turning point. The next year, the liberals in AID and in the House International Relations Committee (renamed from the Foreign Affairs Committee) successfully lobbied both State and the Committee's Chairman, Tom Morgan, and the result was the submission of two separate bills.

[113]U. S. Senate Foreign Relations Committee, *Foreign Assistance Act: Report on S. 2335*, 2 August 1973, p. 4.

[114]Interviews. Also see James D. Grant, "An Analysis of the Congressional Foreign Aid Initiative of 1973," unpublished paper, Harvard University, 12 May 1975.

[115]U. S. House of Representatives, Committee on Foreign Affairs, *Report on the Foreign Assistance Act of 1974*, pp. 73–74.

By the time Congress began redrafting the International Development and Food Assistance Act of 1975, it was evident to many that Congress, in the words of one internal AID memorandum, "is well ahead of the Executive Branch" both in terms of reducing the AID budget less and in directing the AID program more towards the goals of a "basic human needs," employment-oriented development strategy as opposed to the growth-oriented, trickle-down strategy of the 1960s.[116]

In 1975, Congress combined the food aid program with the development assistance bill, and mandated that at least 75 percent of the Title I Funds of PL 480 would go to the neediest countries, i.e., not for short-term political or strategic purposes.[117] Language was also added to encourage the President to negotiate an international system of food reserves. The drive toward depoliticizing the food program as an instrument of U.S. foreign policy ironically followed acceptance of a recommendation of the Bolling Committee, which divided food aid jurisdiction between the Agriculture and Foreign Affairs Committees. It was the latter Committee which recommended to the House that food aid be used more for humanitarian purposes, and less for political and strategic purposes.

Congress was also in front of the Executive in a number of other important areas. It reversed the drift toward loans instead of grants. In fiscal year 1974, 60 percent of the funds transferred by AID were loans, but by 1975, Congress had tipped the scales to grants, particularly to the poorest countries. Secondly, a two-year authorization was accepted for both the economic and the security assistance acts. Thirdly, Congress facilitated a shift toward multilateral assistance. In 1965, 2 percent of U.S. foreign assistance was channelled through the multilateral development banks; in 1970, the figure was 14 percent; and in the years, 1972–74, the average was 23 percent.[118]

In this most recent phase of the foreign aid program, 1973–1976, Congress became the principal arena for redirecting and reshaping U.S. foreign assistance policy. In addition, Congress grew more confident of its own foreign policy judgments and began to legislate more specific foreign policies using the aid bill as the vehicle. That is the subject of the next chapter, but first, I shall summarize certain patterns in the policy process that extend throughout the history of postwar foreign aid policy.

---

[116]Internal staff memorandum, Agency for International Development, July 1976, p. 7. Executive branch requests from 1970 to 1976 declined by 29 percent in current prices and 55 percent in real terms. The Appropriations Committees reduced the requests less than that, and less over time. In fiscal year 1970, the Senate Appropriations Committee reduced the request by 45 percent, but by fiscal year 1977, only by 1.6 percent.

[117]Congressional Quarterly, *Almanac*, 1975, pp. 332–43.

[118]*Development Issues: U. S. Actions Affecting the Development of Low-Income Countries*, The First Annual Report of the President, transmitted to the Congress, 1975, p. 30.

CONGRESS AND FOREIGN AID POLICY: SOME RECURRING PATTERNS

In every change of the legislative mandate on foreign aid, from the European Recovery Program to the International Development and Food Assistance Act of 1975, the same set of questions have been posed with different answers given by each branch.

For example, with only a few exceptions, the Executive has shown a decided preference for multiyear authorizations and grants rather than loans, whereas Congress has insisted, sometimes as in the case of Senator Morse on constitutional grounds, more often for political reasons, on single-year authorizations, and loans as opposed to grants. The explanation for this divergence is simple and institutional. The less often the Executive has to return to Congress, the less power Congress has over the direction of the program and the less influence Congress can have over U.S. foreign policy. Secondly, Congress faces the taxpayers, who fund the programs, whereas the administrators of the foreign aid program face the foreigners who receive the benefits. What you say depends to a great extent on to whom you're listening.

Congress has had clear preferences on the questions how to organize and with whom to staff the new agencies established to administer the aid program. There is a tendency in Congress to think that the more independent the agency is of the State Department, the better run it will be. Similarly, Congress has used its influence to ensure that the director of the aid program has a background which reflects the world of business more than that of diplomacy. Indeed, Congress has been consistently exercised about the question whether the U.S. private enterprise system has been sufficiently represented in the foreign aid program in its ends as well as its means: business should be more involved in the aid program; the promotion of private investment (both U.S. and foreign) should be one of the program's aims; and the program should be run more "businesslike."[119] Whether Congress or the President is Democrat or Republican, these three themes have been pursued more vigorously by Congress than by the President throughout the history of U.S. foreign assistance policy.

Congress's public budgetary process was described as irrational until Aaron Wildavsky studied the Executive's budgetary process and discovered that the process more nearly resembles "incremental muddling" than a rational decision-making process, defined as a comprehensive search for the best alternative on a cost-benefit basis. Both the Executive and Congress tear

---

[119]See David Davis, "The Price of Power: The Appropriations Process for Seventeen Foreign Affairs Agencies," *Public Policy* 18 (1970): 355–381. Davis found that Congress is much more generous to those agencies which are run in a "business-like" manner and which have "business-like" purposes.

at the margins of the budget; sometimes one tears harder than the other. Congressional reductions seem less responsible and more heartless, but that is at least partly because the Executive's budgetary decisions are less visible, and Congress involves itself less in the Executive's process than the other way around.

The difference between a private decision-making process in which few outside actors participate and a public process in which participation is widespread is critical in explaining many of the different positions taken by Congress and the Executive. For example, both branches have singled out individual countries for punishment by reduction or termination of aid—indeed, the Executive does it for almost every country with each appropriation request—but there are relatively few cases of Executive retribution which are either widely known or controversial. Every case of congressional action, however, is known and controversial, in part because the Executive tries to resist these changes. For example, Congress for a long time singled out India, the United Arab Republic, and Indonesia for their neutralism, while after 1961 the Executive sought more flexibility. Yugoslavia also was treated more like an adversary than a potential or tacit ally.[120]

Congress has shown itself to be more responsive to the public mood, and often just as inarticulate. The widespread discontent in the country with the conduct of the Vietnam War was reflected in Congress's frequent desire to do something with the aid bill but its inability to arrive at any consensus on what that should be.

Similarly, with regard to specific policies, Congress has rather consistently stood for a more forthright promotion, protection, and articulation of U.S. interests abroad. Thus, congressmen have often, quite correctly, been referred to as "unexcelled expediters" when it comes to protecting U.S. citizens abroad.[121] On more general questions, Congress is open and public about the conditions which it believes the United States should expect from recipients of America's largesse. Congress has, therefore, taken positions in support of greater restrictions on the sales of arms abroad, the promotion and protection of U.S. foreign direct investment, the protection of fundamental human rights of all people, the protection of U.S. fishermen abroad, and the application of punitive sanctions on both bilateral as well as multilateral aid when such interests are violated unjustly. Congress has been more preoccupied with the problem of the flow of narcotics to the United States from developing countries, and it has pushed the Executive to devise programs of cooperation with these countries to impede such trade, and punitive sanctions if the country is not sufficiently cooperative.[122]

[120]Nelson, *Aid, Influence, and Foreign Policy*, p. 56.

[121]John D. Montgomery has written: "Where constituents' interests are involved, Congressmen are unexcelled as expediters." Montgomery, *Politics of Foreign Aid*, p. 221.

[122]Concern over the transport of narcotics from aid-recipient countries to the U. S. was evidenced by Congress as early as 1951. See Montgomery, *Politics of Foreign Aid*, p. 204.

Certain individual Legislators have taken special interest in particular programs; they define the program, elicit support from colleagues to pass these programs, and prod AID to implement them properly. Examples of this are Senator Charles Percy's long-standing interest in women in development, Senators Fulbright and Gruening's interest in population policy, and Senator McGee's interest in the American Schools and Hospitals program abroad.

Congress has not only tended to be more niggardly than the executive in its appropriations, but also has tended to feel that U.S. instruments of trade—for example, merchant ships and U.S. products—should be given special preference. When the balance of payments issue was a serious problem from 1959 through the 1960s, the Executive agreed with Congress that U.S. aid should be tied to the purchase of U.S. goods and services. In 1971, President Nixon decided to abandon this policy of "additionality,"[123] yet it persists. In fiscal year 1974, over 75 percent of total expenditures for development assistance was spent in the U.S.[124]

Every significant change in the foreign aid program by Congress, whether it was Vandenberg's reorganization of the Administration's idea of the Economic Cooperation Administration or the rewriting of the bill in 1973, involved assistance from outside groups, like Brookings or the Overseas Development Council. Generally, it was the Congress which turned to these institutions rather than the other way around, but the direction of first contact is not so important as the fact that the final policy reflected Congress's long-standing inclinations.

Private interest groups, however, have played virtually no part in the development of the overall foreign aid program, though such groups have occasionally been mobilized on behalf of a specific concern or in response to requests from parts of the government. The defeat of the foreign aid bill in 1971 and the defeat of the 1974 appropriations for the International Development Association spurred those Legislators with special concern for these issues to mobilize private groups in support of their passage. The strategy of Legislators lobbying lobbyists to put pressure on their colleagues was successful in both instances,[125] and the coalition of groups brought together for that purpose has remained as an important source of public support for the program, particularly with regard to those Legislators who are either apathetic or not greatly involved in the program.[126] As Barber

[123]William Seelbach, "The Decision to Rescind Additionality Requirements on A.I.D. Grants and Loans," in Hamilton Studies, Murphy Commission, app. H, vol. 3, pp. 116–26. The study unfortunately overlooked the role of the Congress in the decision.

[124]*Development Issues*, 1975, 48.

[125]Interviews.

[126]The principal groups involved are the United Nations Association, the Overseas Development Council, the Interreligious Task Force on U. S. Food Policy, the League of Women Voters, and the Members of Congress for Peace Through Law. These and as many as fifty other groups meet periodically to plot legislative strategy for the foreign aid program.

Conable has pointed out, the Legislator has a good deal more flexibility on foreign aid legislation where his constituents are not affected directly than on much of domestic policy legislation,[127] and this can mean either the favorable passage and support of foreign aid laws or their defeat.

In summary, Congress and the Executive have pushed-and-pulled on the foreign aid program since its beginning; and there are relatively consistent patterns to the policies each branch has articulated and pursued. Congress has generally preferred single-year authorizations, loans rather than grants, economic rather than military assistance, an independent administering agency rather than one controlled by the State Department, a businesslike program run by a businessman in order to promote the private enterprise system, larger budgetary cuts, a number of specific programs, a large proportion of the aid to be spent on U.S. products carried in U.S. ships, and the more forthright promotion, protection, and articulation of U.S. interests abroad than the Executive, which prefers quiet and flexible diplomacy.

All of these congressional preferences, however, do not add up to a development strategy or to a foreign aid program. Since the Second World War, there have been four such programs, and with the exception of the most recent one, all have been formulated within the executive branch. The Marshall Plan, the Mutual Security Act, the Foreign Assistance Act and the Alliance for Progress—all have been created by the Executive, and with a concerted public relations campaign, they have been sold intact to the Congress.

The most recent "New Directions" aid package was developed in the Congressional arena for three reasons: a group of liberal Legislators eager to compensate for Executive apathy by developing a new and constructive approach to the developing world; private research organizations with *the idea* for a new development strategy; and a competent group of congressional staff able to fuse the idea from the outside groups and the eagerness from the Legislators into a viable bill.

---

[127]In his Arlie House paper. This point is confirmed by O'Leary, *The Politics of American Foreign Aid* (N.Y.: Atherton Press, 1967), p. 46–48, 58; Montgomery, *Politics of Foreign Aid*, p. 198.

10

CONGRESSIONAL FOREIGN POLICY BY AMENDMENT, TWO CASES: INVESTMENT DISPUTES AND HUMAN RIGHTS

Santa Claus inevitably ends up wearing a badge.[1]

—*Gustav Ranis*

Like trade and investment policy, U.S. policy on foreign assistance in the postwar period has been the product of an interactive process between two branches, each with different biases and priorities. Yet Congress's influence in the overall shaping of the foreign aid program, while important, was not as critical as in either trade or investment policy. This conclusion is somewhat surprising given the time Congress has devoted to the foreign aid program and the reputation it has acquired for handicapping U.S. foreign policy by its inept handling of the aid bill. In a critique of Congress's role in making U.S. foreign policy, for example, Stanley Hoffmann placed special emphasis on Congress's "destructive power in the realm of foreign aid."[2]

The apparent paradox between a Congress which is less influential in shaping the general contours of U.S. aid policy and a Congress which is said to savagely assault the aid bill annually is explained in two ways. First, most scholars draw their conclusions about Congress's active and negative influence from its unwillingness to permit multi-year authorizations, its repeated desire to cut the Administration's budgetary request by 10-20 percent, and its occasional but nonetheless controversial disagreements with the Executive on the proper course for U.S. foreign policy. There is no inherent reason why any of these congressional preferences should be considered negative, unless one presumes that the foreign policy perogative

---

[1]Gustav Ranis (ed.), *The United States and the Developing Economies* (N.Y.: W. W. Norton and Co., 1973), p. xx.

[2]Stanley Hoffmann, *Gulliver's Troubles, Or the Setting of American Foreign Policy* (N.Y.: McGraw-Hill, 1968), p. 256.

should be solely that of the Executive, or unless one believes that the President's policy is always the best. It is true that the legislative result may be an impractical or even counterproductive foreign policy, but as this chapter will show, the Executive must also bear a significant part of the burden for such failures.

A second explanation for this apparent paradox is that Congress has shown less interest, at least until recently, in changing U.S. policy on foreign economic recovery or development—i.e., the overall strategy of the foreign assistance program—than it has on specific foreign policies. It is, in contrast, much more intent on using foreign aid as a vehicle to make statements, some binding, on foreign developments or countries.

Congress makes such statements by amending foreign aid bills. Although the Foreign Assistance and the Security Assistance Acts are the primary vehicles, Congress can and does attach these policies to any legislation from the Sugar Act to the Trade Act to the Defense Production Act which in any way transfer resources from the U.S. to another country. By reducing, redirecting, or terminating the transfer or "give-away," as many Legislators call it, Congress expresses its sense of the world and seeks to keep the State Department or the administering agency responsive to its judgment of U.S. priorities.

It is this characteristic of foreign aid policy—the unilateral transfer of resources from one country to another—which distinguishes it from other areas of foreign economic policy. Instead of the norm of "reciprocity" which governs trade policy or "national treatment" which defines the acceptable range of national law in investment policy, foreign aid policy involves a trade, which is sometimes barely acceptable, between two fundamentally different kinds of commodities: resources and influence. The donor grants aid allegedly for general goals like economic development, but it also expects in return *special* behavior from the recipient.

Because the two commodities—resources and influence—are not legitimately interchangeable in any marketplace, but the home, the relationship between the donor and the recipient always exhibits a paternal awkwardness. Unlike any other trade, the transfer of aid can sometimes leave both donor and recipient worse off than before. That is one reason why Senator J. William Fulbright preferred multilateral to bilateral aid:

> *The crucial difference between bilateral and international aid is the basic incompatibility of bilateralism with individual and national dignity. Charity corrodes both the rich and the poor, breeding an exaggerated sense of authority on the part of the donor and a destructive loss of self-esteem on the part of the recipient.*[3]

[3]Sen. J. William Fulbright, *Arrogance of Power* (N.Y.: Random House, 1966), p. 255.

It is natural and understandable for the recipient to seek as much assistance with as few conditions or "strings" as possible, and conversely for the donor to insist on as little aid and as much influence as possible. The recipient comes to believe that it is its *right* to receive assistance, while the donor believes it is its *right* to set the terms.[4] The United States, like all donors, believes in its right to set the terms, and both the Executive and Congress share this belief. Unlike most other donors, however, the U. S. Government is internally divided between Congress and the Executive on the definition of the terms and their mode of enforcement.

The central questions in this chapter are: How are those specific foreign policies made? What are the dynamics of interaction between the two branches, and do they exhibit any consistent patterns? Which branch is pushing which, for what purpose, and to what effect? Why does Congress sometimes "tie" the Executive's hands, depriving the Executive of the flexibility often needed to conduct effective diplomacy?

In the discussion of trade preferences and East-West trade policy in chapter six, I suggested several explanations for why certain issues in the trade bill were amicably resolved and others were not. In this chapter, those hypotheses will be tested by examining two issues intensively, and mapping the process by which the respective policies of the two branches converged and diverged. The two cases describe the process by which Congress and the Executive used aid as an instrument to protect U.S. foreign investment and to defend human rights.

TWO CASES

In 1962, Congress attached an amendment, subsequently named for its sponsor, Sen. Bourke Hickenlooper, to the Foreign Assistance Act requiring the President to suspend U.S. assistance to a country if it expropriates U.S. foreign investment and does not make provisions for "prompt, adequate, and effective compensation." The Hickenlooper amendment was only the most dramatic of the many statements of concern by Congress and the Executive over the treatment of U.S. investors overseas, and the desire to use the foreign aid program as the instrument for addressing this issue. Since 1973, concern in the United States over the violations of human rights by foreign governments stimulated a similar attempt to use the aid program to try to correct these abuses. Amendments were attached to the bilateral economic

---

[4]This pattern of interaction is hardly confined to nations. It's inherent in any paternalistic relationship. For example, with regard to the emerging paternal relationship between the University and the Federal Government, see "Federal Aid, Not Intervention Needed by Education, says Bok," the President of Harvard University, *Annual Report, 1974–75.*

and military assistance acts and to the Inter-American Development Bank Act of 1976 for the purpose of using U.S. assistance as a lever.

The two issues have several points in common and a fundamental difference. Respect for the rights of property and of people are central tenets in the American political creed. At different points in U.S. history, the sense of mission, which has always been an important motive and guide in U.S. diplomacy, has embodied this creed and projected it abroad.[5] A classic example of this American tendency to assume that what is good for America must necessarily be good for the world is the following statement by a congressman from Pennsylvania in a debate on the Foreign Assistance Act of 1962:

> Mr. Speaker, all of us in this country view with alarm the attempts that are being made by one of our Latin American neighbors to take over certain industries in which American capital has been invested in large amounts. We regard such attempts as unwarranted intrusions by a national government into the realm that is traditionally that of private enterprise in the truly American sense of the word. It is not, we say firmly and unequivocally, something that we would do here in the United States and, therefore, it is not something that should be done in any democratic Latin American nation.[6]

The issues differ in that the property which is of concern to U.S. foreign policy is American while the citizens' rights are those of foreigners. The most important similarities between the two issues, from the perspective of this analysis, is that Congress to a great extent first articulated U.S. government concern on this issue; it remained deeply involved in the development of policy; and to a great extent, it defined and imposed a U.S. foreign policy over the objections of the executive branch. While there was little disagreement between the branches on the importance of the two interests, there was considerable difference of opinion on the relative importance of these goals within the panoply of American interests, on the proper instruments which should be used to pursue these goals, and the ways in which the instruments should be used.

Congressional concern for the two issues rather neatly spans the

[5]Arthur A. Ekirch, Jr., *Ideas, Ideals, and American Diplomacy* (N.Y.: Appleton-Century Crofts, 1966), chap. 2.

[6]*Congressional Record*, U. S. House of Representatives, 2 June 1962, p. 9823. The congressman, in an ironic twist, juxtaposed the remarks of U. S. Ambassador to Brazil, Lincoln Gordon, who criticized the Brazilian government for over-extension into the private sector and the remarks of Chairman of the Federal Power Commission, Joseph Swidler, who criticized the Eisenhower administration for limiting the powers of the FPC over the power industry. (pp. 9823–24)

decade and a half since the beginning of the Foreign Assistance Act. The treatment of U.S. investors by developing countries was a continuing preoccupation on Capitol Hill from 1961 until the Hickenlooper amendment was made discretionary in 1973. Since then, Congress has remained interested in the issue, but not obsessed. The human rights issue began to attract increasing attention at the time when interest in investment disputes abroad was waning, and in the 1970s human rights issues became central in the debates on the foreign aid program.

In foreign aid policy, more than in other areas of foreign economic policy, few issues elicit interest and pressure from groups on both sides at the same time. The power of the Irish lobby on the British loan has been replicated by Greek-Americans on aid to Turkey and Jewish-Americans on aid to Israel. On those issues, countervailing groups are generally absent. The two cases examined in this chapter are similar in that the groups interested in the issue are on only one side, but they are different in that business groups are predominantly interested in investment disputes while religious and academic groups are pressing on the human rights issue.

The two cases thus provide an opportunity to test a radical economic theory which postulates that U.S. foreign policy is largely at the service of U.S. multinational corporations.[7] In an article on the origins of the Hickenlooper amendment, Charles Lipson suggests that U.S. policy on investment protection largely conformed to the preferences of large U.S. multinational corporations, and can be explained by that fact.[8]

That proposition will be tested not by examining the "most likely" case of the Hickenlooper amendment alone, but by examining that case in juxtaposition to the case on human rights, and by inquiring whether the policy process can be considered independently of the play of interest groups. One would not expect academic or religious groups to exert the same kind or as much influence as business groups did in investment disputes. Moreover, business would have an additional incentive to prevent passage of human rights amendments since they could jeopardize other U.S. interests, notably business interests, in a country. On the other hand, if the process rather than the groups shape policy, one would not be surprised to find Congress making policy on human rights much as it did on investment disputes and without regard to the interests of multinational corporations. In short, a comparison of the policy-making process for both cases could yield some important conclusions on how U.S. policy is made.

[7]Proponents of this view include Harry Magdoff, *The Age of Imperialism*, N.Y.: Monthly Review Press, 1969; Gabriel Kolko, *The Roots of American Foreign Policy* (Boston: Beacon Press, 1969 1969); and David Horowitz, *Corporations and the Cold War* (N.Y.: Monthly Review Press, 1969).

[8]Charles H. Lipson, "Corporate Preferences and Public Policies: Foreign Aid Sanctions and Investment Protection," *World Politics* 28 (April 1976): 396–421. I am indebted to Charles Lipson for sharing his research on this case.

U.S. POLICY ON INVESTMENT DISPUTES

Since the Marshall Plan, both Congress and the Executive have viewed U.S. foreign direct investment as an important component of the U.S. foreign aid package for two reasons. Public funds were considered insufficient to the task, and there was a consensus that private enterprise was the best instrument to stimulate economic growth, and therefore it should be promoted everywhere.[9] Though the government provided political-risk insurance for U.S. foreign investors as early as 1949, there was no real need for the government to formulate a comprehensive policy on mistreatment of U.S. investors abroad until the Cuban Revolution.

If Cuba was the "inspiration," in Senator Fulbright's words, for reviewing U.S. policy on foreign investment, then the expropriation of several American-owned power plants by a Governor of the Brazilian state of Rio Grande do Sul provided the immediate cause. In July 1959, Senators Johnston of South Carolina and Bridges of New Hampshire introduced an amendment to the Mutual Security Act which would have required the President to deny foreign assistance to a government which expropriates American property without "adequate, effective, and prompt compensation."

The State Department opposed the amendment, and Senator Fulbright repeated their position on the floor of the Senate: "It is unlikely that countries can be deterred in any fashion from taking action of this kind by the threat of withdrawal of U.S. assistance." "Instead of being deterred," Fulbright argued, "certain countries would only be irritated."[10] Since the Mutual Security Act already contained a provision which gave the President the authority to terminate assistance if he found such action to be in the national interest, there was no need, in the view of Fulbright and the State Department, for new restrictions. "I think we should trust the President in these cases," Fulbright said, and the Senate apparently agreed with him, since the mandatory amendment was defeated 44-39-15.[11]

Even those, like Fulbright, who opposed the amendment, made clear their support for the principle that expropriation was permissible only if compensation was forthcoming. Fulbright, however, opposed the idea of using foreign aid for political purposes, such as promoting or protecting foreign investment. His colleagues were more sympathetic to a point of view expressed by Senator Johnston: "Lend and give, if we must, to those

---

[9]President Kennedy stated at a news conference where he expressed his opposition to the Hickenlooper amendment that "private capital is necessary in Latin America. . . . There isn't enough public capital to do the job." (*Presidential Papers* 1962, John F. Kennedy, News Conference, 7 March 1962, 75.

[10]*Congressional Record*, 2 July 1959, p. 12586.

[11]Ibid., p. 12587.

who believe in at least some of the fundamental principles so near and dear to all Americans."[12]

On July 8, Senator Bridges introduced a modified "permissive, rather than mandatory" version of his original amendment. The new one would suspend assistance rather than prohibit it, and it permitted the President the discretion to waive the amendment in the national interest or if the government had either paid adequate compensation or was no longer expropriating property. Fulbright challenged this amendment on the same grounds as before, but this time the amendment passed over his objections, 59-32-7.[13]

When in 1961, President Kennedy sent his foreign aid message to Congress, the Johnston-Bridges provision was omitted. Instead, there was an entire Title (III) devoted to Investment Guarantees which were intended to provide a sound and secure investment climate for U.S. corporations. One billion dollars was requested to guarantee investments against expropriation or confiscation, inconvertibility of funds, or loss due to war, revolution, or insurrection. Also, another $5 million was requested for doing preinvestment studies.[14] But neither investment guarantees nor threats of denying foreign assistance deterred Cuba or Brazil from undertaking a new round of expropriations, and after a subsidiary of ITT was expropriated by a Brazilian Governor, ITT President Harold Geneen turned to Senator Bourke Hickenlooper, ranking Republican on the Senate Foreign Relations Committee, for help.[15]

In Committee mark-up on the Foreign Assistance Act of 1962, Hickenlooper introduced an amendment applicable to all expropriations in the past as well as the future. Within ninety days of an expropriation, the Foreign Claims Settlement Commission would be required by this amendment to complete an evaluation of the claim, and if compensation was not forthcoming, U.S. foreign assistance would be automatically terminated. Hickenlooper later described the State Department's reaction to his amendment: "The State Department raised all kinds of objections. They wrote memorandums [sic]; they appeared before the Committee; they said, in effect, 'We will protect American rights. Please do not write any such laws. Some of the countries will take offense at us and will not take our money.' The Committee held a hearing, and considerable influence was brought to bear by administration sources to soften the amendment."[16]

[12]Ibid., p. 12586.

[13]Congressional Quarterly, Almanac, 1959, p. 159.

[14]Congressional Quarterly, Almanac, 1961, p. 293.

[15]Jerome Levinson and Juan de Onis, The Alliance that Lost its Way: A Critical Report on the Alliance for Progress (Chicago: Quadrangle Books, 1972), p. 144.

[16]Congressional Record, 2 October 1962, pp. 21615–16.

President Kennedy himself at a news conference on March 7, 1962 not only demonstrated his familiarity with the amendment and the issue, but underlined his opposition: "I can think of nothing more unwise than to attempt to pass a resolution at this time which puts us in a position where we sanction a national government for the behavior of one of its state governments."[17]

At hearings, Secretary of State Rusk presented the administration's case: "There can be no difference between us, Senator [Capehart], on the objective of doing everything that we can to create the right kind of environment for private investment. But I do think that such a [mandatory] provision would create very severe complications in our relations with other governments."[18]

The difference between Congress, which wanted the American case made clearly and forcefully to foreign governments, and the State Department, which leaned toward a cautious, quiet, and private approach and examined implications overlooked by Legislators, was clear in many of the exchanges at the hearings.

Senator Capehart. I don't see that it [the denial of assistance] is a breach of relations. It seems to me we can very frankly say to a country: 'We want our people to invest in your country, and we want to help you economically, but if you don't want to accept our terms, which are that if you expropriate any of our property without paying the fair value for it, we will just have to quit doing business with you. We just are not going to give you any economic aid. You can do it if you wish—we are not saying that you cannot expropriate. We are simply saying if you do, and don't pay the fair price for it, we are not going to tax the American taxpayers any further to loan or give you any money.' What is wrong with that?

Secretary Rusk. Senator, I think there is another concern I would feel on the other side of the ledger on this point.

If we are going to tie American policy by law to the private investor overseas, to the extent that you suggest, then I think that we of necessity must reassure ourselves as to the operations, the conduct, the financial structure, and the other aspects of those private investors.[19]

Rusk's point was viewed more as an excuse for inaction than as a suggestion for future policy, and this theme recurred throughout the

[17]*Presidential Papers*, 1962, John F. Kennedy, News Conference, 7 March 1962, p. 75.

[18]U. S. Senate, Committee on Foreign Relations, *Hearings on Foreign Assistance Act 1962*, p. 31.

[19]Ibid., p. 32.

hearings. The Congress wanted to legislate, and State resisted, arguing that authority for administrative action already existed, and that new legislation was neither necessary nor desirable.[20] In an appendix to the hearings, the State Department provided a detailed, six-point case against the amendment, and because the arguments are well-put and have been repeated often since then, an outline of the points follows:

1. *The amendment would lend credibility to the Communist argument that the only purpose of the U.S. aid program was to promote the extension of private capitalism abroad;*

2. *It would put U.S. foreign policy "at the mercy of one unreasonable action by a foreign official";*

3. *It might retard some vital economic and social reforms, particularly those like land reform which are bound to impinge on sizeable U.S. investments in Latin America;*

4. *It might well "commit our whole policy into the hands of one intransigent American citizen";*

5. *The oversight of host government court decisions by the Foreign Claims Settlement Commission would be considered gross interference in their judicial process on an issue, compensation, which is difficult to judge even if there were some agreement on objectives; and*

6. *"Finally, flexibility rather than a rigid rule is required. . . . The interests of the United States require the balancing of many factors . . ."*[21]

In the end, the department was successful in modifying the amendment so that a one-year delay was permitted before the Executive would have to suspend assistance. The House recommended six months, and the final conference report gave the host government "within a reasonable time (not more than six months) . . . to take appropriate steps" before the President (rather than the Foreign Claims Commission) would have to suspend assistance. Hickenlooper called those "weasel words," leaving the "gate wide open for the Executive or the State Department to say that the steps were reasonable or were appropriate . . . "[22]

Hickenlooper succeeded in eliminating the national interest waiver on the floor of the Senate, and in getting the law to apply retroactively to all those expropriations which had occurred since January 1, 1962, thus including the expropriation of a telephone company in Brazil belonging to

[20]Ibid., p. 33.
[21]Ibid., pp. 557–58.
[22]*Congressional Record*, 2 October 1962, p. 21616.

ITT. After trying to defeat it, the State Department and the President changed strategies and tried and succeeded in watering down the amendment by including the clause allowing for "appropriate steps" to be taken before U.S. action would be considered.

The amendment passed (by voice vote) because Senators perceived a genuine threat to a legal principle. As Hickenlooper himself said, if the U.S. didn't put a stop to the first illegal expropriations, they would spread "like a prairie fire."[23] And liberals, like Hubert Humphrey, were in complete agreement: "It was an amendment which I believed was needed to counter the reckless abandon that seemed to be prevailing in certain countries relating to the expropriation of American property." If this behavior goes unpunished, Humphrey continued, "a fire [will be] . . . set loose which will consume the values and principles for which this country stands."[24]

The bill was signed into law on August 1, 1962, but of course, it did not stop the fire. What it did do, however, was shift the brunt of the congressional offensive from the expropriating government to the State Department, which was charged with implementing the law. "The ink on that act is scarcely dry," said Hickenlooper on October 2, "but today, I am persuaded that this provision of law [is] . . . being disregarded by the State Department, and the spirit of the law is not being put into effect. For some reason, which I do not know, this provision is being soft-pedaled."[25] At issue was the alleged failure of the State Department to inform the Honduran government that the land reform bill under consideration by their legislature could, if incorrectly applied, lead to a suspension of U.S. assistance.

Hickenlooper, Sen. Leverett Saltonstall, and Speaker of the House John McCormack—the latter two from Massachusetts—had been contacted and kept informed of developments by the United Fruit Company, whose property in Honduras would undoubtedly have been affected by the land reform law.[26] These three Legislators were disturbed that the only thing they learned when they contacted the State Department was that they already seemed to have more information than State. The Legislators were supported by Senator Morse who was primarily concerned about the violation of international law and by Senator Gruening who feared that widespread expropriations would impede Honduras's economic development.

In the light of the discussion in Congress on the Honduras issue, it is easier to understand the Kennedy Administration's expeditious move to

[23]*Congressional Record*, 8 May 1962, p. 9940.

[24]*Congressional Record*, 11 February 1963, p. 2136.

[25]*Congressional Record*, 2 October 1962, p. 21618; also see pp. 21616–21.

[26]For copies of the letter and telegrams, see *Congressional Record*, 2 October 1962, p. 21618.

suspend foreign assistance to Ceylon on February 8, 1963 after Ceylon's failure to adequately compensate American oil corporations for seizure of assets. A memorandum from Secretary of State Rusk to President Kennedy confirms the importance of the congressional consideration in making the decision: "American businessmen and Congressmen have widely applauded our action [in Ceylon]; failure to suspend under the circumstances would have had adverse repercussions on the Hill and elsewhere . . . "[27]

At the same time, the State Department began to apply subtle and "non-overt economic pressure" by delaying decisions on loans to Peru until there were indications that the government's dispute with the International Petroleum Company, a subsidiary of Standard Oil of New Jersey, was moving toward settlement.[28]

Congress, however, was less troubled with expropriations in 1963 than it was with "creeping nationalizations." Argentina, for example, nullified contracts with U.S. oil companies without mentioning compensation, and Congress debated whether nullification of contracts was covered by the Hickenlooper amendment. Hickenlooper and Morse decided to resolve any ambiguity by introducing an amendment to broaden the coverage of the amendment.[29]

Afraid that the Hickenlooper-Morse amendment would open the flood-gates to a wave of restrictive amendments, the State Department adopted a strategy of accepting, indeed complimenting, Hickenlooper's initiative of the year before, but at the same time, resisting any new amendment.[30] Though he testified in 1962 that the amendment was ill-conceived, Rusk in 1963 said: "Our experience thus far has meant that the [Hickenlooper] amendment has been a good thing."[31] The strategy was partly successful; new restrictive amendments were defeated, but the Hickenlooper-Morse amendment to extend coverage to disputes involving nullification or repudi-ation of contracts passed. The new act was signed on December 16, 1963.

The relationship between Congress and the executive branch on this issue soon assumed an almost routine pattern. Prior to testifying on the Hill on every variety of foreign assistance bill, including the Sugar Act, the State Department would recommend to its embassies overseas that they try to resolve all outstanding investment disputes. A typical cable sent to an

[27]Cited in Lipson, "Corporate Preferences", p. 410.

[28]The freeze continued from 1963 to 1966. See Gregory Treverton, "United States Policy-Making Toward Peru: the IPC Affair," in app. 1, vol. 3, in Appendices to the Murphy Commission Report, pp. 205–11.

[29]*Congressional Record*, 13 November 1963, p. 21761.

[30]David Bell, A.I.D. Administrator, in a memorandum to the President, wrote: "We hope we can draw the line against further restrictive amendments offered from the floor." (Cited by Lipson, "Corporate Preferences" p. 407)

[31]Quoted by Lipson, "Corporate Preferences" p. 407.

embassy on this issue would read: "Government of——should understand that failure to resolve pending cases could affect their quota level [for the Sugar Act, or for foreign assistance] or, under one proposal, result in a special fee on their sugar exports to the U.S."[32] Then, elaborate briefing books would be compiled with details on all outstanding cases so that the official who testified would be prepared to respond to questions from congressmen and Senators. In the case of the Sugar Act, the Legislators could directly confront the lobbyists of the foreign governments, and as Rep. W. R. Poage, then Chairman of the House Agriculture Committee, did in a statement to a lobbyist representing the Bolivian government, link the Bolivian interest in a sugar quota with the U.S. interest in adequate compensation for its overseas investors.

> *Chairman Poage. This is not the only case in the world that comes before us, and we come up here and say that we do not want to give quotas where our people are not properly treated in nations, and I believe in that philosophy. . . . Of course, I know some have said, we can sweep it all under the rug, but we are not going to do that sort of thing.*
>
> *. . . it is going to be several months before we have the Sugar Act ready to go to press, and I do know that things can be changed in the Sugar Act during that time. I think that it would be worth your time to suggest to your government that it would be well to try to work this thing out or get it into some judicial channels where we would know that the matter was going to be handled. I am not trying to hold a knife to the Bolivian Government's throat and say they have to pay any certain amount. Maybe they ought not to pay anything. But they ought at least to be in a judgment on this thing and to make it without too much delay.[33]*

Excluding Cuba, where there were 5800 cases of expropriation, the total number of cases involving the expropriation or nationalization of American businesses in the period 1961–68 was fifty-one.[34] Generally,

---

[32]See my "U.S. Sugar Politics and Latin America: Asymmetries in Input and Impact," in app. 1, vol. 3, in Appendices to the Murphy Commission Report, p. 227. Under the 1962 Sugar Act (PL 87-535), the President also was required to suspend the sugar quota of any nation which expropriated U.S. property without adequate compensation, but the President was permitted to waive the suspension if the national interest so required. (See Congressional Quarterly, *Almanac, 1962,* 127) *Sugar Act Extension,* 1974, 93rd Congress, 2d sess., February–March 1974, pp. 452–53.

[33]Hearings before the Committee on Agriculture, House of Representatives, *Sugar Act Extension, 1974,* 93d Congress, 2d sess., February–March 1974, pp. 452–53.

[34]Department of State, Bureau of Intelligence and Research, "Disputes Involving U. S. Foreign Direct Investment,: July 1, 1971 through July 31, 1973," unclassified research study, 28

corporations preferred to negotiate directly with the host government; they would involve the State Department only if serious problems arose. If the State Department was not particularly helpful, the corporation would turn to its congressman or Senator. State Department officials all readily concede that they are likely to be more responsive when a Legislator contacts them, or when they believe a particular corporation is likely to turn to Congress for assistance.[35]

By the late 1960's, after re-evaluating the impact of the Hickenlooper policy on their relations with host governments, many corporations turned less and less to Congress for help and less to the State Department as well. In 1968, for example, when Congress examined the option of denying Peru a sugar quota because of an investment dispute with IPC, an affiliate of EXXON, W. R. Grace and Company with sizeable holdings in Peru testified against such an action. Naturally, the denial of a sugar quota would disrupt U.S.-Peruvian relations and adversely affect Grace's interests. Grace and other U.S. corporations had come to believe that flexibility in dealing with these disputes was much more effective than the blunt instrument of the Hickenlooper amendment.[36] When in April 1969, the President chose not to invoke the amendment as he was required to do, the response from some in Congress was "passive pressure,"[37] and from others it was relief. The Senate Foreign Relations Committee heard testimony from a number of private witnesses, and all concluded that Hickenlooper was ineffective and some-times counterproductive, and that it should be repealed.[38] Senator Javits also said that he thought "the chances for repeal are good."[39]

Between 1969 and 1971, there were more expropriation disputes, sixty-four, than in the previous seven year period, and between 1971 and 1973, there were eighty-seven new disputes.[40] When the amendment passed in

February 1974. [Thereafter INR Memorandum] Also see International Economic Report of the President, 1975, p. 54.)

[35]Harry Weiner, a former Foreign Service Officer, reported that representatives of nongovernmental groups believed their influence on the State Department was greater when they worked through Capitol Hill. (See Harry Weiner, "U. S.-Brazilian Relations: Non-Governmental Organizations and the Fifth Institutional Act," app. 1, vol. 3, in Appendices to the Murphy Commission Report, p. 255.)

[36]"U. S. Sugar Interests [owned by W. R. Grace] in the country could become a casualty of a law intended to protect them." Unclassified memorandum, Intelligence and Research Bureau, Department of State, 20 February 1969.

[37]Jessica Pernitz Einhorn, Expropriation Politics (Lexington, Mass.: Lexington Books, 1974), pp. 53–54.

[38]U. S. Senate, Committee on Foreign Relations, Hearings Before the Subcommittee on Western Hemisphere Affairs: U. S. Relations With Peru, 91st Congress, 1st sess., April 1969. In this hearing, see the statements by Luigi Einaudi (p. 38), Prof. Harry Kantor (p. 31), Richard Lillich (pp. 55, 63).

[39]Ibid., p. 81.

[40]INR memorandum, p. 8.

1962, there was no discernable disagreement within the business community, but by the late 1960s, with more experience in dealing with these problems, the business community began to divide on the appropriate instrument for dealing with the problem. On the one side, the hard-liners were provoked by the spread and increase in the number of expropriations, and their case was articulated by Secretary of the Treasury John Connally who said that the United States should "get tough" with Latin American countries that expropriate American holdings because, as he put it: "We don't have any friends there anyway."[41] At the same time, however, the Council of the Americas, a business association which represents 90 percent of the U.S. corporations with investments in Latin America, polled its members and found that 76 percent of its members thought that the Hickenlooper amendment had "outlived its usefulness."[42]

Thus, two positions emerged, and they faced each other in the executive, the congressional, and the business arenas in almost a continuous round of debates between 1971 and 1973. Surprisingly, policy was made in each of the three arenas with remarkably little direct contact with actors in the other arenas. More often, a hard-line actor in, for instance, the Executive, would characterize the debate in Congress in such a way as to strengthen his position in the executive debate.[43] But in Congress, the hard-line position would derive strength from the seeming unresponsiveness of the Executive.

The resultant policy, however, in all three arenas was unusual in the way it balanced the many and diverse interests and perspectives. In the Executive, the hard-liners won a tough-sounding statement on expropriation policy by the President on January 19, 1972, but the soft-liners won a statement that really said little that was new, and furthermore, implementation of Presidential policy was delegated to a forum in which they had a preponderant influence.[44] In Congress, the hard-liners won by extending the Hickenlooper concept to multilateral assistance with the passage of the Gonzalez amendment to the Inter-American Development Bank Act of 1972, which required the President to instruct the U.S. Executive Director to

---

[41]Quoted in Einhorn, *Expropriation Politics* p. 96.

[42]Robert Swansbrough, *The Embattled Colossus* (Gainesville: University Presses of Florida, 1976), chap. 10. Business was hardly unanimous on this issue. In an exchange at a House hearing, Rep. Thomas Rees said that in his travels through Latin America, "I didn't find an American businessman who supported the Hickenlooper amendment." However, Daniel Danielan, President of the International Economic Policy Association, a research group for large corporations, disagreed: "It all depends on who you talk to and at what level." (See U. S. House of Representatives, Subcommittee on International Finance of the Committee on Banking and Currency, *Hearings: To Authorize the U. S. to Provide Additional Financial Resources to the Asian Development Bank and the Inter-American Development Bank*, 26 October 1971, p. 162.

[43]"From the Executive Branch one hears such talk about the fear of Congress in this matter." (Einhorn, *Expropriation Politics*, p. 54)

[44]Ibid., pp. 117–18.

the Bank to vote against a loan to any government that expropriates U.S. property without adequate compensation. There was no resistance to this congressional initiative from either Treasury or the White House.[45]

The next year, the soft-liners in Congress succeeded in attaching a waiver provision to the Hickenlooper amendment, permitting the president to continue assistance to a country if he finds that it is in the national interest to do so. The modification, in the words of one authority on the issue, in effect "defused, if not actually repealed" the original amendment.[46] Congressmen Charles Whalen, Dante Fascell, and John Culver tried to have the amendment deleted entirely, but they were defeated on the House floor by Rep. Henry Gonzalez.[47] In the Senate and in Conference, the waiver provision won with the passive support of the President.[48] The Council of the Americas is reported to have lobbied for the discretionary amendment,[49] but there were many individual corporations which continued to prefer the mandatory language, and that position continued to have its supporters in Congress and the Executive.

U.S. POLICY ON INVESTMENT DISPUTES: ALTERNATIVE EXPLANATIONS

In an assessment of the Alliance for Progress, Jerome Levinson and Juan de Onis argue that the only reason Congress wrote the Hickenlooper amendment was because the doors of the executive branch were closed to them in the early years of the Kennedy Administration.[50] This explanation overlooks the interaction between Congress and the Executive in the last years of the Eisenhower Administration when the Johnston-Bridges amendment laid the groundwork for the policy enunciated and expanded by Hickenlooper.

A cogent explanation for the development of the policy on investment disputes is offered by Charles Lipson in an article in *World Politics*. He

[45]The attitude of Treasury in the fall of 1971 when Gonzalez decided to introduce his amendment was ambivalent, according to Einhorn. On the one hand, they would have preferred a clean bill. On the other hand, they supported the policy Gonzalez was advocating, and they needed bargaining leverage in their struggle with the State Department. There may not have been support from Treasury for the amendment, as Einhorn says, but there wasn't any resistance either, and in the end, Treasury *did* use it "as an instrument of leverage" against State. (Ibid, p. 89)

[46]Richard P. Lillich, "Requiem for Hickenlooper," *American Journal of International Law* 69 (January 1975): 97.

[47]For Fascell and Whalen's statements, see *Congressional Record*, 26 July 1973, p. H6715.

[48]Lipson, "Corporate Preferences," p. 414–15.

[49]Ibid.

[50]Levinson and de Onis, *Alliance that Lost its Way* pp. 12, 143–144. Also Swansbrough, *Embattled Colossus*, chap. 6: "Alliance for Progress: The Forgotten Businessman."

argues that the policy developed in accord with the preferences of the largest multinational corporations, but this argument has great difficulty dealing with the significant divisions in the business community, as well as in Congress and the Executive, and the apparently inconsistent policies which emerged from the debate in these three arenas. Furthermore, if the corporate preferences argument best explains U.S. government policy, then why was it necessary, particularly in a period when the Republicans controlled the Executive but not the Congress, for the MNC's to take their case to the Congress at all?

Until the late 1960s, the positions of the Executive and of Congress remained relatively consistent internally, and the two branches related to one another in an adversary-like way. The Executive wanted as much discretion as possible. "Working quietly but forcefully behind the scenes is a far better way to bring about the results we are after."[51] This statement by an AID Administrator reflects the Executive's desire to pursue an interest privately, and in a way that preserves sound and smooth diplomatic relations with the host government.

Congress, on the other hand, wanted to define the terms of the U.S. relationship, and the only way to assure this would be implemented was to draft a public law. To Congress, it was fair and appropriate to deny aid to a country that did not compensate a U.S. company for expropriating its property. It is not a coincidence that the Executive wanted to pursue the interest privately, and the Congress sought to do it publicly. Even when Treasury took a hard-line position during the Connally tenure, it still opposed restrictive legislation, as Jessica Einhorn noted: "The Treasury, no matter what its departmental views on expropriation questions, still shared the general Executive Branch opposition to Congressional directives reducing the flexibility or control of the President over foreign affairs."[52]

Because the administration of the Hickenlooper policy did not appear to conform to legislative intent, Congress tightened the mandate, thereby reducing the Executive's discretion, and it extended the concept to other foreign aid-type bills, like the Fisherman's Protective Act of 1967 and the Sugar Act. The Executive struggled unsuccessfully to defeat these additional restrictions. With the exception of a handful of large multinational corporations, like the United Fruit Company and ITT, few MNC's were involved in this first phase of the debate between Congress and the Executive.

When the second wave of nationalizations occurred in the late 1960s, many in Congress, the Executive, and in business had come to the conclusion that Hickenlooper-type legislation was counterproductive and should be repealed.[53] If repeal was not feasible, then a national interest waiver should

[51]Memorandum by A.I.D. official David Bell, quoted in Lipson, "Corporate Preferences," pp. 408–09.

[52]Einhorn, *Expropriation Politics* p. 87.

[53]For example, the Commission on U.S.–Latin American Relations recommended the

be added to the legislation. Interestingly, policy made in this phase was largely made by independent and uncoordinated actions by Congress and by the executive. Instead of direct interaction, in this period the Executive and the congressional debates influenced each other largely by "anticipatory reactions," with tacit coalitions forming across branches.

Still, one can see a certain trend in the way the policy developed in this period. The trend was toward permitting greater discretion to the Executive, and ironically, it came at the behest of an assertive Congress. That the Congressional initiative in 1973 was taken by a group of liberals who were never very sympathetic to the amendment anyway is not as important as the fact that their initiative was not resisted by those conservative Congressmen who were. Two of the reasons why conservatives permitted the Hickenlooper amendment to become discretionary in 1973 were the passage of the Gonzalez amendment in 1972 and the demonstration by the Executive in January 1972 that it had internalized this congressional concern.

The Gonzalez amendment, which appears anomalous in a trend toward greater discretion, was in fact much more flexible than the Hickenlooper amendment of 1962. Though the Gonzalez amendment did not contain a national interest waiver, the President could refrain from invoking the statute as long as "good faith negotiations are in progress." The Hickenlooper amendment was not repealed in 1973, but by introducing a waiver provision, it was effectively repealed. The congressmen who lead the assault were not being pushed by liberal businessmen, nor by the State Department. If anything, they were doing the pushing, trying to secure an endorsement from the President.

In summary, in the early years of U.S. policy on investment disputes, the legislative-executive model was helpful in explaining why the policy was so tightly drawn by legislation, and why countries with relatively insignificant investment disputes like Ceylon and Peru were treated so harshly by the U.S. By the second phase, the concerns of Congress had been internalized by the executive branch, the law of anticipatory reactions was working smoothly, and thus Congress could readily agree to the relaxation of legislative constraints on the Executive. At the same time, however, that Congress permitted the Executive more flexibility in the use of bilateral assistance, it extended the same rule to multilateral assistance.

U.S. POLICY ON HUMAN RIGHTS

With the leadership of Eleanor Roosevelt, the concern of Americans for the protection of fundamental human rights was embodied in the U.N. Charter

---

repeal of the Hickenlooper and Gonzalez Amendments in its October 1974 Report, *The Americas In a Changing World.*

and the Human Rights Commissions established at the end of the Second
World War. In this brief period, according to Louis Henkin, the United States
was "second to no other major country in the international effort to
establish, promote, and maintain human rights."[54]

This moral element in U.S. foreign policy was not discarded, but it was
transformed by the Cold War into a crusade against Communism, and
ideological preconceptions combined with overriding security considerations
to preclude the even-handed approach to international moral problems
originally evisaged by the U.N. Charter's founding fathers. Americans were
reluctant to criticize the inhumanity of allies like Taiwan, South Korea, or
South Vietnam for fear that it would jeopardize the strategic struggle against
Communism.

For a short time in the early years of the Alliance for Progress, U.S.
foreign policy recaptured a concern for democracy and human rights as a
guiding criterion for U.S. relations with the governments of Latin America,
but these concerns were soon overtaken by more pressing security and
economic interests.[55]

The current salience of the human rights issue can, in part, be
attributed to a decline in both the security threat and the persuasiveness of
the Cold War ideology—both of which followed U.S. failure in Indo-China
and the early success with detente. The first concern of those Legislators
who abandoned the Cold War rationale, was to seek some distance for the
United States from those countries which it had supported but which
flagrantly abused the rights of their citizens.

In 1971, Senator Frank Church organized a series of hearings in the
Foreign Relations Committee on torture and repression in Brazil.[56] Distressed over the large amounts of U.S. military and economic assistance to a
regime which routinely tortured and imprisoned many of its citizens,
Church insisted that AID reassess its program and seriously consider ending
it. The State Department responded that it was U.S. policy not to impose
American standards abroad, and it would therefore be inappropriate to
punish Brazil for violations of its own citizens' rights.

Privately, the State Department passed the congressional message to
the Brazilian government, and instructed AID to undertake a major reassess-

[54]Louis Henkin, "The United States and the Crisis in Human Rights," in Symposium:
Human Rights and U. S. Foreign Policy, Virginia Journal of International Law (1974), 653.

[55]See Robert Packenham, Liberal America and the Third World: Political Development
Ideas in Foreign Aid and Social Science (Princeton: Princeton University Press, 1973), pp.
93–98; Joseph Page, The Revolution That Never Was (N.Y.: Grossman Publishers, 1972); Tom
J. Farer, "International Human Rights: U. S. Policy and Priorities," Symposium: Human Rights
and U. S. Foreign Policy, Virginia Journal of International Law (1974), 641–643.

[56]U. S. Congress, Senate Committee on Foreign Relations, Subcommittee on Western
Hemisphere Affairs, United States Policies and Programs in Brazil: Hearings, 92d Congress,
1st sess., 4, 5, and 11 May 1971.

ment of the aid program to Brazil.[57] The conclusion of the study was that the aid program should gradually be phased out, and the public rationale for this conclusion was Brazil's recent and rapid economic progress. Privately, one AID official conceded that the material amassed by Church's committee and the pressure by Church and his liberal colleagues on the aid program were important reasons for the agency's study, and figured prominently in its final decision. From fiscal years 1971 to 1972, the level of U.S. economic and military assistance to Brazil was reduced from $129.7 million to $41.8 million.[58]

Congress's attention was diverted from human rights until August 1973 when Rep. Donald Fraser (D-Minn.) began a systematic and comprehensive study of the issue of the "international protection of human rights" in the subcommittee which he chaired on International Organizations and Movements of the House Foreign Affairs Committee. Fraser was one of the four young liberal congressmen in the House Foreign Affairs Committee who was permitted to chair a subcommittee and obtain staff as a result of the new rules which had been adopted by the House Democratic Caucus in January 1971.[59] By December, his subcommittee had heard from forty-six witnesses, and by March of 1974, the subcommittee had drafted and issued its report, *Human Rights in the World Community: A Call for U.S. Leadership.* The report included twenty-nine specific recommendations on ways in which human rights considerations could become "a regular part of U.S. foreign policy decision-making."[60]

While Fraser remained chairman, his subcommittee was very active in this field, scheduling regular hearings and meeting periodically with State Department officials. Many of the recommendations in the original report were eventually accepted by the department and implemented, albeit reluctantly. And Fraser's credibility and influence within the House as well as with the State Department has been unusually high for an "outsider."[61]

At the same time as a general record on the issue of human rights was being compiled, a violent military overthrow of a democratic government in Chile presented Congress with a concrete case to tests its conception of

[57]This case was constructed from interviews, many of them conducted while I was a consultant to the Murphy Commission in the summer of 1974.

[58]*Overseas Loans,* 40.

[59]The others were John Culver, Benjamin Rosenthal, and Lee Hamilton. See John Maffre, "Congressional Report: New Leaders, Staff Changes Stimulate House Foreign Affairs Committee," *National Journal,* 19 June 1971, pp. 1314–16.

[60]U. S. Congress, House Committee on Foreign Affairs, *Human Rights in the World Community: A Call for U. S. Leadership,* Report of the Subcommittee on International Organizations and Movements, 27 March 1974, p. 3.

[61]For a discussion of the roles played by "outsiders" and "insiders" in the legislative process, see my "Congress' Impact on Latin America," pp. 264–66.

the role human rights should play in U.S. foreign policy. On September 11, 1973, the Socialist government of Salvador Allende which had governed Chile for three politically precarious years, was overthrown, and Allende was killed. Thousands of Chileans, representing a wide spectrum of political views, were arrested, detained without charges, and many were tortured. There were a number of Americans who were among those arrested, and their fates were not known for a while.

Rep. Dante Fascell, chairman of the Subcommittee on Inter-American Affairs of the House Foreign Affairs Committee (HFAC) and Sen. Edward Kennedy, Chairman of the Senate Judiciary's Subcommittee to Investigate Problems Connected with Refugees and Escapees, began hearings on the political and human rights situation in Chile on September 28, 1973. Upon concluding hearings, Senator Kennedy, disturbed about the intensity of repression in a country with a long history of constitutionalism, introduced an amendment to the Foreign Assistance Act of 1973 which would have barred any funds for military assistance or credits to Chile. The amendment would have denied the $1 million in grants and $10 million in credit sales for fiscal year 1974 which the Administration had requested. It passed the Senate by voice vote.

In the House, however, a comparable amendment introduced by Rep. Robert O. Tiernan and supported by Rep. Michael Harrington was resoundingly defeated, 102-304, and Rep. Otto Passman provided one reason: "Chile pulled away from Communism. We have a democracy forming in a very friendly country, and we would be flying in the face of this new government if this amendment were adopted."[62] In Conference, the Kennedy amendment on denying military aid to Chile was deleted but his two other "sense of the Congress" resolutions were retained. Sec. 32 of the Foreign Assistance Act of 1973 stated: "It is the sense of the Congress that the President should deny any economic or military assistance to the government of any foreign country which practices the internment or imprisonment of that country's citizens for political purposes." Sec. 35 was more explicit and mentioned Chile twice, first urging the President to relay a special message to the Chilean leadership to respect the rights of its citizens, and the second requesting the Inter-American Commission on Human Rights to undertake a mission to Chile.

Despite this congressional expression of concern, the Administration not only failed to give any indication to Congress that it transmitted its message to the new government in Chile, but in fact, it dramatically increased its level of economic and military assistance to the Chilean regime. By November 1973, two months after the coup, the Administration extended two commodity credit loans totalling $52 million to the new Chilean government. In the last full year of the Allende government, fiscal

---

[62]Quoted in Congressional Quarterly, *Almanac*, 1973, pp. 181, 186.

year 1973, the U.S. granted $2.5 million in Food for Peace grants and loans; in FY 1974, the Administration requested $37 million. In addition, the Administration doubled its request for military aid to Chile after the coup.[63] It was clear that the Administration intended to send a very different message to Chile and to other countries than what Congress intended.

As a result of the widespread allegations of torture and repression by the military junta, several international commissions sent groups to Chile to assess the accuracy of the allegations. A three-member Commission of International Jurists, which included Covey Oliver, a former Assistant Secretary of State, issued a thirty-eight page report in September 1974 on its visit the previous April. The report was viewed as a serious indictment of the Chilean government's activities; and it singled out and condemned the Chilean Intelligence Services for engaging in torture, arbitrary arrest, and illegal detention.

The Inter-American Commission on Human Rights, on the basis of a twelve-day tour of Chile in the summer of 1974, issued a 175-page report in December 1974 charging the Chilean government with "extremely serious violations of human rights," including extensive torture of political prisoners. The Chilean government responded with a 125-page rebuttal attacking "certain surprising and disturbing conclusions in conflict with the real state of affairs."[64]

Both Fraser and Kennedy held another round of hearings, dividing their time between questions on the situation in Chile and probes about U.S. policy toward the junta. On July 23, 1974, Kennedy asked Acting Assistant Secretary of State for Latin America, Harry Shlaudeman, how the State Department could justify its request for expanded assistance to Chile in the light of Sections 32 and 35 of the FAA 1973. Shlaudeman responded:

> The phrasing of the section creates some uncertainty regarding its relevancy to the Chilean situation. The Chilean Constitution's state-of-siege provisions empower the retaining of individuals without trial. The Government of Chile says there are no political prisoners or prisoners of conscience and that those detained are detained for reasons of public security or because they are or shall be charged with crimes under statutes predating the coup . . .
>
> Senator Kennedy. . . . I don't think that Congress intended that the

---

[63]For a breakdown of all forms of U. S. economic assistance to Chile from 1967 to 1977, see U. S. House of Representatives Subcommittee on International Organizations of the Committee on International Relations, *Hearings: Chile, The Status of Human Rights, and Its Relationship to U. S. Economic Assistance Programs,* 94th Congress, 2d sess., April and May 1976, app. 6, p. 118. [Hereafter Chile Hearings, April—May, 1976].

[64]Organization of American States, General Assembly, Observations by the Government of Chile on the Report on the Status of Human Rights in Chile," prepared by the Inter-American Commission on Human Rights" (Washington, D. C.: OAS, 1975), p. 2.

decision about whether there are political prisoners in a country to be made by the host government. Your response said that in our consultations with the Government of Chile we have been assured that those who are being held, they are being held because of public security questions or violations of the law prior to the state of siege. But as I understand—and this is from the Chilean Constitution—a state of siege can only be declared by the assembly, which of course has been suspended. So getting assurances that there is no political torture from the Chilean Government and then finding out that there is no political prisoners because the Chilean Government says so. I find that really isn't what we had in mind. I guess we will have to change that . . .

But I question your relying upon the Chilean Government. . . . Did you do any investigation of this? . . . Can we find out if anything we do up here in Congress makes any difference at all?[65]

While Congressional advocates of a strong policy on human rights grew increasingly frustrated by the unresponsiveness of the Executive, the debate within the State Department grew more heated. A superficial bureaucratic analysis would have predicted that AID would silently and eagerly devour the budget increase requested by the Administration for Chile, but such a conclusion would have overlooked AID's two other organizational imperatives: the self-perception of AID as an economic development organization, one uncomfortable at being used for transparently political purposes; and a sensitivity to congressional concern derived from intensive, critical, and annual congressional oversight of AID's legislation and budget.

Acutely sensitive to mounting congressional displeasure with Executive policy, Daniel Parker, the Administrator of AID, tried unsuccessfully to convince State that the requests for a dramatic increase of aid to Chile would probably jeopardize the entire program. Instead of reducing the requests, as Parker recommended, a strategy was devised to try to "put out the fires" on Capitol Hill. Teams of State Department officials from the Chile-Bolivia desks and from the Congressional Liaison Office met with key Legislators on the four Committees which handle the aid legislation to inform them of the current political situation in Chile, the limits of American influence, and the intention of the Administration to ask for an increase in aid. Among the key Legislators consulted were Fascell from

[65]U. S. Senate, Hearings Before the Subcommittee To Investigate Problems Connected with Refugees and Escapees of the Committee on Judiciary, Refugees and Humanitarian Problems in Chile, part 2, 93rd congress, 2nd sess., 23 July 1974, p. 62. [Hereafter Kennedy Hearings, part 2].

HFAC; Passman and Shreiber from House Appropriations; Brooke, Chiles, and Inouye from Senate Appropriations; and McGee from the Senate Foreign Relations Committee. All were either friends of the AID bill or were hostile to the effort to cut assistance to Chile. When it became clear that the aid bill was in trouble, they redoubled their efforts and spoke with more than thirty Legislators including many conservatives who had been hostile to Allende but were apathetic on human rights.

In the meantime, AID Administrator Daniel Parker tried to get State to relent. A compromise was finally worked out with the Inter-American Affairs Bureau (ARA). The decision to immediately increase aid to Chile would be postponed while "Consultation Teams" were sent there to investigate Chile's capacity to use an expanded foreign assistance program. Many of the congressional critics were not informed of this compromise, but Kissinger tried to mollify them by appointing in the fall of 1974 Special Assistants on Human Rights to be attached to the Regional Assistant Secretaries. This organizational change along with the selection in April 1975 of a coordinator of a new Office of Humanitarian Affairs to be attached to the Deputy Secretary's office were both recommended by the Fraser report on human rights.

The motives behind this organizational change as well as its significance was called into question by a series of news articles by Seymour Hersh in the *New York Times* in September 1974. First, on September 8th, Hersh disclosed a seven-page letter from Rep. Michael Harrington to Sen. Fulbright and Rep. Thomas Morgan, Chairman of the House Foreign Affairs Committee, asking them to investigate a massive campaign from 1970 to 1973 by the U.S. to "de-stabilize" the Allende government in Chile.[66] Harrington had been permitted to read the minutes from a secret briefing given by CIA Director William Colby to the House Armed Services Subcommittee on Intelligence in which Colby provided details on the extensive and covert involvement by the CIA in Chilean affairs. This testimony contradicted the statements of several State Department officials to the Senate Foreign Relations Committee who had insisted that the United States had not interfered in Chilean affairs. One year before, Assistant Secretary of State Charles Meyer testified before the Senate Foreign Relations Committee: "We were religiously and scrupulously adhering to the policy of the Government of the United States . . . of nonintervention. We bought no votes, we funded no candidates, we promoted no coups."[67] Harrington's letter provided evidence contradicting every one of Meyer's points.

---

[66]Seymour Hersh, "C.I.A. Chief Tells House of $8 million campaign against Allende in 1970–73," *New York Times*, 8 September 1974. This and other articles by Hersh and others on this issue as well as on human rights issues as they relate to Chile have been reprinted in Kennedy Hearings, part 2, pp. 261–283.

[67]Reprinted in Kennedy Hearings, part 2, p. 265.

Then, on September 27th, Hersh reported that Secretary Kissinger scrawled on a memo to U.S. Ambassador to Chile David Popper "to cut out the political science lectures" when he learned that Popper was repeatedly bringing up the issue of human rights with the leaders of the military junta that overthrew Allende. This disclosure went to the heart of the issue of State's responsiveness to the congressional will. Before Popper had gone to Chile, he met with a group of congressional staff representing Legislators who were most concerned with the issue of human rights in Chile. The meeting was a stormy one,[68] but the congressional message was clear, and apparently received. One State Department official said that before the rebuke from Kissinger "there used to be a cable a week on the issue telling us how he [Popper] was complaining [to Gen. Augusto Pinochet, leader of the Chilean junta]. I don't see that he's doing it any more."[69] Apparently, Kissinger was irritated that Popper raised the issue in a discussion of military assistance with Oscar Bonilla, the Chilean Minister of Defense. Kennedy was particularly vexed since the intention of his amendments to the FAA 1973 was to have human rights issues raised in just such meetings.

Increased mistrust by Congress of the Executive could not help but follow from these disclosures. While professing noninterference in Chilean affairs, the Executive had apparently subverted a democratic government in Chile, and then aggressively supported, by credits and assistance, a repressive military junta in the same country. Moreover, the Secretary of State reprimanded an ambassador for taking a congressional mandate seriously. Congress decided to clarify its mandate. On October 1 and 2, 1974, Senator Kennedy introduced two amendments, one to the Foreign Assistance Act of 1974 and the other to a continuing resolution on foreign aid; both would set ceilings on $25 million on all assistance to Chile but would prohibit the use of these funds for any military assistance or credit sales. The amendment to the continuing resolution was deleted in Conference, but the amendment to the FAA 1974 was approved by Congress and signed into law by the President on December 30, 1974.[70]

Chile, of course, was not the only subject of congressional concern on human rights. The FAA 1974 also had a provision (sec. 26) which required

[68]Interviews with four Congressional staffers who participated in that meeting.

[69]Quoted in Seymour Hersh, "Kissinger Said to Rebuke U.S. Ambassador to Chile," *New York Times,* 27 September 1974; reprinted in Kennedy Hearings, part 2, 272–273.

[70]PL 93-559 (88 Stat 1795). When the State Department showed some reluctance to implement the provision, Sen. Kennedy sent a letter to Secretary of State Henry Kissinger in which he restated the provision (sec. 25), made clear his intent as its author, and provided portions of the congressional debate on the issue in the U. S. Senate. Hearings Before the Subcommittee to Investigate Problems Connected with Refugees and Escapees of the Committee on Judiciary, Refugees and Humanitarian Problems in Chile, part 2, 94th Congress, 1st sess., 2 October 1975, pp. 79–80. [Hereafter Kennedy Hearings, part 3]

the President to report to Congress on the status of human rights in Korea if he intended to make a loan to the government in excess of $145 million allotted for fiscal year 1975. Congress also wrote a more general provision (sec. 502B) stating "the sense of the Congress that, except in extraordinary circumstances, the President shall substantially reduce or terminate security assistance to any government which engages in a consistent pattern of gross violations of internationally recognized human rights." Taking into account his exchange with Shlaudeman, Kennedy sharpened the language of this provision by stating that the State Department should be guided in their determination of human rights violations "by appropriate international organizations, including the International Committee of the Red Cross and any body acting under the authority of the United Nations or of the Organization of American States." For those governments which the President wanted to give aid but which were engaging in gross violations, the President was required to "advise the Congress of the extraordinary circumstances necessitating the assistance."

In disregard of congressional intent, though technically within the bounds of the law, the State Department provided the Chilean junta with a total of $112 million in economic assistance in fiscal year 1975; $20 million of economic assistance from AID (therefore under the $25 million ceiling), $30 million in housing guarantees, $57.8 million in Title I PL 480 food assistance and $4 million in Title II programs.[72]

In 1975, the pattern which had characterized the interaction between the branches in previous years was repeated. On May 19th, the President sent the foreign economic assistance bill to Congress requesting a total of $102 million for Chile. The Administration also proposed $55.1 million of food aid to Chile, which was 85 percent of the total food aid requested for Latin America. When congressional critics pointed out that there were several Latin American countries which were in far greater need than Chile (the per capita income of Haiti was $123, Honduras $276, Chile $793), Administration witnesses justified the request by stating that Chile was traditionally a wheat-consuming country which had suffered their most severe agricultural short-fall in recent history.[73]

As the Organization of American States General Assembly was preparing to consider, among other things, a report on human rights violations in

[72]These statistics were supplied by A.I.D. to Kennedy's Committee, but there is some discrepancy between these and those reported in *Overseas Loans* (41), which shows for fiscal year 1975 a total of $95.5, exclusive of Housing Guarantees (which are not given) and Export-Import Bank Loans which were $23 million. Of the $95.5 million, $31.3 million were loans and grants from A.I.D. (therefore above the ceiling) and $62.4 million were PL 480. Also, in apparent violation of the law, $700,000 in military assistance grants were given.

[73]U. S. Congress, House of Representatives, Committee on International Relations, *Hearings: International Development and Food Assistance Act of 1975*, 94th Congress, 1st

Chile, several Legislators told the State Department that its behavior at the meeting was as much a concern of their's as was the behavior of the Chilean government. Assistant Secretary of State William D. Rogers worked closely with Rep. Fraser's staff, and the result was a statement which both Fraser and Kennedy commended. Whereas previous American spokesmen had been reluctant to raise the issue, Rogers stated forthrightly: "We do not regard human rights as an exclusively domestic concern." And noting the congressional interest, he stressed that "this agenda item represents a test of the system. . . . In a sense, all of us are on trial here—all of us, in our capacity to articulate a continuing standard and to develop fair and effective procedures for the application of that standard to individual cases."[74]

Yet the final resolution passed by the General Assembly of the O.A.S. postponed a review of Chile's treatment of political dissidents until the U.N. Human Rights Commission, which had received permission to investigate conditions in Chilean political prisons, issued its report. Immediately before the investigating team was to leave, however, the Chilean junta cancelled the investigation, charging that it was a Soviet plot to "promote agitation." Chile offered as an alternative to select its own commission and conduct its own investigation. The cancellation provoked a surprisingly strong public reaction from U.S. Deputy Secretary of State Robert Ingersoll.

In the mark-up on the International Development and Food Assistance Act of 1975, Congress set a ceiling of $90 million for *all* economic assistance to Chile, and extended the amendment of the previous year dealing with reports related to the granting of security assistance to the area of economic assistance. The amendments introduced by Rep. Thomas Harkin and Senators Abourezk and McGovern prohibited any economic assistance to the "government of any country which engages" in gross violations of human rights "unless such assistance will directly benefit the needy people in such country." The provision (sec. 116) set out the criteria the Administration should use to judge such violations and the procedure by which its determination should be reported to Congress.

Shortly after the passage of this amendment, the State Department sent its report to Congress required by sec. 502B of the security assistance part of the foreign aid bill of the previous year. In conversation and correspondence with Senator Allen Cranston, Kissinger had promised this report in December 1974, then again in January 1975, and a third time in early August. On November 5th, Cranston sent another letter to the

---

sess., July 1975, pp. 32, 33, 43. The Library of Congress studied this question for Senator Kennedy and concluded: "It is clear also that Chile is experiencing severe shortages of wheat. Total consumption for 1974 is actually less than in 1971; however, 1974 production is only about half what it was in 1971. As a result, 1974 imports are more than double 1971 imports. On this ground, Chile's needs seem to be quite real." (In Kennedy Hearings, part 3, pp. 111–13.)

[74]Rogers's statement is reprinted in Kennedy Hearings, part 3, pp. 95–96. For the resolution adopted at the OAS General Assembly, see pp. 96–98.

Secretary of State reminding him of the promises and the law. On November 18, Assistant Secretary of State for Congressional Relations Robert J. McCloskey, replied on behalf of Secretary Kissinger, reiterating the department's problem with his request and questioning "the efficacy of publicly branding nations whose internal policies we may be in a better position to influence by other means."[75]

Accompanying the letter was an unsigned report, which was, in Rep. Donald Fraser's judgment, "primarily a defense of the State Department's apparent intention not to comply with the law."[76] The *New York Times* reported that the Department had originally intended to meet the requirements of the law by submitting in-depth country analyses of the human rights situation in countries receiving security assistance, but after obtaining these analyses from the U.S. Embassies abroad, Kissinger overruled the idea on the grounds that virtually all aid recipients were violators, and it would serve no useful purpose to specify them. The report to Congress concluded that "many states appear to be in violation of various rights and freedoms; [that] repressive laws and actions . . . are not extraordinary events in the world community. . . . These are all too common." "In view of the widespread nature of human rights violations in the world, we have found no adequately objective way to make distinctions of degree between nations." Therefore, "quiet but forceful diplomacy" rather than "public obloquy" was the best policy prescription.[77]

Of course, there were many in Congress who disagreed with that assessment, and they reacted by tightening the relevant amendments to the Security Assistance Act of 1976, a biannual authorization introduced on October 30, 1975. In that bill, the State Department did not request security assistance for Chile, and although they tried to present that as a significant concession, they also admitted that a Kennedy amendment prohibiting all such assistance could be passed easily again.

The clash between the State Department and Congress continued through 1976 with the department grudgingly and reluctantly taking the human rights issue more seriously, and Congress enlarging its scope of concern. Hearings were held on the situation in a number of countries, including Haiti, Uruguay, and the Philippines, as well as on Chile and South Korea.[78] Just as the policy on treatment of U.S. foreign investors was first applied to bilateral assistance and later through the Gonzalez amendment to

---

[75]The letter is reprinted in the *Congressional Record*, 20 November 1975, p. S20557.

[76]*New York Times*, 19 November 1975. Cranston called the report "a cover-up."

[77]Ibid.; unsigned report is reprinted in *Congressional Record*, 20 November 1975, p. S20557 ff.

[78]For the list of hearings, see hearings Before the Subcommittee on International Organizations of the Committee on International Relations of the House of Representatives, Human Rights Issues at the Sixth Regular Session of the Organization of American States General Assembly, 94th Congress, 2nd sess., 10 August 1976, p. v.

multilateral assistance, the congressional concern for human rights was extended in 1976 to multilateral assistance by the Harkin amendment to the Inter-American Development Bank Act. Sec. 28 of the Act directs the U.S. Executive Director of the Bank to vote against any loan to any government which grossly violates its citizens' human rights.[79]

Congress also began to apply the formulae initially devised for Chile to other countries. In September 1976, Congress sent a Security Assistance Act to the President that prohibited military assistance to Uruguay. Representative Edward Koch, who was the sponsor of the relevant amendment, said:

> In the past year I have come to fully comprehend the terror that the Uruguayan regime is inflicting upon its own people. I have also learned that the State Department, regrettably, is not as much aware of that situation. This cut-off of military assistance to Uruguay will hopefully set U.S. policy toward that country straight: we are not going to assist the Uruguayan military regime in the repression of its own people. While the amount of assistance—$3 million—is modest, the prohibition is an important precedent.
>
> The Uruguayan regime is not alone as the oppressor of its own people. Chile, Brazil, Argentina, and many other nations in Latin America seem to have no regard for the basic human rights of their peoples. This cut-off should send a message to those regimes as well.[80]

LEGISLATIVE-EXECUTIVE RELATIONS AND U.S. POLICY ON HUMAN RIGHTS

> We have generally opposed attempts to deal with sensitive international human-rights issues through legislation—not because of the moral view expressed, which we share, but because legislation is almost always too inflexible, too public, and too heavy-handed a means to accomplish what it seeks.[81]
>
> —Secretary of State Henry Kissinger

> Suppose you are in the Pinochet government and you read about the votes in the General Assembly and our protestations about the

[79]PL 94-302, enacted 31 May 1976. (90 Stat. 591)

[80]News Release, Congressman Edward I. Koch, September 15, 1976, "Hill Conferees Agree to Koch Amendment Ending Military Assistance to Uruguay."

[81]"U. S. Policy on Rights Backed by Kissinger," *New York Times*, 20 October 1976, p. 3.

meeting in Santiago and our protestations about the human rights
meetings and so on, and yet our Ambassador and A.I.D. mission
was continuing to negotiate new loans and new assistance.

What would be the message you would get?[82]

—*Rep. Donald Fraser*

If one were a foreigner, but not in the Pinochet government, and one
examined the policy of the U.S. Government on human rights between 1973
and 1976, the conclusion would no doubt be that U.S. policy was striking in
its inconsistency. Some American leaders loudly denounced violations
abroad; others scrupulously avoided any public statements on the subject.
There was not only a great deal of aid to Chile in this period, but there were
also a great many restrictions on that aid. Sometimes, aid to countries
accused of gross violations increased; other times, it was reduced or denied.
How can the apparent inconsistencies and the very real shifts in policy be
explained? Which of the many theories or lenses—interest groups, corporate
preferences, congressional committees, bureaucratic politics, or the legislative-executive process—is more helpful in explaining these inconsistencies,
as well as the policy itself? The analysis in the previous section has relied on
the legislative-executive process as the best framework for understanding
and explaining how the specific foreign policies on human rights were
developed and why inconsistencies and shifts occurred. Amendments to
foreign aid bills were identified as some of the most important dependent
variables—i.e., specific foreign policies—and the legislative-executive process which determined the content of these amendments was mapped.

Amendments find the Congress and the Executive exchanging their
traditional roles. Congress drafts and initiates; while the Executive delays
and amends. Amendments, especially those attached to foreign aid bills,
function as levers at three levels of the political process: (1) as a lever by
which the United States can insist that developing countries recognize obligations, whether they be postal debts or compensation for nationalizations,
or adopt an internal or external policy, for example on human rights, which
is more "agreeable" to Americans;[83] (2) as a lever by which Congress can
insist that the executive branch be responsive to the legislative will; and
(3) as a lever by which private or constituent interests can use the Congress
to pressure developing countries.

[82]Chile Hearings, April–May 1976, p. 36.

[83]One U. S. Embassy official told me that each year the Embassy would inform the Latin
American government that the foreign assistance or PL 480 checks had arrived with instructions
from Washington saying that they could be collected only after outstanding postal debts,
obligations on military purchases, or investment disputes were settled. Such pressure was
effective in 'lubricating' host government bureaucracies, but was generally ineffective if the
particular issue was 'politicized,' i.e., had already been decided at a higher level.

It appears that the perception of leverage increases as one moves away from the conduct of diplomacy—from the Executive to Congress to the private sector. For example, in a dispute with Ecuador and Peru over seizure of American tuna boats, the tuna industry believed the U.S. government had all the resources necessary to effect a desirable outcome; the State Department believed there was little that could realistically be done; and Congress took a middle position. Rep. Thomas Pelly testified in an effort to tie the sugar quota to the dispute: "It seems to me if our own State Department refuses to institute actions under an effective treaty, then the Congress must take the only kind of action at its disposal to end this tuna war."[84]

While there were still many Legislators in the 1960s and early 1970s who believed that the United States had the power to compel appropriate behavior by developing countries on problems such as investment disputes, the liberals at the front of the human rights issue had learned the central lesson about the limits of U.S. power by the war in Indo-China, and their arguments therefore rested upon a very different rationale. Senator Kennedy articulated it:

The power to change conditions in Chile—now evidenced in a growing flow of refugees—clearly rests with the junta. But there is little evidence of much change. And I am deeply distressed over the junta's lack of response to legitimate international concerns.

The power to alter United States policy clearly rests with us. And our government has a responsibility to the American people and its Representatives in the Congress, to insure that every effort is being made to make our policy live up to the standards and ideals for which our nation stands.[85]

Moral self-esteem, the desire to avoid close association with repressive governments, and the wish to contribute to the alleviation of suffering abroad are three themes which are deeply embedded in this congressional effort. Representative Donald Fraser restated the second with great force:

Why do we want to be associated with that kind of government [Chile]? What interest do we have in the United States of being tied to a government that is not only going after the Far Left, whatever threat they pose, but now is going after the Christian Democrats down there? What interest of the United States is being served by this close relationship, can you tell me?[86]

[84]U. S. Congress, House Committee on Agriculture, *Hearings: Extension of the Sugar Act, 1971,* 92nd Congress, 1st sess., p. 221.

[85]Kennedy Hearings, part 2, p. 4.

[86]Chile Hearings, April–May 1976, 36.

The State Department prefers "quiet but forceful diplomacy," and so not surprisingly, State Department officials didn't adequately answer Fraser's question.[87] Robert McCloskey, former State Department spokesman, provided the rationale for this preferred strategy: "There can always be legitimate criticism that we [the State Department] didn't say enough publicly about what we were doing privately, but that's a choice we make in the belief that it was not necessary for the United States to be making public pronouncements if it was doing what it felt was right privately."[88] Or, as Assistant Secretary of State Jack Kubisch explained to Senator Kennedy:

> It is one thing for our newspapers or for private citizens to make charges or make complaints or appeal to the Chileans. It is something else for U.S. Government officials or the executive branch to lean hard publicly on a regime since to do so might make them feel that they are required to dig in their heels and resist us publicly, or not have anything to do with us, or discuss the matter with us.

> We are really trying to follow a fine line by being as restrained as we can publicly, by making statements true to what we believe in and are concerned about, and privately doing everything we can to try and improve the situation.[89]

Kennedy, like Fraser, was deeply disturbed that the United States, alone among all the world's democracies, should be the principal, indeed the sole, means of support for the junta, but he was also interested in results, and would have considered trading the one for the other. "What makes you believe that the private approach has been more useful or has been more productive, in terms of what has been happening, than a public approach?" he asked. Kubisch said that twenty-four out of twenty-seven Americans who were detained by the Chilean regime were released and that an exchange of views had been permitted, but his answer clearly didn't satisfy Kennedy mainly because the release of American citizens, he felt, could have been accomplished without paying such a high price.[90]

[87]The State Department official, Deputy Assistant Secretary Hewson Ryan answered: "I would not characterize the relationship as close." Then later: "I am afraid that I cannot agree with you on that, sir. The aid program is based on the legislative structure that the development assistance proposed for Chile should go to the neediest. Mr. Kleine [Deputy U. S. Coordinator, Alliance for Progress], I believe, has made a rather forceful case that the aid program has. Our other relationships are extremely limited. We have no military training or assistance program going at this time.

"Of course we have a substantial American colony there. We have substantial American investments. The Chileans pay their bills." (Ibid.)

[88]*Washington Post*, 15 August 1974, p. A22.

[89]Kennedy Hearings, part 1 (23 September 1973), p. 41.

[90]Ibid., pp. 41–42.

The debate over a public vs. a private strategy is not just a debate over which is more effective; it is a debate between Congress and the Executive over style, prerogative, and policy. As we have seen, Legislators, who are also politicians, have very different interests and respond to very different incentives than bureaucrats, who are also diplomats. Legislators press forward with new ideas, programs, and rhetoric; diplomats resist excesses and respond to routine. Secondly, by arguing for a "quiet" and private strategy, the State Department is also arguing for a free hand to conduct foreign policy, while the Legislators, who prefer to remain involved in policymaking and who do not always trust that the *free* hand will be used for the right ends, quite naturally prefer a public strategy in which they can watch the action and readily participate.

But the arguments over style and prerogative only mask the more central disagreement between the branches on policy and priorities, and it is this disagreement on policy which is most likely to lead to conflict. The differences in style only exacerbate the relationship; they do not necessarily lead to disagreement. The State Department viewed the human rights issue as "a part of a large relationship; that is, a part which has to be weighed against other parts."[91] The "other parts" include the full panoply of U.S. interests: economic, commercial, foreign investment, and national security. "State," said one official, "wants a government that can pull Chile together in the long-term."[92] The department did not believe that it could have much effect on the junta on the human rights issue, but that whatever influence it could have, would be enhanced by offering assistance to the regime. Were assistance terminated, several Foreign Service Officers argued, any hope of moderating the repressiveness would be gone.

These arguments were made in the first rounds of the legislative-executive debate in 1973 and 1974. Congress, of course, strongly disagreed with the arguments, and viewed the unparalleled support for the regime as damaging in itself of U.S. national interests. Nor were they able to get an answer to the simple question: even if one accepts the State Department argument, why give so much assistance? (More per capita economic assistance went to Chile in this period than to any other country in Latin America.)[93] So, amendments were introduced; hearings were held to try to answer questions and obtain evidence. The State Department reacted reflexively by trying to get the amendment deleted, and failing that, to dilute it by making it a nonbinding sense of the Congress resolution, and if that

[91]See testimony of Harry Shlaudeman, Deputy Assistant Secretary of State (ARA) to House International Relations Subcommittee on Inter-American Affairs and International Organizations and Movements, *Hearings: Human Rights in Chile*, 93rd Congress, 2nd sess., pp. 132–33.

[92]Interview, summer, 1974.

[93]Chile Hearings, April–May 1976, p. 117.

didn't work, then to try to add a national interest waiver. This amendment making-and-braking process has characterized the interaction of the two branches on many foreign policy issues.

In the human rights area, the lack of responsiveness to the congressional will ensured that each year the amendments would be more tightly worded. No better statement of the reason for tightly-worded amendments can be found than the following "additional view" of Rep. Michael Harrington to the Report of the Committee on Foreign Affairs on the Foreign Assistance Act of 1974:

> The amendments which limit the discretionary authorities of the executive branch, by specifically providing Congress with a disapproval mechanism over certain types of assistance programs, should be recognized as an indication of growing congressional frustration at the increasing tendency of the executive branch to ignore the statutes enacted by Congress.[94]

This same process has also governed the determination of policy on other issues, for example the cutoff of military assistance to Turkey in 1975.[95] Nor is the "feeling" of unresponsiveness unjustified. As the following report by a *New York Times* correspondent who travelled with Kissinger on a trip through Latin America in 1976 shows, the Secretary of State was clearly delivering the message that he wasn't concerned about the human rights issue: "Both supporters and opponents of the Brazilian Government view Washington's concern with human rights as more a product of Congressional pressure than initiative from the Executive Branch."[96]

Generally, Congress "ties the Executive's hands" when the latter has failed to demonstrate sufficient attention to the congressional mandate to be trusted with discretion. In the debate on legislation authorizing the use of troops to ensure a safe evacuation of Americans from Indo-china, Rep. Donald Fraser summarized the dilemma:

> The distrust of the Executive Branch runs so deep in this chamber that members are afraid that any discretion, any grant of authority, to the Executive Branch will open the door to allow the Executive Branch to again try to make one more effort to do what ten years failed to do.[97]

[94]Chile Hearings, April–May 1976, p. 117.

[95]See my "Coping with Congress's Foreign Policy," *Foreign Service Journal* 52 (December 1975): 15–18, 23; interviews.

[96]Jonathan Kandell, "The Latins and the U.S.: Kissinger's Tour Just Made More Clear That Congress Complicates Relations," *New York Times*, 27 February 1976, p. 2.

[97]*Congressional Record*, 23 April 1975, p. H3143.

The resultant policy is one that develops by fits and starts. Congress prods and pushes the Executive to rearrange its priorities, and gradually important cleavages in the Executive begin to open. In the human rights area, Assistant Secretary Rogers, the Special Assistants on Human Rights attached to the regional Assistant Secretaries, James Wilson, the Coordinator on Humanitarian Affairs, and Deputy Secretary Robert Ingersoll, to whom Wilson reported, all became respected allies of congressional leaders on this issue. In a hearing, on October 2, 1975, Senator Kennedy acknowledged their contribution,[98] and at another point, Fraser publicly commended a speech by Rogers in which he appears to contradict Kissinger's position that there was "no adequately objective way to make distinctions of degree" of gross violations. Rogers said that "there *is* a yardstick of public inhumanity. Every country is represented somewhere on it . . . there are differences of degree . . . and there are in the end qualitative thresholds."[99]

In the same way that liberal Legislators point out these cleavages and try to exploit them, officials in the State Department also try to take advantage of the actual and potential differences between Legislators. And often, the department does not have to go looking for these differences. In a hearing in December 1975 on the foreign aid appropriations bill, Representative Edward Koch pressed Secretary Kissinger to make human rights an important concern of the State Department and to consider—if not actually deliver—a cutback in assistance to South Korea if Gen. Park Chung Hee's policies grew any more repressive.[100] Barely five minutes later, Subcommittee Chairman Otto Passman tried to get Kissinger to justify the repression in South Korea in terms of their grave security threat. Said Passman: "It is touch and go, and you either have strict discipline in that country or there will be no South Korea. Is that a fair evaluation?"[101]

It is significant that in those cases where there are countervailing objectives—in the Korean case, a security interest is evident and widely accepted—the resulting policy is more flexible. But in the case of Chile and in the general area of human rights, Passman's views were unrepresentative of the Congress and were overruled in favor of a congressional policy which gave high priority to the issue of human rights. Indeed, the differences

[98]Kennedy Hearings, part 3, p. 4.

[99]In an address before the Pan-American Society in Boston on November 4, 1975, reprinted with a short statement by Rep. Donald Fraser who called it "responsive to the concerns that many members of Congress have expressed regarding the need for foreign policy to be responsive to the human rights dimension of international relations." (*Congressional Record*, 11 February 1976, pp. E397–8.)

[100]U. S. House of Representatives, Subcommittee on Foreign Operations of the House Appropriations Committee, *Hearings: Foreign Assistance and Related Appropriations for 1976*, part 4, 94th Congress, 1st sess., November–December 1975, p. 72.

[101]Ibid., p. 74.

within branches on this issue as well as on investment disputes were never as important as between branches.

A new ranking of priorities is not accepted in a single year, or even in two or three years by a bureaucracy, particularly when its leadership remains resistant to the new ranking, but progress in elevating the concern for human rights is unquestionable. On June 9, 1976, Secretary of State Henry Kissinger made a strong statement on the issue at the O.A.S. General Assembly Meeting in Santiago, something which he would not have done two years before.[102] One State Department official confirmed the rearrangement of priorities, and its cause: "We are," he said, "taking a more aggressive view of human rights than we would have taken without a Congress."[103] And finally on January 1, 1977, after failing to comply for more than a year with FAA 1975 (sec. 502B) requiring reports on the status of human rights in countries receiving U.S. security assistance, Secretary Kissinger submitted six such reports to the House International Relations Committee.[104]

INTERESTS AND GROUPS AND CONCLUSIONS

The discussion, thus far, of the development of human rights policy has been strictly in terms of the Congress and the Executive. What role did outside groups play, and does that help to explain other foreign policies made as a result of interbranch disagreement? In the case of the Hickenlooper amendment, Congress's policy was interpreted by one scholar as being a function of corporate preferences, but if we compare the two cases, other variables appear more salient and important.

In the human rights case, there were various academic and church groups who were involved with the issue, but these groups were not responsible for putting the item on the congressional agenda, nor could it be said that they triggered the interested Legislators to introduce resolutions. Nor were the Legislators responding to constituent pressure of any sort. Indeed, while Kennedy and Fraser are both identified in Washington as the principal congressional advocates on this issue, few of their constituents would identify them as such. And the two subcommittees they chair generate more information and send more literature to interest groups than they receive.

On the other hand, Congress has hardly been the only institution to have taken a new interest in this field. New organizations like the Institute

[102]Reprinted in Chile Hearings, April–May 1976, pp. 121–25.

[103]Interviews.

[104]Bernard Gwertzman, "U. S. Says Six Nations Curb Human Rights," *New York Times*, 2 January 1977, pp. 1, 14.

for International Policy have been established to deal specifically with this issue, while other organizations, which are already known and established, have had a phenomenal growth in their membership in the last few years. Amnesty International, for example, which tries to help political prisoners, has grown from nineteen to one hundred chapters in the U.S. and its financial contributor list has increased from two thousand to forty thousand in just four years from 1972 to 1976.[105] The literature has grown just as much and just as rapidly.[106] Thus, congressional interest in the subject has reflected and paralleled a growing concern throughout the country for the rights of citizens at home and abroad, but it is incorrect to say that congressional interest is a function of this national concern. It preceded it, and continues to flourish without obvious electoral incentives.

Thus, the important factors in explaining congressional policy on human rights include: Legislators, who are respected as authorities in the field, who are effective, and who are willing to devote the time and the energy to the issue; a competent staff; and the absence or the relative weakness of a countervailing leader, group, or principle. Although Multinational Corporations like ITT may have been responsible for putting the issue of protection of foreign investment on the congressional agenda, the solidity and breadth of congressional interest in the issue of investment protection had less to do with corporate preferences than with support of an important and unquestioned principle, the protection of U.S. citizens abroad. As Gregory F. Treverton found in a case study of the IPC investment dispute:

> To a substantial extent, 'liberals' and 'conservatives' found common ground in concern about threats of expropriation in Latin America, the former because they had embraced an ideology of the Alliance in which foreign investment bulked large and the latter because they were generally outraged by threatened seizures of United States property.[107]

After the new policy on investment disputes was legislated, Congress repeated its concern with every renewal of the foreign aid bill, while, at the same time, extending its policy to other foreign aid-type bills. As a result, each year the State Department brought larger and larger briefing books

[105]*Washington Post*, 7 August 1976. For a list and description of other organizations, see Nigel S. Rodley, "Monitoring Human Rights Violations in the 1980s," paper prepared for the 1980s Project of the Council on Foreign Relations in New York, mimeo, pp. 13 ff.

[106]See, e.g., University of Notre Dame Law School, Center for Civil Rights, *International Human Rights: A Bibliography, 1970–76* (Notre Dame, Indiana: Univ. of Notre Dame Press, June 1976), 118 pages.

[107]Gregory F. Treverton, Murphy Commission Studies, App. I, vol. 3, p. 206.

filled with details on the status of every expropriation dispute to Capitol Hill. If the defense of U.S. investments was given priority over other U.S. interests,[108] it was mainly because the State Department failed to balance the various interests from fear of congressional censure, or from the desire to avoid Congress altogether.[109]

Thus, the relationship between the branches is critical in understanding the development of those specific foreign policies which begin as congressional expressions of concern and become binding amendments to a foreign aid bill. The universe of such policies has expanded at an exponential rate since the late 1960s.[110] There is no question that the recent rapid growth is a reflection, in considerable part, of the breakdown in a foreign policy consensus which followed in the wake of Vietnam. But it is also true that the amendment making-and-braking process has existed as long as there has been a foreign aid bill. Fundamentally, foreign policy is a question of integrating goals, and Congress is increasingly interested in defining those goals and in making sure that they are integrated in the way Congress intended.

Joan Nelson has observed that "there is a strong tendency in the Executive Branch not only to gloss over conflicts among goals in defending proposed or actual actions before Congress and the public, but also to minimize such conflicts in its own deliberations."[111] The reason for this executive behavior has been explained in terms of style, prerogative, and policy. The Congress, for similar reasons, has a tendency to stress other priorities; and in the integrative and interactive process, trust and responsiveness are essential. When it is lacking, disagreement and conflict are likely, and the resulting policy may not only fail to accomplish the goals set by either Congress or the Executive, but in fact might undermine both.

While Congress of course can write laws, the power of the Executive in the legislative process, even when it is just the amendment-making process, is very great indeed. In the short-term, the Executive can often succeed in deleting the amendment; in the medium-term, they dilute it; and in the long-term, they have got to learn to live with it. The alternative is self-defeating foreign policies.

---

[108]Richard J. Bloomfield, "Who Makes American Foreign Policy? Some Latin American Case Studies," unpublished paper, Center for International Affairs, Harvard University, 1972.

[109]See my "Congress's Impact on Latin America," pp. 266–67.

[110]See Committee on International Relations, *Congress and Foreign Policy, 1974 and 1975*, committee print, published in August 1975 and 1976.

[111]Joan M. Nelson, *Aid, Influence, and Foreign Policy*, (N.Y.: MacMillan, 1968), p. 30.

IV

CONCLUSIONS: OF LENSES, POLICIES, AND PROCESSES

11

THE POLITICS OF U.S. FOREIGN ECONOMIC POLICY: IMPLICATIONS FOR POLICY AND PROCESS

> . . . for in so complicated a science as political economy, no one
> axiom can be laid down as wise and expedient for all times and
> circumstances, and for their contraries.[1]
>
> —Thomas Jefferson

MOMENTOUS EQUATIONS: MORTGAGING THE FUTURE?

"While we *do* have a world economy," Maurice Strong, former Executive Director of the United Nations Environmental Program, said, "we *do not have* an effective world system of economic management."[2] The development of such a system to cope with the problems of international economic interdependence is increasingly engaging the attention of foreign policy-makers in the United States and other nations, and its importance is likely to expand. In trade, investment, oceans, food, and energy, the rudiments of coordinating mechanisms and international structures are being shaped, not always successfully, by the nations of the world. The United States, for example, assumed the leadership in gaining international agreement for a Financial Support Fund to help finance the mounting energy bills of the industrialized countries, but Congress was cool to the idea. "We bent over

[1]"Letter to Benjamin Austin," in Merrill D. Peterson (ed.) *The Portable Thomas Jefferson* (N.Y.: Viking Press, 1975), pp. 549–550.

[2]Quoted in remarks by Sen. Hubert Humphrey, *Congressional Record*, 29 January 1976, p. S797.

backward to do what Henry [Kissinger] wanted," said one European diplomat in Washington, "and now he can't deliver."[3]

Congress has arrived at a new prominence and importance in foreign policy-making from two different directions. It has been drawn into a more significant role by the nature of the new agenda, which includes those domestic and foreign policy issues in which Congress has always played a large role. From a different direction, the excesses, abuse, and misuse of Presidential power culminating in the Watergate affair, have induced Congress to assert itself in curbing the Executive and redressing the balance of power. In brief, new issues have *pulled* Congress into the foreign policy-making arena, while Presidential failures and abuses have *pushed* Congress into a larger role in national policy-making. In doing so, Congress has found a new self-confidence in its foreign policy judgments, and it has accumulated the resources in terms of staff, legislative support systems, and procedures for obtaining information from the Executive, with which it can formulate independent judgments.

That responds to the question of whether Congress will be involved, but it doesn't answer the question of whether Congress and the U.S. Government will be able to cope effectively with issues of interdependence. Will increasing congressional involvement bias the outcome toward narrow and special interests and a short-term vision of America's future? Walter Lippmann applied himself to that question a generation ago, and his answer was pessimistic:

> *In general the softer and easier side reflects what we desire and the harder reflects what is needed in order to satisfy the desire. Now the momentous equations of war and peace, of solvency, of security and of order, always have a harder or a softer, a pleasanter or a more painful, a popular or an unpopular option. It is easier to obtain votes for appropriations than it is for taxes, to facilitate consumption than to stimulate production, to protect a market than to open it, to inflate than to deflate, to borrow than to save, to demand than to compromise, to be intransigent than to negotiate, to threaten war than to prepare for it.*

> *Faced with these choices between the hard and the soft, the normal propensity of democratic governments is to please the largest number of voters. The pressure of the electorate is normally for the soft side of the equations. That is why governments are unable to cope with reality when elected assemblies and mass opinions become decisive in the state, when there are no statesmen to resist*

[3]Quoted in "Plans for Energy Oil Financing," *New York Times*, 29 September 1976, pp. 1, 65.

*the inclination of the voters, and there are only politicians to
excite and to exploit them.*

*There is then a general tendency to be drawn downward, as by the
force of gravity, towards insolvency, towards the insecurity of
factionalism, towards the erosion of liberty, and towards hyperbolic
wars.*[4]

Since 1955 when Lippmann identified the choices, the new salience and
importance of issues of interdependence has, if anything, altered the agenda in
such a way as to make the choices even starker, and the prognosis more pessimistic than before. More than either domestic *or* foreign policy issues, issues
of interdependence which overlap both, involve especially difficult trade-offs
between: particular and collective interests; short-term, concrete and long-
term, rule-sustaining interests; economic and political, security, or ecological objectives; domestic and diplomatic interests; and sovereignty and
autonomy. The special difficulty is that it is the essence of these issues that
one side of each trade-off—the particular, short-term and concrete, the
economic, the domestic, and the sovereign instinct—is over-represented in
the U.S. political process, while the other side is under-represented.

Lippmann's conclusion is also the predicted outcome of the congressional theories and the interest group theories, and therefore it was framed as
a question rather than an answer for this study. In seeking an answer to the
question of whether these issues of the future will be managed effectively, I
identified and isolated a body of case material on issues which exhibited
many of the same characteristics as these future issues. The logical candidate was foreign economic policy which previously had incorporated many
of those issues, like trade, investment, oceans, energy, which are presently
referred to by the more "modern" appellation as "issues of interdependence."

My intention was to examine U.S. foreign economic policy over a
significant time span, cover a number of different policy-areas, and submit
this body of case material to three sets of questions: (1) When faced with the
kind of choices defined by Lippmann, which foreign economic policies were
chosen? (2) How can those outcomes be explained? Which of the five lenses
best explains these outcomes? and (3) What are the relative advantages and
contributions of using each lens? To what reforms in policy and process is
the analyst pointed?

Earlier studies of the politics of U.S. foreign economic policy were
criticized in chapters one and two for pretending to cover more than they
did. U.S. foreign economic policy envelops almost all of domestic and
foreign policy and begins with our nation's birth, and needless to say, this

---

[4]Walter Lippmann, *Essays in the Public Philosophy* (N.Y.: Mentor, 1955), p. 42.

study does not attempt to be that encyclopedic. Instead, three policy-areas—trade, investment, and foreign assistance—were selected because they represent three of the four central areas of foreign economic policy. The fourth, monetary policy, is almost the prototype issue of interdependence in the sense that national policies on interest rates are transmitted internationally quicker and with more impact than any other foreign economic policy. But monetary policy was not selected as a case because its politics do not have the deep constituent roots that characterize the trade-offs defined above.

An additional step toward specifying the dependent variables was taken in order to make the analysis more manageable. U.S. trade policy was analyzed from 1929 to 1976 with special stress placed on the major trade lens as the spine of U.S. trade policy.

U.S. investment policy was examined, though not as intensively or as systematically as trade policy, and a slightly different mode of analysis for addressing the central questions of this book was adopted to take into account the historical differences in the development of investment policy. A distinction was made between parent and host government investment policy, and the former was subject to an analysis of the relative contributions of Congress, private groups, and the Executive to its development for the period 1960 to 1972. Since host government investment policy has many more of the characteristics of issues of interdependence than parent investment policy, and since it has been formulated in a comprehensive way only very recently and therefore permitted a more detailed study, an entire chapter was devoted to an analysis of the formulation of that policy.

Though foreign aid is not likely to play as large a role in future U.S. foreign policy as it has in the last thirty years, U.S. foreign assistance policy was selected for two reasons: first, there will inevitably be foreign aid components in other policies of interdependence, and secondly and more importantly, the policy-making process of foreign aid contains important lessons for the way in which Congress and the Executive interact.

In trade, investment, and aid policy, officials confront choices between particular and collective interests:

—in trade policy, the choices are between liberal or protectionist policies or between the delegation of highly restricted or the delegation of discretionary powers to the President;

—in investment policy, restrictive vs. discretionary, the extraterritorial reach of U.S. policy toward U.S. MNC's abroad vs. an arms-length policy, exclusionary vs. open policies on foreign direct investment in the United States;

—and in foreign assistance policy, the tradeoffs are between the relative weight given to a single interest vs. balanced interests and overall relations, the delegation of restricted vs. flexible powers to the Executive, and legislating mandatory sanctions vs. a national interest waiver which permits discretionary application.

U.S. FOREIGN ECONOMIC POLICIES: THE DEPENDENT VARIABLE

While aware of the extent to which trade, investment, and aid policies are interrelated, I will nonetheless proceed inductively from a definition of each to a summary statement of U.S. foreign economic policy in the period under consideration.

U.S. Trade Policy, 1929–76

The passage of the Smoot-Hawley Tariff Act in June 1930 represented at once the high point in U.S. tariffs in the twentieth century and a watershed in U.S. trade policy. It was the last time Congress set tariffs on a product-by-product basis, and it was the last time the Executive played a largely passive role in the legislative process.

In the 1934 Reciprocal Trade Agreements Act, Congress delegated to the President the power to reduce tariffs by 50 percent of their current levels by negotiating most-favored-nation agreements with foreign governments on a bilateral basis. During hearings, Congress reached an understanding with the Executive that tariffs would not be reduced on those products which would suffer injurious competition from imports. To ensure that this understanding would be enforced, Congress inserted a provision in the bill which required that private witnesses be given the opportunity to state their case in public hearings to be held prior to bilateral negotiations.

These central principles have guided U.S. trade policy since the 1934 Act: tariffs and trade barriers should be reduced; the Executive should negotiate with foreign governments, rather than Congress setting tariffs on individual products; the principle of reciprocity should govern new agreements; and the liberalizing process should be gradual, permitting of temporary exceptions for manufacturers of specific products especially vulnerable to severe or unfair import competition.

Informed by these principles, U.S. trade policy has retained a general consistency, though unquestionably there have been deviations from these principles. Within the framework defined by these principles, there have been several important shifts in U.S. trade policy which have permitted a widening assault on the world's trade barriers and an expansion of world trade: from bilateral to multilateral agreements, from product-by-product negotiations to linear tariff reductions, from a peril-point provision to adjustment assistance, from tariffs to non-tariff barriers (NTB's).

In 1947, after Congress had renewed and enlarged the President's negotiating authority by permitting the reduction of tariffs by 50 percent of 1945 rates, the United States shifted from a bilateral track to a multilateral one, negotiating within the framework of the multinational General Agreements on Tariff and Trade (GATT). In 1962, Congress transferred the responsibility for conducting trade negotiations from the State Department to the White House Special Trade Representative and from a product-by-product technique to a linear reduction formula by which tariffs on an entire sector of products could be reduced. At the same time, Congress enacted a "radical" executive idea of compensating "injured" industries not by tariffs or quotas which might induce retaliation, but by adjustment assistance.

In the sixth, "Kennedy Round" of multilateral trade negotiations, tariff barriers were reduced to such a low level that nontariff barriers—e.g., quantitative restrictions, health and safety regulations, and the wide range of domestic policies which affect international trade—became more important than tariffs. Negotiating the reduction, harmonization, or elimination of NTB's, however, is qualitatively different than negotiating tariffs because the former involves the alteration of domestic law. Therefore, in drafting the negotiating authority for the Executive to use in the current Tokyo Round, Congress suggested a number of new procedures to directly involve itself in negotiations (through ten Congressional Advisers and Staff) and in the ratification of new agreements (by requiring an affirmative veto on all NTB's). Because of these changes, Congress is playing, for the first time in American history, an active role in international negotiations.

Since 1934, the tariff and trade barriers of the United States and other nations have been reduced, gradually but consistently, and world trade has dramatically increased. Widening areas of domestic economies have been forced to adjust more often and more rapidly to imports, and the adjustment process has not always been easy or smooth. In the United States, domestic industries occasionally have sought governmental protection from import competition. While rarely obtaining what they request—generally a legislated product quota—these industries and the labor unions which have increasingly supported their efforts, nonetheless, *have forced Congress to consider certain proposals for coping with the increased national vulnerability resulting from the relentless opening of the world economy.*

First used in the 1934 Trade Act to insure prior consultation with affected industries, the "escape clause" was broadened and formalized in 1945 and incorporated into bilateral trade agreements and later into the GATT. However, the State Department, which was the Administration's negotiator at the time, lost the confidence of Congress by its unresponsiveness to petitioning groups. Disturbed by this unresponsiveness, Congress legislated a specific escape clause and then a peril-point provision, which was an "automatic" formula to keep tariffs from declining to a "dangerous"

level. Both provisions were tightened as the threat to declining industries increased and the responsiveness of the Executive declined. In addition, Congress transferred the negotiating authority from State and urged the Executive in certain special cases to negotiate voluntary agreements to restrain trade. Each of these changes was viewed as "protectionist," but its real effect was not to insulate certain industries from the impact of trade but to permit their gradual adjustment to international trade. Moreover, Congress never excluded any single, named product from MFN trade negotiations. Rather than legislating specific product provisions, Congress drafted generalized rules about unfair trade practices, administrative relief due to disruptive trade competition, or adjustment assistance. By declining to redress special grievances with specific solutions, Congress side-stepped the entire logrolling problem. At the same time, however, the political process was not insensitive to the plight of genuinely threatened or injured groups since the general and impartial administrative rules were developed to respond to their needs.

In summary, U.S. trade policy from 1934 to 1976 is characterized by liberalness, a gradual but consistent attempt to contribute to the opening of the international economic system by a reduction of the national barriers to trade. As table 13 demonstrates, U.S. tariffs have been continually and consistently reduced over the last fifty years, and U.S. and world trade have soared. The supposed passing of U.S. hegemony in 1971 has not had a noticeable effect on either U.S. barriers or U.S. or world trade.

Congress has recently increased its involvement in trade policy for two reasons: to assure that the liberalizing process has appropriate adjustment mechanisms as well as fair and equitable administrative procedures; and to handle the unique problem of nontariff barriers. As barriers to trade are levelled, more and more national policies, once viewed as purely domestic, will be seen as conferring advantage on the exporters of one nation, and therefore disadvantage to a local, competing industry. The response to this kind of problem will be either competitive, beggar-thy-neighbor increases in export subsidies (or whatever domestic policy is the source of the problem) or harmonization and reduction of the trade barrier. Thus, a wider range of domestic policies will be drawn into the vortex of international trade policy, and that is one reason why the Congress's role in the future will be even greater than at present.

The Ricardian principle of comparative advantage has been learned, and few—other than elements in the labor movement—would question the proposition that free as opposed to less free trade means greater prosperity. The issue is no longer free trade vs. protectionism, or open vs. a closed world, but rather how can the world economy be kept open and opening? How to organize orderly and peaceful change? How to minimize the dislocations due to rapid adjustment and specialization? And how to ensure that the benefits

TABLE 13   Trends in Trade and Tariffs, 1928–78

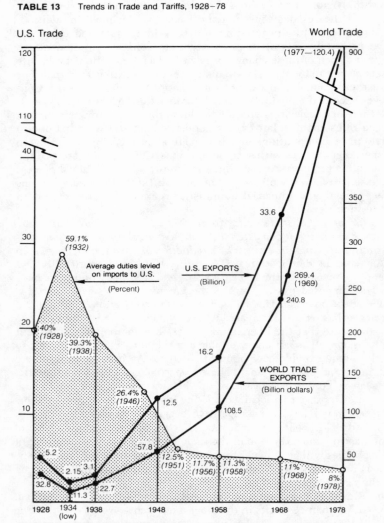

U.S. Trade

World Trade

Average duties levied on imports to U.S. (Percent)

U.S. EXPORTS (Billion)

WORLD TRADE EXPORTS (Billion dollars)

59.1% (1932)

40% (1928)

39.3% (1938)

26.4% (1946)

12.5% (1951)

11.7% (1956)

11.3% (1958)

11% (1968)

8% (1978)

(1977—120.4)

33.6

269.4 (1969)

240.8

16.2

108.5

12.5

57.8

5.2

2.15   3.1

32.8

11.3

22.7

1928   1934 (low)   1938   1948   1958   1968   1978

Note.—U.S. Export totals include military grant-aid and foreign merchandise. (U.S. Department of State, "The Trade Debate," Department of State Publication 8942, Washington, D.C., January 1979, p. 6.)

of increased world specialization are distributed more equitably? Trade policy, in brief, is embarked on a steady course toward reducing artificial barriers to trade, and the questions at issue currently coalesce around its margins rather than at its core.

The apparent debate between restricted or discretionary negotiating authority has also been misleading. Although special groups have often triggered congressional interest, Congress has only moved to deny the Executive negotiating flexibility when the Executive has failed to demonstrate sufficient responsiveness to the legislative mandate. In trade policy, in particular, Congress often inserts an "escape-valve" in legislative provisions, reducing the relevance of the apparent dichotomy between restrictiveness and discretion. Congress writes general rules to be administered by an impartial, nonpartisan International Trade Commission (formerly the Tariff Commission) and its intent is not to grant a quota or relief for any one industry or sector, but only that the process, i.e., the determination of *all* of the trade cases, be fair and equitable. *If the Congress is obsessed with any facet of trade policy, it is certainly not to assist special groups, but to see that the International Trade Commission is free from all—including congressional—distorting influences.* Thus, Congress's increased involvement does not, by any means, necessarily mean a restrictionist or protectionist policy; indeed, with an agreeable legislative-executive process, it could auger well for the future of U.S. trade policy.

Foreign Investment Policy, 1960–76

Since 1960, the starting date of the analysis of U.S. policy on foreign direct investment, U.S. investment policy has been characterized by gross inconsistency, fragmentation of responsibility, and a total absence of conceptual clarity. There have actually been two U.S. policies on investment— one for outward and one for inward investment—and although one would expect the two policies to share several standards or rules, this has not, in fact, been the case. One Congressional Staff summarized the differences by frankly stating that U.S. policy on outward investment denies the validity of the Calvo Doctrine, which maintains that a host government has exclusive legal jurisdiction over all corporations in its domain, while it supports the Calvo Doctrine as it applies to foreign investment in the United States.[5] What this means is that the U.S. has long-standing restrictive and exclusionary laws prohibiting foreign ownership in a wide variety of sectors, including communications, natural resources, and merchant shipping, while it has barely tolerated similar laws affecting U.S. corporations in other countries.

---

[5]From unpublished minutes of a conference on "U.S. Multinational Corporations and Investment Disputes in Latin America," December 17, 1975 at the Embassy of Argentina, sponsored by the Commission on U.S.-Latin American Relations.

U.S. parent investment policy has always consisted of a number of separate strands; each one has been developed and administered independently. At times, one of these strands, for example, balance of payments considerations, has been more important than the others, sometimes to the extent that other important considerations were ignored or overlooked by policy-makers. From 1960 to 1972, the continual deficit in the U.S. balance of payments preoccupied U.S. policy-makers and prompted them to try to limit the flow of capital abroad. Controls on the flow of foreign direct investment abroad were voluntary in 1965 and mandatory in 1968, but the stated purpose of these controls was to limit the outflow of capital, not reduce the stock of foreign direct investment. In fact, neither outcome occurred.

Other strands of U.S. parent investment policy include the extraterritorial application of U.S. antitrust policy, taxation of foreign-earned income, the Trading with the Enemy Act, and the promotion and protection of foreign investment. Each of these policies was made and administered by different governmental agencies, and the implications of these policies for U.S. foreign relations were infrequently considered. With the exception of U.S. policy on investment disputes, U.S. parent investment policies rarely harmed U.S. relations with other countries. In the few cases where relations were disturbed, for example, with the application of the Trading with the Enemy Act to U.S. corporations in France in the early 1960's, an intergovernmental consultation mechanism was devised to prevent the recurrence of such problems and to permit flexible application of the general rule.[6] Thus by ad hoc measures and by remaining sensitive to complaints from abroad, U.S. parent investment policy gradually, though not very systematically, took into consideration the various interests which were affected by the policies.

Although there were individual policies on taxation, balance of payments, and investment insurance, which marginally influenced the direction and to a lesser extent the composition of U.S. foreign direct investment, the U.S. government never formulated an overall plan or policy, comparable to what France did in its Five Year Plan,[7] to direct the flow, composition, and nature of U.S. direct investment. And conversely, while U.S. corporations investing overseas had to adjust to individual U.S. Government policies, corporations, in large part, made their decisions to invest, divest, or alter the terms of their investment on the basis of economic criteria—market, labor costs and productivity, and technology—and to a lesser extent

---

[6]See William L. Craig, "Application of the Trading with the Enemy Act to Foreign Corporations Owned by Americans," *Harvard Law Review* 83 (1970). Also, Raymond Vernon, *Sovereignty At Bay: The Multinational Spread of U.S. Enterprises* (N.Y.: Basic Books, 1971), p. 278.

[7]"France Enters the 1970s," *Business International* (Paris, 1970), p. 13.

the political climate of the host country rather than as a result of U.S. parent investment policies.

Compared to U.S. parent investment policy, U.S. host government investment policy has contained even more strands, was even more fragmented and inconsistent, and was administered by more agencies on the federal level in addition to state-level economic development agencies. Several times in U.S. history, concern over the sale of U.S. property to aliens escalated and led to restrictive and sometimes exclusionary policies and legislation. Until 1973, the most recent instance of such concern occurred in the 1920s, when Congress and several states passed banking legislation, which was highly discriminatory to aliens.

In 1973, after two devaluations, the U.S. became an economically attractive place for foreign direct investment, and after a number of controversial take-overs by foreigners of U.S. corporations and after rumors spread of large-scale Japanese investment in U.S. farms and natural resources, congressional and executive attention quickly focused on the issue. The Executive approached the issue more systematically under the aegis of the Council on International Economic Policy Working Group on Foreign Investment, which was established in the summer of 1973. But congressional attention as reflected by the proliferation of resolutions on the issue served essentially the same purpose: to focus the discussion on alternative proposals to deal with inward investment.

Congress discussed these proposals within the framework of three subcommittees, all of them oriented, in varying degrees, toward the international dimension of the problem. The resulting policy developed by fits and starts. Beginning with an eighteen month, one-shot benchmark study of foreign direct and portfolio investment undertaken by the Commerce and Treasury Departments, the Executive rather reluctantly adopted a policy of monitoring and doing periodic benchmark studies of foreign direct investment. Congress continually pushed the Executive toward more controls, oversight, and regulations of inward investment, and while resisting such prods in the congressional arena, the Executive frequently implemented some variation of the idea by Executive Order in order to keep congressional hands off the executive prerogative. For example, the President established the Committee on Foreign Investment in the U.S. in May 1975 to oversee new large-scale investments by corporations owned by foreign governments. This was done by Executive Order not long after administration witnesses testified against legislation intended to do practically the same thing. The only difference was that Congress wanted such a Committee to have the power to prohibit foreign investment. While not accepting that point, the Executive did pledge to Congress that it would initiate consultations with various governments as a way to avoid the need to prohibit their investments.

In general, however, the various strands of U.S. host government investment policy were never woven into a single, cohesive fabric. Although the government completed the massive study on inward investment, it has not yet catalogued the state laws on inward investment, nor has it attempted to draw the divergent policies of inward and outward investment together into a single policy based on a common set of principles. However, like the latter, the policies on inward investment have not as yet elicited any serious foreign complaint from abroad. In early 1973, a number of restrictive and exclusionary resolutions introduced in Congress did elicit some concern, but these bills were never even subject to congressional hearings let alone enacted.

To recapitulate, U.S. parent investment policy remains composed of a series of separate strands with no overall rationale or goal. U.S. policy on inward investment, however, has assumed more coherency since 1973 and has gradually become more regulative and data-conscious, though not more restrictive or exclusionary.

Foreign Assistance Policy, 1945–76

The four major initiatives of U.S. foreign assistance policy in the postwar period have all shared one core principle: the United States would gain influence abroad in return for transferring resources. Indeed, the Marshall Plan for the economic recovery of Western Europe was initiated on a unilateral basis by the United States only after the United States had experienced the frustration, heavy burden, and limited influence (over both program direction and recipient) of working through the United Nations Relief and Rehabilitation Agency.[8]

For the first three initiatives, spanning the period 1948 to 1973, the overriding interest in U.S. foreign aid policy was security-related, to use American resources to win friends and influence governments in the Cold War. As the definition of U.S. security interests changed during this period so too did the rationale and the direction of the foreign aid program.

In the first period, 1948–53, the European Recovery Program was intended to strengthen the economies of Western Europe to combat both starvation and Communism. After the Communist victory in China and the invasion of South Korea, the U.S. Government redirected its foreign assistance to providing military assistance to those "front-line" governments bordering the U.S.S.R. and China, including South Korea, Taiwan, the Philippines, Indo-China, Thailand, Pakistan, Iran, Turkey, and Greece. During this second period from 1951 to 1961, the U.S. Government placed its greatest emphasis on providing military materiel and training for our friends on the rim to defend themselves against the possibility of conventional warfare by Communist governments.

    [8]Charles P. Kindleberger, "U. S. Foreign Economic Policy, 1776–1976," *Foreign Affairs* 55 (January 1977): 406–07.

By 1961, the threat of direct warfare with Communist governments had receded and had been replaced by the earlier Cold War fear that the Communists would seize power by exploiting poverty. U.S. security interests were again defined as promoting economic recovery and/or development in order to prevent a Communist victory; but this time, the direction of assistance was toward the backward and poorer countries. The Agency for International Development and the Alliance for Progress were both begun in 1961, the first to administer the distribution of resources to the poorer countries, and the second as a massive public initiative to help contribute to the economic development of the poorer countries of the western hemisphere.

The fourth, and most recent, initiative was a genuine collaborative effort, involving Congress, several executive officials, and private research organizations. Unlike previous initiatives, this took the developmental and humanitarian goals of previous foreign aid programs seriously, targetting foreign assistance to the poorest sectors in the poorest countries. However, it is testimony to the durability of security objectives that the major proportion of foreign assistance is still channelled toward programs and countries related more to security (Indo-China before 1974; the Middle East since) than development objectives.

Until 1970, the Cold War rationale which underlay the three foreign aid programs was accepted by the vast majority of Legislators; a consensus existed on the direction and purposes of U.S. foreign policy. This, of course, did not mean that Congress and the Executive were in complete agreement on all aspects of the foreign aid program. On the contrary, there were often disagreements, and these are evident in the annual authorization and appropriations hearings. At certain times, Congress said the Executive was not prosecuting the Cold War actively enough; at other times, that the Executive was relying on military assistance too much and loans too little. Congress wanted the Executive to use private investment more as a supplement to public assistance, and to do so, Congress proposed a number of programs to promote investment and eventually to protect U.S. investors.

The two branches rarely agreed on the proper organizational structure of the agency responsible for administering the aid program. Congress wanted aid to be used to influence the internal and external policies of recipient nations, and while the Executive agreed on the principle that influence should accompany aid, it disagreed on the purposes and the style—public vs. private—of giving aid. However marginal these differences may appear, in fact, they represent the cutting edge of the aid program and of U.S. foreign policy to those countries receiving aid.

Two issues—human rights and investment disputes—where the disagreements between the branches were well known and Congress was deeply involved in steering U.S. foreign policy toward new definitions of U.S. interests, were analyzed in depth in order to obtain clues about the foreign policy-making process on foreign aid. In both issues, congressional concern was first manifested in "sense of the Congress" resolutions, which were gradually tightened if the Executive or foreign governments failed to demonstrate sufficient responsiveness.

In investment disputes, Sen. Bourke Hickenlooper introduced an amendment to the Foreign Assistance Act of 1962 which made the continuation of U.S. assistance to a particular country contingent on that country's fair treatment of U.S. investors. This policy was extended to other areas— multilateral assistance, sugar quotas, fisheries protection; in 1973, another provision was added which permitted the discretionary application of the Hickenlooper amendment.

In the case of human rights, Congress began to articulate in 1973 its concern with the treatment of fundamental human rights by countries receiving U.S. assistance. Although intended to be mandatory, the first round of amendments were diluted by the vigorous lobbying of the executive branch, and the result was two "sense of the Congress" resolutions which were completely ignored by the Executive. Once again, unresponsiveness led to a tightening of these provisions, making a government's receipt of military and, in 1975 economic, assistance sufficient cause for the submission of a report on the status of human rights in that country from the State Department to Congress. Should Congress decide that the report states the violations of human rights more cogently than the case it makes for continued assistance, the Congress could by law veto such assistance.

The process by which Congress reconciles the trade-off between delegating discretionary authority to the President or tightly prescribing his powers is most clearly seen in the analysis of foreign aid policy. Congressional choice is not at the mercy of overweening "special interest subconstituencies" as many have maintained.[9] *Rather the choice is more a function of executive responsiveness and leadership than it is of congressional irresponsibility or lack of responsibility.* Similarly, the congressional decision to place the weight of the foreign aid program to a particular country on a single interest to the exclusion of other U.S. interests in the country is rarely due to a systematic and rational choice, nor is it a result of the continual bargaining between bureaus or branches, but rather to the fact that such bargaining has broken down. To put it another way, to be able to maintain *any* influence, the donor must occasionally demonstrate his willingness to cut off all aid in pursuit of a single interest. Similarly, Congress is sometimes moved to terminate aid to demonstrate the depth of its concern about a particular issue to the Executive.

More important, U.S. aid policy throughout the postwar period has been a generous program motivated by and largely serving security objec-

[9]Bayless Manning, "The Congress, the Executive, and Intermestic Affairs: Three Proposals," *Foreign Affairs* 55 (January 1977), 306.

tives related to the pursuit of the Cold War. Development objectives have not been unimportant, but they have never—even in the current period—been overriding. Congress has exhibited a host of specific preferences on the tactics, strategies, and goals of foreign aid, and with several important exceptions, these preferences are generally combined with those of the Executive and shaped into a coherent whole.

U.S. FOREIGN ECONOMIC POLICY: A SUMMARY STATEMENT

How can the course and the substance of U.S. foreign economic policy since 1934 be described? Certainly, it is too broad and complex to be summarized in any meaningful way in a single sentence. It was in response to a request for just such a statement that one member of President Eisenhower's Cabinet told James Reston, a *New York Times* journalist, in 1956: "We don't have a foreign economic policy. We have forty-nine foreign economic policies."[10] Yet it is not essential or even important to describe all forty-nine policies in order to get a flavor of the general structure and tone of policy.

There are clues to the different dimensions of a summary statement of U.S. foreign economic policy in the analysis of each of the policy-areas. U.S. trade policy has always been and still remains central, the spine of U.S. foreign economic policy, and as such, it reveals several fundamental principles which have guided U.S. foreign economic policy. First, it reveals an unequivocal belief in the economic and political benefits which accrue to all nations and peoples with the *freer flow* of goods, services, and capital across national borders. The goal of U.S. trade policy has been *freer* trade rather than free trade; the former recognizes that too many barriers to trade exist, and that most, but not necessarily all, should be reduced or eliminated, whereas "free trade" presumes no barriers. Secondly, U.S. trade policy reveals a belief that the *process* of reducing such barriers should be a *gradual* and an equitable one which fairly distributes both the benefits and the burdens of trade and which helps noncompetitive industries *adjust* to the changes wrought by freer trade. Thirdly, it reveals the belief that international *agreements* can only endure if they are based on rules which are genuinely *reciprocal and nondiscriminatory.*

U.S. investment policy is, in some ways, trade policy and, more generally foreign economic policy in its most inchoate state. If progress is evident in the relations between nation-states in the postwar period, one of its causes as well as one of its effects is the growing recognition that the double standard in international relations—what you do is our business, but

---

[10]Cited in Holbert Carroll, *House of Representatives and Foreign Affairs* (Boston: Little, Brown and Co., 1966), p. 73.

what we do is not your business—is unproductive and self-defeating. As nations and policy-makers have come to understand this—that "domestic decisions" have international implications—they have been more disposed to fashion reciprocal agreements for smoothing the rough edges of domestic policies that irritate other nations.

In the area of U.S. foreign investment policy, there has been a slow but discernible movement away from the double standard of separate policies for U.S. foreign direct investment abroad and foreign investment in the U.S. The distinction between rules on U.S. resources and rules on access by Americans to foreign resources, however, is a long-standing characteristic of U.S. foreign economic policy. Herbert Hoover, for example, claimed there was no connection between the promotion of U.S. exports, which he vigorously advocated, and high tariffs by the United States on foreign imports, which he also recommended. However, the collapse of world trade which followed foreign retaliation to the Smoot-Hawley tariffs were lessons learned by future Presidents, and the roughest edge of the double standard in U.S. trade policy disappeared.

The progress of multilateral trade negotiations (MTN) in the postwar period forced nations to consider a widening net of "double standard" national policies. Technically, by placing nontariff barriers on the MTN agenda, governments have agreed to negotiate virtually all national policies which in any way confer an unfair advantage on home country industry.

In investment policy, there has not been the same need or even a similar process by which domestic (host investment policy) and international (parent investment policy) policies could become more congruent. In a few isolated cases, for example, New York State banking legislation in the 1950s, credible threats of retailiation by European governments induced the adoption by the United States of nonrestrictive host government policies (similar to our expectations as a parent government). If France or Great Britain, for example, decide to use their MNC's for a specific (foreign policy) purpose, as the U.S. did with the Trading with the Enemy Act, or if other governments intrude on U.S. host government space in other ways on a regular basis, that may provide the sense of urgency needed to harmonize both sets of policies.

A second insight into foreign economic policy which one can derive from an analysis of U.S. investment policy relates to the level and kind of barriers to trade or prohibitions to investment which a nation is always likely to retain. Complete interdependence means complete vulnerability to outside forces, and as Eisenhower said, as long as wars are possible, some degree of national self-sufficiency and self-determination is necessary. The question is how and where to draw the line. The national security argument can always be stretched to include assistance to specific economic interests, and therefore these interests can be expected to argue for an expanded concept.[11] When properly framed, the question adopts a single standard and asks whether the U.S. would be satisfied if the same definition were accepted by a country prescribing rules for U.S. investments. U.S. investment policy has not yet progressed to that stage, but it is unquestionably approaching it. In the interim, U.S. policy has recognized and is sensitive to both dimensions of the problem, and although it has developed by fits and starts, and at times it has shown exclusionary inclinations, in fact, the final policy has been both gradual and internationalist.

The analysis of U.S. foreign assistance policy has provided insights into the foreign policy-making process and particularly the question of how and why amendments are passed denying the President the flexibility to conduct foreign policy effectively. *Automatic and nondiscretionary amendments are often the result of an interactive process in which Congress tries to impose new goals or a new ranking of goals for U.S. foreign policy, but is confronted by an Executive which is resistant or unresponsive.* On the other hand, U.S. trade and aid policy provide instances in which the two branches had different or divergent goals but were nonetheless able to integrate them into a single, relatively coherent policy. Whether the government passes an automatic, nondiscretionary policy, often self-defeating, or a well-integrated policy, depends on the negotiating process between Congress and the Executive. The best way to assure the latter is for the Executive to consult regularly with congressional leaders and to demonstrate responsiveness to legislative mandates.

In the 1976 *International Economic Report,* President Gerald Ford defined the goals of U.S. foreign economic policy succinctly as "freer trade and enhanced global economic stability and prosperity."[12] Our analysis suggests that a more complex definition is required, one which includes several potentially competing goals, such as minimizing domestic unemployment and assuring that injured groups (industry and labor) receive a fair hearing and adequate relief from disruptions due to increased interdependence. In the process of translating these general goals into specific policies, the government has sometimes veered treacherously close to highly protective or restrictive policies, like legislated product quotas, highly discriminatory bills on foreign investment, or automatic sanctions on foreign aid. And deviations, for example, on voluntary export restraint agreements, have occurred. *Yet the end product, particularly on the major policies mandated by laws passed by Congress, has been a foreign economic policy which has pressed the United States toward increased interdependence, not toward greater insulation from its effects.*

[11]See Irving Kravis, "The Current Case for Import Limitations," in Williams Commission Report, vol. 1, pp. 157–58.

[12]International Economic Report of the President, 1976, p. iii.

In an earlier section, I referred to the process in which Congress veers towards parochialism but ends up with a liberal and global policy as the cry-and-sigh paradox. In order to understand, describe, and explain the process and the policy, I identified five different lenses that the analyst could use. In choosing a lens, the analyst should not only look for the one which best explains and predicts the policy, but one which provides him with the clearest picture of the obstacles and the landmarks in the development of policy, and therefore assists him in perceiving the areas in need of improvement.

SELECTING A LENS

Unlike many political analyses which attempt to explain governmental failure or misjudgment,[13] we are in the happy position in this study of looking for explanations for success. U.S. trade and investment policies have feigned parochialism, but in the end, have chosen the far-sighted path. U.S. assistance policy has adjusted its objectives to a changing world, sometimes at the direction of one branch; sometimes at the other's preference.

Structuralism

The structuralist argument—that the passing of American political and military hegemony after 1971 would lead to a series of U.S. policies characterized by their protectionism—is a powerfully cogent one, which turns out, however, to be altogether misleading. The structuralists were in full flower when the Burke-Hartke bill was introduced in 1971 and again when the Dent-Gaydos bill on foreign investment was introduced in 1973; both bills, they argued, signalled the end to American internationalism. The voluntary export restraint agreements on textiles and steel were, its advocates maintained, further indications of the validity of this argument. But neither Burke-Hartke nor Dent-Gaydos passed; indeed, internationalist policies triumphed over these bills, and various multilateral negotiations began to reduce and harmonize the barriers to trade and investment, not to raise them. Secondly, the voluntary restraint agreements were not just the result of pressure politics by declining industries, but of a massive and relatively recent surge of imports. Moreover, the agreements were not permanent, but rather temporary; and they did not shut out imports or even reduce them, but permitted a marginal and orderly increase in imports. Furthermore, compared to the impact of the Trade Act of 1974, these agreements were of marginal importance.

---

[13]See I. M. Destler et al., *Managing An Alliance: The Politics of U.S.-Japanese Relations* (Washington, D.C.: Brookings Institution, 1976); Graham Allison, *Essence of Decision* (Boston: Little, Brown and Co., 1971).

Similarly, in foreign aid policy, after bottoming out in 1971 with the Senate's rejection of the foreign aid bill, Congress organized a coalition on behalf of a more humanitarian and aggressive development policy. If anything, the post-1971 foreign economic policy of the United States revealed a nation more certain and secure in its global position and perspective than at any point in the postwar period. It may be true that the capacity of the United States to affect global economic policies has been reduced, but U.S. foreign economic policies were still pointed vigorously toward an open and liberal world.

Bureaucratic Politics and Process

Though it may be the most popular and widely-used theory of U.S. foreign policy, the bureaucratic argument has proven entirely inadequate in explaining U.S. trade, investment, and aid policy. Bureaucratic fissures were not the cause of inconsistencies in these policies, nor could one say, as the bureaucratic hypothesis does, that an understanding of these fissures was necessary and sufficient for an understanding of U.S. foreign economic policy. Indeed, the utility of the model was severely tested, and found wanting. It contributed greatly to an understanding of the negotiations in the executive arena, but was not helpful, except for providing insights into the bargaining process, in the private arena or in the final legislative arena. Ironically, it was perhaps most helpful in explaining why, after struggling fiercely for a nuance in a Presidential statement, the bureaucracies were singularly ineffective in the final arena that mattered—Congress—or on the critical dependent variable—the law.

On the most important issues in trade policy that separated Congress from the Executive, the Executive, for all practical purposes, was generally united. There were exceptions, of course; for example, on adjustment assistance, where bureaucratic struggles helped influence the outcome in the legislative-executive debate, but these instances were few and relatively minor compared to the many in which the Executive brought a unified policy and strategy to Capitol Hill. The same was true for investment policy and aid policy.

Interest Group Theory

Interest groups did not play an insignificant role in the development of U.S. foreign economic policy, but their role was different from what one might expect. Rather than *dictate* to Congress, they *triggered* Congress to address issues which may have been ignored. Congress, however, rarely legislates for specific items; rather, it generalizes about particular items, and when the argument for the general point is persuasive, the chances of particular groups influencing a policy's direction are reasonably good.

There is no available explanation for the popularity of this theory, except perhaps the one suggested by Richard Hofstadter in his book *The Paranoid Style in American Politics*.[14] The American public, he wrote, needs personalities, groups, events to focus its discontent and to take the "heat" or blame, as the case may be, for mistakes. Special interest groups are easy targets. But the private arena could not be considered the critical decisional locus for explaining either trade, investment, or aid policy. On the big issues, like the Trade Act of 1974, the Foreign Investment Study Act, or the International Development and Food Assistance Act of 1975, *there were too many groups on too many sides of too many issues, and consequently, the groups tended to cancel themselves out in influence, leaving the lone Legislator free to take his cue from wherever he wished.* And in the important issues where there are no countervailing groups, the Executive can more than match the political punch of any single group. While several individual Legislators may need to make the case for the special group for constituency-related reasons, the entire Congress is likely to be swayed by the general, not the special, interest arguments. Indeed, Congress generally displays an instinctively negative reaction to self-serving arguments.[15]

By a second test, the interest group argument is found wanting. The distribution of the benefits of U.S. trade policy did not correlate with the interest groups which had the greatest political impact on the making of policy. The three industries which have participated most actively in making trade policy—steel, textiles, and shoes—have hardly prospered as a result of trade policy. A case could be made that these three industries have declined more slowly as a result of trade policies, but a counter-case—that these industries have declined *because* of those policies which intended to help them—has been made just as effectively.[16] Regardless, the argument that several trade policies have impeded the rapid decline of these industries hardly substantiates the theory that special interests determine or even heavily influence the course of U.S. trade policy.

Congressional Behavior Theories

Theories of congressional behavior do for Congress what bureaucratic theories do for the Executive; they provide a guide to the arena, a list of the

---

[14]Richard Hofstadter, *The Paranoid Style in American Politics* (N.Y.: Vintage Books, 1967).

[15]In the case studies on interest groups developed in the *National Journal*, reporters often mention this congressional tendency to react negatively to self-serving arguments. One example is the fact that the labor union lobbyists have greater credibility and effectiveness on social welfare issues rather than on specific labor issues, like repeal of 14 (b). (See Alan Eherhalt, "AFL-CIO: How Much Clout in Congress?" *Congressional Quarterly Weekly Report*, 19 July 1975, pp. 1531–39.)

[16]C. Fred Bergsten, "Crisis in U. S. Trade Policy," *Foreign Affairs* 49 (July 1971): 619–35.

players in the game, and a description of the rules. By focusing on members' goals and on recruitment patterns, one of these theories is helpful in explaining why one Committee is more likely to produce an aggregated product than another.[17] But, in general, the cluster of theories predicted, incorrectly, that U.S. foreign economic policy would be distributive, short-term, and parochial.

Interbranch Politics

The foreign economic policies analyzed in this study were the product of a continuous, interactive process involving both the legislative and executive branches. While coalitions were sometimes organized between bureaus and Committees, the rule in many of the policies analyzed was that Congress and the Executive approached issues as coherent, unitary organizations with decided preferences and predispositions in each issue. Whether these preferences were molded into a single policy depended to a great extent on the degree of trust and responsiveness which flowed in both directions between the branches. This lens also helped us to focus on the extent to which Congress affected the legislative and, to a lesser extent, the administrative process in the Executive, and the extent and manner in which the Executive weighted the debate in the Congress.

The two most important aspects of U.S. foreign economic policy which require explanation are the consistent liberalness in the overall structure of U.S. foreign economic policy and the occasional restrictive and protectionist policies. There are many varieties of these inconsistent nonliberal or restrictive policies: (1) The "pure" distributive, pork-barrel type. Examples are the provisions of the Trade Act which explicitly exclude certain products from the generalized system of tariff preferences or the voluntary export restraint agreements which are implemented before a finding of injury due to imports is determined. (2) The policy that is aimed not toward an issue but toward the agency administering the policy. Examples of this occurred with greater frequency in foreign aid policy, particularly human rights and investment disputes, but they are also found in the detailed instructions given to the Special Trade Representative in the Trade Act and in the Jackson-Vanik amendment. (3) The policy that forcefully articulates U.S. interests abroad and has the effect, sometimes intended, other times not, of strengthening the hand of U.S. negotiators in a difficult international bargain. Examples include the Mills bill on textile quotas and various congressional resolutions affecting countervailing duty or antidumping issues. (4) The policy intended to confer upon U.S. groups the same advantages enjoyed by foreign groups. The debates on foreign investment in the U.S. and on the "additionality" issue of foreign aid provided examples of

[17]Richard Fenno, Jr., *Congressmen in Committees* (Boston: Little, Brown and Co., 1973).

this policy-type which deviates from the overall structure of U.S. foreign economic policy.

All four of these varieties of inconsistency are best explained by the legislative-executive model, although the first kind—purely distributive—is also explained by interest group theory. The other three varieties cannot be adequately explained except by a framework which views two unitary actors—Congress and the Executive—with different predispositions and priorities. Indeed, each of these kinds of inconsistency was predicted by one of the hypotheses suggested by the lens in chapter two.

Alone among the five lenses, the interbranch politics lens predicted a foreign economic policy which continually probed and pressed the outer boundaries of the global economic system, intent on widening rather than narrowing it. The model's greatest utility is in identifying three critical variables responsible for the process by which protectionism and provincialism have been successfully resisted: (1) Executive leadership in the legislative process; (2) congressional cohesion; and (3) an efficient, mutually responsive legislative-executive process.

To Schattschneider, in his analysis of Smoot-Hawley, "pressure groups" seemed to be the most salient and important variable in trade policy-making. Another look at Smoot-Hawley in the context of U.S. trade law through the Trade Act of 1974, however, suggests the importance of other variables—in particular, Presidential leadership in the legislative process. Smoot-Hawley provides the classic example of the legislative consequences when Presidential leadership is either errant or absent. Hoover not only failed to exercise leadership at critical points on important issues, but he, in fact, misdirected the Congress by submitting a special interest, protectionist message, thereby encouraging protectionist predilections rather than resisting them. There were two other cases—President Johnson's trade message in 1967–68 and Nixon's in 1969–70—where errant or half-hearted Presidential attention diffused rather than focused congressional debate in such a way that the President lost control of the process. On the other hand, when Presidents mobilized broad-based, highly visible public campaigns for a trade bill, particularly when accompanied by White House-sponsored lobbying efforts, for example, with the Randall Commission on Foreign Economic Policy, the 1961 Ball Task Force, or the Williams Commission on International Trade and Investment Policy in 1971, the President remained effective and the policy remained responsible.

While Presidential leadership is important, its real contribution is in the way it weights the congressional debate, which is, of course, decisive in explaining trade policy. *The failure of Congress to withstand parochial pressures in 1929–30 is not nearly so interesting or instructive (for the scholar of the government process) as is Congress' recurrent success in resisting such pressures in every trade bill since then.* The capacity of Congress to fragment a general policy into a multitude of special interest policies is well known; but the capability of Congress to exercise self-discipline and keep the log from rolling is often overlooked, even though it is achieved more often in more important issues.

The need for self-insulation from special pressures is well recognized by Legislators. Rep. John Anderson, in the debate on whether to accept the closed rule in considering the Trade Act of 1974, warned the Congress of the consequences of rejection: "I have no doubt about the effect. A glut of amendments will rain down upon this body that would have the purpose of exempting and protecting every product and labor sector from both the real and imagined dangers of freer trade."[18] Rep. Samuel Gibbons explained why the process would be unavoidable: "Under an open rule, it becomes incumbent upon every member sitting here to try to defend the interests of his own district."[19] Thus, Congress has adopted certain procedures—like the closed rule in the House and cloture in the Senate—and it has delegated important powers to impartial agencies—like the International Trade Commission—in order *to keep itself from* fragmenting general policy. In addition, there are tacit rules—for example, on trade bills, no specific product should be mentioned—which generally are adhered to and succeed in keeping the legislative debate on the general policy level.

The third variable—the legislative-executive process—has been discussed in great detail above. A high degree of trust and responsiveness between branches is crucial to the successful merger of different branch preferences into a single government policy. The foresight to consult beforehand by the Executive and the Congress's willingness to informally exchange views in a nonadversary manner are two parts of this variable. The other two are the Executive's responsiveness to the congressional will and its consequence, and the Congress's willingness to trust the Executive with the discretion necessary to conduct flexible and effective diplomacy.

The overall foreign economic policy of the United States has remained consistent and liberal due to the existence and interaction of these three variables: executive leadership, congressional cohesion, and the legislative-executive process. The interbranch politics model, from which these three variables are derived, has therefore provided the best of the five lenses for describing, explaining, and understanding U.S. foreign economic policy. Prior to testing the model against the second set of criteria—i.e., whether it is helpful in pointing the analyst toward improvements in policy and process, I want first to address the question, to what extent can the interbranch politics lens be considered new? This is not the first study which has focused on the interaction between Congress and the Executive. How does the interbranch politics lens differ from those in previous studies? What does it contribute?

[18]*Congressional Record*, 10 and 11 December 1973, p. 40495.
[19]Ibid., p. 40499.

A CHOICE OF METAPHORS: WHO'S IN THE
DRIVER'S SEAT?

Robert Dahl has succinctly described the relationship between Congress and
the Executive in policy-making by a metaphor in which the Executive is the
car-driver and Congress applies the brakes.[20] This vision of the political
process is widely shared by political scientists and the American public. The
Executive defines and initiates policy, and the Congress, in Stanley Hoffmann's words, destroys, delays, and deters.[21] Dahl's metaphor and its wide
acceptance are indicative of the preoccupation of political scientists with the
importance of "initiative" as not only a defining but also a determining
concept in the governmental process.

The interbranch politics lens does not attempt to test the validity of the
Dahlian metaphor, except in so far as it questions and then revises its
assumptions. Upon a different set of assumptions, a modified metaphor is
constructed. The word "govern" derives from the Latin "gubernare" and,
appropriate to the Dahl metaphor, it means "to steer." Unlike the prevailing
conception which places Congress in the back seat, the interbranch politics
lens assumes that both Congress and the Executive have the capacity to
steer the car of state. There are times when Congress, for various reasons,
has the capacity to turn the car, say left, even if the Executive prefers to go
straight or right; at other times, the Executive turns against the wishes of the
Congress.

Unlike other legislative-executive theories, interbranch politics builds
upon organization theory as interpreted for public bureaucracies by Graham
Allison and others. Using the interbranch lens, both branches can be viewed
as coherent, unitary actors with different sets of predispositions, and with
differing capabilities to translate predispositions into policy. Policy is the
result of the interaction between the branches, and if policy is less than or
other than the rational pursuit of agreed objectives, it is, according to the
new lens, due more to the *process of interaction* than to any other variable
implicit in any of the other lenses. To return to the metaphor, if the car
brakes abruptly or if it veers out of control, it is misleading and inaccurate to
blame Congress, interest groups, bureaucracies, or the "system"; the blame
should be deposited on both ends of Pennsylvania Avenue.

[20]Robert A. Dahl, *Pluralist Democracy in the U.S.: Conflict and Consent* (Chicago:
Rand, McNally, 1967), p. 136. Louis Henkin uses almost the same metaphor in *Foreign Affairs
and the Constitution* (N.Y.: W. W. Norton and Co., 1976), p. 123.

[21]Stanley Hoffmann, *Gulliver's Troubles or the Setting of American Foreign Policy*
(N.Y.: McGraw-Hill, 1968), pp. 255–56. See also *Toward a Modern Senate*, Final Report of the
Commission on the Operation of the Senate (Washington, D.C.: G.P.O., December 1976)
p. 33.

IMPROVING THE PROCESS

> *It would be very helpful if you will ask yourself what it is that you would do different than what we are doing, keeping in mind that you may not know what we are doing.*[22]
>
> —Secretary of State William P. Rogers,
> to the Senate Foreign Relations
> Committee
>
> *It will be prudent for the Executive to keep in close touch with Congress, which feels about the fait accompli much as nature does about vacuums.*[23]
>
> —William Diebold, Jr.

The second, and in some ways the most important, test of the utility of a new lens is whether it is better than other lenses in pinpointing defects or problems in the policy and the process in a way that clarifies possible improvements. Each lens selects from a wide range of variables those which it considers most critical in the policy-making process, and the selection has obvious policy implications. The interest group lens, for example, assists the analyst in focusing on pressure groups, and the obvious implication from such studies is that a process should be found to keep these groups from influencing policy in a way which will harm other interests. The bureaucratic politics lens points the analyst toward improving the coordination process between executive bureaus so as to assure that parochial bureaucratic interests do not determine policy.

The interbranch politics lens suggests that the best way to understand policy and improve it is to focus on the relationship between Congress and the Executive. Moreover, it suggests that the cause of policy failures—defined in this case as self-defeating foreign policies—is the inability of both branches to integrate their respective priorities and goals and conceptions of the means necessary to achieve both.

This study contains numerous cases of foreign policy successes and failures. The questions which the analyst interested in improving the foreign policy-making process would want to address are: Why do successes occur, and how can we replicate the conditions responsible for the favorable outcome? Why do failures or conflicts between the Executive and Congress occur, and how can those variables causing such conflicts be inhibited or

---

[22]Cited in Thomas L. Hughes, *The Fate of Facts in a World of Men: Foreign Policy and Intelligence-Making* (N.Y.: Foreign Policy Association, Headline Series, December 1976), p. 33.

[23]William Diebold, Jr., "U. S. Trade Policy: The New Political Dimension," *Foreign Affairs* 52 (April 1974): 477.

eliminated? How can the process be modified so as to ensure that the outcome reflects balance rather than bias, a long-term vision rather than short-term expediencies, and a general rather than a particular interest?

In the previous part of this chapter, I suggested three variables which are salient in the interbranch politics lens and responsible for the open and global foreign economic policy of the United States: (1) Presidential leadership; (2) congressional self-discipline; and (3) a legislative-executive process characterized by equal and reciprocal flows of trust and responsiveness. Only the President can ensure the existence and replication of the first variable.

As regards congressional cohesion, there are a number of procedures and organizational reforms which Congress could implement to encourage a broader and more statesmanlike approach to issues of interdependence. The usual prescription for congressional fragmentation, extending at least as far back as Woodrow Wilson's recommendation for a Parliamentary-type system,[24] is strong party leadership. While important, this is hardly the only way to assure the triumph of centripetal tendencies.

The foreign policy-making process needs to be altered so that the chances of a Legislator being confronted by pressure groups on only one side of an important issue are minimized. A lobbying disclosure bill which is aimed not at restricting private lobbyists but encouraging the participation of public, general interest, or issue-oriented groups would be one useful approach to this problem. In foreign policy issues where a particular American group has a dispute with a foreign government, it would also be helpful for Legislators to be able to hear the other side of the issue directly from foreign governments. While representatives of foreign governments should not (and could not) be required to testify before congressional hearings, their participation should be respectfully invited.[25]

Theoretically, if a Committee's bill reflected the concerns of all members of Congress, there wouldn't be any need for amendments on the floor of Congress. As chairman of the Ways and Means Committee, Wilbur Mills seemed to have attained that ideal often, and thus he found it easy to take his major bills to the House floor with a closed rule (permitting no or few amendments) from the House Rules Committee. The need to discourage the passage of particular amendments and encourage the debate on general policy amendments is sufficiently important in the realm of foreign economic policy to justify a new kind of rule by the House Rules Committee. To make such a rule practical and useable, the various Committees of

[24]Woodrow Wilson, *Congressional Government: A Study in American Politics* (originally published 1885; reprint ed., Gloucester, Mass.: Peter Smith, 1973).

[25]A study on this subject was done by the Library of Congress, and the author, Jonathan Sanford, found no grounds for barring the testimony of foreigners to congressional hearings. Jonathan Sanford, "Congressional Testimony by Foreign Officials and Citizens," reprinted in *Congressional Record*, 15 June 1976, pp. E3346–3347.

Congress need to keep their deliberations open and responsive to non-Committee Legislators. In the Senate, a modified cloture rule which permitted only general and germane amendments (determined by the Parliamentarian) would be a significant step to parallel reforms in the House Rules Committee.

To provide a long-term focus in Congress, a bipartisan planning committee in each Chamber should be established and should meet separately and together) periodically to consider the legislative calendar for the entire two-year Congress and adopt an agenda, a set of legislative priorities, and a timetable for accomplishing the calendar.[26]

These reforms would hopefully facilitate the long and broad approach by Congress. The need for better liaison between the branches is greater than ever before, and will require a new awareness by the Executive that inadequate consultative procedures may well result in poorly-integrated foreign policies.

Many of the most glaring failures in U.S. foreign policy in recent years have occurred because of disagreement between the branches on the means and ends of a particular foreign policy.[27] For example, on the issue of human rights violations abroad, Congress believed U.S. policy should be vigorous, public, forthright, and willing to use sanctions and many kinds of levers to affect a foreign country's behavior. The Executive under the Nixon and Ford Administrations believed that U.S. policy should be quiet, private, and handled independently of other interests in a way which would not jeopardize them or our overall relations with the particular country. *The result of this disagreement in ends was a sharper disagreement in means: in frustration of the Executive's unresponsiveness, Congress denied the Executive the flexibility to conduct foreign policy in a way which conceivably could have contributed to the alleviation of the repression abroad.* A similar process governed the development of U.S. policy on investment disputes.

The way to avoid these failures is obviously not to try to prevent policy disagreements from occurring. They are both inevitable and healthy; the Founding Fathers established a government of separate institutions with different "wills" in the belief that truth was more likely to emerge from the interaction of independent institutions than from the dictates of one branch. The attention of reform-minded analysts is more profitably focused on ways to improve the adjustment process after disagreements occur than on ways to prevent disagreements. To take one example: instead of fighting the Jackson-Vanik amendment from the beginning to the end when the entire U.S.-Soviet trade agreement of 1972 was scrapped, Kissinger would have done himself and his own vision of U.S. interests a service if he had either

[26]For a variation on this idea, see *Toward a Modern Senate*, pp. 44–47.

[27]See my "At Odds on Ends: Congress vs. President," *Journal da Tarde*, (Sao Paulo, Brazil) 5 July 1976.

agreed to separate the Soviet trade issue from the Trade Act or acknowledged early the thrust of the congressional concern, demonstrated his support, and worked on tactics to ensure the success of that integrated policy.

The U.S. government has been called "weak" because of the divisions between Congress and the Executive,[28] yet the bargaining between branches can be a source of considerable strength either intentionally, as in the case of the Mills bill on textiles, or unintentionally, as in the case of the congressional debate of the Fisheries Management and Conservation Act (S. 961) to extend U.S. fishing jurisdiction to a distance of 200 miles offshore. In the latter case, the threat of congressional action finally induced those governments, whose fleets were overfishing in American offshore waters, to seriously negotiate for reduction in their catch. As the *Washington Post* editorialized: "The threat of unilateral enactment of a 200 mile fisheries zone did in fact mobilize a previously laggard State Department and gave it the club it needed for successful fisheries negotiations with other countries." The results included a new agreement in September 1975 of the International Commission for Northwest Atlantic Fisheries (ICNAF) to drastically reduce foreign fishing while allowing some increase in the catch of American fishermen. The three largest foreign fishing operations—those of the U.S.S.R., Poland and East Germany—have been cut by mutual consent to about 50 percent of 1974 levels. In addition, subsequent negotiations with the Japanese resulted in a reduction of their harvest of king crabs.[29] In this case, the *threat* of congressional action furthered American interests in the international environment; but the effects of the passage of the law in ealy 1976 were more ambiguous. The State and Defense Departments and foreign affairs committees of Congress were afraid that the law would threaten Law of the Sea negotiations, while domestic committees and departments thought it might expedite those negotiations, and even if it didn't, that it would promote more interests than it would harm.

The fundamental problem in making foreign policy is that one's judgment is necessarily based on a guess about the future. Whether Congress' guess is likely to be better or worse than that of the Executive is, of course, impossible to predict. But the important point is that neither branch has a monopoly on the truth or on foresight. In a discussion of U.S.-Soviet relations, Francis O. Wilcox, who was both a Staff Director of the Senate Foreign Relations Committee and an Assistant Secretary of State, restated that point: "If Congress has frequently seemed to be going in one direction

[28]Stephen D. Krasner, "State Power and the Structure of International Trade," *World Politics* 28 (April 1976): 317–347; and Peter J. Katzenstein, "Transnational Relations and Domestic Structures: Foreign Economic Policies of Advanced Industrial States," *International Organization* 30 (Winter 1970).

[29]For the congressional debate, a copy of the *Washington Post* (4 November 1975) editorial, and other news articles, see *Congressional Record*, 19 January 1976, pp. S 135–6.

and then in another, that is partly because it is a collection of poorly coordinated, strong-minded individuals. But more importantly, it is because that is the way the White House and the Kremlin have moved as well."[30]

IMPROVING THE POLICY

Rather than a description of U.S. foreign economic policy or an advocacy brief on behalf of a particular policy, this study has examined and analyzed the politics which have shaped the contours and the content of U.S. foreign economic policy. The unstated, underlying normative assumptions have been that freer trade, nondiscriminatory investment laws, and a development-oriented foreign assistance policy are the correct goals of the three areas of foreign economic policy analyzed in this study. The analysis therefore concentrated on the political process by which policies move toward or away from those goals rather than an analysis of the goals themselves. By understanding the determining variables, one is better prepared to rearrange them in a way which will improve the policy. The assumption, in brief, is that the process can be managed.

To return to the original questions, congressional assertiveness and involvement is likely to increase in the economic issues of interdependence which seem likely to preoccupy policy-makers more in the future than they have in the past. Congress has always been deeply involved in the formulation of U.S. foreign economic policies, and since the new issues of interdependence exhibit the characteristics—particularly the kinds of trade-offs—of U.S. foreign economic policies, one is drawn to the conclusion that the congressional role in U.S. foreign policy will correspondingly increase.

There is no special reason why the relationship between the branches should be hostile or the policy resulting from their interaction flawed. With the proper input of Presidential leadership, congressional self-discipline, and mutual respect and trust between branches, foreign economic policy could accelerate its progress toward the goals listed above. American global hegemony may have passed, but if this analysis is correct, then the global economic system need not close. In fact, the opportunity for greater openness and cooperation between nations comes at just the time when America's ability to manage its own affairs on the road to managing interdependence seems most promising.

[30]Francis Orlando Wilcox, *Congress, The Executive, and Foreign Policy* (N.Y.: Published for the Council on Foreign Relations by Harper and Row, 1971), p. 133.

BIBLIOGRAPHY

Note: Interviews with over two hundred government officials from Congress and the executive branch and with many people working for nongovernmental organizations were a major source of information for this book. I began the interviews in June 1974 as a consultant to the Commission on the Organization of the Government for the Conduct of Foreign Policy and have continued interviewing people on a regular basis since then. Because most of the interviewees requested confidentiality, I will not identify them.

ACHESON, DEAN. *A Citizen Looks at Congress.* New York: Harper and Brothers, 1957.

ALLISON, GRAHAM T. *The Essence of Decision.* Boston: Little, Brown and Co., 1971.

BACCHUS, WILLIAM. *Foreign Policy and the Bureaucratic Process: The State Department's Country Director System.* Princton, New Jersey: Princeton University Press, 1974.

BAILEY, STEPHEN K. *Congress in the Seventies.* New York: St. Martin's Press, 1970.

BALDWIN, ROBERT E. *Non-Tariff Distortions of International Trade.* Washington, D.C.: Brookings Institution, 1970.

BAUER, RAYMOND, ITHIEL DE SOLA POOL, and LEWIS ANTHONY DEXTER. *American Business and Public Policy.* Chicago: Aldine-Atherton, 1972.

BECKETT, GRACE A. *The Reciprocal Trade Agreements Program.* New York: Columbia University Press, 1941.

BEHRMAN, J. N. *National Interests and the Multinational Enterprise: Tensions Among the North Atlantic Countries.* Englewood Cliffs, New Jersey: Prentice-Hall, 1970.

BERGER, RAOUL. "The Presidential Monopoly of Foreign Relations," *Michigan Law Review* vol. 71, no. 1 (November 1972): 1–58.

BERGSTEN, C. FRED. "Crisis in U.S. Trade Policy," *Foreign Affairs* 49 (July 1971): 619–35.

———. "The New Economics and U.S. Foreign Policy." *Foreign Affairs* 50 (January 1972): 199–222.

BERNSTEIN, MARVIN D., ed. *Foreign Investment in Latin America.* New York: Alfred Knopf, 1966.

BIBBY, JOHN F., and ROGER H. DAVIDSON. *On Capitol Hill: Studies in the Legislative Process.* 2d ed., Hinsdale, Illinois: Dryden Press Inc., 1972.

BOLLING, RICHARD. *Power in the House.* New York: E.P. Dutton and Co., 1968.

BONAFEDE, DOM, DANIEL RAPOPORT, and JOEL HAVEMANN. "The President Versus Congress: The Score Since Watergate," *National Journal,* 29 May 1976, pp. 730–748.

BROOKINGS INSTITUTION. *The Formulation and Administration of United States Foreign Policy.* Study prepared at the request of the Committee on Foreign Relations, U.S. Senate. Washington, U.S. Govt. Print. Off., 1960.

BROWN, WILLIAM ADAMS, JR., and REDVERS OPIE. *American Foreign Assistance.* Washington, D.C.: Brookings Institution, 1953.

BROWNE, MARJORIE ANN, and LOIS MCHUGH. *The Role of Congress in Foreign Policy Making: A Selected Bibliography.* Washington, D.C.: Congressional Research Service, 13 August, 1975.

BUCKWATER, DOYLE W. "The Congressional Concurrent Resolution: A Search For Foreign Policy Influence," *Midwest Journal of Political Science* 14 (August 1970): 434–458.

"Bureaucracy: Some Case Studies." Introduction by FRANCIS E. ROURKE. *National Journal Reprints.* (1975–76 ed.).

CALLEO, DAVID, and BENJAMIN ROWLAND. *America and the World Political Economy.* Bloomington, Indiana: Indiana University Press, 1973.

CAMPS, MIRIAM. *The Management of Interdependence.* New York: Council on Foreign Relations, 1974.

CARROLL, HOLBERT N. *The House of Representatives and Foreign Affairs.* Boston: Little, Brown and Co., 1966.

CATER, DOUGLASS. *Power in Washington: A Critical Look at Today's Struggle to Govern in the Nation's Capital.* New York: Vintage Books, 1964.

CHAMBERLAIN, LAWRENCE D. *The President, Congress, and Legislation.* New York: Columbia University Press, 1946.

CHEEVER, DANIEL S., and H. FIELD HAVILAND, JR. *American Foreign Policy and the Separation of Powers.* Cambridge, Massachusetts: Harvard University Press, 1952.

CLAUSEN, AAGE R. *How Congressmen Decide: A Policy Focus.* New York: St. Martin's Press, 1973.

COHEN, BENJAMIN J., ed. *American Foreign Economic Policy:* Essays and Comments. New York: Harper and Row, 1968.

————. *The Question of Imperialism—The Political Economy of Dominance and Dependence.* New York: Basic Books, 1973.

COHEN, BERNARD C. *Foreign Policy in American Government.* Boston: Little, Brown and Co., 1965.

COHEN, STEPHEN D. *International Monetary Reform, 1964–69: The Political Dimension.* New York: Praeger, 1970.

"Congress." Introduction by RICHARD F. FENNO, JR. *National Journal Reprints.* (1975–76 ed.).

Congress and Foreign Relations. Annals of the American Academy of Political Social Science, vol. 289, September 1953: entire issue.

Congressional Decision Making for National Security: A Statement by the Research and Policy Committee of the Committee for Economic Development. New York: Committee for Economic Development, 1974.

COOPER, RICHARD N. *The Economics of Interdependence: Economic Policy in the Atlantic Community.* New York: McGraw-Hill, 1968.

————, ed. *A Reordered World: Emerging International Economic Problems.* Washington, D.C.: Potomac Associates, 1973.

————. "Trade Policy is Foreign Policy." *Foreign Policy,* 9 (Winter 1972–73).

CORWIN, EDWARD S. *The President: Office and Powers 1787–1957: History and Analysis of Practice and Opinion.* New York: New York University Press, 1957.

CRONIN, THOMAS E. *The State of the Presidency.* Boston: Little, Brown and Co., 1975.

CULBERTSON, WILLIAM SMITH. *International Economic Policies: A Survey of the Economics of Diplomacy.* New York: D. Appleton and Co., 1931.

———. *Reciprocity.* New York: McGraw-Hill, 1937.

CURTIS, THOMAS B., and JOHN ROBERT VASTINE, JR. *The Kennedy Round and the Future of American Trade.* New York: Praeger, 1971.

DAHL, ROBERT A. *Congress and Foreign Policy.* New York: W. W. Norton and Co., 1964, 2d edition.

DAM, KENNETH W. *The GATT—Law and International Organization.* Chicago: University of Chicago Press, 1970.

DANIELS, JOHN D. *Recent Foreign Direct Manufacturing Investment in the U.S.* New York: Praeger, 1971.

DE GRAZIA, ALFRED, ed. *Congress: The First Branch of Government.* Washington, D.C.: American Enterprise Institute for Policy Research, 1966.

DE RIVERA, JOSEPH. *The Psychological Dimension of Foreign Policy.* Columbus, Ohio: Charles E. Merrill Publishing Co., 1968.

DESTLER, I. M. *Making Foreign Economic Policy.* Washington, D.C.: Brookings Institution, 1980.

———. *Presidents, Bureaucrats and Foreign Policy: The Politics of Organizational Reform.* Princeton, New Jersey: Princeton University Press, 1974.

DIAMOND, ROBERT, A., ed. *Origins and Development of Congress.* Washington, D.C.: Congressional Quarterly, 1976.

DIEBOLD, WILLIAM, JR., *The End of the I.T.O.* Princeton, New Jersey: Princeton University Essays in International Finance, no. 16 (October 1952).

EAGLETON, THOMAS F. *War and Presidential Power.* New York: Liveright Publishers, 1974.

EINHORN, JESSICA PERNITZ. *Expropriation Politics.* Lexington, Massachusetts: Lexington Books, 1974.

EVANS, DOUGLAS. *The Politics of Trade: The Evolution of the Superbloc.* London: MacMillan, 1974.

EVANS, JOHN W. *The Kennedy Round in American Trade Policy.* Cambridge, Massachusetts: Harvard University Press, 1971.

FAITH, NICHOLAS. *The Infiltrators: The European Business Invasion of America.* New York: E.P. Dutton and Co. Inc., 1972.

FARNSWORTH, DAVID N. *The Senate Committee on Foreign Relations.* Urbana, Illinois: University of Illinois Press, 1961.

FEIS, HERBERT. *Foreign Aid and Foreign Policy.* New York: St. Martin's Press, 1964.

FENNO, RICHARD F., JR. *Congressmen in Committees.* Boston: Little, Brown and Co., 1973.

FISHER, LOUIS. *President and Congress: Power and Policy.* New York: Free Press, 1972.

FRYE, ALTON. "Congress: The Virtues of its Vices." *Foreign Policy*, 3, (Summer 1971): 108–125.

———. *A Responsible Congress: The Politics of National Security.* New York: McGraw-Hill, 1975.

FROMAN, L. A., JR. "Review, American Business and Public Policy." *American Political Science Review*, 57 (1963): 671–72.

———. *The Congressional Process: Strategies, Rules and Procedures.* Boston: Little, Brown and Co., 1967.

GALLAGHER, HUGH G. *Advise and Obstruct: The Role of the Senate in Foreign Policy Decisions.* New York: Delacorte Press, 1969.

GALLOWAY, GEORGE B. *The Legislative Process In Congress.* New York: Thomas Y. Cromwell, 1953.

GARDNER, RICHARD N. *Sterling-Dollar Diplomacy; Anglo-American Collaboration in the Reconstruction of Multilateral Trade.* Oxford, England: Clarendon Press, 1956.

GILPIN, ROBERT. *U.S. Power and the Multinational Corporation: The Political Economy of Direct Foreign Investment.* New York: Basic Books, 1975.

HACKER, LOUIS M. *Foreign Investments in America's Growth.* Washington, D.C.: U.S. Information Service, 1967.

HARRIS, JOSEPH P. *Congress and the Legislative Process.* New York: McGraw-Hill, 1967.

———. *Congressional Control of Administration.* Washington, D.C.: Brookings Institution, 1964.

HELLMAN, RAINER. *The Challenge to U.S. Dominance of the International Corporation.* New York: Dunellen, 1970, p. 19.

HENKIN, LOUIS. *Foreign Affairs and the Constitution.* New York: W.W. Norton and Co., 1975.

HILSMAN, ROGER. "Congressional-Executive Relations and the Foreign Policy Consensus," *American Political Science Review.* 52 (September 1958): 725–745.

HOFFMANN, STANLEY. *Gulliver's Troubles or the Setting of American Foreign Policy.* New York: McGraw-Hill, 1968.

HOROWITZ, DAVID. *From Yalta to Viet Nam.* Middlesex, England: Penguin Books, 1967.

HUITT, R. K., and R. L. PEABODY. *Congress: Two Decades of Analysis.* New York: Harper, 1969.

HUMPHREY, HUBERT H. "The Senate in Foreign Policy," *Foreign Affairs* 37 (July 1959): 525–536.

HUNTINGTON, SAMUEL P. "Transnational Organizations in World Politics." *World Politics* 25 (April 1973).

Institute for International and Foreign Trade Law, *Proceedings of the Conference on Foreign Direct Investment in the United States,* Washington, D.C.: Brookings Institution, 1970.

JACKSON, JOHN E. *Constituencies and Leaders in Congress: Their Effects on Senate Voting Behavior.* Cambridge: Harvard University Press, 1972.

JACKSON JOHN H. *World Trade and the Law of G.A.T.T.* New York: The Bobbs-Merrill Company, 1969.

JAVITS, JACOB K. "The Congressional Presence in Foreign Relations," *Foreign Affairs* 48 (January 1970): 221–234.

JEWELL, MALCOLM E., and SAMUEL C. PATTERSON. *The Legislative Process in the United States.* New York: Random House, 1966.

JOHANNES, JOHN R. "Policy Innovation in Congress." Morristown, New Jersey: General Learning Press, 1952.

KALIJARVI, THORSTEN, and CHESTER E. MERROW, eds. *Congress and Foreign Relations.* In: *The Annals of the American Academy of Political and Social Science* 289 (September 1953) edited by Thorsten Sellin. Philadelphia, Pennsylvania: American Academy of Political and Social Science, 1953.

KATZENBACH, NICHOLAS. "Comparative Roles of the President and the Congress in Foreign Affairs," *Department of State Bulletin,* 47 (September 11, 1967): 333–336.

KATZENSTEIN, PETER J. "International Relations and Domestic Structures: Foreign Economic Policies of Advanced Industrial States," *International Organization* 30 (Winter, 1976): 1–46.

KELLY, WILLIAM B., JR., ed. *Studies in United States Commercial Policy.* Chapel Hill, North Carolina: University of North Carolina Press, 1963.

KEOHANE, ROBERT O., and JOSEPH S. NYE, JR. *Transnational Relations and World Politics.* Cambridge, Massachusetts: Harvard University Press, 1973.

——. *Power and Interdependence: World Politics in Transition.* Boston: Little, Brown, and Co., 1977.

KINDLEBERGER, CHARLES P. *American Business Abroad: Six Lectures on Direct Investment.* New Haven, Connecticut: Yale University Press, 1969.

——, ed. *The International Corporation.* Cambridge, Massachusetts: Massachusetts Institute of Technology Press, 1970.

——. *Power and Money.* New York: Basic books, 1970.

——. "U.S. Foreign Economic Policy, 1776–1976." *Foreign Affairs* 55 (January, 1977): 395–417.

KINGDON, JOHN W. *Congressmen's Voting Decisions.* New York: Harper and Row, 1973.

KISSINGER, HENRY A. "Domestic Structure and Foreign Policy." *Daedalus* 95 (Spring 1966): 503–29.

LARKIN, JOHN DAY. *The President's Control of the Tariff.* Cambridge, Massachusetts: Harvard University Press, 1936.

LEVINSON, JEROME, and JUAN DE ONIS. *The Alliance that Lost its Way: A Critical Report on the Alliance for Progress.* Chicago: Quadrangle Books, 1972.

LILLICH, RICHARD. "The Diplomatic Protection of Nationals Abroad: An Elementary Principle of International Law Under Attack." *American Journal of International Law* 69 (April, 1975).

LODGE, HENRY CABOT. *The Senate and the League of Nations.* New York: Charles Scribner's Sons, 1925.

LOWI, THEODORE. "American Business, Public Policy, Case Studies and Political Theory." *World Politics* 16 (July 1964): 676–715.

——. *The End of Liberalism: Ideology, Policy, and the Crisis of Public Authority.* New York: W.W. Norton and Co., 1969.

——, ed. *Legislative Politics U.S.A.* 2nd edition. Boston: Little, Brown and Company, 1965.

——. "Four Systems of Policy, Politics and Choice." *Public Administration Review* 32 (July/August 1972): 289–310.

——. *The Politics of Disorder.* New York: W.W. Norton and Company, Inc., 1974.

MACKENZIE, KENNETH C. *Tariff-Making and Trade Policy in the U.S. and Canada: A Comparative Study.* New York: Praeger, 1968.

MALMGREN, HAROLD, B. *International Economic Peacekeeping in Phase II.* Atlantic Council of the United States. New York: Quadrangle Books, 1972.

MANLEY, JOHN F. *The Politics of Finance.* Boston: Little, Brown, and Co., 1970.

——. "The Rise of Congress in Foreign Policy Making." In *Seven Polarizing Issues in America Today.* Philadelphia: American Academy of Political and Social Science, *Annals*, 397 (September 1971): 60–70.

MANSFIELD, HARVEY, C., JR., ed. *Congress Against the President.* New York: Praeger, 1975.

MATTHEWS, DONALD R. *U.S. Senators and Their World.* New York: Random House, 1960.

MAYHEW, DAVID R. *Congress: The Electoral Connection.* New Haven: Yale University Press, 1974.

MCCONNELL, GRANT. *Private Power and American Democracy.* New York: Vintage Books, 1966.

MEIER, GERALD. *Problems of Trade Policy.* Oxford, England: Oxford University Press, 1973.

MITCHELL, DANIEL J. B. *Labor Issues of American International Trade and Investment.* Baltimore: The Johns Hopkins University Press, 1976.

MONROE, WILBUR F. *International Trade Policy in Transition.* Lexington, Massachusetts: Lexington Books, 1975.

MONTGOMERY, JOHN D. *Foreign Aid in International Politics.* Englewood Cliffs, New Jersey: Prentice-Hall, Inc., 1967.

————. *The Politics of Foreign Aid: American Experience in Southeast Asia.* New York: Praeger, 1962.

MOORE, CLAYTON F. "How a Tariff Bill is Passed." *Congressional Digest: The Pro and Con Monthly* (June/July, 1929): 164–66.

MORAN, THEODORE H. "Foreign Expansion as an 'Institutional Necessity' for U.S. Corporate Capitalism: The Search for a Radical Model." *World Politics* 25 (April 1973): 369–86.

MORSE, EDWARD. "Crisis Diplomacy, Interdependence, and the Politics of International Economic Relations." *World Politics* 24, supplement (Spring 1972): 123–50.

NELSON, JOAN M. *Aid, Influence, and Foreign Policy.* New York: MacMillan, 1968.

NIEHUSS, JOHN M. "Foreign Investment in the U.S.: A Review of Government Policy." *Virginia Journal of International Law* 16, 1 (Fall, 1975): 65–102.

O'LEARY, MICHAEL KENT. *The Politics of American Foreign Aid.* New York: Atherton Press, 1967.

OPPENHEIMER, BRUCE IAN. *Oil and the Congressional Process: The Limits of Symbolic Politics.* Lexington, Massachusetts: Lexington Books, 1974.

ORFIELD, GARY. *Congressional Power: Congress and Social Change.* New York: Harcourt Brace Janovich, 1975.

PACKENHAM, ROBERT A. *Liberal America and the Third World: Political Development Ideas in Foreign Aid and Social Science.* Princeton: Princeton University Press, 1973.

PASTOR, ROBERT A. "Development-Inducer or Dependency-Seducer? U.S. Multinational Corporations in Africa," *Harvard Political Review* 3 (Fall 1974). With Antoine W. Van Agtmael.

————. "Congress's Impact on Latin America: Is There a Madness in the Method?", pp. 259–272, and "U.S. Sugar Politics and Latin America: Asymmetries in Input and Impact," pp. 221–232, *The Conduct of Routine Economic Relations: U.S. Foreign Policy-Making to Latin America,* ed. by Abraham F. Lowenthal, in Volume III, Appendix I, Commission on the Organization of the Government for the Conduct of Foreign Policy (Murphy Commission). Washington, D.C.: Government Printing Office, June 1975.

————. "Coping With Congress's Foreign Policy," *Foreign Service Journal* 52 (December 1975): 15–18, 23.

————. "On the Congressional Effort to Influence U.S. Relations with Latin America: Congressional Foreign Policy at its Best," *Inter-American Economic Affairs* 29 (Winter 1975): 85–94.

————. "President vs. Congress: At Odds on Ends," *Jornal da Tarde,* Sao Paulo, Brazil, July 5, 1976, p. 26.

PATTERSON, GARDNER. *Discrimination in International Trade; The Policy Issues 1945–1965.* Princeton, New Jersey: Princeton University Press, 1966.

PEARSON, JAMES CONSTANTINE. *The Reciprocal Trade Agreements Program: The Policy of the United States and its Effectiveness.* Gettysburg, Pennsylvania: Times and News Publishing Company, 1942.

POLSBY, NELSON W. *Congress and the Presidency.* Englewood Cliffs, New Jersey: Van Nostrand, 1964.

PREEG, ERNEST. *Traders and Diplomats.* Washington, D.C.: The Brookings Institution, 1973.

————. *Economic Blocs and U.S. Foreign Policy.* Washington, D.C.: National Planning Association, 1974.

PRICE, DAVID E. *Who Makes the Laws? Creativity and Power in Senate Committees.* Cambridge, Mass.: Schenkman, 1972.

RATNER, SIDNEY. *The Tariff in American History.* New York: D. Van Nostrand Company, 1972.

RIPLEY, RANDALL B., and GRACE A. FRANKLIN. *Congress, the Bureaucracy, and Public Policy.* Homewood, Ill.: Dorsey Press, 1976.

ROBINSON, JAMES A. *Congress and Foreign Policy-Making: A Study in Legislative Influence and Initiative.* Rev. ed. Homewood, Illinois: Dorsey Press, 1967.

ROURKE, FRANCIS E. *Bureaucracy, Politics and Public Policy.* 2nd edition. Boston: Little, Brown and Company, 1976.

RUSSETT, BRUCE M., and ELIZABETH C. HANSON. *Interest and Ideology: The Foreign Policy Beliefs of American Businessmen.* San Francisco: W.H. Freeman and Co., 1975.

SANFORD, JONATHAN, and MARGARET GOODMAN. "Congressional Oversight; and the Multi-lateral Development Banks." *International Organization* (Autumn, 1975): 1055–64.

SAYRE, FRANCIS BOWES. *The Way Forward: The American Trade Agreements Program.* New York: The MacMillan Company, 1939.

SCHATTSCHNEIDER, E. E. *Politics, Pressures and the Tariff: A Study of Free Enterprise in Pressure Politics, as Shown in the 1929–30 Revision of the Tariff.* New York: Prentice-Hall, Inc., 1935.

————. *The Semi-Sovereign People: A Realist's View of Democracy in America.* New York: Holt, Rinehart and Winston, 1960.

SCHLESINGER, ARTHUR M., JR. "Congress and the Making of American Foreign Policy." *Foreign Affairs* v. 51 (October 1972): 78–113.

————. *The Imperial Presidency.* Boston: Houghton Mifflin, 1973.

STALEY, EUGENE. *War and the Private Investor: A Study in the Relations of International Politics and International Private Investment.* New York: Doubleday, Doran, and Co. 1935.

STENNIS, JOHN C., and J. WILLIAM FULBRIGHT. *The Role of Congress in Foreign Policy.* Washington, D.C.: American Institute for Public Policy Research, 1971.

TASCA, HENRY J. *The Reciprocal Trade Policy of the United States.* Philadelphia: University of Pennsylvania Press, 1938.

TAUSSIG, G. W. *The Tariff History of the United States.* 7th edition. New York: G.P. Putnam's Sons, 1922.

TRUMAN DAVID B. *The Governmental Process.* New York: Alfred Knopf, 1951.

————, ed. *The Congress and America's Future.* Englewood Cliffs, N.J.: Prentice-Hall, 1965.

TUGWELL, REXFORD G., and THOMAS E. CRONIN, eds. *The Presidency Reappraised.* New York: Praeger, 1974.

United Nations. Department of Social and Economic Affairs. *Multinational Corporations in World Development.* New York: United Nations, 1973.

URI, PIERRE, ed. *Trade and Investment Policies for the Seventies.* New York: Praeger, 1971.

U.S. Commission on the Organization of the Government for the Conduct of Foreign Policy. *Report.* Washington, D.C., U.S. Govt. Print. Off., June 1975.

U.S. Congress. House Committee on Government Operations. *Extent of Control of the Executive by the Congress of the United States.* Washington, D.C., U.S. Govt. Print. Off., 1962.

U.S. Congress. House Committee on International Relations. Library of Congress. Congressional Research Services. Foreign Affairs Division. *Congress and Foreign Policy: 1974.* April 15, 1975. 94th Cong., 1st. sess. Washington, D.C.: Government Printing Office, 1975.

U.S. Library of Congress. Legislative References Service. *Resolved: that executive control of United States foreign policy should be significantly curtailed.* A collection of excerpts and bibliography relating to the Print. Off., 1968.

United States Tariff Commission. *Operation of the Trade Agreements Program, June 1934–April 1948.* Washington, D.C.: Government Printing Office, 1949.

VERNON, RAYMOND. *Multinational Enterprises and National Security*. Adelphi Press, No. 74. London: Institute of Strategic Studies, 1971.

———. *Sovereignty at Bay: The Multinational Spread of U.S. Enterprises*. New York: Basic Books, 1971.

VOGLER, DAVID. *The Politics of Congress*. Boston: Allyn and Bacon, 1974.

WALL, DAVID. *The Charity of Nations: The Political Economy of Foreign Aid*. New York: Basic Books, Inc., 1973.

WALLACE, DON, JR. "The President's Exclusive Foreign Affairs Powers over Foreign Aid: Part I and Part II." *Duke Law Journal* v. 1970, April and June 1970: 293–328.

WALTZ, KENNETH N. *Foreign Policy and Democratic Politics: The American and British Experience*. Boston: Little, Brown and Company, 1967.

WESTERFIELD, BRADFORD. *Foreign Policy and Party Politics: Pearl Harbor to Korea*. New Haven: Yale University Press, 1955.

WESTPHAL, ALBERT C. F. *The House Committee on Foreign Affairs*. New York: Columbia University Press, 1942.

WILCOX, FRANCIS ORLANDO. *Congress, the Executive, and Foreign Policy*. New York: Published for the Council on Foreign Relations by Harper and Row, 1971.

WILLIAMS, BENJAMIN H., *Economic Foreign Policy of the United States*. New York: McGraw Hill, 1929.

WILSON, JOAN HOFF. *American Business and Foreign Policy, 1920–1933*. Lexington, Ky.: University of Kentucky, 1971.

INDEX

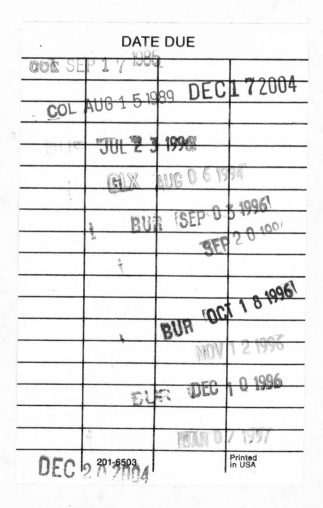